P9-BBO-701

# Multicultural Counseling:
## Context, Theory and Practice, and Competence

# MULTICULTURAL COUNSELING:
## CONTEXT, THEORY AND PRACTICE, AND COMPETENCE

JERRY TRUSTY, EUGENIE JOAN LOOBY AND DAYA SINGH SANDHU
(EDITORS)

**Nova Science Publishers, Inc.**
*New York*

**Senior Editors:** Susan Boriotti and Donna Dennis
**Coordinating Editor:** Tatiana Shohov
**Office Manager:** Annette Hellinger
**Graphics:** Wanda Serrano
**Editorial Production:** Jennifer Vogt, Matthew Kozlowski, Jonathan Rose and Maya Columbus
**Circulation:** Ave Maria Gonzalez, Indah Becker, Raymond Davis,
          Vladimir Klestov and Jonathan Roque
**Communications and Acquisitions:** Serge P. Shohov
**Marketing:** Cathy DeGregory

*Library of Congress Cataloging-in-Publication Data*
*Available Upon Request*


ISBN 1-59033-267-9.

Copyright © 2002 by Nova Science Publishers, Inc.
          227 Main Street, Suite 100
          Huntington, New York 11743
          Tele. 631-424-NOVA (6682)          Fax 631-425-5933
          E Mail: Novascience@earthlink.net
          www.novapublishers.com


All rights reserved. No part of this book may be reproduced, stored in a retrieval system or transmitted in any form or by any means: electronic, electrostatic, magnetic, tape, mechanical photocopying, recording or otherwise without permission from the publishers.

The authors and publisher have taken care in preparation of this book, but make no expressed or implied warranty of any kind and assume no responsibility for any errors or omissions. No liability is assumed for incidental or consequential damages in connection with or arising out of information contained in this book.

This publication is designed to provide accurate and authoritative information with regard to the subject matter covered herein. It is sold with the clear understanding that the publisher is not engaged in rendering legal or any other professional services. If legal or any other expert assistance is required, the services of a competent person should be sought. FROM A DECLARATION OF PARTICIPANTS JOINTLY ADOPTED BY A COMMITTEE OF THE AMERICAN BAR ASSOCIATION AND A COMMITTEE OF PUBLISHERS.

*Printed in the United States of America*

# CONTENTS

# INTRODUCTION

## *Jerry Trusty*
Pennsylvania State University

Our American cultural heritage—as well as our human heritage—includes war and peace, love and hate, racism and acceptance, integration and segregation, tolerance and intolerance, rational and irrational thought and action, hope and despair, destruction and growth. Multicultural counseling seeks to understand this heritage and how it influences our individual and collective being. Multicultural counseling offers frameworks for helping counselors understand the cultural heritages and worldviews of people from various groups, and it offers frameworks for helping people from various groups function effectively in our pluralistic society.

Perhaps no recent chain of events has affected our views of the world and our views of people more than the events beginning on September 11, 2001. This is now a marked date in our minds. On and after this day, our individual and collective perceptions of ourselves, our nation, and our world changed. We suddenly lost security and realized vulnerability. We experienced all the emotions associated with loss: numbness, sadness, fear, anger, guilt, frustration, anxiety, worry, confusion. We felt for those thousands who lost much more than we lost. We heard emotions manifested in the words of our family members, coworkers, friends, the media, and our leaders. We saw people's actions in response to these events. We saw a reborn American nationalism; but we also saw hostile acts against more innocent people, people who looked Middle-Eastern. Blame was spread widely by a few, mostly from those at political and social extremes. Some people reacted to events by coming together with other people and groups, while some reacted by distancing themselves from others. The tolerance of all was tested and is continuously tested, and much cognitive and emotional dissonance exists around how we individually and collectively view ourselves and our fellow humans.

Multicultural identity, multicultural being, and multicultural counseling are all about tolerance, acceptance, and prizing of diversity. Yet do we tolerate those who are intolerant; do we accept those who are not accepting of others; do we prize those who do not prize diversity; and to what degree do we tolerate, accept, or prize? These are difficult questions, but we do have guidance from multicultural counseling in answering them. For example, models of identity development offer insight into how people define themselves and adapt in our pluralistic society. These models explain the processes through which people move, hopefully coming to a point where they are accepting of themselves, selectively accepting of the good in others from all groups, and dedicated to helping others. Multicultural counseling helps us understand individuals, and how individuals are influenced by their experiences, families, sociopolitical and socioeconomic environments, cultural heritages, personal agency, and by their uniqueness. The multicultural perspective is a broad and flexible perspective, a perspective aimed at enhancing our ability as counselors to help people from an increasingly diverse population.

This edited book was designed as a text for graduate-level multicultural counseling courses. The content was structured to meet the accreditation standards of the Council for Accreditation of Counseling and Related Educational Programs (CACREP). However, the content of the book is appropriate for all trainees and practitioners in the helping professions. In most chapters of the book, case examples are provided to illustrate application of models and concepts to work with clients and students. Because counseling-students' personal development is important to their development of multicultural competence, class and small-group experiential activities are included in most chapters. The goal of the text is to provide knowledge and experience for developing multicultural competence in counselor-trainees, counselors, and others in the helping professions.

This text was designed to give broad coverage of several areas and groups encountered in multicultural counseling, thereby serving as a basis for developing multicultural counseling competence. Consistent with CACREP Standards, material is included regarding culture, race, ethnicity, nationality, age, gender, sexual orientation, mental and physical characteristics, families, religion and spirituality, socioeconomic status, identity development, acculturation, multicultural theories, community strategies, racism and discrimination, and advocacy and social justice. The text also covers topics that are currently gaining deserved attention in the multicultural counseling literature. For example, *biracial identity development* is covered in the chapter on identity development; and *forgiveness* is covered in the chapter on religion and spirituality in counseling. Multicultural counselor supervision and the training of multiculturally competent counselors are covered in several chapters in the text.

When racial-ethnic groups are addressed in the book, the focus is geared mainly toward the five largest, officially-designated U.S. racial-ethnic groups, namely, African Americans, Asian Americans, Hispanic Americans, Native American Indians, and White Americans. Authors in all chapters are careful to acknowledge variability within these and other groups, thereby seeking to dispel erroneous generalizations regarding people who identify with particular groups. The authors also seek to provide broad and varying perspectives on the development of individuals within groups.

In Chapter 1, Drs. Jerry Trusty, Patrick Davis, and Joan Looby provide some of the important historical context for understanding and helping diverse groups of people. They draw broadly on literature from history, sociology, social psychology, social anthropology, assessment, psychology, and multicultural counseling to trace meaningful events and evolving perspectives on various groups of people in our country.

In Chapter 2, Drs. Tina Richardson and Elizabeth Jacob describe current issues and contemporary perspectives on multiculturalism and multicultural counseling. The focus in Chapter 2 is mainly on the salient issue of training multiculturally competent counselors.

Racial, ethnic, and cultural identity development is the topic of Chapter 3. Drs. Richard Henriksen and Jerry Trusty present a thorough introduction to various identity development models for various groups of people.

Drs. Timothy Smith and Scott Richards provide religious and spiritual contexts for multicultural counseling in Chapter 4. They demonstrate the relevance of religious and spiritual being to multicultural counseling, and they present a model of spiritual identity development.

Chapter 5 focuses on multicultural counseling theories. Ms. Sheilah Wilson and Dr. Daya Sandhu provide frameworks for understanding and appropriately applying various theories and models to counseling.

Counseling ethnically diverse families is the topic of Chapter 6. Dr. Joan Looby and Ms. Tammy Webb present characteristics of families from non-White U.S. groups, and they offer guidelines for counseling with families from these groups.

Dr. Liza Conyers is the author of the chapter on disabilities (Chapter 7). Dr. Conyers traces evolving perspectives on disabilities, and she underscores the importance of understanding disabilities in psychosocial and sociocultural contexts.

In Chapter 8, Dr. Mark Pope focuses on counseling people from gay and lesbian culture. Dr. Pope describes the controversy surrounding perspectives within multicultural counseling. Special multicultural counseling competencies for working with gay and lesbian clients are also presented.

Dr. Roger Herring contributed the chapter on multicultural counseling for career development (Chapter 9). Dr. Herring discusses the applicability of career development theories and models to diverse groups, and he offers multiculturally sensitive career interventions.

Multicultural group counseling is the topic of Chapter 10. Drs. Michael Mann and Changming Duan reveal perspectives on culturally homogeneous and heterogeneous groups, and they present suggestions for group work with people from various racial-ethnic groups.

Chapter 11 focuses on interpersonal skills in multicultural counseling. Dr. Sylvia Fernandez, Dr. Jerry Trusty, and Ms. Reba Criswell underscore the importance of communication and empathy in multicultural counseling competence.

Drs. Roger Herring and Carmen Salazar contributed Chapter 12, the chapter on non-Western helping modalities. They present several models that have their roots in non-Western cultures, and they provide various perspectives on helping and healing.

The last chapter (Chapter 13) is by Drs. Karin Jordan, Jesse Brinson, and Colleen Peterson. This chapter is on multicultural counseling supervision. The authors discuss issues pertinent to multicultural supervision, and they offer a framework for helping counselor trainees select an effective supervisor.

The editors of this book, Drs. Jerry Trusty, Joan Looby, and Daya Sandhu, thank all the chapter authors for their contributions.

# Chapter 1

# HISTORICAL CONTEXT OF MULTICULTURALISM IN THE UNITED STATES

**Jerry Trusty**
Pennsylvania State University
**Patrick E. Davis**
University of North Carolina, Greensboro
**Eugenie Joan Looby**
Mississippi State University

## INTRODUCTION

To understand our values and our culture, we must understand our history. To understand clients with whom we work, we must understand their individual and collective experiences and perceptions. Therefore, knowing and understanding the history of relations among groups in the U.S. enhances counselors' knowledge and understanding of self and others. Parrillo (1994) defined ethnocentrism as a state in which people see their own group as paramount and other groups are judged according to that standard. Parrillo maintained that North Americans' ethnocentrism is not entirely a deliberate choice. Ethnocentrism is in many ways a natural result of developing within our familiar environment. It is a natural result of our human history and our history as a country. Some people "don't want to hear our history." Granted, our history can be painful; and painful words are written in this chapter. Avoidance of pain is natural and understandable. However, as counselors, we do not avoid our clients' pain; and we do not avoid the heritages of our clients.

The purpose of this chapter is to provide some historical context for relationships among racial-ethnic groups in the U.S. Whereas the authors acknowledge that history is important to understanding groups defined by means other than race and ethnicity (e.g., gender, lifestyle, disability status), the focus of this chapter is on the four largest, non-White U.S. racial-ethnic groups, Native American Indians, African Americans, Hispanic Americans, and Asian Americans. Some historical background for other groups is provided in subsequent chapters of this book. The historical background provided in this chapter is by no means inclusive or exhaustive. Our purpose is to present many influential historical events and processes experienced by people in our country. We first present the historical, ideological bases of racism and dominance, and how this legacy is manifested in contemporary society. We next discuss the historical role of psychology and counseling in oppression. We then describe influential experiences of people from each of the major, non-White racial-ethnic groups in the U.S.

# RACISM AND DOMINANCE

## Racism and Dominance in Historical Context

It is common for people from a particular culture to make comparisons of their culture to the cultures of others, and to believe that their culture is superior (McLemore, 1980). It is natural for people to think that the values they hold are the "right" set of values, otherwise they would not hold those values. There is historical precedence for economically or militarily dominant cultures perceiving superiority over other cultures. For example, the Greeks—whose culture preceded the Roman Empire—perceived all groups surrounding them as barbaric. Later, the Romans viewed the people of the British Isles as culturally inferior. Later still, the people of Britain came to view cultures other than theirs—especially those in Africa and America—as inferior (Parrillo, 1980). In recent historical periods, perceptions of cultural superiority and ethnocentrism parallel perceptions of racial and ethnic superiority (Marden & Meyer, 1973; Ropers & Pence, 1995).

From the general perspective of superiority, various dimensions of superiority emerge, including social superiority, religious superiority, moral superiority, racial superiority, and psychological superiority—to name a few. For example, perceptions of religious superiority (among other dimensions) led to the crusades of the Middle Ages; beliefs of racial superiority were a main part of the "justification" of slavery. Such conceptualizations of superiority are required for "moral" and "civilized" people to dominate or oppress other people (Ropers & Pence, 1995). Racism differs little in the contemporary context. Atkinson, Morten, and Sue (1993), referring to current racism, pointed out that an ideological, biological conceptualization of race is the basis for racism. Racism, in turn, is the basis for discrimination.

Human history is replete with examples of racism, prejudice, discrimination, and even murder and genocide; and these negative beliefs and actions are based on superiority-inferiority logic (Ropers & Pence, 1995). For example, Africans were seen as "an inferior species" and Native American Indians were "savages," and therefore people belonging to these groups could be enslaved or killed (Parrillo, 1980, 1994). Prejudice and racism are part of our collective human heritage and collective unconscious, and they are part of our American cultural heritage. Ropers and Pence (1995) stated, "We as a culture have socially decided that African Americans, Latinos, Native Americans, women, working-class people and poor, and gays, lesbians, and bisexuals are 'less' favored groups, and that it is therefore acceptable to treat them unequally" (p. 47). Ropers and Pence illuminated the direct connections of these contemporary attitudes, beliefs, and behaviors in U.S. society to our U.S. history.

Early colonization bears a strong influence on contemporary racism (Ramirez, 1999; Ropers & Pence, 1995). Colonization often constituted "ownership" of the property (home) of a native or residing people, and often meant ownership of the people themselves, particularly if the people were non-White. For example, the English's treatment of White people in the North American Colonies differed greatly from the treatment of Native American Indians in America and Africans in colonial Africa (see McLemore, 1980; Parrillo, 1994, 1996). In the American Colonies, White people were allowed to own shares in the companies (e.g., the Virginia Company), and were given other democratic rights (McLemore, 1980); whereas Native American people were driven from their homes, enslaved, and killed (Parrillo, 1994; Ropers & Pence, 1995).

Europeans needed justification for this dominance and ownership, and the justification was found through "religion" and "science." With regard to the religious basis, slavery and genocide were seen as part of "God's plan" for the White race—the "White man's burden" to dominate and lead the world. The scientific basis was a convenient ideology—a "biologically-defined" dichotomization of races as inferior or superior (Ropers & Pence, 1995). Although the world has a long history of war and domination, this "doctrine of White supremacy" is a relatively new phenomenon, being born in European colonialism and gaining momentum through the years (McLemore, 1980; Ropers & Pence, 1995). Parrillo (1994) asserted that most historians agree that although many early civilizations perceived themselves as superior to others, their perceived superiority was based on culture and not on race. Although racism has likely always been with us, its origins are attributed to colonialism in the 16th and 17th centuries, when it became a major justification for domination.

It is important to remember that many of the true driving forces behind colonization were economic in nature. The English, Dutch, French, Spanish, and Portuguese competed around the world for the resources that colonies could bring. In fact, the possibility of precious minerals was a major lure. For these European countries, falling behind economically might mean falling behind militarily (McLemore, 1980). Therefore, although the stated reasons for dominance of other people were so-called religious and scientific reasons, economics were the underlying reason. Perhaps it is difficult for "moral" and "civilized" people to provide economics as a reason for racism, dominance, or genocide. As the reader will see in subsequent sections of this chapter, economics have been, and continue to be, a driving force behind U.S. immigration policies. Economics are also a driving force behind perceptions of and behavior toward various groups of people. And again, economics are not always the stated reason for actions (see Parrillo, 1980, 1994).

Soon after the "discovery" of the Americas by Columbus, the Spanish and Portuguese were first in exploration and colonization. Later, the English began to colonize the East Coast of North America. The Dutch made attempts at establishing colonies along the East Coast, but they were not as successful as the English because more English people immigrated to North America. New Amsterdam became New York, and the English companies, the English settlers, and the English government controlled the East Coast from Virginia to Massachusetts. This was the first instance in which the dominant, Protestant, English population in America was forced to accommodate diversity. In New York, there were people from many European countries. However, the process of inclusion was relatively smooth in this early phase in our nation's development (McLemore, 1980).

Parrillo (1996) pointed out that early North American settlers did not form a homogeneous group. People from countries other than England, and even from within

England, differed greatly in language, customs, and religious beliefs. People most often interacted with others who shared their origins; and whereas there was general adjustment to a largely English political system, people were not pressured to culturally assimilate. Parrillo (1996) described the early settlements in North America as a "patchwork quilt of ethnic diversity" (p. 40). Those who fought for independence from Britain were likewise diverse. Parrillo noted, for example, that over 5,000 Blacks served in the Colonial Army. Cultural distinctions among White groups (e.g., Scotch-Irish, French, Dutch, Germans) faded when they united against their common enemy in the Revolutionary War, and when they shared a common victory. The ideals of rights to life, liberty, and pursuit of happiness and that all men are created equal were expressed by the new nation; but these rights were not yet extended to women and people who were not White (Parrillo, 1996).

However, these ideals were attractive to many hopeful people around the world; and many chose to come to the U.S. to experience these freedoms. Ethnic communities that had blended into the early mainstream of the country were revitalized as more immigrants came. New ethnic communities were also created (Parrillo, 1996). Some who were new to this country and many already in this country were readily accepted and quickly integrated into U.S. society. However, some in this country and some new to this country were not readily accepted and integration was resisted. Instances of smooth acceptance and contentious non-acceptance are described later in this chapter.

Vontress (in Ponterotto & Pedersen, 1993, p. xii) noted that although racism is inconsistent with basic American ideology, it is part of our American cultural heritage. The historical evidence supporting this conclusion is strong. Many contemporary Americans believe that although racism, prejudice, and discrimination still exist, they are no longer a pervasive problem in this country. Dovidio and Gaertner (1991) observed that whereas many White Americans currently express lower levels of overt racism than in years past; racism and discrimination continue in a new, more indirect, complex, and potentially sinister form. According to Ponterotto and Pedersen (1993), in our contemporary social structure, White Americans are likely to deny the existence of prejudice against persons of color, and likely to deny their own prejudices.

The trouble with this way of thinking, behaving, and being is that prejudice and discrimination are often subtle and beyond our awareness. Discrimination can be unintentional, especially when the perpetrator does not know or understand the victim. Discrimination can be institutional, emanating from a set of rules and parameters established by and for a particular, usually dominant, group of people. It can result from seemingly innocuous acts of omission or commission. Discrimination could result from a split-second, nonverbal behavior communicated from a counselor to a client. As Ponterotto and Pedersen (1993) expressed, it is easy for people to ignore or rationalize away these realities, and not deal with the cognitive dissonances created by acute perceptiveness; and therefore, prejudice and its products—racism and discrimination—are denied; and the status quo is maintained. For these reasons and others, our ethical standards (American Counseling Association, 1995) make explicit statements underscoring the importance of counselors (a) being aware of their own values, (b) understanding how these values impact counseling and clients, (c) understanding clients in context, and (d) respecting diversity.

## The Role of Psychology and Counseling

The professions of psychology and counseling have not been innocent bystanders in the oppression of people, especially those who differ from the norm. Ramirez (1991, 1999) noted that psychology was initially a science of individual differences. However, it soon became a science of the norm, used to judge those who differed from that norm of functioning and behavior. That "most desirable composite" of personality traits, behavior, adjustment, and adaptation became the standard by which others were judged. In fact, racial-ethnic differences were sometimes used to validate judgements and describe traits. Ramirez (1991) gave an example of an early developer of intelligence tests using a racial-ethnic group to describe the low-intelligence trait. The early test-developer failed to realize that cultures and environments define intelligence and adaptation, rather than the inverse. That is, the personal characteristics, abilities, skills, and coping that help people adapt to and effectively operate on their environments are not universal across environments; and naturally, what is valued in one culture is not necessarily valued in another.

Intelligence tests have been and continue to be one of the most sinister tools of oppression and conformity (Ramirez, 1991, 1993; Ropers & Pence, 1995). Ropers and Pence (1995, p. 77-78) noted that the same test developer used in the Ramirez example above also believed that people's social class (socioeconomic status) results from biological differences. There are also contemporary psychologists who purport an evolutionary cause for "low intelligence." Some psychologists, in the past and recently, have asserted that lower intelligence of African Americans is a main cause of U.S. social ills (Ropers & Pence, 1995). This is the "science" of intelligence testing used to support the "doctrine of White supremacy." Psychologists--in the past and recently--have used their assertions to argue for limiting immigration, withholding help for less-fortunate individuals and groups, and even for creating a more "genetically desirable" population (see Ropers & Pence, 1995). Could selfish economics also underlie this "logic?" There are many other psychologists who vigorously oppose these assertions of biologically determined intelligence, and they oppose proposed "social-problem solutions" based on this ideology (see Ropers & Pence, 1995).

When authors write of intelligence, the word that is often erroneously omitted is the word *measured*. That is, authors should use the terminology, *measured intelligence*, thereby not supporting the illusion that intelligence is something that exists in an objective sense, something that can be precisely and validly measured in all cases, and something that is uniformly meaningful across the universe. Intelligence is a hypothetical construct, and the definition of that construct and the measurement of that construct depends on the particular theory of intelligence on which that construct is based. For example, some intelligence theorists include interpersonal intelligence, social intelligence, or musical intelligence as components of the construct, noting that intelligence is not only academic, and that the *academy* is culturally defined, reflecting a particular worldview (see Drummond, 2000; Thorndike, 1997). Most reasonable people would agree that interpersonal abilities help us adapt to a wide variety of environments. If your environment is an orchestra, musical ability surely helps you adapt to and function in that environment.

We refer the reader to the following resources for information on the more culturally sensitive and ethical approach to intelligence testing and testing in general: American Counseling Association (1995), Anastasi (1988), Dana (1993), Drummond (2000), Thorndike

(1997). Also, this topic and the counseling perspective are elucidated more fully in subsequent chapters of this text, most notably in the chapter on career development.

Counseling theories and methods have also been used as tools of discrimination and oppression. Counseling theories are explanations of behavior. They describe behavior in terms of adjustment and maladjustment, adaptation and maladaptation. Theories delineate causal relationships among variables. Theories might attribute maladjustment to clients' irrational thinking or an ill-functioning family system or a lack of self-awareness or resource-awareness. Besides delineating cause, it is important for counselors to be aware that all counseling theories emanate from culture. Jackson (1995) noted that until very recently, the perspective of counseling was *monolithic*. That is, counseling was based on a single view of the world, the Anglo-European view. Ivey (1995) termed this the *naïve Eurocentric approach*—terminology suggesting unintentional discrimination. Sue and Sue (1999) referred to this phenomenon as *ethnocentric monoculturalism*. The ethnocentrism described by these authors bears many similarities to the broader ethnocentrism described earlier.

Most counseling theories were developed in the middle- to latter-years of the 20th century. Most were based on and supported by research with samples from U.S. mainstream, White, Western culture. Most were developed for people in mainstream culture, and counseling itself was of, by, and for mainstream culture. Many theories reflect the individualistic focus of Western culture; and many ignore the influences of several important variables, including culture, gender, race-ethnicity, socioeconomic status, environment, discrimination, institutional barriers, socialization, values, person-environment-fit, and so forth (see Atkinson, Morten, & Sue, 1993; Ramirez, 1991, 1999). Perhaps the most objective evidence of the shortcomings of counseling is the underutilization of counseling services by people who are outside the U.S. mainstream (see Leong, Wagner, & Tata, 1995).

According to Jackson (1995) and Ivey (1995), counseling is now shifting to a pluralistic or multicultural perspective, a perspective that is much more flexible in addressing the needs of those who differ from the mainstream. This multicultural perspective involves focusing on the commonalities and differences across cultures and groups, and focusing on the commonalities and differences within cultures and groups. This perspective involves seeing our clients and ourselves for what we really are, cultural beings (Ivey, Ivey, & Simek-Morgan, 1993; Ramirez, 1991, 1999).

# NATIVE AMERICANS

## Pre-Columbian America

When the first Europeans arrived in North American, this land was already multicultural, and had been for thousands of years. By 9500 B.C., Native Americans lived throughout what is now the United States. The use of land by people of these First Nations mirrors land use in the United States in the early 19th century, with productive agriculture in the Southeast and Midwest, fishing in the Great Lakes, and meat production on the Plains. There were six major language groups among the First Nation peoples (Kehoe, 1999). Within these groups, there were over 200 diverse languages, with many dialects; and there were some languages that were unique to particular groups (Parrillo, 1996). There were general cultural areas determined somewhat by geography, yet there was long-distance trade across North America (Kehoe, 1999).

Similar to tribal societies in other parts of the world, a clan system or friendship system served as the basic building blocks of societies. Some societies were matrilineal, with property passed down from mother to daughter, and husbands joining the wife's family. Roles for women and men varied greatly among groups, depending on geography, food production, and cultural orientation. In some groups, women had considerable political power, and some even fought in battle (Parrillo, 1996).

In many of the North American tribes, the social organization was egalitarian and democratic (e.g., the Iroquois, see McLemore, 1980; Parrillo, 1994). In these groups, heredity did not determine leadership, and the leader was the most capable person. However, some groups were not democratic. Along the Northwest Coast, there were two distinct classes, freemen and slaves. Slaves were captured in raids, and their children became slaves. Freemen were rank-ordered according to social status, and the number of slaves held was one indicator of social status (Parrillo, 1996).

By the 10th century A.D., there were urban areas in North America. The largest city was Cahokia, near present-day St. Louis. Population estimates are difficult to make, but there were at least 10,000 residents. An estimated area of 20,000 square miles was ruled from Cahokia (Kehoe, 1999).

## Invasion and Conquest

The "discovery" of America by Columbus marked the beginning of the invasion and conquest of the First Nations. Europeans and Native Americans fought all across North America for 400 years. However, disease took a greater toll than actual warfare. According to Kehoe (1999), many devastating epidemics came through Mexico as a result of early Spanish incursions and conquests. After generations of exposure to diseases such as smallpox, diptheria, measles, and cholera, Europeans had developed immunity. However, Native Americans had no resistance to these and other diseases. Kehoe maintained that no Europeans that came to America after 1650 saw the First Nations as they were before. Kehoe compared the scene in North America to that in Europe after the Black Death had taken one-third to one-half of its population. Parrillo (1996) noted that whole villages, and even whole tribes were decimated by disease. When Spain, France, and England actively engaged in colonizing North America, the existing population was considerably weakened socially, economically, politically, and militarily by disease (Kehoe, 1999).

The Native Americans were not without support. Las Casas, a Spanish bishop living in the New World, argued in Europe on the behalf of Natives. In 1517, he met with the King of Spain, relaying the decimation of the Native population and asking for another workforce to replace them. Las Casas informed the King that Africans were better adaptable to the type of labor needed. Parrillo (1994) wrote, "It is cruelly ironic that the humane efforts of Las Casas on the Native Americans' behalf led to the brutalization and exploitation of black people and racial discrimination against them for over 400 years." (p. 225)

As early as 1598, the Spanish began colonization and American Indian slave-trade in the Rio Grande Valley. Years of war in this area led to the subjugation of Native populations. The Native Nations in California constituted a dense population. The Spanish established concentration-camp style missions in this area; and later, Natives were removed from their homes. Soon after the U.S. takeover in 1848, Native Americans were shot, for sport, by miners and ranchers; and they were bought and sold as slaves. Native Americans were not allowed to testify in court against White people. By 1900, California Native Americans were outnumbered by Native people from other First Nations who were forced from their homes in the east (Kehoe, 1999).

In the eastern part of what is now the United States, Whites were the minority for many years. As White settlers and Native Americans interacted, each group grew to distrust and dislike the other. Europeans saw the land and resources for what they could become and for what profit they could bring. Native Americans, in contrast, saw the land for what it was (see Parrillo, 1994, 1996). Settlers could not understand the Native Americans' resistance to Christianity; and Native Americans could not understand the settlers' use of punishment for social control (Parrillo, 1994). McLemore (1980) noted that the English and the English colonists gave up on "civilizing the savages."

As the number of settlers grew to a critical mass, and when economic strength became adequate for survival independent from Native Americans, settlers were suddenly ready to drive the Native inhabitants from their land. This began in Virginia and in New England in the early 1600s (Kehoe, 1999; Parrillo, 1994). By the late 1600s, the colonists had a relatively tight grip on the East Coast (Kehoe, 1999).

On the frontier of the colonies, tribes and members of tribes were enlisted as allies of the British, French, and later of the United States. However, in many cases, becoming an ally brought no reward or help in return (see Koehe, 1999). In the North, many Iroquois fled to British Canada in the late 1700s. Those remaining were forced to disperse and work on European-style family farms (Kehoe, 1999). In the South, five tribes were termed *Civilized Tribes*, namely, the Cherokee, Muscogee (Creek), Choctaw, Chickasaw, and Seminole. They were considered civilized by White people because many from these tribes easily adapted to European-style commerce, farming, and lifestyle (Daniels, 1962; Kehoe, 1999). Whereas some adapted and some became economically successful, many chose to fight rather than assimilate (see Daniels, 1962; Parrillo, 1994). Kehoe noted that these five tribes gave up much land in the early 19th century, culminating in the Trail of Tears, the forced removal of people of these tribes from the Southeast to reservations in the West. Many died in this forced expulsion. For example, of 13,000 Cherokee who began the trip, fewer than 9,000 are estimated to have survived the move to Oklahoma (Parrillo, 1994). In the Midwest and the Plains, Native Americans were steadily pushed from their ancestral lands. Across the 19th century, there were many bloody battles associated with these expulsions. Many who were forced from their homes returned to intermarry with settlers and blend into the new culture (Kehoe, 1999), and some sought to reclaim their birthplaces. For example, today there are relatively large numbers of Choctaws living near their birthplace, Nanih Waiya, in Eastern Mississippi; and there are relatively large numbers of Choctaws in Southeastern Oklahoma.

## Dominance

Parrillo (1994) noted that the racism, prejudice, and discrimination directed toward the Native Americans served as a model for later domination of African Americans, Hispanic Americans, and Asian Americans. Ropers and Pence (1995) likened the treatment of Native Americans to ethnic cleansing. For example, in 1755 in Boston, the local government paid bounties to settlers who brought evidence that they had killed Native Americans.

Because tribes differed so greatly from one another, and because the nature and degree of contact of White people with tribes varied greatly, the "doctrine of White supremacy" was not easily or readily applied to Native American Indians. Early White settlers, to resolve this cognitive dissonance, designated all Native Americans as "Indians." McLemore (1980) wrote, "They were all given the label 'Indian,' and they soon were regarded as permanently alien, unassimilable, and ineligible for full membership in the new host society being created" (p. 33). As late as 1903, the U.S. Supreme Court referred to Native Americans as "a dependent race," "ignorant," and concluded that they needed to be ruled by "Christian people" of the United States. It was not until 1924 that Native Americans, as a group, were considered full citizens of the U.S. (Kehoe, 1999).

In 1831, the U.S. Supreme Court deemed Indian nations "domestic dependent nations," whose laws and treaties were subordinate to decisions of the U.S. Government. For an example of how this policy was applied, the Lakota agreed to a treaty in 1868 that retained a reservation including the Black Hills. In 1876, the Black Hills were removed from the reservation by the U.S. Government so gold could be mined from the area. Later the U.S. opened much of the reservation for Euro-American homesteading (Kehoe, 1999).

In the middle of the 19th century there was a noted shift in U.S. policy toward Native American Indians. The former policy of annihilation and expulsion gave way to a policy of segregation and isolation. Most reservations were established in this period, and they now number more than 300. In 1871, Congress made Native Americans wards of the government. Parrillo (1994) wrote, "Americanization became the goal" (p. 237). Children were sent to assimilationist boarding schools; Natives' "pagan" religion was not allowed; and attempts at assimilation were pervasive and consistent. Though perhaps not intended, these policies and practices had further negative effects on Native Americans (Kehoe, 1999).

## Movement toward Pluralism

In the 1930s, the U.S. Government moved from a policy of forced assimilation to a policy of pluralism. The new policy encouraged tribal self-government, traditional customs and languages, and Native religious practices. In the 1950s, the government attempted a relocation program to move Native people into urban areas. This action frightened many Natives, especially because the director of the program was the former administrator of the Japanese American relocation program during World War II. Of the 40,000 Native Americans who participated in this program, more than 10,000 returned to reservations (Parrillo, 1994). Over the last four decades, public and political sentiment have come to be much more positive toward Native Americans. Some political and social efforts have been fruitful. For example, the civil rights movement had some positive outcomes for Native American Indians.

Although there have been successes, little has changed in the quality of Native American life; and discrimination continues (Parrillo, 1994; Ropers & Pence, 1995).

Whereas mainstream societal attitudes toward Native Americans have improved somewhat, more progress is needed (Watts, 1993). To demonstrate, Markstrom-Adams (1990) analyzed the content of novels about Native Americans published during the 1970s and 1980s. The analysis revealed a less stereotypical and more culturally sensitive attitude in these novels as compared to earlier works. However, a study by Haertel, Douthitt, Haertel, and Douthitt (1999) demonstrates the subtle nature of contemporary gender-racial discrimination. They found that research participants rated a Native American Indian woman job candidate lower than a White man, although the two candidates had identical vitae and audiotapes.

## AFRICAN AMERICANS

Beginning in the early 1500s, millions of Africans were transported from the Western coast of Africa, across the Atlantic, to the West Indies and the American colonies (Thorpe, 1961). European domination of Africans often began on slave ships (Smythe, 1976). Conrad (1966) asserted that the actual culture of slavery began on the ships. Tannenbaum (1946) recounted how, while on board, captured Africans were chained together while lying down, with little room for movement. Coombs (1972) pointed out that crowding captives into ships maximized cargo capacity, therefore maximizing the crew's reward. This practice often made it impossible for the African to turn over or to sit up during the several-months voyage from Africa to the New World. Brawley (1924) recounted how many Africans suffocated to death, whereas many died from diseases caused by unsanitary conditions.

Steckel and Jensen (1986) discussed the Parliamentary decision to investigate the high death rates among enslaved Africans occurring on slave ships in the Middle Passage. Smythe (1976) asserted, "Mankind has experienced few tortures so ghoulish and uncivilized as the transportation of slaves from Africa to the New World, known as the Middle Passage" (p. 5). The Parliamentary inquisition determined that the tight packing of the African cargo led to high fatality rates on the ships. This practice precipitated diseases such as flux (abnormal flowing of fluid from the body), dysentery (severe diarrhea with flowing of mucus and blood), mortification of the bowels (local death of living tissue), and consumption (wasting away of the body). Also inadequate food supplies and suicide contributed to the high fatality rate. Although some writers question the accuracy of the statistics, Sterba (1996) estimated that forty- to sixty-million Africans died during American slavery. Elkins (1959) compared American slavery with the Jewish Holocaust, whereas Sterba compared slavery to both the Jewish Holocaust and the conquest of Native American Indians. Sterba insisted that although each was unique, they all share significant commonalties.

Coombs (1972) stated that virtually all of the captured and enslaved Africans were made to participate in a period of "seasoning" in the Caribbean Islands prior to reaching their final destinations in North America. Coombs maintained that newly-captured Africans were considered more dangerous and more strong-willed than seasoned or "broken-in" slaves, and therefore not preferred by North American slave owners. Seasoning consisted of a myriad of lessons inculcated to the slaves via whippings, withholding of food, and similar cruelties until the slave more readily accepted his or her enslaved, inferior condition.

## Socialization of African Slaves

Albanese (1976), in the work *The Plantation School*, argued that slavery and the plantation itself served as educational institutions. Slavery served as an effective acculturation tool for establishing and inculcating specific cultural norms to Whites and Blacks. Phillips (1959) argued that no "better" school existed for socializing Blacks to assume their inferior status as slaves. Albanese maintained that slave behaviors that failed to conform to the slave master's intentions were systematically expunged from the slave's behavioral repertoire. To demonstrate this point, Albanese related that Blacks who refused to abdicate their individuality and culture by assimilating into this new cultural form (accepting their enslaved condition) were "sent to professional Negro breakers and to be broken" (1976, p. 185). McAdoo (1997) described slave masters' absolute power over slaves, and the brutality that masters exercised. Researchers maintain that there remains little, if any, African in the African American. Kardiner and Ovesey (1951) stated, "The most conspicuous feature of the Negro in America is that his aboriginal culture was smashed, be it by design or accident" (p. 39). They insisted that this basic principle, as it affects present-day African Americans, can not be overestimated.

Kardiner and Ovesey (1951) noted that the only means of resistance for African slaves was flight (running away). Katz (1968) observed that through acts of violence and cruelty, slave owners inculcated effective lessons to slaves who ventured to participate in acts of protest. As an example, Katz reported how Lillburn Lewis (nephew of Thomas Jefferson) discouraged his slaves from running away by making an example of a captured run-away. Katz related that Lewis gathered all of the slaves into the outhouse, and started a huge fire. Upon tying the 17 year old slave to a meat block, and amidst pleas for mercy, Lewis commenced chopping the boy into pieces beginning at his ankles and tossing the boy's severed body parts into the fire, while lecturing other on-looking slaves of the impropriety and consequences of disobedience. Katz wrote, "and so were the arms, head, and trunk, until all was in the fire" (1968, p. 200).

## Socialized Black Inferiority

American socialization of Africans was based on Euro-American racist ideology, which insisted upon the inherent inferiority of African and Black people (Grier & Cobbs, 1968; Horton, 1994; Parrillo, 1994). Powdermaker (1939) maintained that White indoctrination of, and insistence upon African inferiority might have been the most debilitating action against African slaves and succeeding generations of African Americans. He pointed out that African slaves in America came to personally believe that they were inherently inferior to Whites. Tannenbaum (1946), who participated in a comparative study of the institution of slavery in Africa, South America, and North America, argued that North American slavery was the most oppressive form of slavery in the world. Morgan (1933) asserted that the North American slave system, unlike others, refused to recognize and respect the humanity of the African slave. Mellon (1988) argued that the goal of slavery was to create within the slave a feeling of complete dependence upon and perpetual, unquestioned inferiority to the White race. Mellon found that this type of socialization distinguished American slavery from slavery in other parts of the world, arguing that American slavery was the most damaging.

Tannenbaum (1946) described how manumission (freeing) of slaves in Spanish countries was often encouraged and practiced. Once manumitted, African slaves easily transitioned into the free society. Tannenbaum established, however, that British and American slavery systems strongly discouraged manumitting slaves. He explained that the few American slaves who were manumitted were kept as close to the slave condition as possible, and assimilation into the free American society became virtually impossible. Phillips (1959) believed that the institution of slavery was quite effective in socializing the slave to accept his inferior status. Black skin, whether slave or free, was evidence of and came to represent the inherent inferiority of the Black race. Morgan (1933) wrote that African Black skin was seen as a "clear representation of evil and godlessness" (p. 15). Blackness was used to justify Africans' condition and ill-treatment (Curry and Cowden, 1972).

Higginbothom (1996) argued that American slavery has had long-lasting, adverse effects on African Americans. Higginbothom presented *The Ten Precepts of American Slavery Jurisprudence*. One goal of slavery was to "presume, preserve, protect, and defend the ideal of the superiority of whites and the inferiority of blacks" (Higginbothom, 1996, p. 1697). In relating the humanly damaging precepts of slavery regarding education, Higginbothom wrote, "Deny blacks any education, deny them knowledge of their culture, and make it a crime to teach those who are slaves how to read or to write" (p. 1697). Regarding Western religious culture, Higginbothom wrote,

> Recognize no rights of slaves to define and practice their own religion, to choose their own religious leaders, or to worship with other blacks. Encourage them to adopt the religion of the white master and teach them that God is white and will reward the slave who obeys the commands of his master here on earth. Use religion to justify the slave's status on earth. (p. 1697-1698)

Interestingly, although virtually no Africans transported to American shores were Christian upon their arrival, statistics demonstrate that presently, the majority of African Americans consider themselves as Christians. The literature suggests that many, if not all, of the precepts Higginbothom (1996) delineated continue to influence African American participation in American society. Higginbothom's first precept regarding the presumed inferiority of African Americans appears to remain etched in American culture.

In the Dred Scott versus Sanford case (a slave who took his master to court to secure his freedom under the Missouri Compromise), U. S. Supreme Court Chief Justice, Roger Taney, responding to the pressure of public sentiment, announced the Court's decision to deny Dred Scott's claim of freedom. Although the decision was not unanimous, Chief Justice Taney argued that Blacks were "beings of an inferior order, and altogether unfit to associate with the white race, either in social or political relations" (Nicolay & Hart, 1914, p. 75). He included in the court's decision that "a perpetual and impassable barrier was intended to be erected between the white race and the one which they had reduced to slavery" (p. 75). He argued that Blacks were so inferior to Whites that the Negro had no rights that Whites were bound to respect, and that a "stigma, of the deepest degradation, was fixed upon the whole race" (Nicolay & Hart, 1914, p. 75). Powdermaker (1939) summed up the ideology of many Whites, stating, "Negroes are innately inferior to White people, mentally and morally." And, "There may be good niggers and bad niggers, but a nigger is a nigger and cannot escape the taint" (p. 23).

Grier and Cobbs (1968) maintained that Blacks absorbed many of the toxins of White society and began to feel about themselves as their country felt about them. Powdermaker (1939) confirmed that assertion by recounting the statement, and belief, of an eighty-year-old Black woman. He quoted her as saying, "The Whites has always been ahead and I suppose they always will be." When asked why she believed this was so, she responded, "A nigger is a nigger" (p. 326). In contemporary North America, African Americans often express similar aversions toward Blackness and African features and characteristics. Anderson and Cromwell (1977) asserted that African Americans adopted the belief and practice of devaluating Black skin and African features centuries ago. They ascertained that within the Black culture, the agreed upon sentiment was the darker the African American's complexion, the more unattractive the individual. Keith and Herring (1991) found that skin tone within the African American community predicted African American occupational opportunities and income more so than individuals' parents' socioeconomic status. Kardiner and Ovesey (1951) claimed that during slavery, "Gradations of color became the fixed method of determining status which persists to this day" (p. 47). Grier and Cobbs (1968) lamented that often the unfortunate Black child exists in a world where even the child's parents can not see beyond the color of their child's skin.

Higginbotham (1996) noted that a primary goal of American slavery jurisprudence was to keep Blacks "as powerless as possible" (p. 1697). This was accomplished in through an extremely biased system of "justice," and by withholding educational opportunities for Blacks. Butchart (1990) contended that people in slave-holding states recognized the emancipatory power of education. They also recognized the potential of education to challenge White American superiority ideology. In order to keep Blacks powerless, Southern states enacted laws to keep slaves ignorant and in awe of Whites by prohibiting slaves from participating in learning to read and write (Jones, 1996). Katz (1968) stated that slave states aimed to "keep the [slave's] mind in abject ignorance and degradation, lest the enslaved should grow dissatisfied, and claim the inalienable rights of humanity" (p. 233). Curry and Cowden (1972) argued that slave owners, through a myriad of often-violent lessons, effectively socialized Blacks and Whites to believe that Blacks were uneducable, and that education was for Whites. Therefore, during the acculturation process of African Blacks in America, White Americans attempted to eliminate education from African American culture. The super-imposed, internalized message that education was for Whites became a fundamental component of African American and White American culture.

## Slavery's Impact on Africans' Personality

Albanese (1976) stated that slavery's mark can be visibly seen today. He asserted, "There are many parallels between the slave family and the modern-day lower-class black family. Both are characterized by a strong mother, instability, poverty and a father either absent or constituting a marginal personality" (p. 165). Albanese determined that the sheer brutality and socialization of slavery led to the eventual destruction of the independent and individual nature of the African, and within a few short years a "Sambo" personality emerged. Albanese noted that ingratiating, cowering, and obsequious behaviors were typical of the Sambo personality. Albanese delineated similarities between slaves' behaviors in the United States and behaviors of Jews discovered in Nazi concentration camps. Kardiner and Ovesey (1951) insisted that the Africans acquired these personality characteristics as they adapted to intensely difficult social conditions.

Curry and Cowden (1972) maintained that although demeaning, ingratiating behaviors were essential to the physical well-being of slaves, they were the very behaviors that slaveholders despised. Horton (1994) argued that although the West Africans sold into slavery often had cultural legacies of bravery and heroism, they underwent vast mental and personality changes in the New World. In a short period, they were converted from warriors to slaves. Blassingame (1972) maintained that regardless of the African slave's previous culture, upon landing in the New World, slaves had to learn the language and culture that their master prescribed.

## After Slavery

This slave-master social system and racial-inferiority theory left an enduring legacy in the United States. After the Civil War, institutionalized and personalized racism continued. Conerly's (1909) writing attests to the pervasive, racist, superiority ideology and vengefulness of Southern Whites after the Civil War. Writing from admitted personal knowledge and experience in the Ku Klux Klan in Mississippi, Conerly (1909, p. 251) boasted about how "justice" was exercised by the Klansmen:

> Before the criminal suspected that danger lurked near him he was in their [the Klan's] clutches. He was then taken to a place presided over by the Grand Cyclops, where witnesses were presented and a thorough investigation had. If adjudged guilty, when day dawned the culprit would be missing and sometimes found in his neighbor's yard, a dead proposition, or found dangling from the limb of a tree.

This passage demonstrates the ubiquity and blinding nature of hate; and from this passage, the self-rightousness of superiority ideology shines through. It is obvious that the victim was judged guilty of crime even before he was in the clutches of the Klan. That is, he was described as a "criminal" before his "trial." The "thorough investigation" appears to have taken place across the course of one night. Conerly's phrase, "a dead proposition," seems a boastful attempt at humor. This passage shows how people try to put "moral" reasoning behind immoral action. The reasoning and action are the cognitive and behavioral dimensions. The affective dimension is the hate that destroys any possibility of empathy for the victim. Evidently, hate was strong; and this "moral" reasoning and "justice" was good enough for many Southern Whites. It is estimated that over 4,000 African Americans were lynched in the Deep South after 1882, and likely thousands more were lynched earlier (Parrillo, 1994). Conerly (1909) was not a radical by Southern standards in the post-Civil War period. It is revealing that Conerly, through his writing, publicly and proudly admitted to knowledge of murder, seemingly without fear of justice.

When reconstruction ended in 1876, and the status of African Americans became a Southern concern rather than a national concern, the "inferior" status of African Americans was once again formalized. Southern politicians received support from the U.S. North and West. That is, in the latter years of the 19th century, immigration was threatening jobs and "racial security." Many dark-skinned immigrants were entering Northern and Western ports; Southern politicians supported California politicians in passing the Chinese Exclusion Act;

and the North and West supported—or at least did not actively resist—segregation laws in the South. In the late 19th century, the U.S. Supreme Court supported "separate but equal" principles, and by the early 20th century, most Southern states had passed *Jim Crow laws*. These laws specified segregation in almost all areas of life (Parrillo, 1994). Parrillo stated, "It is impossible to exaggerate the impact on a society of legalizing such discriminatory norms." (1994, p. 365)

Whereas racial superiority ideology was strong and pervasive in the South, it was much more variable in the North. There was no universal acceptance of racial superiority ideology in the North. Segregation was, in general, not supported by laws in the North; but was upheld by common practice. That is, Whites were expected to maintain the status quo, and African Americans were expected to accept their minority status (Marden & Meyer, 1973).

In 1954, the U.S. Supreme reversed its prior "separate but equal" principle in *Brown v. Board of Education of Topeka*. The court concluded that segregation policies are inherently unequal, and they generate a sense of inferiority in those who are excluded (Ropers & Pence, 1995). This ruling extended much further than schools, however. It was an assertion by the Court that all laws imposing segregation were unconstitutional. In essence, the ruling undermined the legal basis of all public discrimination in the U. S. (Marden & Meyer, 1973).

Through tireless determination and bravery of civil-rights leaders and otherwise "ordinary" people, the Civil-Rights Movement began to take hold in our country. Boycotts, sit-ins, freedom marches, and voter registration drives were successful. One by one, Jim Crow laws were challenged and eliminated, new rights were gained, and public desegregation was accomplished (Parrillo, 1994). According to Parrillo, the "Civil Rights Act of 1964 was the most far-reaching legislation against racial discrimination ever passed" (p. 375). It outlawed public discrimination and gave the U.S. Attorney General broad powers to enforce laws. Through the latter decades of the 20th century, the number of African American elected officials increased dramatically. There are many indicators of recent socioeconomic progress by African Americans, including gains in educational achievement, income, and occupational prestige (Parrillo, 1994; Smith, 1997; U.S. Census Bureau, 2000).

The prejudices associated with African American history and experience are ubiquitous yet subtle. For example, the very words used to designate groups, *white* and *black*, carry dichotomous, polar connotations (e.g., good and evil, comfort and fear, inclusion and exclusion). A person might be *blacklisted* or *blackballed*. Given the connections between racial and religious superiority ideology, it seems no accident that connotations of *white* and *black*, and *light* and *dark* used as adjectives and nouns in the Christian Bible are generalized to races, and reflected in our language and therefore in our thinking processes. Parrillo (1994) stated, "Slavery may end, segregation may end, but some people still believe blacks are inferior" (p. 355). Parrillo (1994) provided a comprehensive perspective on this phenomenon: People draw conclusions about other people from their observable world, their "objective reality." From their vantage point, people may observe that African Americans are unemployed and poor, live in dangerous neighborhoods, are receiving government assistance, or do not achieve in school. What people sometimes fail to realize is that this so-called, so-perceived "objective reality" is only a temporal reality, a snapshot. It is a reality that is objectively observed at a particular point in time, but this reality has been socially constructed over hundreds of years. As Parrillo (1994) stated in referring to African Americans' experiences in the United States, "overcoming 200 years of social conditioning is not easy." (p. 355). The impact of social conditioning was especially strong considering its nature. It was highly aggressive and totally dominating for African Americans. In addition, it is difficult for White people to overcome 400 years of racial-superiority social conditioning.

## HISPANIC AMERICANS

### General Profile

Hispanics in the United States comprise a population sharing diverse migration histories, acculturation experiences, and experiences with prejudice, racism, and discrimination, but are tied together by similar linguistic heritage--the Spanish language (Burgos-Ocasio, 2000; Flores, 2000). As noted by Gonzalez (1997), the term "Hispanic" is a federal designation used to classify individuals who reside in the United States and claim a lineage or cultural identity with Spain. Several researchers (Gonzalez, 1997; Lee, 1999; Sue & Sue, 1999) have articulated the concerns of many Hispanics that the term *Hispanic* implies a homogeneous group and ignores individual heritages, that some Hispanics prefer to be identified differently (e.g., Latino, Chicano, Mestizo, Mexican American), and that some prefer to be identified by their country of origin. Axelson (1999) believes that Hispanic ethnic identity is sometimes a function of not only acculturation but also current political, economic, and social circumstances.

The Hispanic population in the United States now numbers more than 35 million, and it is projected that by 2050, one of every four Americans will be Hispanic (Flores, 2000; The Learning Network, 2001). The rise in numbers is attributed to high birth rates and immigration. Flores (2000) maintained that the numbers do not include undocumented immigrants, assimilated Hispanics--those who label themselves as Americans and de-emphasize their Spanish heritage, and full-blooded Indians from Mexico and South America. Despite rapid growth, the Hispanic population in the United States continues to be underestimated.

### The Spanish Conquerors

Although extremely diverse, the Hispanic population shares a common connection with the Spanish conquistadores and Christopher Columbus who introduced the Hispanic culture to the Western hemisphere. Burgos-Ocasio (2000) pointed out that the Spanish conquistador Juan Ponce de Leon is credited with founding Florida in the 1500s; and prior to 1700, Mexicans were residing in what is now the Southwestern United States. Further, the Spanish explorers had established settlements in the Southwest and West, including what are now the states of California, Texas, Arizona, New Mexico, Texas, Nevada, Utah, Colorado, and Wyoming (Axelson, 1999; Gonzalez, 1997). The Spanish presence in the "New World" extended from 1492 until 1898 when the Spanish American War saw Spain relinquishing its last two colonies-Cuba which became an independent country, and Puerto Rico, which was annexed by the U.S. (Parrillo, 1994).

There are more than 21 distinct Hispanic groups in the United States today. The largest groups include Mexican Americans, who constitute approximately 64% of the Hispanic population, and number 13.5 million; Puerto Ricans, who number around 2.7 million, and make up more than 10% of the Hispanic population; Cubans, who number more than one million and make up close to 5% of the Hispanic population; and Hispanics from Central and South America who make up more that 13% of the Hispanic population (Peterson & Gonzalez, 2000). Hispanics now outnumber African Americans as the nation's largest minority group, and it is projected that by 2020, the Hispanic population in California will outnumber the non-Hispanic population (Flores, 2000; The Learning Network, 2001).

The migration history and experiences of Mexicans, Puerto Ricans, and Cubans in the United States will be examined because these groups share a long, historical, sometimes tumultuous relationship with the United States. It is important to point out that Hispanics from Central and South America (13.4% of the current Hispanic population) have replaced Puerto Ricans as the second largest Hispanic population in the United States (Flores 2000; Peterson & Gonzalez, 2000).

## Mexican Americans

Mexican Americans constitute the largest and fastest growing of the more than twenty-one different Hispanic groups in the United States (Flores, 2000; Lee, 1999; Sue & Sue, 1999), and many regional variations exist within this population. The increase in numbers has been attributed to high birth rates and immigration. Gonzalez (1997) contended that these numbers are likely underestimated because of the numbers of undocumented immigrants who have entered the United States from across the Mexican border seeking a better life for themselves and their families. Presently, the largest numbers of Mexican Americans live in California and Texas (Baruth & Manning, 1999; Gonzalez, 1997). Flores (2000) explained that large numbers of Mexican Americans inhabited California before it became part of the United States, and since 1970, the immigration rate of Mexican Americans to California has been high.

Mexican Americans can trace their origins to the Spanish conquistadores who left Spain for the Americas seeking land, gold, wealth, and religious domination, by plundering the Indian cities and conquering the indigenous Aztec peoples (Mexico: A Country Study, 1996). The conquistadores who settled in the Southwest from the 16th century until the Mexican War of Independence with Spain in 1821 embarked on a mission to eradicate the indigenous culture and "civilize and Christianize" the Native inhabitants. Axelson (1999) noted that they imported their language, culture, values, and religion, founded colonies and Catholic missions in New Mexico, Texas, California, and Arizona, and intermarried with the Native American Indian population, producing offspring called Mestizos who represent the majority of today's Mexican population.

Axelson (1999) maintained that from 1821 to 1848, there was extreme tension among the United States, Texas, and Mexico. Gutierrez (1999) noted that in the 1820s there was thriving trade between Texas and U.S. states and territories to its east. Many from the U.S. were moving into Texas. U.S. Government envoys led unsuccessful attempts to buy Mexico's northern provinces, and the Mexican government made unsuccessful attempts to colonize Texas. By 1835, many Anglo and Mexican Texans desired independence from Mexico. Texas won its independence in 1836, but tensions continued between Mexico and the Texas Republic. Texas was annexed by the U.S. in 1845, and war between the U.S. and Mexico raged from 1845 to 1847. In 1848, the Treaty of Guadalupe Hidalgo was signed. The agreement ended the war, relinquished the northern third of Mexico's territory to the U.S., and offered citizenship to any Mexicans inhabiting the area (Gutierrez, 1999; Mexico: A Country Study, 1996). The annexed territories include present-day Texas, New Mexico, Arizona, Utah, Nevada, California, most of Colorado, and portions of Wyoming (O'Rourke, 1998).

There were between 75,000 and 100,000 Mexicans who remained in the annexed territories. Mexican officials had hoped that the citizenship rights they had negotiated for their former citizens would protect them. However, growth in the Mexican immigrant and Anglo-American populations in the U.S. West undermined the Mexican Americans' social and political status, reinforced their ethnic minority status, and "hastened them down the path toward a subordinate status in their own homelands" (Gutierrez, 1999, p. 376). Discrimination continued into the 1900s with many Mexicans in the Southwest losing valuable land, being mercilessly exploited, and becoming, in essence "a conquered people" (Axelson, 1999, p. 126).

Mass migration to the United States came from the desire to escape poverty and political turmoil, and to provide better lives for their families. Regarded as a source of cheap labor by the agriculture, mining, railroad, textile, and other industries, Mexican laborers--especially undocumented workers--were mercilessly exploited by powerful farmers, ranchers and industrialists who often forced them to work in inhumane conditions, violated their rights, and treated them as third class citizens (Lee, 1999). Further, because many were illiterate, and a came across the border illegally, the ever present threat of being "rounded up" and deported remained constant.

Presently, the economy of the United States is fueled by Mexican labor. Axelson (1999, p. 126) maintained:

> Today, many of the agricultural, business, and manufacturing enterprises in parts of the country are so dependent on Mexican labor that they would have difficulty continuing without it. The political and financial influence of these employers, along with the proximity of the two countries and the enormous length of border makes it difficult, if not impossible to prevent immigration.

There have been efforts between the United States and Mexico to stem the tide of undocumented Mexican immigrants into the U.S. Randall (2001) pointed out that in 1924, the U.S. Border Patrol was established, and between 1929 and 1935, it succeeded in deporting thousands of Mexican Americans and their families without the benefit of court hearings. In addition, Axelson (1999) mentioned that in 1942, the Bracero program was established—a program designed to import inexpensive Mexican labor to the United States. Although most of the braceros returned home to Mexico upon expiration of their contracts, non-sanctioned immigration continued and the program finally expired in 1964. During the economic recession of the mid 1950s, the U.S. Immigration and Naturalization Services launched a massive program, termed *Operation Wetback*, directed at deporting undocumented workers (Axelson, 1999; Randall, 2001). Through this operation, more than 3 million "undocumented" Mexicans were deported, and less than 2% were granted a formal hearing. Therefore, many who were deported had no chance to prove their documented status (Parrillo, 1994). This action further strained the already fragile relationship between the Mexican and Anglo American communities.

Through the last half of the 20th century, people in Mexico and in the U.S. continued to advocate for undocumented Mexican immigrants, seeking rights to fair and equitable treatment under the United States Constitution. In 1982, the Supreme Court ruled that children of undocumented workers are entitled to a free public education (Axelson, 1999). Other legal rulings which have affected Mexican Americans include The 1967 Bilingual Education Act, The 1968 Elementary and Secondary Education Act, The 1974 Ethnic Heritage Act which granted an education for children with English language difficulties, The Amendment to The Voting Rights Act of 1965 which sought protection for language groups, and The Immigration Reform and Control Act of 1986 which sought, among other things, to grant amnesty to undocumented Mexican immigrants (Randall, 2001).

Mexican Americans have been active socially and politically, and have gained recognition by advocating for the rights of migrant workers (e.g., Cesar Chavez). However, a legacy of political and economic oppression, poverty, unemployment, illiteracy, prejudice, ethnocentrism, and discrimination continues to affect their psyche and full acceptance into the dominant society (Flores, 2000; Sue & Sue, 1999). For example, Arbona (1995) noted that Hispanic Americans with lighter skin tone experience less discrimination than do Hispanic Americans with darker skin—a colorism similar to that described earlier regarding African Americans.

Parrillo (1994) maintained that the very diversity of the Mexican American population makes it difficult to establish a unified political agenda. Therefore, Mexican Americans are underrepresented in many local and state governments across the U.S. Southwest and West. The educational attainment of Mexican Americans is also a concern. Reed and Ramirez (1997) reported that only 8% of Mexican Americans age 25 and over have completed a bachelor's degree, whereas 25% of non-Hispanics in that age range have completed a bachelor's degree. Gutierrez (1999) illuminated the concern effectively: If political efforts to deny access to public education for undocumented Mexicans are successful (e.g., California's Proposition 187), the main means of social mobility for many Mexican Americans vanishes, and a growing underclass grows more rapidly.

## Puerto Ricans

The Puerto Rican population currently accounts for over 10% of the Hispanic population in the United States. Discovered in 1493 by Christopher Columbus, Puerto Rico remained under Spanish rule until 1898 when it was ceded to the United States by Spain at the end of the Spanish American War (Randall, 2001). Most of the island's indigenous population was destroyed by the Spaniards. Beginning in the early 1500s, the population was supplanted by African slaves brought to the New World (Fitzpatrick, as cited in Burgos-Ocasio, 2000). Thus Puerto Rican culture is a mixture of Spanish colonial culture, African, European, and Native Indian influences (Garcia-Preto, 1996). Because of economic opportunities, the majority of Puerto Ricans are concentrated in New York and New Jersey; however, Puerto Ricans live in all fifty states (Burgos-Ocasio, 2000; Flores, 2000; Sue & Sue, 1999).

Axelson (1999) pointed out that from 1900 until 1974, as an unincorporated territory of the United States, the island was governed by officials appointed by the President of the United States. In 1948, the island elected its first governor, as a result of the amended Jones Act, and in 1952 gained commonwealth status (Randall, 2001). As a United States commonwealth (free-associated state), Puerto Rico enjoys close social, economic, and political ties to the United States; however its political status is ambiguous (Whalen, 1999). Although United States citizens since 1917, Puerto Ricans do not vote in presidential elections, do not have elected congressional representatives, nor do they pay federal taxes (Axelson, 1999). Puerto Ricans continue to struggle with some major political issues including statehood versus commonwealth status versus independence (Whalen, 1999), and the U.S. military bombing exercises on the island of Vieques.

Axelson (1999) and Ortiz (1996) explained that limited employment opportunities and impoverishment brought on by industrialization and technological advancements forced many Puerto Ricans to migrate to the United States mainland in search of better economic opportunities. But many who left their homeland hoped to return. Many came as temporary contract laborers and agricultural workers, whereas others have filled service and clerical positions. However, high rates of poverty, unemployment, poor educational preparation, and female headed, single parent households continue to limit the full participation of many in mainstream society (Axelson, 1999; Bailey & Ellis,1993; Dana, 1993; Sue & Sue, 1999). One factor related to the lower socioeconomic status of Puerto Ricans is the cultural ethic that discourages women from working outside the home (Parrillo, 1994). Although the socioeconomic status of Puerto Ricans as a group is well lower than the U.S. average, there is much socioeconomic within-group variability. For example, about 40% of Puerto Ricans have incomes at or above the U.S. median income, and 10% have incomes sufficient to be classified as affluent (Parrillo, 1996).

Puerto Ricans living in the U.S. mainland have generally maintained a strong ethnic and cultural identity. Even for many third-generation, mainland Puerto Ricans, there is a strong commitment to bilingualism. Community life centers around family networks, ethnic neighborhoods (barrios), churches, and businesses. Many community activist organizations have developed over previous decades, and Puerto Rican women have played a prominent role in activism. For example, groups of women worked for and won bilingual education for children. Other groups have been instrumental in increasing access to higher education (Whalen, 1999). Fortunately, many Puerto Ricans are free to migrate between the United States and their homeland without the threat of deportation. Presently, many are choosing to return to Puerto Rico where they can maintain their strong ethnic and cultural identity and participate fully and equally in the economic, social, and cultural community.

## Cubans/Cuban Americans

Discovered by Columbus in 1492, Cuba was regarded as one of the most valuable Spanish colonies in the Caribbean. Axelson (1999) reported that it was settled by Spanish conquistadores, who in their quest for wealth and riches, managed to eradicate the more than one million Native Ciboney Indians. Beginning in the early 1500s, the Spanish began replacing the original manual labor force with African slaves. In 1898, the Spanish American War ended Spanish domination of Cuba, and it was governed by the United States military until 1902, which saw the election of a constitutional government (Axelson, 1999). The United States continued to play an active role in Cuba until the 1959 Cuban revolution. As Axelson (1999, p. 31) wrote, "Although the United States government lent its support, its influence was seen as undesirable to the cultural and revolutionary movement. American-owned sugar plantations, cattle ranches, oil refineries, and other businesses were seized."

When Fidel Castro came to political power, he created a Marxist state; consequently, relations between Cuba and the United States soured considerably (Burgos-Ocasio, 2000). In 1961, Cuba and the United States ended diplomatic ties, and in 1962 commercial air travel and open immigration ended between the United States and Cuba (Randall, 2001). Soon after the revolution, there was mass migration of Cuban citizens to the U.S., notably to Miami, New Jersey, and New York, and others went to Puerto Rico, Mexico, and Spain.

In 1961 a group of Cuban exiles attempted to invade Cuba in the Bay of Pigs expedition. The 1,500 Cuban refuges were trained by the U.S. Central Intelligence Agency (CIA), and the action was supported by several other U.S. agencies. In just a few days, the invaders were captured or killed. Several months later, Cuba released 1,000 of the captured invaders in exchange for medical supplies and infant food (Axelson, 1999). Axelson (1999, p.132) continued the series of events, writing,

> In 1964 with the strong persuasion of the United States, the Organization of American States (OAS) voted political and economic sanctions against Cuba, barring hemispheric countries from conducting trade or other relations with Cuba. Prior to the blockade, the United States had provided 90% of Cuba's imports. Cuba was thus forced to turn to the Soviet Union and other Eastern European countries to buy goods.

Today, changing world politics have left Cuba to fend for itself, and relations between Cuba and the United States remain tenuous. However, to garner the support of the Cuban American community Castro "released 3, 600 political prisoners in 1979, half of whom went to the United States under a special parole program. In return, he encouraged Cuban Americans to return as tourists and to renew relationships with relatives and friends. . . in Cuba" (Axelson, 1999, p. 132).

The first Cuban exodus to the United States in 1959 included older, affluent, middle and upper class professionals who were welcomed as political refugees. Most came to Miami and New York, and initially, long-time residents in those areas were concerned that Cubans would overburden social-service systems (Parrillo, 1994). However, the new immigrants quickly adjusted to United States culture. Their strong capitalist orientation resulted in thriving businesses in banking, textiles, furniture, real estate, food, cigars, and trade (Burgos-Ocasio, 2000; Dana, 1993; Flores, 2000; Parrillo, 1994).

The second Cuban exodus into the United States, referred to as the Mariel boatlift, saw more than 125,000 Cubans migrating to Florida from April through August of 1980 (Axelson, 1999; Randall, 2001). Unlike the first wave of Cuban immigrants, this group consisted of working class individuals, prison inmates, mental patients, and all other "undesirables" that Castro wished to banish from Cuba, and many could not speak English (Axelson, 1999; Dana, 1993). This migration was sanctioned by Castro, and while welcomed initially by Americans, there was concern as to whether or not the United States could accommodate the refugees. Although many were detained in refugee camps across various states, and given special refugee status, they were eventually placed with sponsors willing to assist with their resettlement (Axelson, 1999; Flores, 2000). In 1984, the United States Immigration and Naturalization Service granted Cubans who were a part of the Mariel boatlift eligibility to apply for permanent residence status (Randall, 2001).

The Cuban population in the United States exceeds one million, with more than 70% identifying themselves as first generation Cuban Americans (Axelson, 1999; Flores, 2000). Whereas the majority of Cubans classify themselves as White and of Spanish heritage, others consider themselves Black, mulatto, Native American, or mixed (Axelson, 1999). Cubans share a common language, Spanish, and a common turbulent history. The majority of Cubans in the United States reside in Miami, and despite their tumultuous past have managed to function effectively in mainstream U.S. culture (Axelson, 1999; Burgos-Ocasio, 2000; Dana, 1993; Flores, 2000). Many people assert that Cuban-Americans were instrumental in making Miami into a thriving economic and cultural center, and that Cuban Americans have brought many other U.S. communities to economic, social, and cultural vitality (see Grenier & Perez, 1999; Parrillo, 1994). Whereas Cubans have become strongly rooted in the U.S., they continue to be strongly nationalistic; and most consider Cuba their home. Many Cuban-Americans have the goal of rebuilding their homeland (Grenier & Perez, 1999).

This section has presented important information on the migration patterns, and historical experiences of three major Hispanic groups in the United States. It is important to keep in mind that although Hispanic groups share some cultural values, they represent more than twenty-one different Spanish-speaking and two Portuguese-speaking countries (Flores, 2000). Also, many people of Hispanic heritage were living in what is now the United States before the United States "owned" those territories, and even before there was a United States. Many individuals of Spanish ancestry strongly believe that the term "Hispanic" does not do justice to the diversity of people found in this population. Thus it becomes important for therapists to recognize that "the appreciation or understanding of individuals in any group, or the group itself, is distinct and unique, and cannot be completely captured by any single generalization or description" (Flores, 2000, p.300).

## ASIAN AMERICANS

### Early Immigration

The first large-scale immigration of Asians into the U.S. began during the 1840s, when many Chinese came to California and the West Coast area in response to the discovery of gold (Marden & Meyer, 1973; Yung, 1999). Most of these Chinese immigrants were men; and because of the scarcity of women in frontier regions, most fell into employment in jobs usually performed by women, such as cooking, cleaning, and other domestic-type jobs (Kitano, 1991). As the need for laborers diminished in subsequent years, the Chinese began to be seen as the "yellow peril." An anti-Chinese, racist movement developed. Chinese were seen as "subhuman," and they were blatantly discriminated against (Sue & Sue, 1993). Chinese miners were killed by mobs of Whites (Takaki, 1993), and these Whites had little fear of prosecution for their crimes because at that time in California, Chinese where not allowed to testify against Whites (Kitano, 1991).

During the 1850s, many laws were passed that discriminated against Chinese laborers. For example, in California, Chinese laundries were taxed and Chinese miners were required to pay special taxes and fees. Chinese were not allowed to own property (Kitano, 1991; Takaki, 1993). At the end of the next decade, the Central Pacific Railroad was completed. Ninety percent of railroad laborers were Chinese, and they became jobless. The resulting competition for jobs fueled racism, leading to increased discrimination and violence perpetrated against Chinese Americans in the 1870s (Marden & Meyer, 1973; Takiki, 1993).

After the collapse of post U.S. Civil War Reconstruction, Southerners in the U.S. supported Californians in the U.S. Congress and the Chinese Exclusion Act of 1882 was passed (Marden & Meyer, 1973). The Chinese Exclusion Act was the first time that the U.S. restricted immigration based on race and national origin. McLemore (1980) stated, "for the first time, American policy accepted the idea that an entire group may be undesirable because of its race or nationality" (p. 71). This act was later extended to include all Asians, and stayed in effect until 1943, when 105 annual entries from China were allowed (Marden & Meyer, 1973). Yung (1999) summed up the message of the Chinese Exclusion Act, writing, "The Chinese were only welcomed as long as their labor was needed to develop the economic infrastructure of the American West." (p. 123)

## The Twentieth Century

Toward the end of the 1800s, Japanese agricultural workers immigrated to the U.S. By the early 1900s, the designation "yellow peril" referred more to Japanese than Chinese. In California, organized labor, the media, and both major political parties opposed further Japanese immigration (McLemore, 1980). In San Francisco, Asian children were segregated into a separate school. This action in California, however, led to friction between the Japanese and U.S. Governments. An agreement was reached that ended segregation of Asian students; and in exchange, the U.S. Government and Japan itself limited immigration to the U.S. (McLemore, 1980; Axelson, 1999). For economic and racist reasons, the Japanese and Korean Exclusion League (later renamed the Asiatic Exclusion League) was formed in the U.S. and in Canada (McLemore, 1980). This group also targeted South Asians (East Indians) in the U.S. West, describing this group to the public as a "menace," and influencing popular media outlets to print disparaging articles (Parrillo, 1980).

Given this environment of mistrust, prejudice, racism, and discrimination, the relocation of over 110,000 Japanese into camps during World War II was allowed (Sue & Sue, 1993). According to Marden and Meyer (1973), "This action was the most unprecedented single national action against a large group of people in American history" (p. 390). Many of those relocated were second- and third-generation Americans (Parrillo, 1980), and two-thirds were U.S. citizens (Tamura, 1999). Parrillo (1980, 1994) described this relocation as *incarceration*, likening camps to concentration camps.

Many camps were hastily built, there was little privacy, sanitation facilities were often not adequate, and physical conditions were often harsh. Centralized dining facilities made it difficult for families to dine together. Camps were surrounded by barbed wire and guard towers (Parrillo, 1980; Tamura, 1999). Many in the U.S. Government began to see a need to contrast the U.S. camps with Nazi concentration camps, and governmental officials began efforts to make the camps as democratic as possible (McLemore, 1980). Thus, conditions in the camps improved, and many young Japanese were allowed to leave camps for schooling in the Midwest and East (McLemore, 1980; Parrillo, 1980; Tamura, 1999).

"National security" was the "official" reason for incarcerating the Japanese from the Western U.S. There was no similar incarceration of Japanese in Hawaii, although Hawaii was more strategic to our national security at the time (Parrillo, 1980, 1994). Parrillo asserted that the difference in treatment of Japanese in Hawaii and the U.S. mainland was primarily due to structural discrimination. In Hawaii, the Japanese were more integrated into the economy (see Tamura, 1999), and there was less racism and hatred (see Parrillo, 1994). In the U.S. West, Japanese were more isolated and there was a legacy of racism toward Asians (Parrillo, 1980, 1994). Likewise, Marden and Meyer (1973) concluded that a national security explanation for internment has little merit. Pressure from public "civic" groups with economic and racist motivations was largely responsible for the decision to relocate the Japanese.

After World War II, Japanese began returning to their previous communities. Many of the same "civic" groups that supported their relocation opposed their return. However, some White church groups and other civic and political groups supported Japanese being able to return to their homes. In 1946, public opinion in California made a turn toward support of the Japanese (Marden & Meyer, 1973). Many Japanese people lost property as a result of incarceration during World War II. Some who were relocated received some compensation for their losses, but compensation was much smaller than actual losses, and returning Japanese were forced to adjust to a lower socioeconomic status (Marden & Meyer, 1973). Parrillo (1980) stated, "they lost property, savings, income, and jobs for which they were never adequately compensated" (p. 289). With regard to Japanese in Hawaii, 80% of Hawaiians killed in World War II were of Japanese ancestry (Marden & Meyer, 1973). Many U.S.-born Japanese American soldiers from Hawaii and from the U.S. mainland served bravely in the U.S. Army in World War II. Units received distinguished service citations for their fighting against the Germans in Italy and France. A Japanese unit helped liberate the Nazi extermination camp at Dachau, Germany. Japanese American soldiers were fighting bravely and dying for this country while parents of some soldiers were incarcerated in camps in the U.S. (see Several, 1998).

## A "Model Minority"

Marden and Meyer (1973) described Japanese Americans in the 1970s as a "model minority." In contemporary American society, Asian Americans--as a group--are described as a model minority (see Leong & Serafica, 1995; Parrillo, 1994). Although this may label may seem enviable, it has four subtle negative consequences. First, it tends to conceal the fact that there is much variability in levels of educational and economic success between and within Asian American groups. Some individuals and groups have struggled successfully, while struggles of other individuals and groups have been frustrated (Leong & Serafica, 1995). Second, individuals from some Asian-American groups tend to have psychological problems; and these problems are likely to be unrecognized or untreated (Sue & Sue, 1993). Also, being stereotyped as high achievers increases stress levels for Asian American youth (Parrillo, 1994). Third, the public often makes unfair, nonobjective comparisons between Asian Americans and other racial-ethnic groups, holding Asian Americans up as a model for others to emulate (Parrillo, 1994). And fourth, the model-minority label contributes to the illusion that there is no discrimination against Asian Americans. Leong and Serafica (1995) provided evidence that educational attainment results in fewer economic rewards for Asian Americans than it does for European Americans. In the contemporary media, Asian Americans are still portrayed in stereotypical caricatures. Although the level of overt discrimination against Asian Americans may have lessened over the last few decades, and although gains have been made by many Asian Americans, racism and discrimination against these groups and individuals continue (Sue & Sue, 1993).

We have presented some of the major historical events and experiences impacting some groups of Asian Americans. Asian and Pacific Islanders are represented by over 25 distinct groups, and there is much variability within and among these groups (Sue & Sue, 1993). Many of these groups do share common experiences. They have all experienced racism and discrimination; and Asian Americans, in general, underutilize counseling services. Even when compared to other U.S. minority groups, Asian Americans underutilize counseling services; and underutilization is not caused by lack of need (Gau, 1996; Nishio & Bilmes, 1993; Root, 1993). The main reasons for underutilization, from synthesis of the literature, seem to be (a) preference for using family and community resources, (b) the lack of counselors who are similar ethnically and counselors' lack of familiarity with Asian Americans' language and culture, and (c) inappropriate interventions used by counselors (Gau, 1996; Leong et al., 1995).

## CLASS AND SMALL GROUP ACTIVITIES

### Ancestry

This is an activity that requires some work outside class, but it is done with the class as a whole:

1. First, have class members take a week or so to research their ancestors and family histories, concentrating on the country-of-origin of surnames of parents, grandparents, great-grandparents, and so forth. Information on when ancestors came to North America or other parts of the World will be useful. Also, other information on particular ancestors (e.g., participation in wars, ancestors' occupations and achievements) will be useful.
2. In class, call out names of countries, areas, parts of the world one at a time (e.g., England, China, North Africa, Ireland, Spain, Poland, etc.). If class members have ancestors from that particular country or part of the world, they stand. To show those standing that their diversity and survival are appreciated, those seated applaud those standing. Those people standing give the surname of the ancestor (if known); and if they have information about that ancestor, they briefly share it with the class. When that group is finished sharing, they sit down; then the class appropriately honors all those from that country or part of the world that did not survive to fulfill their dreams or experience freedom in this country. For example, in the case of African American groups, the class might take a moment of silence to honor those who died on ships, plantations, battles, or who died as slaves. The activity proceeds through all groups represented by the class. Most class members will stand several times. If some groups are not represented by the class (e.g., Hispanic American groups), the class should appropriately honor those groups. If Native American groups are not represented, they should be honored, especially those tribes that occupied the geographic area of the university.

3.  An additional, optional component of the activity would be to have class members make a collage or other visual representation of their cultural heritages. This could be done collectively or individually.

## Mixed Messages

1.  Form into groups of 4 to 7 people.
2.  Have each group member list 3 positive and 3 negative messages that were passed down to them regarding specific racial-ethnic groups. These messages came from parents, teachers, leaders, the media, and so forth.
3.  Have members take turns sharing their negative messages.
4.  As messages are shared, the group discusses the nature and origins of these messages. How were these messages communicated? In what context were these messages communicated? What dimensions of superiority-inferiority "logic" were the bases for these messages? What is the historical basis of these messages? Are these messages part of our cultural heritage?
5.  Have members take turns sharing their positive messages. How were these messages communicated? In what context were these messages communicated? What were the origins of these messages?
6.  Process the activity by answering the following questions: Which type of message was more difficult to remember, positive messages or negative messages? Were positive and negative messages sometimes communicated together (e.g., we treat people with respect, but . . . )? Were the messages more often subtle or were they obvious? How did the quality and content of messages differ depending on characteristics of group members--age, make-up of communities, socioeconomic status, racial-ethnic group, geographic region, urban/suburban/rural, parents' history, religious background? How did these messages affect how you viewed specific racial-ethnic groups in the past—how you view groups now? What can counselors do to counter the effects of negative messages?

## REFERENCES

Albanese, A. (1976). *The plantation school.* New York: Vantage Press.

American Counseling Association (1995). *ACA code of ethics & standards of practice.* Alexandria, VA: Author.

Anastasi, A. (1988). *Psychological testing* (6th ed.). New York: Macmillan.

Anderson, C., & Cromwell, R. (1977). "Black is beautiful" and the color preference of Afro-American youth. *Journal of Negro Education, 46,* 76-88.

Arbona, C. (1995). Theory and research on racial and ethnic minorities: Hispanic Americans. In F. T. L. Leong (Ed.), *Career development and vocational behavior of racial and ethnic minorities,* (pp. 37-66). Mahwah, NJ: Lawrence Erlbaum Associates.

Atkinson, D. R., Morten, G., & Sue, D. W. (1993). *Counseling American minorities: A cross-cultural perspective* (4th ed.). Madison, WI: Brown & Benchmark.

Axelson, J. A. (1999). *Counseling and development in a multicultural society* (3rd ed.). Pacific Grove, CA: Brooks/Cole.

Bailey, A. J., & Ellis, M. (1993). Going home: The migration of Puerto-Rican born women from the United States to Puerto Rico. *Professional Geographer, 45(2),* 148-158.

Blassingame, J. W. (1972). *The slave community.* New York: Oxford University Press.

Baruth, L. G., & Manning, M. L. (1999). *Multiultural counseling and psychotherapy: A lifespan perspective*( 2nd ed.). New Jersey: Prentice-Hall.

Brawley, B. (1924). *A short history of the American Negro.* New York: MacMillan.

Burgos-Ocasio, H. (2000). Hispanic women. In M. Julia (Ed.), *Constructing gender: Multicultural perspectives in working with women* (pp.109-138). California: Brooks/Cole.

Butchart, R. (1990). Recruits to the "army of civilization": Gender, race, class, and the freedmen's teachers, 1862-1875. *Journal of Education, 172,* 76-87.

Conerly, L. W. (1909). *Pike County, Mississippi, 1798-1910, pioneer families and Confederate soldiers, reconstruction and redemption.* Reprinted in E. R. Williams, Jr. *Source records from Pike County, Mississippi.* Easley, SC: Southern Historical Press.

Conrad, E. (1966) *The invention of the Negro.* New York: Paul S. Eriksson.

Coombs, N. (1972). *The Black Experience in America.* New York: Twayne.

Curry, R., & Cowden, J. (1972). *Slavery in America.* Itasca, IL: F.E. Peacock.

Dana, R. H. (1993). *Multicultural assessment perspectives for professional psychology.* Boston: Allyn and Bacon.

Daniels, J. (1962). *The devil's backbone: The story of the Natchez Trace.* New York: Mc Graw-Hill.

Dovidido, J. F. & Gaertner, S. L. (1991). Changes in the expression and assessment of racial prejudice. In H. J. Knopke, R. J. Norrell, & R. W. Rogers (Eds.), *Opening doors: Perspectives on race relations in contemporary America* (pp. 119-148). Tuscaloosa, AL: University of Alabama Press.

Drummond, R. J. (2000). *Appraisal procedures for counselors and helping professionals* (4th ed.). Upper Saddle River, NJ: Merrill.

Elkins, S. (1959). *Slavery: A problem in American and institutional and intellectual life.* New York: Grosset & Dunlap.

Fitzpatrick, J. P. (1971). *Puerto Rican Americans: The meaning of migration to the mainland.* Englewood Cliffs, NJ: Prentice Hall.

Flores. M. T. (2000). Demographics: Hispanic populations in the United States. In M. Flores & G. Carey (Eds.), *Family therapy with Hispanics* ( pp. 297-321). Boston: Allyn & Bacon

Gau, H. (1996). *Perceptions regarding utilization of professional counselors among non-client Chinese Americans: A qualitative study.* Unpublished doctoral dissertation, Texas A&M University-Commerce.

Garcia- Preto, N. (1996). Latino families: An overview. In M. McGoldrick, J. Giordano, & J. K. Pearce (Eds.), *Ethnicity and family therapy* (pp.141-154*).*. New York: Guilford Press.

Gonzalez, G. (1997). The emergence of Chicanos in the twenty-first century: Implications for counseling, research, and policy. *Journal of Multicultural Counseling and Development, 25,* 94-106.

Grenier, G. J., & Perez, L. (1999). Cubans. In E. R. Barkan (Ed.), *A nation of peoples: A sourcebook on America's multicultural heritage* (pp. 138-155). Westport, CN: Greenwood Press.

Grier, W., & Cobbs, P. (1968). *Black rage.* New York: Basic Books.

Gutierrez, D. G. (1999). Mexicans. In E. R. Barkan (Ed.), *A nation of peoples: A sourcebook on America's multicultural heritage* (pp. 372-390). Westport, CN: Greenwood Press.

Haertel, C. E. J., Douthitt, S. S., Haertel, G., & Douthitt, S. Y. (1999). Equally qualified but unequally perceived: Openness to perceived dissimilarity as a predictor of race and sex discrimination in performance judgments. *Human Resource Development Quarterly, 10,* 79-89.

Higginbotham, L. (1996). The ten precepts of American slavery jurisprudence: Chief justice Roger Taney's defense and justice Thurgood Marshall's condemnation of the precept of Black inferiority. *Cardozo Law Review, 17,* 1695-1711.

Horton, H. (1994). The legacy of slavery. *New England Journal of Public Policy, Summer-Fall,* 259-269.

Ivey, A. E. (1995). Psychotherapy as liberation. In J. G. Ponterotto, J. M. Casas, L. A. Suzuki, & C. M. Alexander (Eds.), *Handbook of multicultural counseling* (pp. 53-72). Thousand Oaks, CA: Sage.

Ivey, A. E., Ivey, M. B., & Simek-Morgan, L. (1993). *Counseling and psychotherapy: A multicultural perspective* (3rd ed.). Boston: Allyn and Bacon.

Jackson, M. L. (1995). Multicultural counseling: Historical perspectives. In J. G. Ponterotto, J. M. Casas, L. A. Suzuki, & C. M. Alexander (Eds.), *Handbook of multicultural counseling* (pp. 3-16). Thousand Oaks, CA: Sage.

Jones, R. (1996). In the absence of ethnicity. *Society,* 44-47.

Kardiner, A., & Ovesey, L. (1951). *The mark of oppression.* Cleveland, OH: The World Publishing.

Katz, W. (1968). *The suppressed book about slavery.* New York: Arno Press.

Kehoe, A. B. (1999). American Indians. In E. R. Barkan (Ed.), *A nation of peoples: A sourcebook on America's multicultural heritage* (pp. 48-74). Westport, CN: Greenwood Press.

Keith, V., & Herring, C. (1991). Skintone and stratification in the Black community. *American Journal of Sociology, 97,* 760-778.

Kitano, H. H. L. (1991). *Race relations* (4th ed.). Englewood Cliffs, NJ: Prentice Hall.

Lee, W. L. (1999). *An introduction to multicultural counseling.* USA: Taylor & Francis.

Leong, F. T. L., & Serafica, F. C. (1995). Career development of Asian Americans: A research area in need of a good theory. In F. T. L. Leong (Ed.), *Career development and vocational behavior of racial and ethnic minorities,* (pp. 67-102). Mahwah, NJ: Lawrence Erlbaum Associates.

Leong, F. T. L., Wagner, N. S., & Tata, S. P. (1995). Racial and ethnic variations in help-seeking attitudes. In J. G. Ponterotto, J. M. Casas, L. A. Suzuki, & C. M. Alexander (Eds.), *Handbook of multicultural counseling* (pp. 415-438). Thousand Oaks, CA: Sage.

Marden, C. F., & Meyer, G. (1973). *Minorities in American society* (4th ed.). New York: D. Van Nordstrand.

Markstrom-Adams, C. (1990). Coming-of-age among contemporary American Indians as portrayed in adolescent fiction. *Adolescence, 25,* 225-237.

McAdoo, H. (1997). *Black families.* Thousand Oaks, CA: Sage.

McLemore, S. D. (1980). *Racial and ethnic relations in America*. Boston: Allyn and Bacon.

Mellon, J. (1988). *Bullwhip days: The slaves remember*. New York: Avon Books.

*Mexico: A country study*. (1996). Retrieved November 15, 2001, from http://lcweb2.loc.gov/cgi-bin/query2/r?frd/csdy:@field (DOCID+mx0013)

Morgan, J. C. (1933). *Slavery in the United States: Four views*. Jefferson, NC: McFarland & Company.

Nicolay, J., & Hart, J. (1914). *Abraham Lincoln: A history*. New York: The Century Company.

Nishio, K., & Bilmes, M. (1993). Psychotherapy with Southeast Asian American clients. In D. R. Atkinson, G. Morten, & D. W. Sue (Eds.), *Counseling American minorities: A cross-cultural perspective* (4th ed., pp. 225-234). Madison, WI: Brown & Benchmark.

O'Rourke, D. (1998). *Our war with Mexico: Re-reading Guadalupe Hidalgo*. Retrieved November 15, 2001, from http://www.findarticles.com/cf_dls/ml1252/n5_v125/20485534/print.jhtml

Ortiz, V. (1996). Migration and marriage among Puerto Rican women. *International Migration Review, 30*(2), 460-484.

Parrillo, V. N. (1980). *Strangers to these shores: Race and ethnic relations in the United States*. Boston: Houghton Mifflin.

Parrillo, V. N. (1994). *Strangers to these shores: Race and ethnic relations in the United States* (4th ed.). New York: Macmillan.

Parrillo, V. N. (1996). *Diversity in America*. Thousand Oaks, CA: Pine Forge Press.

Peterson , N., & Gonzalez, R. C. (2000). *The role of work in people's lives: Applied career counseling and vocational psychology*. Pacific Grove, CA: Brooks/Cole.

Philips, U. (1959). *American Negro slavery*. Gloucester, MA: Peter Smith.

Ponterotto, J. G., & Pedersen, P. B. (1993). *Preventing prejudice: A guide for counselors and educators*. Newbury Park, CA: Sage.

Powdermaker, H. (1939). *After freedom*. New York: The Viking Press.

Ramirez, M., III (1991). *Psychotherapy and counseling with minorities: A cognitive approach to individual and cultural differences*. New York: Pergamon Press.

Ramirez, M., III (1999). *Multicultural psychotherapy: An approach to individual and cultural differences* (2nd ed.). Boston: Allyn and Bacon.

Randall, V. (2001). *Hispanic/Latino Americans: Laws and policies*. Retrieved November 15, 2001, from http://academic.udayton.edu/race/03justice/hislaws.htm

Reed, J., & Ramirez, R. R. (1997). *The Hispanic population in the United States: March 1997 (update)*. U.S. Census Bureau, Current Population Reports [On-line]. Retrieved September 30, 1999, from http://www.census.gov/population/www/socdemo/hispanic/ho97-1.html

Root, M. P. P. (1993). Guidelines for facilitating therapy with Asian American clients. In D. R. Atkinson, G. Morten, & D. W. Sue (Eds.), *Counseling American minorities: A cross-cultural perspective* (4th ed., pp. 211-224), WI: Brown & Benchmark.

Ropers, R. H., & Pence, D. J. (1995). *American prejudice: With liberty and justice for some*. New York: Plenum Press.

Several, M. (1998). Nikkei Veterans Monument. Retrieved November 12, 2001, from http://www.usc.edu/isd/archives/la/pubart/Downtown/Little_Tokoyo/veterans.html

Smith, T. M. (1997). *Findings from the condition of education 1996: Minorities in higher education*, (NCES Publication No. NCES 97-372). Washington, DC: U.S. Department of Education, National Center for Education Statistics.

Smythe, M. (1976). *The Black American: Reference book.* Englewood Cliffs, New Jersey: Prentice-Hall.

Steckel, R., & Jensen, R. (1986). New evidence on the causes of slave and crew mortality in the Atlantic slave trade. *Journal of Economic History, 46,* 57-77.

Sterba, J. (1996). Understanding evil: American slavery, the Holocaust, and the conquest of the American Indians. *Ethics, 106,* 424-448.

Sue, D., & Sue, D. W. (1993). Ethnic identity: Cultural factors in the psychological development of Asians in America. In D. R. Atkinson, G. Morten, & D. W. Sue (Eds.), *Counseling American minorities: A cross-cultural perspective* (4th ed., pp. 199-210). Madison, WI: Brown & Benchmark.

Sue, D. W., & Sue, D. (1999). *Counseling the culturally different: Theory and Practice* (3rd ed.). New York: John Wiley & Sons.

Takaki, R. T. (1993). *A different mirror: A history of multicultural America.* Boston: Little, Brown & Co.

Tamura, E. H. (1999). Japanese. In E. R. Barkan (Ed.), *A nation of peoples: A sourcebook on America's multicultural heritage* (pp. 311-329). Westport, CN: Greenwood Press.

Tannenbaum, F. (1946). *Slave and citizen: The Negro in the Americas.* New York: Alfred A. Knopf.

The Learning Network (2001). *Population of the United States by race and Hispanic origin: 2000 census results.* Retrieved November 15, 2001, from *http://In.infoplease.com/ipa/A0762156.html*

Thorndike, R. M. (1997). *Measurement and evaluation in psychology and education* (6th ed.). Upper Saddle River, NJ: Merrill.

Thorpe, E. (1961). *The mind of the Negro.* Baton Rouge, LA: Ortlieb Press.

U.S. Census Bureau (1995). *Hispanic today.* Washington, DC: U.S. Government Printing Office.

U.S. Census Bureau (2000). Educational attainment. U.S. Census Bureau, Education, Educational Attainment. Retrieved March 17, 2000, from *http://www.census.gov/population/www.socdemo/educ-attn.html*

Vivas-Maldonado, J. L. (1974). *Historia de Puerto Rico.* New York: L.A. Publishing.

Watts, T. D. (1993). Native Americans today: An outer view. *Journal of Alcohol & Drug Education, 38,* 125-130.

Whalen, C. T. (1999) Puerto Ricans. In E. R. Barkan (Ed.), *A nation of peoples: A sourcebook on America's multicultural heritage* (pp. 447-463). Westport, CN: Greenwood Press.

Yung, J. (1999). Chinese. In E. R. Barkan (Ed.), *A nation of peoples: A sourcebook on America's multicultural heritage* (pp. 119-137). Westport, CN: Greenwood Press.

# Chapter 2

# CONTEMPORARY ISSUES IN MULTICULTURAL COUNSELING: TRAINING COMPETENT COUNSELORS

**Tina Q. Richardson**
Lehigh University
**Elizabeth J. Jacob**
University of Scranton

## INTRODUCTION

The recent shift to focusing on multicultural issues within the counseling profession has led to counselor education programs implementing a variety of strategies to address the complex and multidimensional issues related to training culturally competent counselors. Kiselica (1998) indicated that there has been an increased emphasis on training professionals to be multicultural providers in a society that is becoming rapidly diverse. This shifting paradigm has led to varying suggestions and models of counselor training (Pedersen, 1988; Sue and Sue, 1990). The increasing trend within training programs has been to require students to take one course on multicultural issues in counseling (Ponterotto, 1996), with arguments also provided for infusion of multicultural issues across the curriculum (Constantine, Ladany, Inman, & Ponterotto, 1996). The emergence of multicultural competencies (Sue, Arrendondo, & McDavis, 1992; Sue et al., 1982) helps define at least in part what characterizes effective training and competent professional development. Competency standards in the related areas of (a) counselors' awareness of their own assumptions, values, and biases; (b) understanding the worldview of the culturally different client; and (c) developing appropriate intervention strategies and techniques moves the profession one giant step closer to identifying what may be considered *best practice* for training competent mental health workers (Sue, Arrendondo, & McDavis, 1992) (See Figure 1). Being able to identify best-practice approaches to multicultural training, and evaluating the effectiveness of competency-based counselor training may be some of the most important contemporary achievements for the counseling profession.

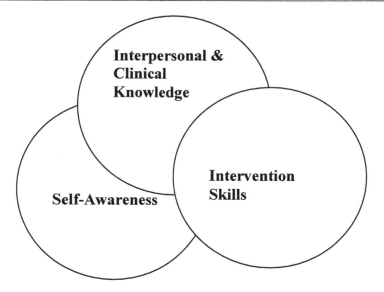

**Figure 1.** Multicultural Counseling Competence

The American Counseling Association's (ACA) Code of Ethics and Standards of Practice (American Counseling Association, 1995) has stated and clarified counselors' responsibility to respect differences and use nondiscriminatory practices. The American Psychological Association's (APA) Guidelines for Providers of Psychological Services to Ethnic, Linguistic, and Culturally Diverse Populations (1993) underscore this principle. Both ACA and APA explicitly express that mental health professionals should aspire to personal awareness in terms of how one's own cultural background, experiences, attitudes, vales, and biases influence the counseling process. The competency standards may be easily adapted to correspond directly with training objectives that are consistent with the profession's ethical guidelines and standards for practice.

The purpose of this chapter is twofold: (a) to discuss how multicultural competencies may be used to shape the learning process for counselor trainees and (b) to identify some contemporary multicultural issues with regard to content areas beyond those of race and culture that must be addressed in multicultural training. Thus, the first half of the chapter defines multicultural counseling and the competencies related to training. The remainder of the chapter identifies some of the multifaceted topic areas that must be addressed for counselors to become competent in our diverse society.

## DEFINING MULTICULTURAL COUNSELING
## AND RELATED COMPETENCIES

Although multicultural counseling has been defined in numerous works, the essence of its meaning is grounded in whether counseling is viewed from an etic or emic approach. Etic perspectives regarding multicultural counseling and human existence suggest that a core set of principles or processes transcend all racial and cultural boundaries. Proponents of etic frameworks contend that aspects of traditional theories are universally applicable to all people or that new culturally inclusive models can be created. Proponents of an emic approach suggest that culture specific perspectives are more appropriate for conceptualizing the human experience, and models of counseling should evolve from and reflect the particular racial or ethnic group.

We prefer Arrendondo 's (1992) definition of multicultural counseling because it reflects both etic and emic approaches to counseling. According to Arrendondo (1998), multicultural counseling refers to preparation and practices that integrate multicultural and culture-specific awareness, knowledge, and skills into counseling. Arrendondo also indicates that the term *multicultural*, in the context of counseling preparation and application, refers to five major racial-cultural groups in the United States and it territories: African American/Black, Asian, Caucasian/European, Hispanic/Latino, and Native American or indigenous groups who have historically resided in the continental United States and its territories. Some scholars might dispute this point. In fact, more agreement may be held for the notion that contemporary interest in the assessment and implementation of multiculturalism and multicultural competencies in the counseling process has its roots in the racial Civil Rights Movement of the 1960s and 1970s (Helms & Richardson, 1996). The activism of the civil rights era contributed to the mental health field paying more attention to the mental health needs of racial and ethnic minority groups (Cook & Helms, 1988). As a result of the recognized prevalence and inappropriateness of "deficit models" for diagnosing the mental health of African, Asian, Indigenous, and Hispanic Americans, it became increasingly common to use the multicultural rubric to incorporate other aspects of human diversity (i.e., ethnicity, gender, sexual orientation, religiosity, etc.) under the multicultural umbrella. It is our perspective that because people are multi-dimensional in that they simultaneously belong to racial, ethnic, gender, religion, age, and class groups as well as affectional orientations, it is neither appropriate nor beneficial to use a narrow perspective to define people or counseling processes. Thus, multicultural counseling should refer to the integration of multiple dimensions of client cultures into pertinent counseling theories, techniques, and practices with the specific intent of providing clients of all socio-demographic and psycho-demographic variations with effective mental health services (Richardson & Molinaro, 1996).

By this definition, multicultural competency does not require a unique set of skills related to any particular cultural characteristic per se; rather competency is a specific type of philosophical orientation--an orientation responsive to the relevant sociopolitical dynamics of race and the multidimensional principles of cultural socialization that are integrated into the counseling process, regardless of the client's ostensible socio-demographic characteristics (Richardson & Molinaro, 1996). The philosophical orientation is something that can be taught and achieved by any trainee or professional who engages in the life-long process of self-knowledge and worldview exploration. Sue et al. (1992) suggested that *universal* and *focused* multicultural approaches are necessary in order to provide effective services in general, because cultural issues need to be seen as central to all counseling, not just in work with clients who have been identified as a racial-ethnic minority or identified as belonging to a "special" population.

The competencies needed to become a skilled counselor must be used to inform practice. Sue and Sue (1990) described a culturally skilled counselor as (a) one who is actively engaged in the process of becoming aware of his or her own assumptions about human behavior, values, biases, preconceived notions, personal limitations, and so forth; (b) one who actively attempts to understand the worldview of his or her clients without negative judgments; and (c) one who is in the process of developing and practicing appropriate, relevant, and sensitive intervention strategies and skills in working with his or her clients. The three characteristics of awareness, knowledge, and skills are used as organizing principles under which the multicultural competencies are defined (Sue et al, 1992).

Pedersen (1988) described multicultural awareness as a professional obligation as well as an opportunity for the adequately trained counselor. As such, multicultural awareness increases a person's intentional and purposive decision-making by accounting for the many ways that culture influences different perceptions of the same situation. Culture is not external to an individual; it exists within the person, and operates as a learned competency. Counselors and trainees then must first engage in a process of self-awareness wherein they explore the fundamentals of their own values, habits, customs, perceptions, and life styles before they focus on an awareness of others. Sue and Sue (1999) indicated that skilled counselors engage in the conscious and intentional processes of examining their worldviews and cultural conditioning. This self-examination becomes reflected in their work with clients. Sue and Sue highlight the importance of knowledge acquisition to increase understanding of groups' and individuals' social and political realities, including relevant historical factors as well as contemporary influences that shape people's lives. Culturally skilled counselors use self-awareness and knowledge of similarities and differences to understand the worldviews of clients, void of the deleterious effects of negative judgments or generalizations. Studies consistently reveal that counseling effectiveness is improved when counselors use modalities and define goals consistent with the life experiences and worldview perspectives of clients. Cultural competence is demonstrated through the active process of transforming awareness and knowledge into the practice of appropriate, relevant, and culturally sensitive intervention strategies and skills.

Sue et al. (1992) indicated that the three characteristics of (a) counselor awareness of own assumptions, values, and biases; (b) understanding the worldview of the culturally different client; and (c) developing appropriate intervention strategies and techniques can be described as having three dimensions of (a) beliefs and attitudes, (b) knowledge, and (c) skills (see Sue et al., 1992 for a detailed listing of their nine competency areas).

We believe that multicultural competence for counselors also involves developing social or interpersonal competence in the three dimensions (see Figure 2). In this context, awareness refers to more than being aware of one's own assumptions, values, and biases which influence social interactions; it refers to acquiring accurate knowledge and meaningful understanding of worldview perspectives and behaviors that facilitate interpersonal relationships across cultural boundaries. Additionally, the combination of social awareness and knowledge can be integrated into social skills that are appropriate for establishing meaningful cross-cultural relationships that reflect mutual respect, positive regard, and significance. According to Herman (1993), an important determinant of successful counseling is the counselors' ability to build a helping alliance with the client, and the quality of that bond determines counseling outcome. Counselors' and clients' interpersonal qualities form that bond (Corey, Corey, & Callahan, 1988) and shape counselors' emotional availability (Zeddies, 1999). The practice of counseling and psychotherapy requires the ability to connect interpersonally with the client. Thus, in order for counselor competence to be developed in the multicultural realm, counselors must simultaneously develop multicultural interpersonal competence (see Figure 3).

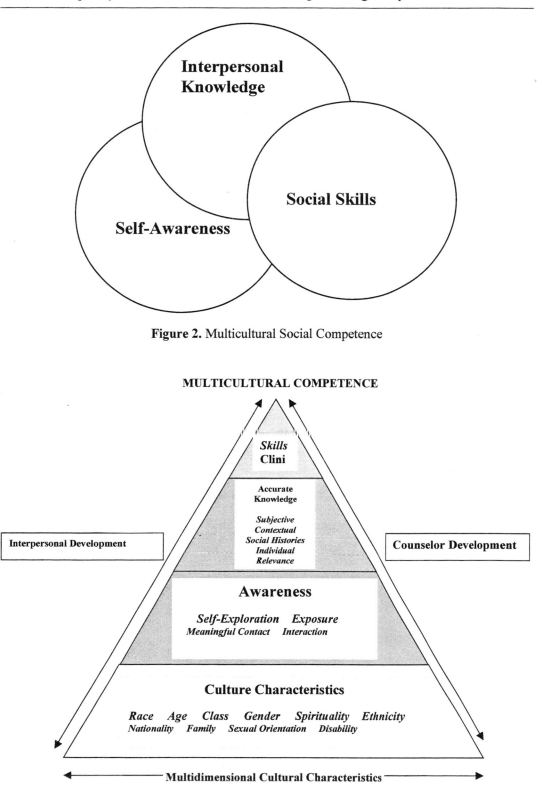

**Figure 2.** Multicultural Social Competence

**Figure 3.** Contemporary Multiculturalism

The process of transforming the competency framework for use in training programs requires competent trainers, creativity, and a supportive environment for trainees to challenge themselves in personally relevant and professionally appropriate ways. Competence of the trainer refers to faculty members who can teach multiculturalism and facilitate student development. Examination of the program's *multicultural agenda* and philosophy must be understood before any training program attempts to develop culturally sensitive counselors. Encouraging students to explore their role as cultural beings is an integral aspect of the learning process and should be undertaken after the program identifies the profession's long-standing and contemporary concerns. Additionally, creativity of the programs' faculty enhances this process.

## EXPANDING MULTICULTURAL CONTENT IN TRAINING

In this section of the chapter, we discuss some broad areas that training programs must address in their attempt to develop culturally competent counselors. The areas include the topics of worldview, race, ethnicity, gender, sexual orientation, age and disability, religion and spirituality. These topic areas do not represent the totality of what must be addressed in order to become multiculturally competent; however, they represent a starting point for understanding the multidimensional nature of human diversity and highlight areas for ongoing professional development and training. In incorporating the multicultural competency and standards in the training of graduate counselor-trainees, counselor educators must take adequate measures to ensure that graduate students in counseling are prepared to work with the depth and diversity presented by individuals from diverse backgrounds. Counselor training programs are challenged to respond to a broad range of diversity issues that trainees will likely encounter in professional practice.

### Worldviews

Ivey, Ivey and Simek-Morgan (1993) suggested that examining one's conceptual framework or worldview is necessary to become culturally competent. According to Sue (1983), worldview is defined as how a person perceives his or her relationship to the world (such as nature, institutions, other people, and things). In other words, an individual's worldview is the framework from which the person perceives and responds to the environment. In the therapeutic relationship, this response framework or worldview influences the interaction between the counselor and the client. In a therapeutic counseling relationship, the interaction of worldviews is vigorous and dynamic. Ivey et al. (1993) and Sue (1983) maintained that for effective multicultural counseling therapy to occur, a counselor must understand the worldview from which his or her responses and reactions emerge as well as understand the worldview of the client.

A counselor must be aware of how his or her worldview affects behaviors during counseling. For example, the values and attitudes inherent in the counselor's worldview affect the counseling relationship in terms of counselor behaviors, therapeutic goals, and treatment planning (Axelson, 1985). In an observational study of same-race groups, Steward (1993) found differences between White and Black female groups in terms of their perceived core issues. Black women initially focused on societal issues, such as racism, whereas White women moved from introductions to problem sharing and exploration of problem etiology. Clearly, a counselor should consider that problem sharing and exploration of problem etiology for people of color might mean exploring the sociopolitical implications of racism or other forms of oppression. However, one of the key factors in establishing culturally appropriate goals is the counselor's own level of comfort and understanding of the client's presenting issues and worldview. For instance, any counselor who is not aware of his or her own worldview and feels uncomfortable or threatened with the client's presenting issues associated with racism or other societal ills, may very well lack the ability to create an understanding and safe environment. The unintended result of encapsulation may be that the counselor imposes his or her own worldview and cultural values onto the client, potentially alienating the client and being viewed with suspicion by the client. Lack of counselor understanding may also lead to erroneous counseling assessments and inappropriate interventions, which in turn may be destructive for the client. The likelihood of these unintended negative results is relatively high, due to fact that many clients are in a vulnerable state when they initially come to counseling.

There are two models related to worldviews that can be used for training purposes to help counselors understand their own values as well as differences among individuals and between groups. The Value-Orientation model identifies a set of core dimensions or human questions that may be pertinent across cultures (Kluckholm & Strodtbeck, 1961). Kluckholm and Strodtbeck (1961) conceptualized four worldview dimensions and three possible responses to the human questions. The first dimension, Time Focus, relates to the temporary focus of human life and the three value orientation responses associated with it are past, present, and future. The second dimension, Human Activity, related to the modality of human activity and the value orientations associated with it are being, being and becoming, and doing. The Social Relations dimension pertains to how human relationships are defined. Relationships can be lineal (i.e., vertical with leaders and followers), collateral (i.e., where consults with friends or family are expected) or individualistic (i.e., where individual autonomy and control of one's own destiny are expected). The last dimension, People-Nature Relationship, refers to the relationship of people to nature. The three value orientations associated with it are subjugation to nature, which means life largely determined by external forces such as God or fate, harmony with nature, or mastery over nature.

Rotter's (1975) concepts of internal-external locus of control and locus of responsibility (Jones et al., 1972) provide a psychological framework for understanding worldview perspectives. According to Rotter's work, people tend to view the location of control over their worlds as either internal or external, contingent upon life experiences and based on their own actions. A person with internal attributions of control believes that one shapes his or her own fate. A person with external attributions of control believes that reinforcing events occur independently of one's actions and that the future is the result of luck or chance. Locus of responsibility refers to the level of blame attributed to individuals or systems. According to Sue and Sue (1999), when these two psychologically independent frameworks are placed on a continuum, they can be used to understand the levels of personal control and responsibility that a client may perceive him or herself to have and how response to the environment are shaped and carried out. These worldview models can also be used to understand the values that are embedded in the counseling process. Trained awareness of these value assumptions can facilitate the process of counselors becoming culturally intentional and multiculturally competent.

## Race and Ethnicity

There is a need for counselor training to promote a thorough understanding of the social constructs of race and ethnicity with particular emphasis on models of racial and ethnic identities. Counselor trainees need to become increasingly proficient in working with rapidly growing diverse populations in terms of race, ethnicity, and cultural variables. Only with a clear understanding of these constructs and with understanding how they impact the identity development of clients can culturally responsive counseling interventions be formulated and integrated into a counselor's repertoire.

This means that counselor training programs and educators should incorporate the dimensions of race and ethnicity into a multicultural curriculum, providing students with clear definitions as they are illustrated in the professional literature and theoretical frameworks which provide various perspectives on how these constructs impact the work of counselor trainees. For example, race is not a scientific, biological classification system determined by physical characteristics (Ponterotto & Casas, 1991; Rose, 1964). Rather, it is a sociopolitical, within-group variable manifested through the process of racial identity development, including the components of identification with a "race" and the roles of racism and oppression (Helms, 1994). Race is believed to be relevant for racial and ethnic minority group members because it is a visible characteristic to which American society ascribes membership and often makes attributes of limitations.

Unlike race, which is often perceived to be a fixed characteristic based on biological or genetic foundations, ethnicity is often seen as more fluid and flexible as well as a largely voluntary choice. Ethnicity has been defined as a distinct social and cultural heritage (e.g., language, religion, traditions) shared by a group of people, and transmitted across generations (Ponterotto & Casas, 1991). Thus, ethnic identity refers to a sense of group identity based upon the extent to which an individual believes he or she shares a common membership with a particular ethnic or cultural group. Although physical characteristics may be included in a definition of ethnicity, one does not have to share the same physical attributes to belong to an ethnic group; and these markers may not be permanent. Based on an investigation of acculturation attitudes of Hispanics and Asian Americans, 13% of the participants stated that they saw their ethnic identity in terms of their physical appearance (Sodowsky, Lai, & Plake, 1991). This ethnic saliency is one dimension of ethnic identity, but the other aspect is whether an individual from a minority group feels a sense of attachment or belonging to his or her ethnic group.

When exploring the construct of ethnicity, it is also important for instructors to provide an exploration of the other relevant ambiguous identity construct of acculturation. Casas and Pytluk (1995) indicated that acculturation is defined as a multidimensional psychosocial phenomenon. It is reflected in psychological changes that occur in individuals as a result of their interaction with a new culture. More specifically, from a psychological perspective, acculturation is the product of cultural learning that occurs as a result of contact between members of two or more culturally distinct groups. It is important to understand that the process of acculturation is accompanied by attitudinal and behavioral changes in individuals who come in contact with a new culture, and that the process involves socialization into an ethnic group other than one's own. The process of acculturation may occur when two or more cultures interact, resulting in several possible outcomes: (1) the host culture absorbs the immigrant culture, or (2) multiculturalism whereby both cultures coexist mutually. On an individual level, exposure to another culture can result in three possible outcomes: (a) assimilation, with the individual adopting the cultural values, attitudes, and behaviors of the host culture and rejecting his or her culture of origin; (b) resistance to assimilation, resulting in resistance to the host culture and retaining the identity of the parent culture; or (c) biculturalism, with an individual adopting characteristics from both the host and parent cultures (LaFromboise, Coleman, & Gerton, 1993). Acculturation is an identity characteristic that receives attention in the multicultural literature for promoting better understanding of ethnic minority concerns, especially for Hispanics and Asian Americans (Arbona, 1995; Jacob, 1998; Jacob & Richardson, 1996; Sodowsky, Kwan, & Pannu, 1995). Trainees must learn how to incorporate race-ethnicity and associated constructs and processes into the delivery of services.

## Gender and Sexual Orientation

The reality that much psychological literature (i.e., theory and research) informing clinical practice is based on the experiences of White males results in necessary concern regarding its generalizability and appropriateness for women (Phillips, 1998). Given some of the socialized differences between men and women in this society, it seems reasonable to question and test the appropriateness of psychological models and intervention strategies for women (Morrow & Hawxhurst, 1998). In order to be competent, counselors must have a comprehensive understanding of gender roles, gender identity, and the effects that both may have on the lives of clients who seek treatment (Dermer, Hemsath, & Russell, 1998). Thus, training programs need to introduce feminist perspectives in the overarching multicultural training provided to all trainees (i.e., men and women). For example, feminist philosophy can be integrated with other counseling modalities to enhance counselor's understanding of the social and political nature of counseling and the personal life experiences of clients (e.g., see Ivey, 2000). A feminist approach to counseling requires that one sees clients' concerns as a combination of personal, cultural, social, and political elements versus simply an intrapsychic struggle void of the larger social context. The assumption that client concerns must be considered alongside their associated core social influences allows clients to recognize the sociopolitical and economic forces causing psychic pain and provides an appropriate reframe in defining pathology. In addition, it enables the counselor to better facilitate and support client empowerment through healthy resistance (Spencer, 1998). Empowerment occurs when both the internal and external conditions of people's lives change in the interests of social equity (Marrow & Hawxhurst, 1998). The catalyst for empowerment is individual and collective political analysis and action. Clearly, counselors must be prepared to analyze gender dynamics and the salient--and often subtle--experiences that affect how and what women and men present in therapy (Weiner, 1998).

Likewise mental health workers must be prepared to work effectively with more than heterosexual client populations. Counselor training should prepare counselors to be effective with clients whose sexual orientations range from homosexual or bisexual to heterosexual. In

1975 the American Psychological Association amended its policy regarding Equal Employment Opportunity to include sexual orientation among the prohibited discriminations listed in the policy statement. This was done two years after the American Psychiatric Association removed homosexuality from their official list of mental disorders. Likewise, the American Psychological Association (APA) adopted the resolution that homosexuality per se implies no impairment in judgment, stability, reliability, or general social and vocational capabilities. Further, the APA urges all mental health professionals to take the lead in removing the stigma of mental illness that has long been associated with homosexual orientations. The American Counseling Association (ACA) takes the same perspective. Training programs need to provide the requisite learning environment (i.e., curriculum and climate) that result in competent delivery of services to clients that span the continuum of sexual orientations (Abeles, 1985).

Counselor training programs must produce graduates that can work with lesbian, gay, and/or bisexual clients whose presenting issues will undoubtedly span the ranges of concerns from relationship difficulties and family concerns to educational and career aspirations as well as coming out and other personal growth and developmental milestones. In reality, counselors must be social advocates; and as such, they must accumulate knowledge that enables them to think critically about heterosexism and homophobia, intervene effectively with individuals, couples, and families, and appropriately empower their clients.

Some major areas in which training programs must focus their efforts include introducing trainees to relevant psychological literature regarding how to change homophobic attitudes (Blumenfeld, 1992; De Cecco, 1985), coming out (Cass, 1979; Davis, 1992; Marcus, 1993; Weinberg, 1973), working with family members (Aguilar-San Juan, 1994; Carrier, 1995; Herek & Capitanio, 1995; Sears, 1991), and working with students (Sears, 1991; Butler, 1990). Training should help counselors avoid making inaccurate attributions regarding sexual orientations and develop a resource base that includes organizations such as the American Civil Liberties Union (ACLU), Parents, Family, and Friends of Lesbians and Gays (PFLAG), and other local organizations for consulting and referrals when necessary. Counselors must also be able to address relevant multidimensional factors such as gender, class, race, ethnicity, and religion that intersect sexual identity and life experiences (Perez, Debord, & Bieschke, 2000).

## Age and Disability

Another underserved population that needs to be included in counselors' multicultural training includes the elderly. By the year 2030, the elderly population (age 65 and over) in the United States is expected to represent 20% of the total population (US Census Bureau, 1995). Census data indicate that the larger portion of the elderly population are women because they live longer, on average. The elderly population represents the full range of social class and ethnic and cultural diversity that exists in the younger population. In order to provide effective services to this population, counselors need to understand the impact that ageism has on the quality of life for the elderly. Ageism refers to the discrimination and negative stereotypes directed toward older people that results in them being viewed as less valued members of society (Atkinson & Hackett, 1998). Counselor training must facilitate trainees' awareness of attitudes about geriatric people that may diminish their therapeutic effectives.

With regard to knowledge, counselors need to be familiar with the range of human growth and development--not just the part of the continuum from birth to middle age. Counselors need to acquire a working knowledge of the mental health trends for this population. One misperception about the elderly is that mental incompetence, senility, or dementia is the norm. In reality, only 5 to 10% of individuals over age 65 and 15 to 20% over the age of 75 years have mild to moderate dementia (American Psychiatric Association, 1997; Marino, Richardson, Greenwood, & Regina, 2000). In situations where an elderly client does seek treatment for dementia, counselors must be able to help both the affected individual and family members deal with the gradual progressive nature of the condition and the stressful impact of care-taking. According to Marino et al. (2000), counselors must take precautions to avoid misdiagnosing depression as dementia and thereby assuming that nothing can be done from a counseling standpoint. In spite of the fact that elderly clients frequently have medical concerns that require coordination with physicians, counselors should be able to provide services related to depression, suicide, substance abuse, sexuality, and discrimination as well as other life issues that are developmentally salient for the client (Sue & Sue, 1999).

Likewise, multicultural training also must prepare counselors to work with clients who have disabilities. According to the U.S. Census Bureau (1995), 49 million Americans have a disability. Of those, 5.8% are children and 53.9% are age 65 and older. Counselor trainees should understand the significance and scope of the Americans with Disabilities Act (ADA), a federal law that mandates nondiscrimination toward disabled individuals. Disability is defined as a physical or mental impairment that substantially limits one or more of the major life activities of such individuals (American Disabilities Act, 1990). In order to provide effective services to clients, counselors must examine their own views of clients with disabilities and work through any biases that may have a deleterious impact on counseling process and client outcomes. They must be comfortable addressing any and all topics relevant to clients' presenting concerns and the effects they may have on families. Counselors must be knowledgeable about clients' disabilities, and be actively involved in learning. In addition, counselors should be aware of resources (i.e., programs, services, opportunities) that will assist the clients' pursuit of major life activities.

## Religion and Spirituality

Another contemporary area that warrants attention is the role of religion and spiritual issues in counseling. According to Stanard, Sandhu, and Painter (2000), as human beings are being recognized as multisystematic organisms, spirituality and religion in human development are gaining legitimacy. Historically, the counseling profession steered away from addressing religion or spirituality issues in the counseling process with clients. However, recently there is an increase in the literature that explores the role of religion and spirituality in counseling. According to Sandhu (in press), spiritual issues in counseling are analogous to the other four forces in counseling (e.g. psychodynamics, behaviorism, humanism, and multiculturalism).

This raises curriculum issues for counselor educators in the training of counselors. Within a multicultural course, issues related to religion and the role of spirituality in working with clients need to be incorporated so that counselor-trainees are prepared to address the relevant topics as they appear in their work with clients. Part of this shift emerges when counselors are examining issues related to working with diverse clients and the role of indigenous helping models arises. Cultural dynamics of indigenous models of helping often include a mandate that counselors are trained to shift from a Western model of helping and explore alternative forms of helping that often may have a religious or spirituality presence in the lives of clients. At times, this shift has clashed with the traditional values and beliefs inherent to the counseling profession—values and beliefs that lead counselors to ignore religion and spirituality in their work with clients. There is a need for counselors to be sensitive to issues of religion and spirituality, and counselors must be culturally competent to manage these dimensions in their work. This arises in an era in which--according to Stanard et al. (2000)--there seems to be new understanding regarding how to unlock the mysteries of healing through belief, faith, and imagination.

The multicultural counseling competencies framework (Sue et al., 1982) becomes critical in the integration of religion and spiritual issues in counseling. This is because there may be direct differences or clashes between a counselor's and a client's values and beliefs along religious and spiritual dimensions. Zinnbauer and Pargament (2000) indicated that many counselors do not receive training on how to recognize and manage religious or spiritual value differences in counseling. To manage value issues, counselors must first be aware of their own value systems and beliefs. Beutler and Consoli (1992) stated that therapists should be subjected to thorough exploration and evaluation of their beliefs. This is one of the reasons why the training of multiculturally sensitive and competent counselors needs to incorporate the role of religion and spirituality as a contemporary issue in working with clients.

In addressing the contemporary issues of religion and spirituality in counselor training, first there is a need to differentiate between the constructs of religion and spirituality. Abels (2000) argued that in many ways, religion and spirituality are different and the same. The overlaps and ambiguity in how these constructs are used interchangeably is a critical reason for counselor-trainees to be able to distinguish and understand each of the constructs separately, and also explore how the dimensions may overlap in their own lives and in the lives of clients. Stanard et al. (2000) indicated that although religion and spirituality share common elements, there are significant differences, which may impact how the constructs provide meaning separately or together in a client's life.

Schwartz and Conley (1996), using Lewis' (1968) definition of religion, described it "as the attitude of individuals in a community toward the powers which they conceive as having ultimate control over their destinies and interests" (pp. 112). Although there is no consensus in the literature on the nature or existence of boundaries between religion and spirituality, Stanard et al. (2000) described religion as the role of adherence to the beliefs and practices of an organized church or religious institution that are institutionalized in religion. The complexities associated with religion may often make it difficult to separate out the values of the individuals involved within counseling because religious convictions often are the part of culture associated with people's deepest convictions. The organized major religions (e.g. Christianity, Islam, Hinduism, Judism, etc.) provide belief systems that may be difficult for another to understand, primarily if the doctrine is radically different from one's own religious orientation. However, counselor-trainees must be willing to understand that in order to appreciate and understand another's belief system, one does not necessarily need to agree with it. In examining the role of religion and how it may impact the lives of clients, counselor-trainees are seeking to understand and respect the differing viewpoints that may shape a client's belief system and exploring how it may give meaning to the life of a client.

Whereas religion may be considered as more of a formalized practice, spirituality may also involve a non-secular component. Abels (2000) described non-secular spirituality as "a set of personal beliefs derived from the individualistic perception of self and his or her relationship to both the natural world and the metaphysical realm" (p. 3). According to Stanard et al. (2000), the construct of spirituality includes the concepts such as transcendence, self-actualization, purpose and meaning, wholeness, balance, sacredness, altruism, universality, and a sense of a Higher Power. As with religion, spirituality deals with meaning, purpose, and morality in a social context. Spirituality can often be ambiguous and difficult for counselor-trainees to fully comprehend because it is often subjective and can be individually defined. As Stanard et al. (2000) highlighted, spirituality is a universal experience with few limitations. The authors explore the assessment of spirituality in counseling and describe selected instruments to aid in the assessment of spirituality. These instruments may be important tools for counselors in helping them gain a better understanding of the role of spirituality in the issues that bring clients into counseling.

Faiver, O'Brien, and Ingersoll (2000) discussed the notion that exploring the role of guilt and its underpinnings to religion is also part of the need to differentiate between religion and spirituality. Counselor-trainees must become familiar with the emerging literature on forgiveness (Benson, 1992; Canale, 1990; Pingleton, 1992; Rosenak & Harnden, 1992; Wahking, 1992). Forgiveness may become a vital part of counseling when there is a religious or spirituality context. In the movement toward appreciating cultural sensitivity, exploration of spirituality issues also becomes relevant in understanding indigenous practices of healing and psychological well-being. Counselor-trainees must begin to understand that the practice of incorporating indigenous practices may be difficult, especially when deeply rooted. Western practices which are an inherent part of counselor-training models may come into contact with equally or more deeply rooted non-Western ways. Morgan (in press) indicated that spirituality and religion may be seen as a *growing edge* for counselors to incorporate in working with clients in the treatment of alcoholism and other addictions.

Counselor trainees need also to be provided with frameworks that explore how to deal with religious and spiritual issues in counseling. Zinnbauer and Pargament (2000), for example, presented a comparison and critique of four models of addressing religious and spiritual issues in working with clients. Also, authors are beginning to explore spiritual identity models as frameworks for counseling (see Richards & Bergin, 1997; Smith & Richards in a subsequent chapter in this text). Such frameworks can be useful tools for helping counselors understand clients and design appropriate treatment interventions with clients for whom spiritual or religious issues are salient. Counselors need to voice openness to discussing religious-spiritual issues with clients, yet they may not be certain how to integrate the issues in working with clients. The worlds of religion, spirituality, and counseling may frequently be at odds, but trainees must begin to recognize that the intersection of these dimensions need not be detrimental for the religious or spiritual client.

## The Challenge of Teaching Multicultural Competence

It is critical for counselor educators to teach much more than awareness and knowledge so that multicultural sensitivity is reflected in counseling competence and therapeutic interventions. It is our experience that the expectation of many programs and students is that self-awareness and a "conceptual" understanding of difference taught in the classroom is not sufficient training. This, as the primary emphasis of training, often does not lead to an accurate understanding of how to implement the understanding into application in the real world. Most trainees enter the arenas of multicultural training and counseling with little prior contact with culturally diverse clients and come in with their own ethnocentric perceptions of the world.

Trainees' expectations tend to cluster mainly under the second competency of gaining knowledge or acquiring skills to work with minority groups. Trainees rarely recognize or expect that self-awareness is a preliminary criterion in the movement towards developing multicultural competence. Multicultural training should be comprehensive, intensive, and inclusive in order to expand and enhance the trainees' prior multicultural learning and help trainees overcome any cultural encapsulation they may bring to counseling. This often becomes an ongoing process of learning where trainees have to develop multicultural competency beyond the realms of a required multicultural course or components of a training program.

For a beginning course on multicultural issues, it is often critical that the emphasis on counselor self-awareness combined with a process of acquiring knowledge and sensitivity is carried as a theme over the entire course of the semester. Most often the students respond well to a combination of didactic and experiential learning components within a supportive environment. This observation seems consistent with Kiselica's (1998) recommendation to provide a learning environment that consists of a combination of challenge and support.

It seems equally important to help students think about how they view the world, very early in the course. In order to encourage insights in this area, students participate in a series of worldview exercises. While this chapter does not permit a detailed explanation of all the activities, there are a few points that can be made. The "lenses" through which one sees the world is shaped by the community in which one grew up and currently lives, the institutions where one was educated and to which one belongs. Likewise one worldview is reflected in the close personal friendships established and maintained, family, mentors, meaningful contacts, leisure activities including the authors and literature one reads, preferences for art, ideals and aesthetics, and so forth. Trainees are asked questions about these issues and the level of diversity reflected in their responses is used to create a visual representation of the worldview lenses. With this heightened perspective, trainees gain a better understanding of what they perceive well and what are possible blind spots or limitations. Needless to say, everybody has some limitations, and recognition of limitations is the basis for identifying growth areas.

Mio (1989) suggests multicultural training should include experiential contact with ethnic minority groups as an essential element of the training process. One-on-one exchange of ideas with another individual can greatly enhance one's experience with members of another cultural group above and beyond factual knowledge about the group. A fascinating observation on the authors' parts is that for many students, this is usually the first time they have reflected on seeing themselves as multicultural beings. In currently teaching multicultural courses at predominantly White campuses, it has also been our experience that often this process is most challenging for students who are White, which is an observation consistent with Kiselica's (1998) recommendations on teaching multiculturalism to Anglo counselors-in-training. An additional benefit in experiential contact with diversity outside of the classroom is that it provides realistic information, supplying an alternative to relying on general "cookbook recipes" in working with culturally diverse clients. Trainees can benefit from linking their personal experiences with diversity to implications for working with clients. Through understanding themselves and their clients as cultural beings, trainees grow in their ability to effectively use the self for helping others. Because the availability of cultural experiential opportunities varies across campuses and settings, instructors will need to structure specific parameters for activities and experiences. Students' self-reflections, done through journaling their experiences, are useful for growth.

We have explored the relevance of how what we refer to as *otherness experiences* impact students' learning and application of the material presented in our teaching. Our students have provided much feedback on the utility of such exercises within the end-of-year student evaluations as well as within the final journal entry that is part of the overall course requirements. One avenue to get students to discuss the application of the material in the course and integration of specific experiential activities is to, within the final journal entry, have students reflect upon and write about the learning process across the course of taking the multicultural class. Ongoing qualitative evaluation of journal entries collected by one of the authors with permission from the students reveals that many students believe that one of the most meaningful experiences in taking the multicultural course has been "forced opportunity" to engage in cultural and social events around diversity. Many of the students at a predominantly White institution admit that they have often never considered moving beyond their encapsulated cultural worldview or social nucleus until having to seek out otherness experiences to complete the course requirements.

A sampling of student responses indicates a favorable response to the assignment with students disclosing realizations and reflections on the self-awareness component of cultural competence. Three selective student responses are included below as examples to show how students have integrated the activities into application. Furthermore, the responses give an indication of students' level of receptiveness to the experiential exercises and the type of learning triggered for the students:

1. *"Going out into the community to experience otherness was good practice for me. Sometimes there is a fear of what is not known. Sometimes my perception may be based on misinformation. I cannot make assumptions based on what I have heard, but rather can be open to experiencing different cultures. It's a chance to enter someone else's perceptions of the world, a chance to experience the world through the client's eyes and see what is different, what is the same".*

2. *"I cannot say enough about the otherness experiences. They were just great. I probably got the most from these experiences. It was real life situations and experiences. There could not have been a better way to develop our thoughts about multicultural issues than to expand our experiences. Sharing our experiences in class is not only fun but it is broadening our awareness. I learned so much from not only my experiences but from everyone else's. Once again, an excellent educational tool"*

3. *The otherness adventure was a very enjoyable form of learning. Forcing students to go out into situations that are uncommon to them was a backhanded way of making the real world more visible. This was an adventure that brought forth more learning as to the different lifestyles and cultures than all of the books available would ever have done. This was "hands on" learning experience and sharing these experiences was a way of venting the different feelings that the adventurer was going through.*

*There were feelings of fear, isolation, friendship... this list could go on and on, but in each case it was a learning process."*

## CONCLUSIONS

Multicultural competence is demonstrated through the active process of transforming awareness and knowledge into the practice of appropriate, relevant, and culturally sensitive intervention strategies and skills. Thus, it is critical for counselor educators to teach--and for trainees to learn--more than awareness and knowledge. It is our experience that trainees' expectations tend to cluster mainly under the second competency of gaining knowledge or the third competency of acquiring skills to work with diverse client populations. Trainees rarely recognize or expect that self-awareness is one of the preliminary criteria in the movement towards developing competence. Like every other aspect of counseling training, multicultural training must be comprehensive, intensive, and inclusive in order to expand and enhance trainees' prior multicultural learning and overcome any cultural encapsulation they may bring to the counseling process.

In fact, Mio (1989) suggested that experiential contact with diverse populations should be an essential element of the training process. Counselor trainees need exchange of ideas and interpersonal interactions with individuals, families, and groups who represent a broad range of human diversity. As a result of these types of interactions, trainees may develop a better awareness of their biases and assumptions and be better able to identify their specific growth areas. It will also enable trainees to have an understanding and knowledge of difference above and beyond factual knowledge of an ethnic, racial, gender, affectional, or religious group. We argue that the counseling relationship should not be the first time a counselor has to confront issues of race, ethnicity, gender dynamics, sexuality, religious diversity, and the like. Additionally, preliminary learning experiences seem likely to lower trainees' anxiety in their initial counseling field experiences. Exposure to some combination of the topic areas previously discussed can serve as important formal and informal mechanisms for multicultural development.

Intentionality on the part of counselor educators teaching courses designed to address social and cultural issues is mandatory in helping trainees embark on the process of multicultural competence. This also mandates that the educator is aware of her or his own parallel processes regarding multicultural competence and how it relates to presence in the classroom in particular and the profession in general. Self-reflection on the part of the educator is necessary so that the individual is able to provide a balance of support and challenge to trainees who may experience a range of reactions and emotions to the process of developing multicultural competency.

## EXPERIENTIAL ACTIVITIES

### 1. Interview Project

Interview people with various cultural heritages and from various racial-ethnic groups. The instructor should determine how many people and whom should be interviewed. It may be desired or necessary to interview some people who are outside the university setting—in the interest of diversity. The instructor should stress confidentiality issues. Have interviewees provide responses to the following questions. The interviewer may need to explain or re-phrase some of the items below.

1. With what culture(s) or group(s) do you identify, belong?
2. What values do you see as of great importance in your culture(s)?
3. How are the values of mainstream U.S. culture different from those you grew up with?
4. Would you share conflicts or stress that this has caused you?
5. Describe the importance of yourself, your family, and other groups in the decision-making process (provide examples). Are decisions made on a collective or on an individual basis?
6. How important is the role of history in your culture and in your family?
7. When people in your culture have problems, to whom do they go for help?
8. What kind of personal qualities would the people of your culture want in the person they go to for help?
9. How might religious beliefs influence the helping process in your culture?
10. How much is it of concern to you and your family if you go for help outside of the family?
11. Have you been in the role of helper in your culture? If so, please describe.
12. What other things do you think counselors need to know about your culture so that we can be better helpers?

Please feel free to use additional questions. Compile your responses into a discussion of similarities and differences. Provide suggestions for working more effectively with culturally different individuals and families. Include a resource list that provides information on working with culturally different individuals or families.

## 2. Small Group Activities

The following are "go arounds" done in small groups in class.

*(Group members should be very supportive in these go arounds. In these, pay close attention to feelings, thinking, behavior—always validate feelings)*

*Go Arounds:*
**The significant experiences in my early life when I recognized prejudice, racism, discrimination**—Process: explore feelings, thinking, behavior associated with experiences—then and now.

**The times in elementary school when I was ridiculed or made fun of**—Process: explore the feelings, thinking, behavior associated with these experiences? What was the basis for my being "picked on" (glasses, weight, height, skin color, freckles, hair texture, socioeconomic status, etc.). What did these experiences teach me—then and now?

**The times in school when I supported or ignored other people being singled out, kidded, or hurt because of some characteristic**—Process: explore the feelings, thinking, behavior then and now.

**The time(s) in my life when I felt most like I *did not* belong**—when I felt most different than others, lonely—Process:

**The time(s) in my life when I felt most like I *did* belong, connected, affiliated**—Process:

## 3. Otherness Experiences

Instructors will need to design this course-long project. The intent is to provide students with a variety of diversity experiences, helping counselor-trainees broaden their perspectives and perceptiveness and helping them build multicultural competence. Components might be attending and interacting at campus intercultural activities, attending various events, interviewing people who are culturally different (see #2 above), analyzing essays or literary passages that reflect different worldviews, viewing movies that reflect difference, and so forth. In short, activities should be designed to help trainees take multicultural risks and develop multicultural coping skills (multicultural competence).

Experiences should cover diversity broadly, including difference related to race-ethnicity, region of the country or world, gender, sexual orientation, life style, age, socioeconomic status, disability status, religion and spirituality, language, and other dimensions of difference available.

After each experience, counselor-trainees reflect on their experience by journaling, including what they learned, how learning occurred, how learning relates to their perceptual schemata, and how learning relates to their functioning as a person and as a counselor. Learning might be framed in terms of multicultural coping skills or multicultural competence. In journaling, students should address their experiences, behaviors, feelings, and thinking (and the interrelationships among these) associated with the experience.

Toward the end of the course, counselor-trainees reflect over the range of activities, tracing change in perspectives and growth toward multicultural coping in terms of the personal self and the counseling self. The focus here is on awareness and growth in their multicultural being. Identity development may also be incorporated.

Although this type of experience is more common to a single course, such activities could be used to span students entire programs, becoming a portfolio-type project.

# REFERENCES

Abeles, N. (1985). Proceedings of the American Psychological Association, Incorporated, for the year 1984: Minutes of the Annual Meeting of the Council of Representatives. *American Psychologist, 40*, 621-653.

Abels, S. L. (Ed.). (2000). *Spirituality in social work practice: Narratives for professional helping*. Denver, CO: Love.

Abreu, J.M. & Atkinson, D.R. (2000). Multicultural counseling training: Past, present, and future directions. *Counseling Psychologist, 28*, 641-656.

Aguilar-San Juan, K. (1994). *The State of Asian America, Activism, and Resistance in the 1990's*. Boston: South End.

American Counseling Association. (1995). *ACA code of ethics & standards of practice*. Alexandria, VA: Author.

*Americans With Disabilities Act*, 42 U. S. C. Sec. 12101 (1990).

American Psychological Association. (1993). Guidelines for providers of psychological services to ethnic, linguistic, and culturally diverse populations. *American Psychologist, 48*, 45-48.

Arbona, C. (1995). Theory and research on racial and ethnic minorities: Hispanic Americans. In F. T. L. Leong (Ed.), *Career development and vocational behavior of racial and ethnic minorities*, (pp. 37-66). Mahwah, NJ: Lawrence Erlbaum Associates.

Arrendondo, P. (1998). Integrating multicultural counseling competencies and universal helping conditions in culture-specific contexts. *The Counseling Psychologist, 26*, 592-601.

Atkinson, D.R., & Hackett, G. (1998). Counseling diverse populations (2nd ed.). Boston: McGraw-Hill.

Beale, A.V. (1986). A cross-cultural dyadic encounter. *Journal of Multicultural Counseling & Development, 14*, 73-76.

Benson, C. (1992). Forgiveness and the psychotherapeutic process. *Journal of Psychology and Christianity, 11*, 76-81.

Beutler, L. E., & Consoli, A. J. (1992). Systematic eclectic psychotherapy. In J. C. Norcross & M. R. Goldfried (Eds.), *Handbook of psychotherapy integration* (pp. 264-299). New York: Basic Books.

Blumenfeld, W.J. (1992). *Homophobia: How we all pay the price*. Boston: Beacon.

Butler, J. (1990). *Gender trouble: Feminism and the subversion of identity*. New York: Routledge.

Canale, J. (1990). Altruism and forgiveness as therapeutic agents in psychotherapy. *Journal of Religion and Health, 29*, 229-301.

Carrier, J. (1995). *De los Otros: Intimacy and homosexuality among Mexican men*. New York: Columbia University Press.

Casas, J. M., & Pytluk, S. D. (1995). Hispanic identity development. In J. G. Ponterotto, J. M. Casas, L. A. Suzuki, & C. .M. Alexander (Eds.), *Handbook of multicultural counseling* (pp. 155-180). Thousand Oaks, CA: Sage.

Cass, V.C. (1979). Homosexual identity formation: A theoretical model. *Journal of Homosexuality, 4*, 219-236.

Constantine, M.G., Landany, N., Inman, A.G., & Ponterotto, J.G. (1996). Students' perceptions of multicultural training in counseling psychology programs. *Journal of Multicultural Counseling & Development, 24*, 241-253.

Corey, G., Corey, M.S. & Callahan, P. (1988). *Issues and ethics in the helping professions.* Pacific Grove, CA: Brooks/Cole.

Davis, P. (1992). The role of disclosure in coming out among gay men. In K. Plummer (Ed.), *Modern homosexualities: Fragments of lesbian and gay experience* (pp. 75-86). New York: Routledge.

De Cecco, J.P. (1985). *Homophobia in American society: Bashers, baiters, and bigots.* New York: Harrington Park.

Dermer, S. B., Hemesath, C. W., & Russell, C. S. (1998). A feminist critique of solution-focused therapy. *The American Journal of Family Therapy, 26*, 239-251.

Faiver, C. M., O'Brien, E. M., & Ingersoll, R. E. (2000). Religion, guilt, and mental health. *Journal of Counseling & Development, 78*, 155-161.

Fourali, C.E. (2000). Beyond opposites: Extending the cultural boundaries of CBT methodology. *Counselling Psychology Quarterly*, 13(2), 135-158.

Fischer, A. R., Jome, L. M., & Atkinson, D. R. (1998). Reconceptualizing multicultural counseling: Universal healing conditions in a culturally specific context. *The Counseling Psychologist, 26,* 525-588.

Kiselica, M.S. (1999). Confronting my own ethnocentrism and racism: A process of pain and growth. *Journal of Counseling & Development*, 77(1), 14-17.

Helms, J.E., & Richardson, T.Q. (1996). How multiculturalism obscures race and culture as differential aspects of counseling competencies. In D. Pope (Ed.). *Counseling for multicultural effectiveness*. New York: Sage.

*Herek, G.M., & Capitanio, J.P. (1995) Black heterosexuals' attitudes toward lesbians and gay men in the United States. Journal of Sex Research, 32, 95-105.*

*Herman, K.C. (1993). Reassessing predictors of therapist competence. Journal of Counseling & Development, 72, 29-32.*

Ivey, A. E. (2000). *Developmental therapy: Theory into practice*. North Amherst, MA: Microtraining Associates.

Jacob, E. J. (1998). *The salience of identity factors for Asian Indians: A comparison of theoretical models*. Unpublished doctoral dissertation. Lehigh University, Bethlehem, PA, 1998. UMI Dissertation Abstracts Index: 9831805.

Jacob, E. J. & Richardson, T. Q. (1996). *The impact of identity issues on the work choices of Asian Indian women*. Unpublished manuscript. Lehigh University.

Jones, E.E., Kanouse, D., Kelley, H.H., Nisbett, R.E., Valins, S., & Weiner, B. (1972). *Attribution: Perceiving the causes of behavior*. Morristown, NJ: General Learning Press.

Kiselica, M. S. (1998). Preparing Anglos for the challenges and joys of multiculturalism. *The Counseling Psychologist, 26,* 5-21.

Kluckhohn, F.R., & Strodtbeck, F.L. (1961). *Variations in value orientations*. Evanston, IL: Row, Patterson, & Co.

LaFromboise, T., Coleman, H. L. K., & Gerton, J. (1993). Psychological impact of biculturalism: Evidence and theory. *Psychological Bulletin, 144*, 395-412.

Lewis, (1968). As cited in Schwartz, S. E., & Conley, C. A. (1996). *Human diversity: A guide for understanding (3rd ed.), (pp. 112)*. NY: McGraw-Hill.

Marcus, E. (1993). *Is it a choice? Answers to three hundred of the most frequently asked questions about gays and lesbians*. San Francisco: Harper.

Marino, D., Richardson, T. Q., Greenwood, L. P, & Regina, J. M. (2000). *The effects of alzheimer's disease and depression on Neuro-Behavioral Cognitive Status Examination Scores*. Unpublished Manuscript.

Mio, J. S. (1989). Experiential involvement as an adjunct to teaching cultural sensitivity. *Journal of Multicultural Counseling & Development, 17,* 38-46.

Morgan, O. (in press). Alcohol problems, alcoholism, and spirituality: An overview of measurements and scales. *Alcoholism Treatment Quarterly*.

Morrow, S.L., & Hawxhurst, D.M. (1998). Feminist therapy: Integrating political analysis in counseling and psychotherapy. *Women & Therapy, 21*(2), 37-51.

Pedersen, P. (1988). *A handbook for developing multicultural awareness*. Alexandria, VA: American Association for Counseling and Development.

Perez, R. M., Debord, K. A., & Bieschke, K. J. (2000). *Handbook of counseling and psychotherapy with lesbian, gay, and bisexual clients*. Washington, D.C.: American Psychological Association.

Phillips, L.D. (1998). Women of color: Integrating ethnic and gender identities in psychotherapy. *Signs, 23*(4), 1096-1097.

Pingleton, J. P. (1989). The role and functions of forgiveness in the psychotherapeutic process. *Journal of Psychology and Theology, 17,* 27-35.

Ponterotto, J. G., & Casas, J. M (1991). *Handbook of racial/ethnic minority counseling research*. Springfield, IL: Charles C. Thomas.

Ponterotto, J. G., Casas, J. M., Suzuki, L. A., & Alexander, C. M. (Eds.). (1995). *Handbook of multicultural counseling*. Thousand Oaks, CA: Sage.

Pope, D. B., &Coleman, H. L. K. (Eds.). (1998). *Multicultural counseling competencies: Assessment, education, and training and supervision*. Thousand Oaks, CA: Sage.

Richards, P. S., & Bergin, A. E. (1997). *A spiritual strategy for counseling and psychotherapy*. Washington, D.C.: American Psychological Association.

Richardson, T. Q., & Molinaro, K. (1996). White counselor self-awareness: A prerequisite for developing multicultural competence. *Journal of Counseling & Development, 74,* 238-242.

Richardson, T.Q., & Silvestri, T. (1999). White identity formation: a developmental process. In R.H. Sheets & E. Hollins (Eds.) *Racial-ethnic identity and human development: Implications for schooling*. Mahwah, NJ: Erlbaum.

Ridley, C. R., Espelage, D. L., & Rubinstein, K. J. (1998). Course development in multicultural counseling. In D. B. Pope and H. L. Coleman (Eds.), *Multicultural counseling competencies: Assessment, education, and training and supervision*, (pp. 131-158). Thousand Oaks, CA: Sage.

Rose, P. I. (1964). *They and we: Racial and ethnic relations in the United States*. NY: Random House.

Rosenak, C., & Harnden, G. M. (1992). Forgiveness in the psychotherapeutic process: Clinical applications. *Journal of Psychology and Christianity, 11,* 188-197.

Rotter, J. (1975). Some problems and misconceptions related to the construct of internal versus external control of reinforcement. *Journal of Consulting and Clinical Psychology, 43,* 56-67.

Sandu, S. (in press). *Spirituality: A multicultural perspective*. Newbury Park, CA: Sage.

Schwartz, S. E., & Conley, C. A. (1996). *Human diversity: A guide for understanding* (3rd ed.). New York: McGraw-Hill.

Sears, J. (1991). *Growing up gay in the South: Race, gender, and journeys of the spirit.* New York: Harrington Park.

Silvestri, T.J., & Richardson, T.Q. (2001). The relationship between white racial identity attitudes and neuroticism, extraversion, openness, and agreeableness. *Journal of Multicultural Counseling and Development, 79,* 68-76.

Sodowsky, G. R., Kwan, K. K., & Pannu, R. (1995). Ethnic identity of Asians in the United States. In J. G. Ponterotto, J. M. Casas, L. A. Suzuki, & C. M. Alexander (Eds.), *Handbook of multicultural counseling* (pp. 123-115). Thousand Oaks, CA: Sage.

Sodowsky, G. R., Lai, E. W., & Plake, B. S. (1991). Moderating effects of sociocultural variables on acculturation attitudes of Hispanics and Asian Americans. *Journal of Counseling & Development, 70,* 194-204.

Spencer, R. (1998). Fostering resistance through relationships in a feminist hospital program. *Women & Therapy, 21*(2), 101-112.

Stanard, P. R., Sandu, S., & Painter, L. C. (2000). Assessment of spirituality in counseling. *Journal of Counseling & Development, 78,* 204-210.

Sue, S. (1983). Ethnic minority issues in psychology: A reexamination. *American Psychologist, 38,* 583-592.

Sue, D.W., Arrendondo, P., & McDavis, R. J. (1992). Multicultural counseling competencies and standards: A call to the profession. *Journal of Counseling & Development*, 70, 477-486.

Sue, D.W., Bernier, J.B., Durran, M., Feinberg, L., Pedersen, P., Smith, E., & Vasquez-Nuttall, E. (1982). Position paper: Cross-cultural counseling competencies. *The Counseling Psychologist, 10,* 45-52.

Sue, D.W. & Sue, D. (1999). *Counseling the culturally different: Theory and practice* (3rd ed.). New York: John Wiley & Sons.

Tomlinson-Clarke, S. (2000). Assessing outcomes in a multicultural training course: A qualitative study, *Counselling Psychology Quarterly*, 13(2), 221-231.

Thompson, C. H. & Neville, H.A. (1999). Racism, mental health, and mental health practice, *Counseling Psychologist, 27,* 155-223.

U.S. Census Bureau. (1995). *Population profile of the United States.* Washington, DC: U.S. Government Printing Office.

Wahking, H. (1992). Spiritual growth through forgiveness. *Journal of Psychology and Christianity, 11,* 198-206.

Weinberg, G. (1973). *Society and the healthy homosexual.* Garden City, N.J.: Doubleday/Anchor.

Weiner, K.M. (1998). Tools for change: Methods of incorporating political/social action into the therapy session. *Women & Therapy, 21*(2), 113-124.

Wohl, J. (1995). Traditional individual psychotherapy and ethnic minorities. In J.F. Aponte, R Young-Rivers, & J. Wohl (Eds.), *Psychological interventions and cultural diversity* (pp. 74-91). Boston: Allyn & Bacon.

Zeddies, T.J. (1999). Becoming a psychotherapist: The personal nature of clinical work, emotional availability and personal allegiances. *Psychotherapy, 36,* 229-235.

Zinnbauer, B. J. & Pargament, K. I. (2000). Working with the sacred: Four approaches to religious and spiritual issues in counseling. *Journal of Counseling & Development, 78,* 162-171.

# Chapter 3

# RACIAL, ETHNIC, AND CULTURAL IDENTITY DEVELOPMENT MODELS

*Richard C. Henriksen Jr.*
Southwestern Oklahoma State University
*Jerry Trusty*
Pennsylvania State University

## INTRODUCTION

*It's so hard for me to cope at school. Everybody I know has a group of kids that look like them to associate with but I don't. How am I going to make friends?*

*My family keeps pressuring me to go into business. I want to do my own thing but I am afraid that I will hurt them if I don't do what they want. In my culture, children do as their family tells them but in this culture people do their own thing. How can I figure out what I am going to do?*

*You don't understand what it means to be a minority in this country. I try as hard as I can but I never measure up to what society wants. I feel like giving up because as long as white people control everything I will probably never get anywhere anyway.*

*Black people ought to just stop crying. Prejudice stopped back during the Civil Rights Movement. Now they get everything and white people don't get anything. If there is any problem in this country it is that white people are being discriminated against because blacks and Mexicans are getting all the jobs even when they are not qualified?*

What is your first reaction to the above statements? Do you see yourself saying them? Do you sense the anger and frustration? How would you as a counselor help each of these individuals work through these issues? Each of the statements suggests not only that many people have difficulties in life when it comes to interpersonal interactions, but also that finding answers to problems is not simple. One of the ways each of these problems could be addressed would be through an understanding of the stage or phase of racial, cultural, or ethnic identity development currently occupied by each of those individuals.

Erikson (1963) suggested that it is when children grow to adolescence that they become concerned with how they are viewed by others in relation to how they view themselves. This period Erikson defined as *Identity versus Role Confusion*. During this time period, young people see the need to belong with a group or groups as vitally important. This it is an integral part of their ego development. Erikson (1963) pointed out that "young people can also be remarkably clannish, and cruel in their exclusion of all those who are 'different,' in skin color or cultural background" (p. 262). In the first example that opened this chapter, the individual is struggling to fit in and feels rejected by his or her peers. This problem of identity development is compounded by the realization that racial, cultural, and ethnic identity development can have a lasting effect on how the individual views the self and therefore how the self is presented to others.

Erikson (1963) noted that identity development peaks during adolescence, and identity development is a life-long activity. The racial, cultural, and ethnic identity development models that will be discussed in this chapter also take the view that identity development is a life-long process. Even though identity development may appear completed, at some point different stages or phases of development can be repeated; and some characteristics of racial, cultural, or ethnic identity development may be skipped all together.

Any discussion of racial, ethnic, or cultural identity development brings with it the need to identify terms. Because there are so many ways race, ethnicity, and culture are defined, it is important that definitions be provided as they are used in the current discussion. Many may agree with how we define these terms, and many may disagree. It is through an active discourse regarding these terms that professionals may come to recognize common definitions.

## Race

There has been a great amount of discussion concerning the description of individuals by race, and whether the term is used as a phenotype description or used in social terms (Atkinson, Morten, & Sue, 1993). In this chapter, race is defined as the phenotype of the individual but is also discussed based on the social definition of race. Phenotype refers to the visible properties of an individual that are produced by the interaction of the genetic makeup of the individual and the environment. In a purely biological sense, race has been broken down into three distinct categories: Caucasoid, Mongoloid, and Negroid. These three categories have served as the foundation for the phenotypic description of people and the basis of racial classifications. This is consistent with Krogman (1945) who defined race as "a subgroup of peoples possessing a definite combination of physical characteristics of genetic origin, the combination of which to varying degrees distinguishes the subgroup from other subgroups of mankind" (p. 49). The physical characteristics of race often consist of elements such as skin pigmentation, facial features, and the color and texture of body hair. Problems often encountered when race is defined by strictly phenotypic means include the lack of recognition of the existence of similarities between races, the assumption of homogenous racial groups, and the lack of recognition of the existence of Biracial and Multiracial individuals (Root, 1996).

Race has also been described in social terms, resulting in a more fluid definition. Atkinson, Morten, & Sue (1993) suggested that "regardless of its biological validity, the concept of race has taken on important social meaning in terms of how outsiders view members of a 'racial' group and how individuals within the 'racial' group view themselves, members of their group, and members of other 'racial' groups" (p. 7). Davis (1991) took on the task of answering the question, "Who is Black?" He noted that *Black* is a designation given to people who have at least one Black ancestor. Phinney (1996b) also stated,

> the psychological importance of race derives largely from the way in which one is responded to by others, on the basis of visible racial characteristics, most notably skin color and facial features, and in the implications of such responses for one's life chances and sense of identity (p. 919).

These concepts of race are also important to our discussion of racial, ethnic, and cultural identity development because of how the social meaning of race influences the process of identity development. Descriptions of individuals by ethnicity are also affected by how ethnicity is defined.

## Ethnicity

A simple definition of ethnicity would be the culture, customs, and traditions of a group of people. However, anytime the definition of a concept is made parsimoniously, information that could have made the concept more understandable is often lost. For example, Phinney (1996b) suggested that *ethnicity* is used to refer to broad groupings of Americans based on race and culture. From this perspective, ethnicity takes on a different dimension because it is viewed as having racial as well as cultural implications. Frable (1997) went a step further and defined ethnicity as the distinctions between groups based on national origin, language, religion, food, and other cultural markers. From these three definitions we can see that ethnicity is a complex means by which individuals are described. Thus, understanding identity development is more involved than just helping a client answer the question, "Who am I?"

Phinney (1996b) pointed out that there are three aspects of ethnicity that impact the psychological well being of individuals: (a) the cultural values, behaviors, and attitudes that distinguish one group from another; (b) the group members' subjective sense of what it means to be a member of the ethnic group; and (c) the experiences associated with minority status, such as discrimination and powerlessness. Ethnicity is also impacted by the current political climate, changes in the historical views of ethnic groups, and the current state of economic forces on society as a whole. Sue and Sue (1999) referred to "the racism and poverty that dominates the lives of minorities" (p. 103). Being a member of an ethnic group could mean having a lower socioeconomic status, less attractive housing, fewer opportunities for advancement, and higher levels of unemployment. Therefore, ethnicity involves more than race and culture. It includes the effects felt by the members of an ethnic group in reference to other ethnic minority groups and the dominant majority group.

## Culture

If race and ethnicity are important to understanding individuals and how they function, then it can be inferred that culture will also have an impact on how the individual functions. As we have seen earlier, ethnicity includes both race and culture. So what is culture? How culture is defined can, like race and ethnicity, influence the way we understand an individual, family, or group of people.

Culture has been defined as, "the way people live; the rules they set for themselves; the general ideas around which they organize their lives; the things they feel are good or bad, right or wrong, pleasurable" (Rose, 1997, p. 9). Linton (1945) defined culture as, "the configuration of learned behavior and results of behavior whose components and elements are shared and transmitted by the members of a particular society" (p. 32). Culture can be viewed as the basic morals, values, and beliefs groups of people claim for themselves, which they pass on from generation to generation. Culture also includes the accepted behaviors of a group. We can then infer that any society or segment of society, which transmits behaviors to the future generations of that society, has a culture (Atkinson et al., 1993).

Cohen (1993) defined culture as "the means by which we make meaning, and with which we make the world meaningful to ourselves, and ourselves meaningful to the world" (p. 196). Culture then is seen through the symbols created by a group of people. Symbols include language, art, music, tools, religion and those other activities that allow individuals and societies at large to recognize those aspects of a group of people viewed as unique. To sum, "culture consists of the values, traditions, social and political relationships, and worldview created, shared, and transformed by a group of people bound together by a common history, geographic location, language, social class, and/or religion" (Nieto, 2000, p. 139). Culture, like ethnicity and race, gives us an inside view of the nature of a group of people.

## IDENTITY DEVELOPMENT PROCESSES

In the following pages we will look at the racial, cultural, and ethnic identity development processes of several groups including African-Americans, Euro Americans, Biracial individuals, Asian Americans, Hispanics, and Native Americans. It is important to remember that these identity development patterns are affected by all the previously stated variables. To view identity development narrowly would be to negate that which makes a group unique. Therefore, it is important to learn about all aspects of the individual, rather than just the identity development process. We should also note that there are more similarities between groups than there are differences.

In this chapter, the process of identity development is limited to the description of racial, ethnic, and cultural identity development processes. Quantitative and qualitative research is limited in the areas of racial, ethnic, and cultural identity development. Much of the available literature is largely anecdotal and theoretical, but it does provide descriptions of identity development that have been useful in quantitative and qualitative research. Whereas modes of identity development have been anecdotal, they have provided researchers and practitioners with a starting point for understanding the racial, ethnic, and cultural identity processes experienced by many individuals who present for counseling services. Colón (1998) illuminated the importance of understanding the racial, ethnic, and cultural identity development of people. Colon stated,

> My sense of who I am has not come to me easily. My beginnings were shrouded by a mysterious tragedy that occurred at the time of my birth, the details of which were withheld from me for decades. I was raised in foster care, receiving only a handful of cryptic visits from my father and completely cut off from my mother. I was given no sense of who my people were, where I came from, or even what my racial and ethnic background was. The defining struggle of my life has been to find the racial, ethnic, and cultural aspects of myself; to uncover the truth of the events that transpired at my birth; and to integrate these discoveries into my sense of who I am. (p. 200)

Colón's words point us to how understanding our racial, ethnic, and cultural heritage is an integral part of who we are as individuals, and his words imply the importance of assisting clients with their understanding of who they are. Additionally, the importance of understanding one's own racial, ethnic, and cultural development is important and necessary so that our own development does not interfere with the counseling process.

It is also important for counselors to understand the differences in identity development among different ethnic groups because even though there may be similarities (Atkinson et al., 1993; Phinney, 1989, 1993, 1996a) there are differences relevant to individual ethnic groups. Counselors should also recognize that identity development models should not be used in isolation but as part of an overall assessment process so that stereotyping of ethnic minority clients may be less likely to occur. Additionally, researchers have suggested that identity development is not dependent on the movement through stages. The models presented in this chapter take the view that racial, ethnic, and cultural identity development involve a stage or phase development process, and that it is important to recognize the stages of development to understand the identity development process of the client.

The early models of racial identity development included models of Black racial identity (Cross, 1971; Thomas, 1971; Vontress, 1971) and Chinese American identity (Kim, 1981; Sue & Sue, 1971). In this chapter we discuss racial identity development models for Black, White, Hispanic, Biracial, Asian, Native Americans, and ethnic/minority individuals in general. The proliferation of identity development models indicates that there is continued and growing interest in identity development research and application to counseling practice. Models of racial identity originally took on typological approaches seeking to identify the stages of development. Current models seek to not only identify stages and phases of development but also seek to understand how an individual moves from one stage or phase to the next. Research has also suggested that individuals may recycle through stages or phases of development or skip parts of the process altogether. Most who have formulated models of racial, cultural, and ethnic identity for various groups have used the Cross (1971) model of Black racial identity development or *Nigrescence model* as a basis. Because of this, we begin our look at racial, cultural, ethnic identity with Black identity development.

## BLACK IDENTITY DEVELOPMENT MODELS

The way in which members of a group perceive their own racial-ethnic group, how they are perceived by members of their own group, and how they are viewed by society at large can affect their psychological well-being (Phinney, 1996b). Bagley and Young (1988) suggested that Black individuals who are secure in relation to their Black culture are more likely to experience a healthy identity development process, as compared to Blacks who are less connected to their cultural heritage. Because of the historical separation from their cultural roots, African Americans are cognizant that their historical heritage has been destroyed and that they have not been fully accepted into mainstream American society. African Americans have long struggled against the degradation of their heritage and their Blackness, which was clearly evidenced during the racial upheaval and the Civil Rights Movement of the 1960s.

Phinney (1996b) suggested that ethnic minority group identity includes both the cultural differences of ethnicity and the phenotypic aspects of race, due to the effects of skin color among African Americans. Breland (1998) noted that the recognition of skin tone differences among Black individuals has led to the use of such terms as dark skinned, brown skinned, ebony, chocolate, and fair skinned. Breland's work stresses that society's view of race is based largely on phenotype, and this affects the racial identity of minority group members. Black individuals with lighter complexions have been given preferential treatment in society since the time of slavery (Bond & Cash, 1992; Ross, 1997). This preferential treatment of light skinned Blacks has caused them difficulty in the Black community (Breland, 1998) in a similar manner to that experienced by Black-White Biracial individuals. Skin color plays a significant role in the interactions among Blacks and Whites and can, as suggested by Phinney (1996b), be a source of discrimination by the White community when judgments are made based on skin color.

Helms (1990) noted that Blacks have long had to struggle to establish pride in their cultural-racial identity. As noted earlier, the development of an identity is critical to an individual's psychological well-being (Erikson, 1963; Phinney, 1993). Cross (1971, 1995) and Helms (1990) have suggested that acquiring a racial identity is a developmental process that incorporates several stages. Phinney (1996b) suggested that by late adolescence most minority young people should have developed ethnic pride and a secure, internalized ethnic identity.

The first models of racial, ethnic, or cultural identity development were based on single race individuals. Racial identity has been conceptualized as an interest in gaining knowledge about one's racial-ethnic heritage, a sense of group belongingness, and the possession of positive attitudes about one's racial-ethnic group (Atkinson et al., 1993; Phinney, 1996b). Early racial identity development paradigms involved models of Nigrescence (the process of converting to Blackness). The most cited model of Nigrescence was developed by Cross (1971) as a result of the experiences of African-Americans during the 1960s. Cross (1971, 1995) pointed out that his model of Nigrescence explained how an individual becomes Black or Afrocentrically aligned. Cross also pointed out that theories of Black identity development were born out of the struggles of Black people to create an identity for themselves. The process of the development of a Black identity is a dynamic process in which an individual progresses in an orderly fashion from one stage to another. It is important to note that not all individuals will pass through all stages or phases of development and many individuals may recycle through the stages or phases. Individuals may stop at one stage and not move to other stages or phases of development.

During the same time period in which Cross (1971) developed his model of Black identity development, Thomas (1971) also developed a model of Nigrescence. This model, like Cross's, suggested that a Black individual will go through several stages in the process of accepting his or her Blackness in a White dominated world. Thomas (1971) put forth a five-stage model of Nigrescence suggesting that Black individuals move from a period in which they *withdraw* into the self prior to examining the self and others. He went on to say that Black individuals begin to *testify* about their feelings of becoming Black as they move toward *processing of information* about the Black culture and what it means to be a Black person. Individuals then begin to *actively* move into the world of Blackness, resulting in a *transcendental* phase in which individuals are able to see themselves as members of the dominant society, irrespective of race and class. The Thomas model begins with the individual rejecting the self and ends with the individual accepting the self. The model suggests that as individuals move through the stages they become able to recognize who they are racially, resulting in acceptance of themselves as racial beings. The Thomas model is similar to the Cross (1971, 1995) model, which also begins with self-rejection. In order to illustrate the utility of the Cross model, it will be discussed based on the following case example.

## Case Example

> Kareem is a 17 year old, African-American, male. He is currently seeking assistance with coming to grips with the loss of his father. He is angry and lashes out at the counselor, who is White, and tells him that he does not understand what its like to be Black. He is also having trouble in school because he says doing "good" in school is a "White" thing. Kareem is not sure the counselor can help him and is not sure he wants to come back. Kareem tells the counselor that he used to trust White people, but since that time so many Whites have hurt him that he does not trust them any more. He also talks to the counselor about not wanting a Black counselor because he does not believe that they are as smart as White counselors. Kareem tells that counselor that he has to get help because he can't go on living like this.

The first thing we notice in this case example is that this individual is seeking help even though he is not sure he can be helped by this counselor. Just knowing that he wants help could put the counselor in a position of being able to develop a therapeutic relationship that could result in Kareem reaching the goal for which he has sought counseling. However, we also note that Kareem has suggested that the counselor may not be able to help him because he assumes that he does not understand the Black experience. Because of this potential for difficulty it is important for the counselor to understand the racial identity process for African-Americans and where Kareem resides in the developmental process. This will give the counselor a starting point for the development of the relationship.

Cross (1971) suggested that an individual must pass through several well-defined stages leading to a Black identity because the Black experience is a process. He suggested that the process results in liberation from seeing the self only as a racial being. Cross identified the five stages of Black identity development as pre-encounter (pre-discovery), encounter (discovery), immersion/emersion, internalization, and commitment. In 1995, Cross revised his model based on his research of the stages. Whereas the names of the stages remained the same, the basic descriptions of the stages were modified based upon research findings.

The first stage *pre-encounter* or pre-discovery focuses on the identity to be changed. The individual is currently neutral to race or even anti-Black. Individuals in this phase place emphasis on other aspects of their personality such as their religion, lifestyle, or profession and avoid references to race. These individuals are often not aware of what it means to be Black in America. They are more likely to have a Eurocentric view, which leaves them primed for a conversion experience. Individuals in this stage are largely influenced by their earlier socialization experiences (Cross, 1995). Kareem is clearly not in this stage of development because he recognizes his Blackness and has pointed out that he does not believe the counselor understands what it means to be Black.

During the *encounter* stage, the individual begins the conversion toward a Black identity. The dominant theme of this stage is an encounter that brings to awakening race relations in society. An experience with racism or discrimination could be the encounter that brings about a new realization concerning the status of race relations between Whites and Blacks. The individual is likely to personalize the encounter and could become riddled with guilt, anger, and resentment over previous views held about the White race and his or her rejection of Blackness. The individual becomes energized and ready to change into a new person (Cross, 1995). Here we note that Kareem has also moved beyond this stage because he tells his counselor that he is Black. He expresses negative feelings toward his counselor as a result of his earlier encounter experiences. Kareem is likely to have had several encounters, which could be an indication of his lack of faith in the ability of his counselor to help him. However, Kareem is likely to be at a more advanced stage of development because of his willingness to work with a White counselor.

Between the encounter and internalization stages, there is a transition that Cross (1995) refers to as *immersion/emersion.* During this stage the old identity is demolished and a new identity begins to emerge. Two phases occur during this phase, which begins with the individual first being fully immersed in the Black culture. The individual rejects everything White and reclassifies himself or herself as Black, Black American, or African-American. This is the result of the individual feeling that something is happening to him or her rather than the individual feeling a part of a growth experience. In the second half of this phase, individuals are able to feel more control over their thoughts and feelings. The intense emotions experienced during the first half of this phase have passed and the individual feels the need for continued growth as he or she moves toward the internalization of a new Black identity (Cross, 1995). Kareem is likely to be at this stage of development because we can sense that he continues to be dominated by a lack of trust in White people as evidenced by some lack of faith in the ability of his counselor to assist him with his problem. Kareem also gives us an indication that he may still be in this stage because he rejects education, seeing it as a White thing. As individuals move through the immersion/emersion stage, they are less likely to see things as Black or White but are able to see utility in the values held by both races. This is evident in the *internalization* stage.

The process of working through the challenges and problems faced during the immersion/emersion phase is what indicates that the individual is internalizing a new identity, and identity that dominates the individual's very existence. During this stage, individuals recognize that they are Black, and they become proud of their Blackness. A *commitment* to Blackness signifies the entrance into the final stage of development. The individual possesses a clear, confident sense of his or her own identity. The individual is flexible in thoughts about self and others, is psychologically open, and has self-confidence in his or her racial identity (Cross, 1995). Kareem could possibly be in the second half of the immersion/emersion phase or the internalization stage. This is evidenced by his willingness to give the White counselor a chance at helping him even though he has doubts. The dissonance experienced by Kareem is evidence that he no longer takes a hard line stance against White individuals and is willing to give them a new chance to gain his trust. This is critical to the development of a therapeutic relationship. If the counselor is able to gain Kareem's trust, then Kareem is more likely to come back for further sessions. Kareem could also be in the internalization stage because he is committed to his Blackness. Even though one of his issues is a seeming rejection of education, education has some importance because he chose to discuss it.

The Cross (1995) model of Black identity development is a tool that points to the racial identity development level of the individual. It provides another opportunity to understand the world of the client and could provide a means for connecting with the client. Understanding the current stage of development occupied by the client provides counselors an expanded, contextual perception of the client's world.

In addition to enhancing psychological and contextual understanding of the client, the stage of identity development could give counselors insight into the client's preferences regarding ethnicity of the counselor (Sue & Sue, 1999), which in turn could reduce early termination. Attention has also been paid to the importance of counselors being sensitive to the cultural background of African Americans. Cultural sensitivity is often viewed as the most important characteristic in a counselor (Pomales, Claiborn, & LaFromboise, 1986). Sue and Sue (1999) also point out that it may be beneficial to inquire about the client's reaction to being in counseling with an ethnically different counselor. This is important because it is often the first impression that an African American holds about the counselor that will determine the outcome of the counseling process.

Identity development should be integrated into the broader context of functioning. Young (1993) suggested that in order for counseling to be effective, counselors need to confront the truth of the African American experience; and counselors should address the spirituality, humanness, and love of love that is innate to the African American. Parham and McDavis (1993) asserted that in working with Black males it is important to solicit the cooperation of the church and local civic groups. These activities may help meet the community needs of African Americans and could increase the likelihood that African Americans participate in the counseling process. Other areas of importance to African American clients would also emanate from the counseling relationship.

Parham and McDavis (1993) suggested that school counselors provide educational seminars on parenting and the developmental process encountered by children. A focus on skills seems particularly useful. The education program provided could be tailored based on the overall assessment of racial identity occupied by the African American population in the school. With regard to adult clients, counselors could assist African Americans with the resolution of identity crises that involve conflicts between the need to adapt to the culture of the world of work and the need to maintain a Black identity.

Helping African Americans, as with any other ethnic minority group, begins with the understanding of self-identity. Outcomes of counseling are largely dependent upon how the counselor uses the self in the counseling process. If counselors are aware of themselves and their cultural being, they are in a better position to see their clients as cultural beings. Counselors are then better prepared to help their clients.

## WHITE IDENTITY DEVELOPMENT MODELS

The study of racial identity development has been focused largely on ethnic minority groups, with a major focus on African Americans. There is a growing attention to the racial identity development of additional ethnic groups, including Asian and Hispanic Americans. White racial identity development has received comparatively little attention. White people may have been raised to believe they have no culture, or they may be confused about their race (Helms, 1992). White people may be reluctant to refer to themselves as White because of their fear of being labeled as racist, or fear of experiencing other negative consequences. The racial identification *White* cannot be separated from the preponderant influence or authority that the White group has maintained over others. More attention is now being directed toward White racial identity development because of the implications for research, training, and counseling, (Behrens, 1997), and because White identity development has such a pervasive influence on society.

*Whiteness* is a fluid concept. That is, Whiteness can be and often is influenced by demographic changes, political realignments, and economic cycles. The concept of Whiteness is forever changing as a result of the changing meaning of race in the larger society (Kincheloe, 1999). It is necessary to remember that the concept of race itself is fluid, and takes on a dynamic quality due to the changes in the landscape of the population.

White identity development is influenced by interactions with African Americans, Hispanics, Asian Americans, Native peoples and other ethnic minority groups. Encounters with minority groups is one cause for many White individuals "to rethink their tendency to dismiss the continued existence of racism and to no longer embrace the belief that racial inequality results from unequal abilities among racial groups" (Kincheloe, 1999, p. 163). Like the models of Nigrescence, White identity development is influenced by and in some part the result of interactions between the majority culture (White) and minority cultures. However, Kincheloe (1999) also points out that research does not indicate what truly constitutes Whiteness.

Historically, Whiteness has been presented as a non-colored, non-blemished pure racial category (Kincheloe, 1999). This was evidenced by Davis (1991) who defined the social construction of Black as being equated with an individual having one-drop of Black blood in his or her ancestry. A Louisiana Supreme Court case (*Jand Doe v. State of Louisiana*, 1986) held up a ruling that an individual with one-drop of Black blood is Black. The idea held that White is a pure racial category has been challenged as a result of changing definitions of Whiteness.

Kincheloe (1999) noted that it was not until the late 1600s that the label Black came into existence. Prior to that time there was no labeling based on skin color even for Africans. It was the advent of slavery in the new world around 1680 that the racialization of people based on concepts of White and Black became reality. The result has been that the racial category *White* has gone through many changes. At one point in time federal and state agencies identified individuals as White, Negro, and Indian. For example, California once classified Mexicans as White and the Chinese as Indian. Chinese Americans were then categorized as

Orientals, Asians, Pan Asians, and Asian Pacific Americans. The result has been that America has attempted to place individuals into heterogeneous categories based on skin tone, hair texture, and eye shape (Kincheloe, 1999). However, because biological characteristics of groups of people are not consistent, there has been a lack of consistency of what constitutes White. This has not been the case for Blacks and has been a more complex dilemma for Biracial individuals.

As we seek to understand the racial identity development of White individuals it is necessary to recognize that White persons have gained a sense of who they are racially by comparing themselves to other groups with an emphasis on comparing themselves against Blacks (Kincheloe, 1999). Haymes (1996) pointed out that to understand White racial identity formation it is necessary to recognize that *white* has been viewed as the opposite of *black* and that *white* has been vested with the privilege of being viewed as pure.

## Case Example

Sally is a thirty-two year old, White, female. She has come to counseling because she is concerned that she is not yet married and has not had a serious long-term relationship. She has come to this African-American counselor because she has heard that he is a very good counselor. She expresses concerns to the counselor because she was raised believing that Blacks were not as smart as Whites and that they were lazy and should never be in a position to tell Whites what to do. She is willing to try counseling with this counselor because of his reputation. She states that she always thought she knew who she was in this world but is now confused. Her parents never focused on her racial heritage and she always viewed herself as American. But now her friends are always talking about what it means to be White and how other minority groups are getting more attention than Whites are. It caused her confusion because she thought that minority groups, especially Blacks, deserved special treatment because of how they have been discriminated against and because they were not as academically talented as Whites. But now she is not sure because Blacks seem to have more opportunity, and Whites are having to give up their rights. Sally is no longer sure what to believe especially since she receives conflicting messages from her White and Black friends and co-workers.

As the case of Sally illustrates, confusion about racial identity is also an issue that can lead White individuals to seek counseling. The problem becomes more complex when the counselor sought is a member of an ethnic minority group, or perhaps more commonly when the counselor is White and the client belongs to a non-White group. We return to this case example after a more thorough discussion of White racial identity development models.

Much of the early research involving racial identity development focused on Black racial identity development with little research involving White racial identity development (Sabnani, Ponterotto, & Borodovsky, 1991; Tokar & Stevenson, 1991). As noted earlier, attention is now being placed on White racial identity development because of the role it plays in counseling (Behrens, 1997) and because of the effects that White racial identity is having on society. Helms (1992) also pointed out that in order for racism to disappear it is necessary for White and non-White individuals to understand the White racial identity development process and how it is affected by racism. Helms (1992) pointed out that the term *White* is used to identify individuals "who exhibit the physical characteristics of White Europeans and have been assimilated and acculturated into White Anglo-Saxon culture as it exists in the United States" (p. ii). While discussing White racial identity development, the Helm's definition of "White" will be used.

Hardiman (1982) developed a model of White racial identity development that focused upon the interactions between Whites and people from minority groups. Rather than seeing White racial identity development as being limited to the effects of interactions with Blacks and Whites, Hardiman saw White racial identity development as being impacted by the interactions between Whites and all other minorities. This model was a model based on racial consciousness. Hardiman (1982) suggested that individuals move through several stages in the racial identity development process that begins with a lack of racial understanding, and proceeding toward development of a non-racist White racial identity.

Hardiman (1982) asserted that White individuals start their journey toward developing a racial identity by first having a *lack of social awareness.* Individuals in this stage are just becoming aware of racial differences and are not yet fully cognizant of the roles and expectations of different racial groups. The individual then moves through a stage of unconscious identification with his or her own racial group and begins to accept the stereotypes of the various minority groups. During this early stage of development, Whites are taught to be aware of people's color but not to mention color in public (Helms, 1992). This stage is referred to as *acceptance* because of the acceptance of and identification with Whiteness. Much of what is learned during the acceptance stage is the result of interactions with White and minority individuals. People move through acceptance toward resistance, which Hardiman refers to as the *transition.* This stage involves feelings of guilt and anger because of discrepant experiences related to what has been learned about the meaning of being White. During *resistance,* White individuals begin to reject the racist teachings they have been led to believe are true. The anger and guilt becomes more intense because the individual is able to recognize that he or she has in many ways conformed to the dictates of racism. Toward the end of the resistance stage the individual begins to develop compassion and appreciation for ethnic minorities. During the final stage, *redefinition,* the individual develops a White identity that is not dependent on racism. The individual is able to identify and recognize the importance and worth of all people regardless of race or ethnicity and moves toward *internalization.* It is during this time that individuals are able to integrate their White identity into all areas of the self without it negatively affecting relationships with their own or other ethnic or racial groups.

The Hardiman model is based on the notion that White individuals will first develop a racist identity before moving toward an identity that is void of racist attitudes and accepting of others. Like the Hardiman (1992) model, the Helms (1984, 1992) model states that an individual moves from a belief in the superiority of Whiteness toward a discovery of the positive nature of being White without the maintenance of racist beliefs. In research conducted by Phinney (1988), it was discovered that White adolescents started their ethnic identity search later than Black adolescents. This may be due in part to White adolescents believing their culture is obvious and their ethnicity has more to do with their relationship to other minority groups. Phinney (1988) also pointed out that ethnic identity search is more likely to occur in college students than in high school students. Blacks demonstrated higher levels of ethnic search and commitment in their college years suggesting the earlier beginnings of ethnic search. Because White individuals are more likely to start their ethnic identity search later than other groups, it is more likely that they will have learned racist views prior to their ethnic search, making it more likely that they will begin the racial identity development process with racist views of other groups.

The Hardiman (1982) model of White racial identity development viewed racial identity development from a group perspective. The Helms (1984, 1990) model of White Racial Identity Development (WRID) takes the view that racial identity development is largely an individual process. However, like other models (Hardiman, 1982, Ponterotto, 1988) of White racial identity development, Helms's (1984, 1990, 1992) WRID model views White racial identity development as a response to both positive and negative experiences with minority individuals.

Helms (1984) originally saw WRID as a five-stage process. In her revised model (Helms, 1990) she identified WRID as a two phase process with each phase consisting of three stages. She described WRID as a developmental process comprised of "abandonment of racism and evolution of a nonracist White identity" (Helms, 1992, p. 24).

The WRID is based on interactions between Blacks and Whites but does have applicability to White individuals interactions with other racial-ethnic groups. The WRID models begins with the selfish understanding that it is better to be born White than to be born a minority, which in and of itself is a racist orientation. Because of its subtly, this orientation is not always in the awareness of the individual. In order to begin the racial identity development process the individual must be able to recognize that racism does exist (Helms, 1992). During the first stage of the WRID, *contact,* the individual is unaware of or ambivalent toward his or her own race and the race of others. Family discussions may spark interest in issues of race but the individual is not aware of the importance or significance of racial issues (Helms, 1990) A young female child, in kindergarten, once told her mother "I want some tan paint." The mother purchased the paint for the child thinking she just wanted to paint a picture. When the child received the paint she began to paint her skin. Alarmed, the mother asked the child why she was painting herself. The child stated, "I want to be like the other girls in my class because they are so pretty." This child displayed an ignorance of race and racial issues because she was not consciously White and the only differences she saw between herself and her class mates was the color of skin (Helms, 1992), which she thought was pretty. Toward the end of the contact stage the individual begins to become aware of race and racial differences. The individual also has begun to recognize the societal rules concerning the interactions of Blacks and Whites. During this time, denial of racial problems becomes apparent. The ability of the individual to overcome this denial will determine if any further movement in the racial identity development process will occur. The individual will remain in the contact stage until he or she is able to recognize that race does matter (Helms, 1990).

Once the individual is able to recognize the significance of race movement toward the stage of *disintegration* can occur. Emergence into this stage occurs because denial of race differences is no longer occurring. The individual has also found that his or her Whiteness is an important characteristic, however, confusion about racial issues also dominates this stage. The individual begins to realize that being White is like a double-edged sword. This is the first time the individual is able to identify as being White and recognizes that there are benefits of belonging to the White group. At the same time, the individual recognizes that being White also means that one is to treat Blacks in a self-indulgent fashion. A moral dilemma ensues that brings about dissonance because he or she can no longer recognize the humanity of all people. It is during this stage that the concept of blaming the victim takes hold (Helms, 1992). A student once said, "If Black people would just do what they have to do they could get what they want." The student did not realize that racism works in many ways to keep minorities from reaching their goals. As Phinney (1988) learned in her research, White students learn that there are advantages to being White and do not want to be part of a minority group due to prejudice and discrimination. The negative aspects of this stage are resolved in one of three ways: (a) through over-identifying with the struggles encountered by Blacks, (b) by trying to protect Blacks from the effects of racism and discrimination (become paternalistic), or (c) through a conscious effort to focus on one's Whiteness, excluding Blacks from social interactions (Helms, 1990). The individual who seeks to exclude Blacks from social interactions places an emphasis on racial differences and promotes segregated experiences due to a lack of knowledge concerning Black people. As the distorted views of Blacks become more complex and ingrained, individuals move toward and enter the *reintegration* stage (Helms, 1992).

The reintegration stage includes an unsympathetic attitude toward minorities and a belief in the superiority of Whites. Blacks are seen as inferior, and there is covert or overt expression of racism. The individual in this stage denies the contributions of minorities and takes credit for all the things that have been developed for the benefit of society. This stage is also the period during which Whites attribute blame to Blacks themselves for their social condition. Whites tend to stay in this stage longer than any other stage because of their membership in the dominant group. In order for the individual to move to the next stage and therefore the next phase of development, it is necessary for the individual to have a moral reawakening that was lost during the disintegration stage. This moral re-awakening allows the individual to leave the racism phase and enter the nonracism phase (Helms, 1990, 1992).

The nonracism phase begins with the *pseudo-independence* stage. This stage begins when the individual is able to bring into focus his or her attitude towards Blacks or other racial-ethnic groups. Individuals at this stage are curious about and find acceptance with both Blacks and Whites. The person no longer holds firm to the belief that Whites are superior to Backs and is able to cope with racial differences at the intellectual level. The individual is able to accept that racism exists but does not admit that Whites as a group or the individual White person has any responsibility for the problem. The White person, for example, might remark "It's not my fault that racism exists. I didn't do anything to hurt anybody and neither did my family." The individual is more comfortable during this stage because he or she is accepted by Whites and is receiving some acceptance from Blacks.

The case example of Sally points out his dilemma and her effort to find the truth. She is confused because her family has taught her many negative things about Blacks, and her friends have reinforced many of her parents' views. However, her own interactions with Blacks have caused her to question what she believes, and she is now willing to investigate and gain new knowledge about Blacks in order to reduce her level of cognitive dissonance. As White individuals are able to realize that just recognizing that racism exists will not lead to its demise, the individual is able to move on to the *Immersion/Emersion* stage.

Helms (1990) included this stage in order to identify the period during which the individual seeks to learn about his or her White history. The individual uses this period to understand the significance of being White. People at this stage take a personal re-appraisal of their Whiteness and are able to take personal responsibility for the continuation of racism. The person develops a moral conscious that understands the suspicions held by Blacks about Whites. The person becomes able to confront racism and other forms of discrimination. As the number of contacts with liked minded Whites and Blacks increases, the individual is able to enter into the last stage of the identity development process, *Autonomy.*

During the autonomy stage the individual is able to accept racial differences without focusing on those differences. People are accepted for who they are not what they represent. The individual is able to develop an appreciation of and respect for cross-racial interactions and is able to accept the cultural norms of other groups (Helms, 1984). Individuals become secure in their identity and seek to nurture their Whiteness (Helms, 1990, 1992).

Thompson (1994) pointed out that the WRID emphasizes "Whites' interactions with and attitudes toward non-whites rather than Whites' identity development as racial beings" (p. 646). Additionally, much of the research that has been conducted on the WRID model has been related to racism and prejudice (Pope-Davis & Ottavi, 1994). It is therefore important to note that the development of a White racial identity must also include how White individuals interact with other races and how these interactions affect the racial identity development process. This is not only true for White identity but also is important in the process of gaining a clearer understanding of the racial identity process in all individuals.

Sue and Sue (1999) noted that it is important, when training White counseling students, to understand how identity development manifests itself in students' personalities. Further, the characteristics associated with a particular identity development level may dictate the objectives and techniques most likely to promote trainee growth. Sabnani, Ponterotto, and Borodovsky (1991) provided a developmental model of identity development in White trainees that could be used during training. Additionally, detailed and specific training exercises were also developed to aid trainees with movement through the identity development process. The goals of training and the related tasks were correlated to the multicultural counseling competencies (see: Sue, Arredondo, McDavis, 1992).

It is also important to note that White racial identity development models make many assumptions that may not be present in all individuals. As with any other racial group, counselors should assess each client individually; determine which characteristics of identity are present; and then conceptualize which techniques and interventions would be most appropriate with the client. Counselors are encouraged to remember that the needs of the client should be placed above all other considerations (Egan, 1998).

## IDENTITY DEVELOPMENT FOR BIRACIAL INDIVIDUALS

Having first looked at the processes of developing Black and White racial identities, we now move into a look at the development of a Biracial identity. Importance has recently been placed on understanding Biracial identity development due to the increased visibility of Black/White interracial relationships and because of the 2000 census. Historically, most of the research on Biracial identity development has been focused on Black/White Biracial individuals because of the link to the period of slavery in this country. Additionally, much of the research on Biracial individuals has focused on the negative aspects of being Biracial; and researchers have often neglected studies that suggest what constitutes mental health in Biracial individuals (Root, 1990).

Salgado de Snyder, Lopez, and Padilla (1982) noted that few studies have included exogamy (marriage outside one's group), even though there has been concern about the emotional and psychological welfare of children who come from mixed marriages. They also observed that even in those studies that have been conducted with interracial children, little attention has been paid to parents' cultural, linguistic, and religious differences. These aspects of individual identity can also affect the racial-ethnic identity development of multiracial individuals.

Early research suggested that Biracial individuals would suffer identity crises because Biracial individuals had no single group with which to identify and because of their marginal status (Parks, 1931; Stonequist, 1937). Teicher (1968) and Gibbs and Moskowitz-Sweet (1991) studied Biracial individuals who were identified as having existing psychological disorders. They concluded that psychological problems were due in part to Biracial participants' marginal status and lack of group identification. In Jacobs' (1992) study, participants were identified as being marginal because they had no single group with which to identify. Studies that focused on the developmental difficulties encountered by multiracial individuals failed to identify the strengths of these individuals and the resources that were beneficial to their development of healthy identities.

In contrast to studies that focused on the negative aspects of Biracial identity and its relationship to psychological disorders, other studies identified positive characteristics of Biracial individuals. Tizard and Phoenix (1995) found that many Biracial individuals maintain positive attitudes about their mixed racial heritage. Field (1996) found that Biracial individuals possess positive self-concepts much like their monoracial peers. Tizard and Phoenix (1995) carried out a qualitative study of Biracial (Black/White) individuals using semi-structured interviews. Fifty-eight Biracial individuals participated in the study with 72% female and 28% male. The majority of the participants indicated that they had positive attitudes about their racial make-up. They were also able to stress the advantages of being a part of more than one racial group. This study raised questions about the view held by many social scientists that Biracial individuals "need to acquire a Black identity and culture [that] implicitly denigrates their mixed background, and denies their right to construct identities that are both Black and White" (Tizard & Phoenix, 1995, p. 1409). The Tizard and Phoenix study suggested that Biracial individuals are more inclined to suffer from psychological stress and anxiety due to their treatment by society at large rather than from the mere fact that they are Biracial.

Root (1990) suggested that Biracial individuals could resolve their racial identity development process in one of four ways. She suggested that no single resolution is identified as healthier than another. Instead she pointed out that any of the four resolutions could be viewed as a healthy outcome of the racial identity development process because they all assume that the individual is able to recognize and accept both sides of his or her racial make-up. Root identified the four resolutions of the identity development process as being (a) an acceptance of the racial identity imposed by society, (b) identification with one racial group in the individual's make-up, (c) identification as a multiracial individual, and (d) identification as a member of a new racial group. Root also asserted that the resolution chosen is employed based on the current circumstances encountered by the individual. This view was supported by research conducted by Henriksen (2001).

The development of a racial, ethnic, or cultural identity has been viewed as a dynamic process that is stage based. This typically means that individuals must successfully complete one stage of the developmental process prior to moving to the next stage. This does not directly account for instances when individuals recycle through the stages or regress back to earlier stages of development. For identity development models to be truly dynamic they should address issues of recycling and regression. There are both dynamic and static models of Biracial identity development.

The first model of Biracial identity development came from the work of Stonequist (1937). His model focused on the "marginal" identity of the Biracial individual. The model encompassed American bias by suggesting that Biracial individuals do not establish concrete identities because they do not belong to a single racial group. Stonequist's Marginal Person Model was a deficit model much like the model postulated by Gibbs (1987). Stonequist took the view that the identity development of Biracial individuals was problematic, and the adjustment process was viewed as marginal. Stonequist saw this marginal status as being a consequence of the fact that Biracial individuals are related to two racial groups but do not belong to either. Gibbs (1987) suggested that multiple racial identities could pose dilemmas for adolescents as they work to develop a cohesive, well-integrated racial identity. The notion was that biracial individuals would develop problems resulting from the ambiguity experienced in their identification with their parents, peer group, and ethnic, racial, or cultural group. The Stonequist model is a descriptive model rather than a stage or developmental model.

As has been pointed out, models of Biracial identity development have not always looked at the stage progression of a racial or ethnic identity. Gibbs (1987) looked at racial identity development in Biracial individuals from an internal conflict perspective (duality of identity). Morrison and Rodgers (1996) took the perspective that Biracial identity development is hindered by a society that views race as significant, with emphasis on single race classifications. Poston (1990) conducted research that suggested that racial identity development is impacted in two primary respects. First, racial identity is impacted by how the individual views him or herself racially, how the individual views others in the same racial-ethnic group, how the individual views individuals who are members of other ethnic groups, and the effects the majority group has on impacting and shaping the individual's attitude as a racial being. Secondly, racial identity development is impacted when the Biracial individual no longer accepts the belief that one must conform to a single racial group in order to be accepted. The importance of Poston's work is evident in the models of Biracial identity development that followed. Poston's (1990) model of Biracial identity development took the perspective that achieving a racial identity is a developmental process.

Poston (1990) posited a tentative model of Biracial identity development in response to the inability to apply models developed for single race groups. He saw the Cross (1971) model of Black identity development and the Morten and Atkinson (1983) general model of minority identity development as being inadequate to describe the identity development process for Biracial individuals because of the models' focus on people who belonged to well-defined groups.

The model of Biracial identity development posited by Poston (1990) not only takes into account the unique experiences of different ethnicities and cultures but also recognizes that a Biracial individual will develop a racial identity based on the incorporation of different aspects of the ethnicity and culture of both parents.

In the first stage of the Poston (1990) model, *personal identity,* the young child is not cognizant of membership in any particular group. Identity is influenced by the family and the child's sense of self-esteem and self-worth. The second stage, *choice of group categorization,* occurs when the individual feels pushed to choose between a majority or minority identity. The individual feels the necessity to identify with a group in order to foster relationships with family, peer, and social groups. Poston also noted several factors that he believed affected the choice of a racial group: (a) *status factors*—including the status of each parent's racial group and the status of peer groups, (b) *social support factors*—including parental and familial influence and acceptance and participation in the cultural activities of other racial groups, and (c) *personal factors*—such as physical appearance (e.g., skin tone, hair texture), cultural knowledge, and age. The next stage is *enmeshment/denial.* During this stage the individual becomes enmeshed in one group and experiences rejection and hostility from the denied group. It is as though the individual has cut off completely one-half of him or herself. The individual experiences feelings of guilt and confusion due to the choice that was made.

The individual is able to move into the *appreciation* stage when he or she is able to begin the process of accepting that he or she possesses multiple racial heritages. The individual maintains a preference for one group identity but no longer rejects the other half of his or her identity. Individuals who enter the appreciation stage are able to find enjoyment in the cultural activities of both parts of their identity. Individuals who enter the final stage of identity development, *integration*, experience a sense of wholeness and an integration of both dimensions of their racial make-up. A sense of self-confidence and self-assurance is gained as the individual develops an integrated self-identity. The Poston model incorporates a life span focus, acknowledging that racial identity development as a dynamic process with no specific beginning and no specific end. However, Kerwin and Ponterotto (1995) noted that the Poston Model of Biracial identity development assumes that all Biracial individuals will experience confusion and maladjustment as a result of being Biracial. This is consistent with previous models (Gibbs, 1987; Stonequist, 1937), but is not supported by other research on Biracial identity development (Henriksen, 2001; Root 1990).

Another of the early models of Biracial identity development was developed by Jacobs (1992) who studied Biracial children. Jacobs found that Biracial children seek to identify themselves with the Black parent but want to possess the qualities of the White parent. Jacobs' research and his clinical experience suggested that preadolescent Biracial children proceed through three qualitatively different stages of racial identity development. Stage I, identified as *pre-color constancy*, is characterized by flexibility and little attention paid to specific colors being used to classify groups. However, Jacobs did point out that children who have suffered from racial prejudice are more likely to avoid the playful exploration of color and its reference to people. In the second stage, *post-color constancy*, which Jacobs suggests is reached by age 41/2, the child is viewed as being able to identify and evaluate colors based on experience with prejudice. The child becomes ambivalent about his or her racial status and recognizes that his or her color is permanent. This stage is also the period during which the Biracial individual is able to develop and internalize a Biracial label and to construct a personal racial identity. During Stage III, *biracial identity*, which Jacobs identified in children aged 8-12, Biracial children discover that their racial group membership is influenced by their skin color but is not determined by their skin color. This is evident in Biracial individuals who display White features and identify as White and deny their Black heritage. The child also learns that racial group membership is determined by parentage, particularly by the minority parent.

Jacobs' (1992) study suggests that one of the major impacts on the racial identity development of Biracial children involves parental labels. This is consistent with other research (Henriksen, 2001; Poston, 1990, Wardle, 1992) which also suggests that interaction with parents and parents' resolution of their own identity development can either positively or negatively impact the identity development of Biracial children. However, Jacobs' assertion that a single instance of labeling is often sufficient for Biracial children to begin exploring racial identity is simplistic.

Wardle (1992) suggested that Biracial identity development is a two-stage process that involves five ecological components: family, minority context, majority context, group antagonism, and community. Wardle suggested that first stage occurs between the ages of three to seven years. It is during this time that the child becomes aware of the racial differences among people and learns the labels and emotional expressions of other racial groups. The child sees race by identifying the physical cues, such as skin color, that differentiate the various racial-ethnic groups in a similar manner as do Whites and Blacks. During the second stage of racial identity development, which is identified as occurring into adolescence, Biracial children continue to define themselves in terms of how they identify who they are, how they feel about their self-identification, and how they feel about the views society maintains concerning them. The model suggests that the outcome of the racial identity development process could be a Biracial identity.

Wardle (1992) asserted that the ecological components of the Biracial racial identity development process can and do affect both stages of development. He noted that children might respond individually to the minority side of their Biracial make-up. He also noted that parents could influence whether the child integrates minority and majority values, attitudes, and behaviors, or identifies with a single group. The parent who is from the majority racial group also influences the Biracial child. The affect of this parent on the child is dependent upon how the parent views him or herself in the context of his or her culture. Extended family members--through their acceptance or rejection of the Biracial child--also affect biracial children. Wardle (1992) suggests that family members, both nuclear and extended, exert the greatest amount of influence on the racial identity development of Biracial children. Group antagonism (opposition expressed concerning membership in a racial group) occurs because of the perceived marginality of the Biracial individual. The Biracial child is caught in a situation in which membership in a racial group is tenuous because the child does not possess a single race identity. The child does not fit into any single group and most likely lacks the support necessary for membership from either or both groups. Wardle suggests that it is the resolution of these conflicts that could determine whether or not the child will develop a healthy racial identity or not. The Wardle model (1992)is based on a positive view of Biracial identity development.

Root (1990) also took a positive view of Biracial identity development. Root's developmental model challenged several existing models, suggesting that Biracial identity development does not cause maladjustment or confusion. Root also identified four general resolutions to the Biracial identity development process. This model suggests that racial identity development is in part dependent upon the way in which the individual is able to cope with racial identification conflicts that occur during critical developmental periods. Conflicts could be affected by political, social, and familial environments. Root suggested that the conflict which causes Biracial people the greatest difficulty is the tension between racial components within oneself. Root noted that this conflict could occur repeatedly throughout the lifetime of the individual. She also suggested that internal conflict could lead to themes of marginality, discrimination, and ambiguity, which are influenced by environmental factors.

Root (1990) suggested that Biracial individuals contend with both parts of their identity throughout their lifetime. Biracial individuals first begin the identity development process when, as children, they become aware of race as a social construct and become aware that they are different from their single race friends. Biracial individuals then give attention to all aspects of their heritage as they develop an identity. Resolution of the identity process occurs when there is no longer an internal need to compartmentalize the different parts of the individual's heritage. The resolution of the Biracial identity development process can consist of one of four general resolutions with no one outcome being more acceptable than the others. The four resolutions assume that the individual is able to identify all aspects of his or her heritage or racial background. The four resolutions include (a) acceptance of the racial label given by society, (b) public identification with a single racial group, (c) identification with both racial groups (i.e., Biracial), and (d) identifying oneself as being a member of a new racial group (i.e., Multiracial). Root noted that the resolution utilized is in part dependent upon the circumstances facing the individual.

As Root (1990) noted, the idea that Biracial individuals could develop a racial identity without becoming maladjusted or confused has had little acknowledgement in the literature. Henriksen (2001) also took the view that the development of a racial identity is not based on individuals coping with maladjustment or confusion. Instead he saw Biracial identity development as a process of search leading to commitment.

In a study conducted by Henriksen (2001), six women and one man took part in semi-structured interviews. Data suggested that Biracial individuals go through several processes or periods leading to the development of a racial identity, rather than going through several different stages. The results of the Henriksen study also suggest that past research-based and anecdotal models of Biracial identity development were in part correct and in part deficient.

Henriksen's Black/White Biracial Identity Development Model (2001) incorporates six periods or processes that could be encountered by Biracial individuals. Results demonstrated that some individuals may experience all six phases or periods, some may experience fewer than six, and some may recycle through the phases or periods. Additionally, like the Root (1990) model, the Henriksen model suggests that Biracial individuals might resolve their identity development via several different means of self-identification.

The first phase or period identified is referred to as *neutrality.* Individuals in this phase are unaware of their own racial classification and of the social implications of race. A 22-year-old Biracial woman described neutrality when she said; "I mean you really don't see color you just compare yourself to other people. . . I wasn't really dark and I wasn't really light. I was like you know coffee with a little extra cream." In this case race involved comparing skin color but had no real importance. Neutrality was also identified in the words of a 20-year-old Biracial female when she said, "In elementary school, I really didn't even know [about race], it didn't even matter." The notion that an individual is classified by racial categories does not enter the individual's consciousness until their parents or peers racially classify them.

The ability to recognize and accept oneself as having a racial identity is the first indication that the individual has entered the *acceptance* phase or period (Henriksen, 2001). During the acceptance phase the individuals accept that they are racially different from their parents and peers but are not aware of what it means to be racially different, nor do they see their racial status as a problem. The words of a 21-year-old Biracial female point out what it means to be in the acceptance phase.

I guess I've always known that I was different because I was always bright [light skinned]. I was always brighter than the other girls and my hair was always like theirs and I would always say . . . I have hair like Tammy, but my skin is like Tonya. They [other children] let you know that you're not like everyone else. (Henriksen, 2001, p. 73)

The acceptance of being racially different could also be the result of negative social interactions. Some participants in the study indicated that they felt sadness and insecurity based on being confronted with the notion that because they had parents of two different races something was wrong with them. Acceptance appears to come at an early age; around the time individuals enter school for the first time. The struggle with seeking out a racial identity begins during this phase and continues throughout the ensuing years of development. This is consistent with Root (1990) who suggested that racial identity development is a life-span process.

Once the individual has accepted that he or she is a racial being movement into the *awareness* phase begins. Awareness is the phase that occurs when individuals develop an understanding of what it means to be racially different from others. This phase is typically accompanied by a significant social interaction which often results in feelings of isolation because of the lack of existence of a reference group. The experiences of acceptance and awareness can be experienced simultaneously or separately. The importance of this phase was identified in the words of the participants of the study who indicated that this period was important to their development of a racial identity (Henriksen, 2001).

Having become aware of the significance of race, Biracial individuals move toward a period of *experimentation.* Experimentation is the period when the Biracial individual seeks to fit into only one part of his or her racial identity

I've just hung around White people to see what it's like and just hung around Black people to see what it's like. Well, like around fourth or fifth grade I hung mostly around White people because underneath from kindergarten to third I hung around with Blacks and Whites and then I was in fourth or fifth grade . . . I still had my Black friends but I didn't hang around with them as much as I did my White friends. And then when I started sixth grade I . . . hung around mostly Black people and then when I went to middle school I hung around White people all the way to the middle year of my freshman year of high school then I started hanging around Black people more . . . and still now but I still hang out with White people when I get the chance. I guess where I live they're not, some people aren't accepting. White people aren't because they go by what their parents say and stuff so they'll hang out with me at school and stuff but outside of school . . . I don't ever get to talk to, hang out with them unless it's a school function or something. (Henriksen, 2001, p. 78)

The words of this 19 year old Biracial woman point out the dilemma faced by many Biracial individuals as they search for a racial identity. Movement through the experimentation period is not just a time when Biracial individuals seek to fit into one racial group; it is also a time when Biracial individuals are most actively involved in seeking their own racial identity. However, the study also suggested that not all biracial individuals move into the experimental period and that recognition of one's identification as a Biracial individual can occur following the awareness phase.

The period of *transition* follows the experimentation period and involves the continuing movement toward a sense of racial self-recognition. Individuals in the transition phase continue to search for a racial group with which to identify. Participants suggested that it was better to find their own identity rather than to choose between two identities and never being sure if you were really being accepted. The idea that one cannot really choose between being Black or White was also indicated because participants realized that they had parents of both races. This is the central theme of the transition period (Henriksen, 2001).

When individuals recognize and decide who they are racially, they enter the final *recognition* phase. It is the time when Biracial individuals state, "this is who I am and I am proud of who I am." Individuals verbally describe themselves as biracial but identify themselves as Black, White, Mulatto, Biracial, or Mixed. Many individuals use a label that is dependent upon the environmental circumstances that are being faced. This is consistent with Root (1990) who identified several healthy outcomes to the developmental process. However, indications that the racial identity development process does not come to a complete end was found in the words of several participants in this study who asked, "Now that I know where I am, where am I going?" (Henriksen, 2001).

The Black/White Biracial Identity Development Model (Henriksen, 2001) aids in the establishment of a clearer understanding of the process involved in developing a racial identity. The model also points out that racial identity development is not necessarily a sequential or stage-wise progression. Phases or periods can occur simultaneously and individuals can recycle through the phases or periods. This study also confirmed the importance of the influences of family and peers. It also identified the importance of a spiritual connection that assisted the individual during the struggle to develop a racial identity. More studies of Biracial identity development are needed to refine and validate this model and other models.

It has been noted that the process of developing a Biracial identity is a complex process that is similar to and different from the development of a Black or White identity. Recognition that Biracial individuals experience a process of racial identity development and the identification of the process and related influences allow counselors to become able to develop counseling interventions that could meet the needs of Biracial individuals. No one approach or theory is the correct one for all Biracial individuals. However, a more thorough understanding of the racial identity development process for Biracial individuals can lead to increased successful counseling outcomes.

## GENERAL MODELS OF IDENTITY DEVELOPMENT

### Case Example

I have never really tried to understand what it means to be a Mexican in America. I have at times asked why do people treat me the way they do because I am an American. I was born here. Most of my friends are White and the few Mexican friends I have are more White than Mexican like me. I see a lot of things on the news about Mexicans and I think I'm not like them. I don't really want to be like them, I just want to be me. My parents talk to me a lot about what it means to be Mexican but I don't really listen to them because I just want to be an American. My friends often ask why I don't pay much attention to my Mexican heritage when it is a part of me. I know that they probably know more about Mexican culture than I know.

I know that I need to learn more about my heritage because by not wanting to learn I am hurting my parents. Being the oldest boy in the family also means that I am a role model for my brothers and sisters. They are all into their Mexican heritage and they ask me if I am ashamed of being Mexican. I'm not sure. I want to know more about who I am but I am afraid that if I do my friends won't want to be my friends any more. I know that when I date White girls we have to sneak around because most of their parents don't like Mexicans. Sometimes I wish I was White and sometimes I wish I were more Mexican. I got really hurt a couple of weeks ago when I tried to get a job and the man told me he only hires Americans. I know I can't hide from who I am and I don't know how to discover who I am. I am really confused and realize that I have to do something.

Ethnic minorities in the United States face many challenges related to their minority status and ethnic identity. As we have seen in the Cross (1971, 1995) model of Black identity development, many African Americans begin their search for an identity by first rejecting their own identity and seeking to become like the White majority. This is also evident in the previous case example. The young Mexican male sees his heritage as being a hindrance to his progress. He is also confused by the messages that he receives from the White community. There are several messages he has received that no longer seem to apply to him. First, he learned that to make it in America you have to assimilate into the culture of the dominant group. This had worked for him; but now it no longer works, resulting in his becoming confused about his place in society. Secondly, he learned the concept of rugged individualism and that he is his own person. However, he is now realizing that his focus on his own needs have pulled him away from his family and his responsibilities to the family. This is a major problem for him because of the importance placed on family respect in Mexican culture. Finally, the young man in this case example has realized that minorities are not afforded the same rights and dignity of the majority group, and this fuels an inner turmoil that pushes him to learn about his identity.

Many minority individuals face the same conflicts encountered in this example. Understanding the complexities of racial, ethnic, and cultural identity development could provide counselors with a means by which they could understand the dilemmas minorities face during the process of finding their identity. In the previous sections, we focused on the racial identity development processes for Black, White, and Biracial individuals. This section turns to a more general perspective on minority and ethnic identity development.

## Minority Identity Development (MID) Model

Most minority groups in America have experienced discrimination in social, economic, and educational arenas. The result is that their view of themselves and others has been affected. Because of the similar experiences of discrimination, Atkinson et al. (1993) developed a model of identity development that they believe "defines five stages of development that oppressed people may experience as they struggle to understand themselves in terms of their own minority culture, and the oppressive relationship between the two cultures [minority and White]." (p. 28). It is important to note that not all individuals will experience all of the stages of the Minority Identity Development (MID) model. Some may begin at later stages rather than the early stages, and some may begin and end at the last stage. The authors of the model suggest that family influences play a prominent role on the developmental process and where the process begins.

The MID model is based on observations of minority clients over a period of years. Stage one of the MID is identified as the conformity stage. Individuals at this stage prefer the culture of the majority group to their own. They feel deficient in the qualities that they perceive as valued by the majority group. Individuals at this stage tend to be self-depreciating, minority depreciating, but majority group appreciating (Sue and Sue, 1999). Individuals at this stage may see their physical features as less desirable and the cultural values of the majority group as more desirable, while seeing their own cultural values as roadblocks (Atkinson et al., 1993).

During the dissonance stage, the individual is made aware that he or she belongs to a minority, non-dominant group. This stage is characterized by a monumental encounter (racism or discrimination) event, and internal conflict is the hallmark of this stage (similar to the Cross, 1971, 1995 model). Minorities begin the process of letting go of their denial system and recognizing that they are members of a minority group. This is accompanied by the realization that their victimization is due to their minority status. Minorities often struggle between being self-depreciating and self-appreciating during this stage (Atkinson et al., 1993).

In the resistance and immersion stage, the individual completely endorses minority views and rejects the views of the majority culture. The person begins to appreciate the self and the group to which he or she belongs, and has a strong desire to eliminate oppression. Internal conflict exists in relation to other minority groups, and there is anger with the majority group (Atkinson et al., 1993). Sue and Sue (1999) note that during this stage individuals experience feelings of guilt, shame, and anger due to their having previously rejected their own group and having collaborated with the White majority to the detriment of their group.

During the introspection stage of the MID model, the minority person becomes uncomfortable with holding rigid views of his or her own group in relation to the majority group. The individual begins to reject the view that there is nothing positive about White culture, and recognizes that other groups do possess positive qualities. The person begins to feel comfortable with his or her own identity, but recognizes that society does continue to maintain barriers to the full expression of minority cultures. The individual becomes more autonomous yet still feels a responsibility and allegiance to his or her group (Atkinson et al., 1993).

Minority individuals experience self-fulfillment, with respect to cultural identity, during the synergistic stage. Dissonance has been resolved allowing greater flexibility and control in relation to interactions to other groups. Objective analysis of the values of other ethnic and racial groups allows the individual to accept or reject aspects of those groups. A commitment to ending oppression is an enduring part of this stage (Atkinson et al., 1993). Sue and Sue (1999) identify this stage as the Integrative Awareness Stage. They suggest that individuals in this stage "have developed an inner sense of security and can now own and appreciate unique aspects of their culture as well as those of U.S. culture" (Sue & Sue, 1999, p. 136).

As with the previously discussed models of Black identity development, this model is based on interactions between minorities and the majority (White) culture. How the individual is able to move through the process of becoming oneself will positively or negatively affect the racial identity of the individual. Phinney (1989) suggested that ethnic identity development begins with a period of search or exploration and concludes with a commitment to one's ethnicity.

## Ethnic Identity Development

Research suggests that ethnicity is a central concern during identity formation for minority-group people. Ethnicity is seen as equal to or more important than religion and politics (Phinney & Alipuria, 1990; Phinney & Chavira, 1992). Ethnic identification is salient because of its relationship to psychological well-being in minority individuals (Phinney, 1989; Sue & Sue, 1999).

Our discussion of ethnic identity development focuses on the model developed by Phinney (1989, 1993, 1996a). Similar to Atkinson et al. (1993) and Sue and Sue (1999), Phinney looked to formulate an ethnic identity development model that would be applicable across various groups. Phinney (1989) sought to understand the process of ethnic identity formation, which involves understanding how the individual recognizes the implications of his or her ethnicity, how the individual makes decisions about the role ethnicity will play in his or her life, and the process of identity formation regardless of the individual's ethnic involvement. This is in contrast to other models of racial-ethnic identity development, which suggest that individuals become more attuned to and involved with their ethnicity as they move through the stages of identity development.

The process of developing an ethnic identity is dynamic, involving changes across time. The process is dependent upon environmental and other contextual conditions, and it varies with the individual (Phinney, 1996b). Phinney also noted that individuals are likely to reexamine aspects of their ethnic identity and maybe return to earlier developmental stages, or recycle through the stages. This is consistent with other models of racial-ethnic identity development (e.g., Henriksen, 2001). Like the MID model of minority identity development, the Phinney (1993, 1996a) model had several influences. Phinney (1993, 1996a) incorporated interview data with descriptions of identity development involving Black identity development (Cross, 1971), Asian American identity development (Kim, 1981), minority identity development (Atkinson et al., 1993), and ego identity development (Marcia, 1966, 1980). Before describing Phinney's (1993, 1996a) model, we provide basic descriptions of the above models which served as a basis for Phinney's model.

The Cross (1971, 1995) model of Nigrescence was described earlier in this chapter. To review this model, it begins with a rejection of Black culture and the acceptance of White culture. After experiencing racism and discrimination, Black individuals then begin the process of developing a Black identity. Black identity development concludes when the individual is able to integrate Blackness, gain a clear sense of identity, and effectively function within a White dominated society.

Kim's (1981) model of Asian American identity development also begins with the rejection of one's Asian heritage. Kim's five stage model consists of ethnic awareness, white identification, awakening to social political consciousness, redirection to Asian American consciousness, and incorporation. Kim pointed out that the Asian American identity development process begins with the family as the model of ethnic identity. The amount and type of cultural knowledge shared in the home could determine early identity attitudes. Like other models (Cross, 1971, 1995; Helms, 1984, 1990; Henriksen, 2001), it is not until the individual experiences discrimination that the self-esteem is challenged resulting in the desire to escape one's ethnicity and seek to identify with White society (Kim, 1981). The Asian American then begins the process leading to the establishment of a positive and comfortable Asian American identity. The Asian American first goes through a stage of knowledge acquisition during which the individual realizes that he or she is a member of an oppressed group and then moves to reconnect with Asian American culture. The Asian American individual becomes angry and fights against oppression. The process of Asian American identity formation ends when the individual is able to recognize his or her ethnicity and there is no longer inner conflict over whether or not to identify with White culture. The qualitative nature of Kim's (1981) work points out how counselors can assess an individual's ethnic identity by simply asking clients to describe their experiences.

Marcia (1966, 1980) formulated four identity statuses based on interviews conducted with college men. The four statuses, as distinguished from stages, include diffusion, foreclosure, moratorium, and identity achievement. Each status is identified by the presence or absence of the search for an identity and the commitment to an identity. Marcia (1980) pointed out that the statuses are not necessarily stages through which the individual progresses, but instead a means by which counselors can identify the current involvement in search of or commitment to an identity. During the diffusion status, the individual is neither searching for nor committed to an identity. The individual may or may not have experienced a crisis period, which could push the individual toward the search for an identity. Individuals are either uninterested in ideological matters or mix ideologies because one outlook seems as good as another. The foreclosure status is exemplified by a commitment to an ideology or identity without search. Foreclosure is accompanied by commitments based on the attitudes and opinions of others which are not questioned and typically involve the internalization of societal values (Marcia, 1966, 1980). The moratorium status is characterized by the presence of an identity search. The individual has experienced a crisis that has led to this search. The final status is identity achievement, which is characterized by a clear commitment to an identity. Those who demonstrate an achieved ego identity will have resolved many of the uncertainties about their future and will have made commitments that will guide their future decision making (Marcia, 1980). Like the models of Kim (1981), Cross, (1971), and Atkinson, Morten, and Sue (1993), the Marcia (1966, 1980) model suggests that the development of an identity occurs over time and moves from the lack of an identity to the achievement of an identity.

Phinney (1988, 1992, 1993, 1996a) took the constructs gleaned from Marcia (1966,1980), Cross (1971), Atkinson, Morten, and Sue (1993), and Kim (1981), and incorporated them with constructs obtained in both quantitative and qualitative research to develop a model of ethnic identity development. Phinney suggested that three stages of ethnic identity could be clearly identified and reliably distinguished instead of the four or five stages found in other models. Phinney (1996a) pointed out that this model of ethnic identity development is provided as a guide to understanding the "variation among young adults in their understanding of ethnicity, rather than as a theoretical explanation of the process" (p. 146). Phinney conducted research with Whites, African Americans, Asian Americans, and Hispanic Americans.

The initial stage of the Phinney (1993, 1996a) model is identified as unexamined ethnic identity. During this stage, ethnicity is given little attention and is characterized by the lack of search or exploration of ethnicity. The child or young adolescent accepts the values or attitudes present in his or her environment, usually those of the parent or parents. If the image is positive, the minority child is likely to develop a positive image of the group. However, if the child is presented with a negative image of the minority group, the child may develop a negative or mixed image of the group. Socialization will also affect whether the minority child will develop positive, negative, or mixed images of other groups (Phinney 1993, 1996a). Phinney (1993) identified two possible subtypes that could occur during this stage, namely, diffuse and foreclosed. The diffuse individual displays a lack of interest in or concern with ethnic identity, whereas the foreclosed individual's views of ethnicity are based on the opinions of others.

The second stage is referred to as ethnic identity search. This stage is described as the period during which the person seeks out knowledge concerning his or her group. Phinney (1993) pointed out that this search may begin due to general influences on ego identity development as described by Erikson (1968). However, like other models (Atkinson, Morten, & Sue, 1993; Cross, 1971; Henriksen, 2001; Kim, 1981), it is likely that the minority individual enters this stage due to increased socialization with other ethnic groups and experience with discrimination. The person is likely to experience mood swings and may harbor anger toward Whites (Phinney, 1993).

In the final stage, achieved ethnic identity, the minority person develops a secure identity within his or her ethnic group. The person is likely to hold a positive own-group view. However, involvement in the group may be limited if other aspects of life gain importance. Phinney (1993) noted that individuals in this stage could vary from acceptance and positive involvement in their ethnic group to preference for separatism as a rational approach to combating discrimination. This is in contrast to the Cross (1971, 1995) model, in which preference for separatism occurs during the immersion/emersion stage.

The value of the Phinney model and the MID model is found in their application to a variety of ethnic groups. The general principles provide counselors a means to easily conceptualize the ethnic identity development process and to identify the current stage of development occupied my minority individuals. The major limitation is that the model is general in nature and does not identify the more specific problems encountered by members of specific minority groups.

Both models have the potential to point out (a) the role oppression plays in the development of a minority identity, (b) the variations of cultural identity between members of a particular minority group, and (c) the potential each member of a minority group has for changing his or her sense of identity (Atkinson, Morten, and Sue, 1993). Other issues relevant to the counseling process can also be addressed using these models as a framework (e.g., the counseling relationship, client preferences). Clients at the various stages of development may present different problems. Understanding the etiology of problems could provide counselors with the information necessary for appropriate interventions. Even though it has been suggested that most minority group members prefer a directive approach to counseling (Sue & Sue, 1999), other approaches may be appropriate depending on the circumstances. Because many minority clients may find it difficult to talk to a counselor who is not a member of his or her ethnic group about problems of oppression, journaling may be an approach to working with ethnically diverse clients. Given the chance to write out their stories may provide them the opportunity to express their feelings without feeling constrained. Counselors could then use the journals as a means to understand the identity development process of the client without putting the client on the defensive.

# IDENTITY DEVELOPMENT FOR ASIAN AMERICANS

Whereas researchers have focused considerable attention on the ethnic and racial identity development of Whites and African Americans, less attention has been focused on Asian Americans (Phinney, 1990). There have been many more theoretical articles than empirical studies (Phinney, 1990), and few studies have used large samples (Ying & Lee, 1999). However, it seems that counselors should be concerned about the identity development of Asian Americans. Phinney (1989), through interviews of Asian American, Hispanic American, and African American adolescents, asked participants if they would prefer to be White rather than their own race or ethnicity. Compared to other racial-ethnic groups, a much higher percentage of Asian Americans responded that they would change their ethnicity to White if they could. Other data from the interviews suggested that Asian Americans were less likely than African Americans or Hispanic Americans to feel ethnic pride. Phinney concluded that Asian Americans tended more toward assimilation than other minority groups. This tendency toward assimilation may be a product of Asian cultures, several of which value conformity, obedience, and adaptability (Ibrahim, Ohnishi, & Sandhu, 1997; Sodowsky, Kwan, & Pannu, 1995; Sue & Sue, 1999; Ying & Lee, 1999), and value collectivism over individuality (Sandhu, 1997; Tse, 1999; Yeh & Huang, 1996). Although several authors have contended that people from ethnic minority groups value collectivism (we orientation), and people in Anglo culture value individualism (me orientation), little empirical research has been done to quantify this difference; and findings from the research that has been done are not consistent. Perhaps the constructs of individualism and collectivism are difficult to quantify (Gaines et al., 1997).

## Stage Models of Identity Development Applied to Asian Americans

Researchers and authors take varying perspectives on the applicability of stage models of identity development for Asian Americans (cf. Sodowsky et al., 1995; Tse, 1999; Yeh & Huang, 1996; Ying & Lee, 1999). We first present research and other literature that focus on the shortcomings of stage models, followed by research and literature that support the effectiveness of stage models.

Yeh and Huang (1996) asserted that stage identity development theories and models are not useful for Asian Americans. They described stage theories as being too fixed, restrictive, and individualistic to readily incorporate familial, social, political, and geographical contexts (i.e., collectivistic contexts). Most stage theories were not developed specifically for Asian Americans; and therefore, many models do not address relevant experiences and values of Asian Americans. Yeh and Huang collected visual and verbal data on Asian American college students' identity development. Visual data came from a projective drawing exercise. The researchers found that participants' relationships with others, their environments, and mainstream U.S. culture had strong influences on their identity development. That is, Asian Americans were more focused on collectivism than individualism in their identity development. Yeh and Huang also found that avoidance of shame drives the identity development of Asian Americans. This result is supported by quantitative research by Kwan and Sodowsky (1997). Kwan and Sodowsky reported that shame was related to the internal, psychological aspects of identity development and to cultural stress in Chinese Americans. In identity development models for other groups (e.g., African Americans), anger is more the driving emotion.

Although Yeh and Huang (1996) provided little information on validation of their qualitative findings, their findings seem logical. Their findings are also consistent with the multidimensional theoretical model proposed by Sodowsky et al. (1995). Sodowsky et al. synthesized a model from the literature that includes (a) internal (psychological) and external (social) forces in Asian American identity development, and (b) an interaction of Asian and American cultural aspects. It therefore seems prudent for counselors to explore the influences of collectivism on Asian American clients' identity development processes. Counselors should conceptualize Asian American clients' in social-situational contexts, and explore the influences of family and other relationships, mainstream American society, and other pertinent groups (Sodowsky et al., 1995; Yeh & Huang, 1996). Also, counselors should be aware of emotions, cognitions, and behavior associated with shame (Sue & Sue, 1993; Yeh & Huang, 1996). Asian Americans may conform to mainstream American standards to avoid the indignity of being different. Counselors should therefore explore the degree to which Asian American clients have experienced discomfort, awkwardness, embarrassment, or humiliation, and how these experiences relate to identity development.

Although authors suggest that identity development models organized by stages are not useful, other authors (e.g., Ibrahim, Ohnishi, and Sandhu, 1997; Kim, 1981; Phinney, 1989; Tse, 1999; Ying & Lee, 1999) speak to the efficacy of stage models, at least for some Asian Americans. Tse (1999) analyzed 39 previously published personal stories of Asian Americans. Participants were of various ages and from diverse Asian groups. The researcher focused on the advanced stages of identity development, ethnic emergence (identity search) and ethnic identity incorporation (achieved identity). Ethnic emergence is the period—usually occurring around late adolescence—of identity exploration before there is a commitment to identity. Identity incorporation is next stage, in which many earlier conflicts are resolved and there is a commitment to an Asian American identity (see Phinney, 1990).

Tse (1999) found evidence of two substages within ethnic emergence. The first substage is *awakening to minority status*. In this substage, participants became more sensitive to issues of race and to the visibility of their minority status. They realized how their race and ethnicity have affected their self-perceptions. For some, this realization was gradual; but for others, it was abrupt. As participants awoke to their minority status, they became more aware of the consequences of their minority status. Some participants also revealed anger at mainstream society.

The second substage within ethnic emergence is *ethnic exploration*. In this substage, participants began exploring their Asian culture. They sought friendships in their own culture. Several participants attempted to learn their ethnic language, and many experienced conflict and difficulty in studying the language. Although participants in this substage grew to feel more pride and belonging in their heritage culture, they eventually concluded that they did not fit wholly into either their heritage culture or American culture. This conclusion led participants to the next stage, ethnic identity incorporation (Tse, 1999).

At this stage, participants began to explore an identity with the Asian American group. Participants found commonality with other Asian Americans, and they intimated that they became more comfortable with their place in American society. They felt pride in themselves and developed positive perceptions of their heritage culture and American culture (Tse, 1999).

The above results are consistent with the latter stages in other models of racial or ethnic identity development (e.g., Atkinson, Morten, & Sue, 1993; Cross, 1995; Kim, 1981). However, these models may not fit for all Asian Americans (Phinney, 1989; Tse, 1999; Yeh & Huang, 1996). For example, Asian ethnic group members who experience a strong community heritage culture may have little need to identify with mainstream culture or Asian American culture.

Ying and Lee (1999) analyzed 342 essays written by Asian American adolescents, ages 12 to 22. The participants represented various Asian cultures, but most were from East Asia. Ying and Lee reported that their results supported both the Phinney (1989) model and the Atkinson et al. (1993) model. Ying and Lee found that integration (accepting both cultures) came after earlier stages: (a) unintegration (accepting neither culture), (b) separation (accepting the heritage culture), and (c) assimilation (accepting mainstream culture); but the order of earlier stages was more consistent with Phinney's model. One major difference between the Phinney model and the Atkinson et al. model is the sequence of progression in identity development. According to Phinney, racial or ethnic identity development begins with separation (accepting the heritage culture); whereas according to Atkinson et al., it begins with assimilation (accepting mainstream culture). Ying and Lee found support for Phinney's model for Asian Americans, in that identity development begins with separation. However, Ying and Lee did not find clear and consistent sequential progression through the various stages of either the Phinney model or Atkinson et al. model. The researchers suggested that environmental variables may have been responsible for this lack of consistency.

Results of Ying and Lee (1999) suggest that counselors should be flexible in using identity development models for conceptualizing Asian American clients. Although stage models may not fit for some Asian Americans, they may fit for others. It seems that if counselors are perceptive and adept in case conceptualization, they would be able to assess the applicability of stage models to particular clients. Counselors could then *match* their models of operation to clients' environmental situations, their world-views, and their needs (see Ivey, 2000; Root, 1993).

Ibrahim, Ohnishi, and Sandhu (1997) suggest that in general, minority identity development models are applicable to South-Asian Americans. However, counselors should view South Asians in the context of British colonization. South Asians who experienced British colonization understand Western values. Yet they tend to have strong ethnic pride and do not tend to deny their cultural heritage. South Asians understand differences between their culture and Western culture, and therefore they may be at higher stages in minority identity development models. For example, people from India experienced being a minority in their own country. However, they did not lose their ethnic identity; and they were adaptable in coexisting with the British. Therefore, they have, as individuals and in some sense as a culture, been successful in progressing in their minority identity development (Ibrahim et al., 1997).

The identity development of South Asians and other Asian Americans must also be viewed in the context of generation in the U. S. (i.e., immigrant, first generation, second generation, etc.; Ibrahim, Ohnishi, & Sandhu, 1997; Sue & Sue, 1993). South Asians who are immigrants may not experience the conformity or preencounter stage. In responding to discrimination or related crises, individuals from first, second, and subsequent generations may move forward or backward to the Resistance and Immersion stage. By becoming secure in their ethnic identity and individuality, they are prepared to move toward integrative awareness and commitment.

Adaptability for Asian Americans, however, may involve conflict. For example, on the one hand, educational and economic achievement are highly valued, consistent with Western values in the U.S (Sue & Sue, 1993). On the other hand, a focus on material possessions may not be consistent with spiritual ideals in the heritage culture. The goal of psychological and spiritual development in many South Asian and East Asian cultures is spiritual purity and oneness with God. Material and intellectual achievement are seen as lower stages of development, and are, in some ways, antithetical to the spiritual ideal (Badarayana, 1960; Ibrahim et al., 1997; Rinpoche, 1994).

## Acculturation Models and Bicultural Models Applied to Asian Americans

The concept of acculturation has been used to study the ethnic and racial identity of Asian Americans. Phinney (1990) described two general models of acculturation. One is a bipolar model. In this model, acculturation is conceptualized on a continuum, with a strong embracing of the culture of birth on one end, and a strong embracing of mainstream culture on the other end. As the individual becomes more acculturated to mainstream culture, the individual relinquishes the culture of birth. In other words, identification with the two cultures is mutually exclusive, and identifying with one culture is dependent on not identifying with the other. This model was termed the acculturation model by LaFromboise, Coleman, and Gerton (1993). The second model described by Phinney is the two-dimensional model (see Berry, Trimble, & Almedo, 1986). In this model, the two cultures are not mutually exclusive, and identifying with one culture is independent of identifying with the other. A person may embrace both cultures strongly, embrace one culture or the other, or embrace neither culture. LaFromboise et al. (1993) termed this model the alternation model, or bicultural model. LaFromboise et al., through a theoretical and subjective analysis of the advantages and disadvantages of various models of acquiring a second culture, determined that the alternation model was the most practically efficacious model for counselors and their clients. Reasons cited were that the alternation model (a) focuses on the individuals' cognitive and affective processes, (b) encourages the client to choose the desired level of participation in each culture, (c) focuses on coping skills in both cultures, and (d) enhances belonging and feelings of being culturally grounded.

There is support for the viability of the alternation model for Asian Americans. Liu, Pope-Davis, Nevitt, and Toporek (1999) reported that for Asian American college students, being identified with Asian culture was positively associated with being identified with mainstream White culture. If identification with the two cultures were mutually exclusive and one-dimensional, then the researchers would have found a negative association. Ying and Lee (1999) also found support for the two-dimensional model across the period of adolescence. They found that younger Asian American adolescents were likely to embrace one culture or the other (the heritage culture or mainstream culture, i.e., the one-dimensional model), whereas older adolescents were likely to be integrated, embracing both cultures (i.e., the two-dimensional model).

There are similarities and differences between the alternation model of LaFromboise et al. (1993) and other racial or ethnic identity models. If the individual has identity with the heritage culture and mainstream culture, and has skills to adapt to and function in both cultures, the individual is bicultural. The concept of being bicultural is consistent with the final stages of many of the racial and ethnic identity development models. For example, in the MID model of Atkinson et al. (1993), in the final stage (synergistic stage), individuals take a broad view on society and cultures, incorporate positive elements from both cultures, gain more cultural flexibility, and are committed to pluralism. Other models (e.g., Helms, 1984; Phinney, 1990; Tse, 1999) have a similar final stage or goal.

There are also differences between the alternation (bicultural) model and many racial and ethnic identity development models. The alternation model does not have fixed stages, and identity development is not conceptualized as a sequential phenomenon. In the alternation model, no dominant culture is assumed, in contrast to identity development models (see LaFromboise et al., 1993; Ramirez, 1991, 1999).

It would be naive to think that there is no dominant culture in the U.S. However, there are particular advantages to using a counseling model in which dominance is not assumed. First, it gives a more balanced treatment of both the culture of birth and mainstream culture. That is, the model makes no inherent judgements about either culture. Second, not assuming dominance can promote self-awareness in clients. By making no judgements, clients take new perspectives of themselves, their heritage culture, and mainstream culture. Third, operating from this nonassumption of dominance can be empowering for clients. Consistencies and inconsistencies between cultures are defined by clients and not by models. When a model makes few assumptions, clients are more likely to drive counseling, rather than counseling being driven by methods or models. The caveat in using such a client-driven model, however, is that counselors would need to help clients think and act within the context of environmental and experiential realities. For example, an assumption of nondominance might lead the counselor and client to ignore important discrimination events in the client's history, or to deny discrimination in the client's current environment.

## HISPANIC/LATINO IDENTITY DEVELOPMENT ISSUES

The Hispanic population is one of the fastest growing ethnic minority groups in the United States (Hunt, 1998; Marcell, 1994; Smart & Smart, 1995). This growth in population poses many new challenges for counselors and counselor trainees as they prepare to provide services for this diverse population. Developing an understanding of the process of identity development is critical to the development of culturally sensitive interventions that will meet the needs of persons from Hispanic-Latino groups.

The study of Hispanic identity development is a relatively new area of research (Bernal & Knight, 1993; Bernal, Knight, Garza, Ocampo, & Cota, 1990; Casas & Pytluk, 1995; Szapocznik, Santisteban, Kurtines, Hervis, and Spencer, 1982). The early emphasis involving Hispanic identity emphasized levels of acculturation and retained ethnic identity (Ethier & Deaux, 1994). Problems with research involving Hispanic identity have involved definitions of the designations *Hispanic* and *Latino*.

Jones-Correa and Leal (1996) pointed out that the terms Latino and Hispanic are used to identify persons who are Mexican American, Puerto Rican, Cuban, and South American. They acknowledged that there is a fierce debate regarding the use of these descriptive terms and their meaning. One point of view is that the term Latino exists because Latin Americans share many cultural commonalities. The competing view is that because the term Latino refers to neither a nation nor states, the term has no specific meaning. Jones-Correa and Leal (1996) observed that the term *Hispanic* also has origins that are not related to the people the term purports to describe. Both of these terms are creations that have been used to describe people who have Spanish-speaking heritages. However, the suggestion of an Hispanic identity, which includes commonalities of cultural traits and historical experience and national coalitions, has not been defined in the literature. Latino leaders have used the term *Hispanic* to suggest that there are commonalities in issues of the various ethnic groups, and *Hispanic* identification has been used to advance the special interests of specific ethnic groups under a single umbrella (Jones-Correa & Leal, 1996). However, the research literature uses the terms Hispanic and Latino interchangeably and do suggest that these means of identification are inclusive of many different ethnic groups (Dana, 1993).

## Factors That Affect Hispanic Identity

Cuellar (1998), through review of the literature, illuminated the variability within Hispanic subgroups. The variations found among Hispanic subgroups are seen vividly in the variations associated with living in two cultures. These variations are acculturation types that include traditional, bicultural, and assimilated types. The traditional individual holds onto and practices the cultural traditions of their country or group of origin. Bicultural individuals maintain aspects of their culture of origin while incorporating aspects of the dominant culture. Assimilated individuals are those who have given up their culture and adopted the majority culture. From these definitions, the reality that Hispanic individuals can differ greatly in ethnicity is made clear. Hispanic identity is also tied to the degree to which people have engaged in assimilation and acculturation of the dominant culture.

Phinney (1989) suggested that the way in which ethnic minorities are socialized results in differences in how individuals view themselves and how they view themselves in relation to others. Bernal et al. (1990) investigated the developmental sequence of ethnic identity. Their results suggested that this process may begin at an early age with the individuals first becoming aware of race and subsequently becoming aware of ethnicity because of the higher level of cognitive ability required. They identified five components to ethnic identity: (1) ethnic self-identification—labeling oneself as a member of a group; (2) ethnic constancy—realizing that one's ethnicity is permanent and not subject to change; (3) use of ethnic role behaviors—although the individual may not be aware that behaviors are ethnic, the individual engages in behaviors that reflect the culture, values, and customs of the ethnic group; (4) ethnic knowledge—becoming aware that there are behaviors, values, customs, and so forth, that are relevant to the ethnic group, and (5) ethnic preferences and feelings—having a preference for one's ethnic group and the associated language, values, customs, and so forth. These characteristics are acquired developmentally through social interactions with their families, communities, and the dominant society. Bernal et al. (1990) also found that like other groups (e.g., African Americans and Asian Americans), ethnic identity emerges developmentally over time.

Studies (e.g., Knight, Cota, & Bernal, 1993; Okagaki & Moore, 2000; Quintana & Vera, 1999) suggest that parental influences on Hispanic ethnic identity development are particularly strong. Knight et al. (1993) conducted a study with Mexican American children that examined socialization of ethnic identity based on parental influences. Their results suggest that the content of what children are taught about their culture could determine what values are internalized. Children could internalize values (e.g., cooperation, respect) that are reflective of how they view themselves and how they perceive membership in the ethnic group. The more children identify with their ethnicity, the more likely they are to behave in a manner that is consistent with those cultural values. The results of the study also indicated that it was the mother's teaching about the ethnic culture rather than the maternal reinforcement style that was most influential in the transmission of cultural values.

In a study conducted by Okagaki and Moore (2000) with young adults of Mexican descent, they found that the participants held beliefs that were very similar to those held by their parents. They were proud of their Mexican heritage and saw it as important for others with a Mexican heritage to learn about their culture. The researchers found that the level of ethnic identity achievement is dependent upon children's perceptions of their parents' beliefs about their ethnic identity. If the parents were not perceived as being authentic in their beliefs about their ethnicity, the children tended not to be accepting of their identity; but if the parents were perceived to be authentic, then the children developed positive views of their ethnic group. Language is also an important factor that affects the ethnic identity of Hispanic individuals.

Gao, Schmidt, and Gudykunst (1994) studied the effects of ethnolinguistic vitality among Mexican Americans. Giles, Bourhis, and Taylor (1977) suggested that the extent to which the language of an ethnic group remains vital is related to three factors: (a) the social status of the group within the society at large, (b) the demographic characteristics of the group, and (c) the perception of institutional support for the group's language. Giles et al. proposed the idea that as the ethnolingustic vitality of a group increases, the likelihood increases that the group will continue to function as a distinctive group in a multilingual setting. Giles et al. also pointed out that if an ethnoliguistic group does not maintain vitality, it will slowly deteriorate. Gao et al. (1994) found that respondents perceived English and the Anglo group as more vital than Spanish and being Mexican American. However, Mexican Americans were perceived as possessing more group pride than their White counterparts. Those who held a strong connection to the language had higher indications of ethnic identity and pride in their ethnic group. The study suggests that for Mexican Americans there is a positive correlation between ethnic identity and ethnolinguistic vitality. There are many other areas that affect the ethnic identity of Hispanic/Latino individuals such as family connections, religion, and employment. The case study that follows points out the complex process involved in the development of an ethnic identity among Hispanics.

## Case Example

Juanita is a young woman from Paraguay who is currently in graduate school. She has been struggling for some time trying to rediscover who she is. She talked about the need to understand the essence of her Hispanic culture in order to understand herself. She sees herself as a member of an expanding ethnic group in the U.S. but does not feel connected. She stated often that she needs to know herself better. She talked about realizing that her people are festive, warm, and alluring and that she often feels embarrassed around them. She often talked about the murals and religious artifacts found in her home and the homes of her relatives and friends back in Paraguay. Her description of Hispanic people spoke of pride and affection. But she also expressed dismay at not feeling as drawn to her own culture as she is to White culture. She often talked about her Catholic faith and how that faith dominates the lives of Hispanics. She communicated with many hand gestures and maintained frequent eye contact but seemed distant at times. Juanita talked a lot about the shame she experienced when she would see Hispanic refugees who had just arrived in the U.S. Her focus was on their physical condition and their lack of grooming. She stated, "All I could see were grubby hands, filthy and unwashed. I was so ashamed that these were the same hands that I saw working the fields in Paraguay." She often talked about the male dominated family structure she finds in her homeland and here in Hispanic communities around the country. She talked about feeling caught between two worlds and wanting both. Juanita talked about how learning her own language was so important and that trying to force Hispanic people to assimilate is not only wrong but harmful. Her shame was also apparent when she said, "This may be easy for me to say that we must learn another language, since I am bilingual, yet I know , as a young child, I forced myself to forget all about those feelings of inferiority and rejection about my ethnic tongue until now." Juanita continues to struggle with her sense of identity but believes she will one day know herself again.

For Juanita, understanding and coming to know herself meant getting back to her roots. She focused on family, religion, language, and culture. Comas-Diaz (1993) points out that to effectively help Hispanic clients counselors need to understand Hispanic cultural values, family dynamics, and the process of acculturation. This is especially true in the case of Juanita because these areas form the basis of her struggles. Juanita found that in her country families were formed on the basis of a patriarchal system in which the father is dominant and females are submissive (Comas-Diaz, 1993). This runs counter to the culture she has experienced in the United States, where she has learned that she is an individual and able to make her own decisions. Traditional male and female roles that would be found in places like Mexico, Puerto Rico, and Paraguay are not reinforced in the United States and results in change that often leads to clashes in the family (Comas-Diaz, 1993). The result is that for many Hispanics, acculturation has led to some loss in ethnic identity leaving the individual asking the question, "Who am I?"

Working with Juanita could be a complex process due to all the cultural influences being exerted upon her. The level of ethnic identity she currently occupies can provide counselors with the ability to more accurately conceptualize the world that Juanita occupies. Comas-Diaz (1993) suggests that a comprehensive perspective that includes physical, emotional, sociocultural, environmental and other factors is critical to the effective delivery of services to Hispanic/Latino populations. The effects of acculturation should also be considered when working with Juanita.

Corsini (1987) defined acculturation as "a process whereby individuals learn about the rules for behavior characteristic of a certain group of people" (p. 7). From this definition we can see that Juanita is having difficulty with the incorporation of U.S. culture while now wishing to maintain her Paraguayan culture. Bicultural models (e.g., Berry et al., 1986; LaFromboise et al., 1993; Ramirez, 1991, 1999) that were discussed earlier in this chapter provide an appropriate framework for helping her. That is, these models could be used to help her embrace her unique self, choose her desired degree of involvement in both cultures, gain coping skills in both cultures, and become flexible in her cognitive and cultural styles (see Ramirez, 1999). Accomplishing these tasks leads to bicultural or multicultural identity. The process of acculturation and bicultural functioning is often difficult for people (Ramirez, 1991; Trusty, 1996), but failure to work with issues associated with coping in the two cultures would be detrimental.

## Identity Development

Ruiz (1990) developed a model of Hispanic-Latino American identity development based on clinical case studies. The purpose of the model was to identity the developmental stages encountered by Hispanics-Latinos in the development of an identity. The development of the model was based upon several assumptions. First, like other ethnic minorities, Chicano, Mexican American, and Latino individuals needed a culture specific model of ethnic identity development to account for their process of developing an identity. Ruiz viewed the general models of racial-ethnic identity development, such as the MID model, as being too broad and not accounting for the specific cultural differences embraced by the many different Hispanic cultures. Second, Ruiz recognized that the marginal status of Hispanic individuals and families served as a major source of maladjustment. Hispanics often encounter high levels of stress stemming from the process of acculturation, which, for some Hispanics, leads to other difficulties (Smart & Smart, 1995). Third, forced acculturation could be detrimental to the psychological well being of Hispanic individuals. Smart and Smart (1995) identified six characteristics of the Hispanic immigration experience that could foster psychological difficulties: (a) discrimination on the basis of skin color, (b) the unique Hispanic emphasis on social and familial ties, (c) illegal immigration, (d) geographic proximity, (e) the legacy of armed conflict, and (f) the Hispanic reliance on physical labor. Smart and Smart noted that these factors need to be taken into account when stress related acculturation issues are encountered. Fourth, Ruiz assumed that the development of pride in one's culture and ethnicity underlies psychological well being and mental health. Finally, pride in being Hispanic provides greater flexibility and freedom when choosing how to live.

The Hispanic-Latino American identity development model begins with what Ruiz (1990) called the *causal stage*. During this stage individuals do not identify with their heritage culture. They have received messages that defame the ethnic heritage of the individual. Similar to the encounter stage of the Cross (1971, 1995) model of black identity development, the individual has experienced an encounter that challenges how the individual previously viewed the self. The person feels humiliated and now questions the vitality of his or her ethnicity. As a result of the negative encounter, the individual moves into the *cognitive stage*. This stage is characterized by three cognitive messages internalized by the individual. First, the individual creates an association between Hispanic group membership and discrimination and poverty. Second, the individual sees total assimilation into the White culture as the only means by which the individual will be able to function in the larger society. Third, the individual views assimilation as the only means by which success in the dominant society can be achieved. The Hispanic individual cognitively decides that in order to make his or way in the dominant society, it is necessary to give up his or her culture and adopt a new one (Ruiz, 1990).

The *consequence stage* is characterized by shame and embarrassment about one's name, accent, skin color, and cultural traditions and customs. The individual becomes estranged from the culture or origin to rid oneself of a negative self-image--possibly resulting in attempts to become mainstream White. The result is that the individual encounters increasing amounts of stress. This stress is a signal that the individual has entered the *working through stage*. This stage is characterized by an increase in ethnic consciousness due to two factors. First, the person finds it increasingly difficult to deny origin, heritage, and self. Second, the person begins to experience a compelling need to reidentify heritage, self , and culture. The individual begins to reincorporate lost fragments of his or her identity. As a result of this reincorporation of one's cultural heritage, the individual is able to move toward the *successful resolution stage*. Like the internalization stage of the Black identity development model (Cross, 1971, 1995), the successful resolution stage is characterized by a acceptance of the individual's culture and ethnicity. The person is secure in the identity with improved self-esteem and resiliency.

Understanding Hispanic-Latino American identity development provides counselors with the opportunity to gain improved insight into the world of this ethnic minority group. Cognitive interventions designed to meet issues encountered at each developmental stage can be developed and employed that could lead to improved psychological well being. Interventions could also improve the ability of the counselor to assist the client with other issues that may be causing the client difficulty. Counselors can assist clients with issues of oppression and help them attain personal and collective liberation (Sue & Sue, 1999). Counselors should also take into account the expectations of the client in the development of treatment strategies and use active, concrete, and problem solving strategies. However, counselors should also be aware that each client is an individual and should tailor interventions to the specific needs of the individual. We refer the reader to resources (Arbona, 1995; Altarriba & Bauer, 1998; Fouad, 1994; Sue & Sue, 1999) supplying general guidelines and recommendations for working with Hispanic American clients.

## NATIVE AMERICAN INDIAN IDENTITY ISSUES

Native American Indians are a heterogeneous group that is comprised of over 450 tribes, more than 150 languages, and approximately 1.9 million identified members (Wilson, 1996, U.S. Bureau of the Census, 1991). However, the growth in the number of Native Americans, since 1960, is not accounted for by birth rate. Much of the growth is hypothesized to come from "ethnic switching," which suggests that individuals who had once identified themselves as White are now identifying as Native American (Nagel, 1995). Nagel (1995) suggests that the ethnic renewal of Native Americans is due to three factors: (a) federal Native American policy, (b) American ethnic politics, and (c) Native American political activism. He points out that for some Native Americans not living on reservations, ethnic identification with their cultural group has been optional. The *Red Power* Native American Indian political activist movement of the 1960s and 1970s provided the impetus for the resurgence in ethnic pride and a movement toward the reclamation of a previously discarded ethnic identity (Nagel, 1995).

There is no generic Native American Indian. There are clan, band, and tribal differences as well as family and political formations that differ widely between groups. Peroff (1997) asserted that ideas about Native Americans and "Indianness" are tied to the past and are often inaccurate. Definitions of "Indianness" include: (a) an ongoing adaptation and adjustment to the White society; (b) a process by which Native Americans maintain boundaries between themselves and Whites; and (c) the renewal of Native American Identities, social organizations, or cultures. What is clear is that rather then allowing Native American Indians to define themselves, mainstream society has continuously determined who is Native American (Garrett, 1999; Peroff, 1997). Currently the U.S. Bureau of Indian Affairs (1988) identifies as Native American any person who has a genealogy that involves Native American ancestry, whose blood origin consists of one-fourth or more Native American, and who is a registered member of a federally recognized tribe or clan. Unlike other ethnic groups who have the ability to self-define, Native American identity is dependent upon the government.

Wilson (1996) related that historically, the United States has attempted to assimilate Native Americans through destroying of their way of life. For one hundred years, it was illegal for Native American Indians to practice their traditional religion and for generations Native American Indian children were forced to attend residential schools, were punished for speaking their native languages and practicing their religion, and were punished for even the most simple expression of their Native American Indian culture. Today, many Native American leaders express commitments to their traditional religions and cultural practices. However, in the literature there are few models that explain the identity development process for Native American Indians. It is likely that the heterogeneity of Native American Indians renders the development of identity models difficult (see Choney, Berryhill-Paapke, & Robbins, R. R., 1995).

McDonough (1998) underscored the importance of having an identity when he wrote,

> Membership in a distinct cultural structure is necessary to enable individuals to develop and exercise their capacity to make meaningful and autonomous choices about how to lead their lives. According to the cultural recognition thesis, it is one's own cultural identity that is fundamental to one's sense of self and the capacity to make autonomous choices; and so it is this cultural identity, and not just any cultural identity that happens to be available, that requires recognition. (p. 470)

Native Americans have long been denied the ability to define their cultural identity and as counselors it is important that we assist Native Americans with their ability to define themselves. To this end, counselors need to be able to provide Native Americans with the opportunity to search for an identity and make a commitment to an identity (Phinney, 1996), if that is their desire. As we have noted earlier, research suggests that the development of an ethnic identity helps to promote psychological well being.

With the absence of identity development models for Native Americans, counselors are challenged to develop an understanding of the worldviews of Native Americans and how enculturation affects the expression of an ethnic identity. It is important to recognize that even though no means by which one can or should describe Native American Indians as a single group exists, there are similarities among Native American cultures that are worthy of recognition.

Wilson (1996) delineated some commonality among Native American Indians' values and worldviews. Native American Indians see a strong interdependency between and among humans and nature. This interdependence has historical and enduring spiritual character. Wilson stated "This shared understanding of the world shapes the life experiences of North America's Indigenous peoples and, in turn, their identity development" (p. 305). That Native Americans are connected by spiritual means is also seen in the ethical ideals shared by several tribes. Brant (1990) identified five ethical principles that seem to emphasize the worldview of the Iroquois, Ojibway, and Swampy Cree peoples: an Ethic of Non-Interference (the idea that you should not interfere in any way with another person), an Ethic That Anger Not Be Shown (the idea that one should not burden others with one's emotional stress), an Ethic Respecting Praise and Gratitude (the notion that it is better to say nothing than to say something that would bring attention to someone and suggest that they have done better or are better than another person), the Conservation-Withdrawal Tactic (emphasis is placed on the need to prepare mentally before acting), and the Notion That Time Must Be Right (the notion that a person should take the time necessary to prepare emotionally and spiritually for a chosen action). Although these ethical principles are not universal among all Native American tribes, traditionally based ethics do exist today and will continue to exist into the future (Wilson, 1996).

Herring (1997) enumerated several values common to Native Americans that he identified as generalizations. Counselors should avoid seeing these values as being evident among all Native Americans Indians. Prejudice and stereotyping can take place when counselors to fail to see each Native American as first being an individual. Common concepts found among Native Americans include *sharing*—the idea that honor and respect is gained by sharing and giving to others; *cooperation*—the collectivist concept that the tribe and family take precedence over the needs of the individual; *noninterference*—Native Americans are taught not to interfere with the lives and decisions of others and to observe rather than act in an impulsive manner; *time orientation*—Native Americans are present focused and have a spiritual connection to the past, whereas planning for the future is less important; *harmony with nature*—Native Americans work toward unity with nature rather than to control nature. These values are similar to the ethics identified previously and are guiding principles for many Native Americans. However, there are also different values maintained by different tribes that are indicative of the unique heritage of the individual tribes. One way of identifying the level of cultural identity of Native Americans has been to identify their level of acculturation to the dominant society.

Vance (1995) noted that there are at least four cultural-self definitions employed by Native American Indians. The first is *traditional*: The individual supports and lives largely in the traditional way, and the person is comfortable with this life. The second self-definition is termed *assimilated*. The person supports and lives according to the dominant White society and is comfortable with this form of existence. The third is *transitional*. The individual adhering to this identification fluctuates between the traditional Native culture and the dominant White culture and often displays dysfunctional ways of coping. The individual is not committed to either culture and is at times unhappy, uncertain, or unaware of his or her personal lifestyle. Deyhle (1998) described this as the "living between two worlds metaphor" (p. 3), the Native American world and the White world. He identifies this self-definition as a deficit model. The individual in transition may be abusive, substance dependent, and display a lack of personal stability. Gale (1991) suggested that when traditional Native values clash with the values of the dominant White society, cultural conflict results.

The final form of self-identification is *bicultural*. Individuals who adopt this self-identification live and support both the traditional Native American Indian way of life and the way of life of mainstream society. These individuals may engage in both tribal and nuclear family patterns of interaction and behavior. In contrast to the other identities, bi-cultural individuals have reconciled cultural differences between their culture and the dominant culture and are comfortable with the reconciliation. This is similar to the final stage in the racial and ethnic identity models for other groups (Cross, 1971, 1995; Kim, 1981, Phinney, 1996a; Ruiz, 1990). This model of self-definition suggests that Native Americans self-define based on their relationship to their culture of origin and the dominant White culture. Whereas this bicultural identity is similar to final stages of racial-ethnic identity models; it differs in that unlike other ethnic minority groups who are immigrants, Native American Indians are indigenous peoples who have had their culture taken away from them and are attempting to reclaim their cultural heritage.

Zitzow and Estes (1981) pointed out that taking the view that Native Americans fall into either traditional patterns or non-traditional patterns of cultural identity are limiting and can subject the client to continued patterns of prejudice and stereotyping. They suggest that understanding Native Americans according to the concept of *heritage consistency* is more appropriate, and affords counselors enhanced ability to identify issues of self-concept, acculturation, internal conflict, identity, and willingness to seek out counseling services. Moving away from the traditional and non-traditional labels allows for the more appropriate designations *Heritage Consistent Native Americans (HCNA)* and *Heritage Inconsistent Native Americans (HINA)* (Zitzow & Estes, 1981). These designations exist on a continuum and allow counselors to recognize that Native Americans are individuals first. Individual Native American Indians are viewed as possessing values related to both heritage consistency and heritage inconsistency. Whatever position the person occupies along the continuum is viewed as acceptable. This model recognizes that Native Americans may be engaging in activities at both ends of the continuum. Zitzow and Estes also asserted that it is not the position that the individual places him or herself on the continuum that is important; rather, it is the concerns and feelings expressed by the individual that are important.

HCNA individuals have a predominant lifestyle and pattern of behavior that reflects the historical traditions of his or her tribal culture. HINA individuals reflect a lifestyle and pattern of behavior that is indicative of the dominant non-Native American cultural pattern. The degree of heritage consistency could be determined in relation to the number of positive responses made by the individual that indicate a similarity of experience resulting in increased heritage consistency. Several factors influence the person's heritage consistency, including geographical location, family members' heritage consistency, religion and philosophy, and personal pride in the culture of the tribe (Zitzow & Estes, 1981). Various other environmental characteristics may also influence heritage consistency.

Individuals with high heritage consistency may experience a number of related counseling or social concerns. Specific issues involved in counseling HCNA individuals include: (a) the sense of security and support may be limited to the reservation and extended family; (b) language barriers may lead to an increased reliance on non-verbal expression; (c) the individual may limit social interactions to only HCNA individuals and my be uncomfortable communicating with non-Native Americans; (d) the person may have difficulty in school due to a lack of necessary basic mainstream learning skills and may have difficulty incorporating the values of non-Native education into his or her own belief system; (e) the individual may experience conflicts between the motivation to learn and being accepted by other HCNA people; (f) the person may find it difficult to establish and carry out long-term goals; (g) keeping emotions to oneself may be viewed as a positive personality trait; (h) the individual may have difficulty making decisions due to prior experience with paternalism from the federal government; and (i) the individual may not understand the expectations of the dominant culture and lack sufficient positive role models (Johnson, Swartz, & Martin, 1995; Zitzow & Estes, 1981). These issues may not be exclusive to HCNA individuals but may also be present with HINA individuals. Counselors should focus on the unique life experiences of the individual in the development of counseling strategies with HCNA clients.

In contrast to HCNA individuals, issues that may lead HINA individuals to counseling include: (a) the individual may express denial and a lack of pride in being Native American; (b) the individual may experience guilt due to a lack of knowledge of Native American cultures and customs; (c) the individual may experience pressure to conform to both Native and non-Native values or beliefs; and (d) the individual may lack both support and belief systems due to a negative image of Native Americans in general (Zitzow & Estes, 1981). Seeing the issues that affect both HCNA and HINA individual indicates the importance of identifying the level of acculturation and self-identity with the individual Native American client.

Zitzow and Estes (1981) also pointed out that when helping Native Americans it is important to respond to them as individuals first while maintaining sensitivity for heritage consistency concerns. Counselors should recognize that a relationship based on mutual trust is necessary for effective counseling. Clients should also be allowed to place themselves on the continuum and discuss what that placement means to them. The concept of heritage consistency could provide Native American Indians with a special tool for self-definition and self-exploration. It can complement counseling theories that first focus on the individual and then focus on issues related to the client. The key is to use the heritage consistency model as a structure to assist Native American clients with the achievement of individual awareness and identity.

## CONCLUSION

Attention devoted to the identity development of individuals has expanded exponentially over recent years. However, racial-ethnic identity development is a relatively new area of focus and many questions remain unanswered, especially for particular groups. Racial, ethnic, and cultural identity development is an individual experience. Whereas some models have applicability across groups, there is much variation in identity development between and within groups. Models can provide counselors with frameworks with which they can come to understand the identity development of persons. Models of identity development should not be used to categorize clients nor to stereotype their patterns of behavior. Rather, counselors should seek to help both clients and themselves with the quest to understand the worldview of the client. The real-life identity development of people is far more complex than can be revealed by any model. The use of identity development models can assist the client with this process and provide opportunities for growth.

Counselors should also become aware of their own racial, ethnic, and cultural identity development, the impact their development has on clients, and how they can use their identity development as a means to foster counselor and client growth. The counselor's most important tool is the self, and to make effective use of that tool it is important to know the self. Identity development is a promising area for expanding our knowledge and enhancing the practice of counseling.

# ACTIVITIES TO ENHANCE LEARNING

1.  Students can interview one or more individuals, either adolescent or adult, from an ethnic group different from their own using an interview similar to one used in research (Henriksen, 2001; Henriksen & Watts, 1999; Phinney, 1989) or develop one that could assist with understanding individual identity development. Interviewees could be asked to identify their racial-ethnic background and that of their parents, and grandparents. They could be asked to describe their own culture and how it impacts their social interactions with members of other ethnic groups and their own ethnic group. Interviewees could also be asked to describe the benefits of being a member of their racial-ethnic group and if they could be a member of another racial group which one would it be and the reasons for the choice. They could also be asked the disadvantages of being a member of their racial-ethnic group. The purpose of the interviews would not be to identify the specific stage of development currently occupied by the individual. Rather, it would be so that students could gain a better understanding of how the racial-ethnic identity development process affects the overall development of the individual. Remember that the best way to understand the ethnic-racial or cultural identity development of clients is to conduct an interview with them (Phinney, 1996a).

2.  Role Play Exercise

The class should be divided into groups of three or more with each group member taking on one of the following roles:

| | |
|---|---|
| A. Counselor: | The counselor is going to work with a client who is of a racial-ethnic minority group that is different from that of the counselor. The counselor should begin the interview by developing a positive relationship with the client and seeking to understand the worldview of the client. |
| B. Client | The client should assume the role of a racial-ethnic minority group member. The client should be aware of (a) the cultural values held by the minority group, (b) the current sociopolitical climate and how it impacts the lives of the members of the minority group, and (c) how the cultural values held by the minority group and current sociopolitical issues affect the counseling process. The client will need to express these constructs in the counseling session. It is important to be genuine and sincere in your role of client. If there were members of different racial-ethnic groups in the class it would benefit the counselors to interview them as well as role-playing students. |
| C. Observers | Observers should examine the dynamics of the interview and offer feedback concerning what was observed. They should also try to put themselves in the place of both the client and the counselor and discuss how they viewed the experience from both perspectives. |

The role play should last from 5 to 10 minutes, and then there should be about 15 minutes of feedback. All participants in the role play should discuss their roles, what they saw occurring, and different approaches that could have been used. Students may also try to identify the current stage of racial-ethnic identity development occupied by the client in the role play. Students should rotate roles until all students have had an opportunity to enact each role.

3.   Interactive Cultural Experience

The course instructor makes name tags (labels) for each student that indicate members of racial-ethnic groups (e.g., educated Black Woman, uneducated Asian American, Hispanic-Latino migrant worker, Native American Indian activist) different from their own group. Labels are to be placed on the left shoulder of each student in a manner that students cannot see their own label but can see other students' labels. Students should not look at their labels. Students then interact with each other—based on label stereotypes— and try to find out as much as you can about as many different people as possible during a 15 minute time period. Students should then come together as a group and discuss the experience. Questions such as: What was it like for you to be a member of _____ ethnic group? How do you sense you were treated? What feelings did you experience during the exercise? What do your experiences tell you about labeling? If you had a client who was a member of a different ethnic group how would you treat him or her? How do you think the client would expect to be treated? This discussion should last 15 minutes or more. This exercise should help students realize some of the experiences encountered by racial-ethnic minorities and give them a better understanding of how identity affects the individual.

4.   Cultural Self-Exploration

Counseling students and faculty can engage in the process of self-exploration. Using the Cultural Self Exploration Questionnaire (Henriksen & Watts, 1999), conduct interviews with family members so that you can develop an understanding of your values and beliefs and the impact family members have had on your identity development. You can then focus attention on your current values and beliefs and look at your own racial, ethnic, and cultural development. The result could be that you come to know yourself more intimately, which could facilitate your relationships with clients.

## REFERENCES

Altarriba, J, Bauer, L.M. (1998). Counseling the Hispanic client: Cuban Americans, Mexican Americans, and Puerto Ricans. *Journal of Counseling & Development, 76*, 389-395.

Arbona, C. (1995). Theory and research on racial and ethnic minorities: Hispanic Americans. In F. T. L. Leong (Ed.), *Career development and vocational behavior of racial and ethnic minorities*, (pp. 37-66). Mahwah, NJ: Lawrence Erlbaum Associates.

Atkinson, D. R., Morten, G., & Sue, D. W. (1993). *Counseling American minorities: A cross-cultural perspective* (4th ed.). Madison, WI: Brown & Benchmark.

Badarayana (1960). *The Brahma sutra, the philosophy of spiritual life*. (S. Radhakrishnan, Trans. and notes). New York: Harper & Brothers.

Bagley, C., & Young, L. (1988). Evaluation of color and ethnicity in young children in Jamaica, Ghana, England, and Canada. *International Journal of Intercultural Relations, 12*, 45-60.

Behrens, J. T. (1997). *Does the White Racial Identity Attitude Scale measure racial identity? Journal of Counseling Psychology, 44*, 3-12.

Bernal, M. E., & Knight, G. P. (1993). *Ethnic identity: Formation and transmission among Hispanics and other minorities.* Albany, NY: State University of New York Press.

Bernal, M. E., Knight, G. P., Garza, C. A., Ocampo, K. A., & Cota, M. K. (1990). The development of ethnic identity in Mexican-American children. *Hispanic Journal of Behavioral Sciences, 12*, 3-24.

Berry, J. W., Trimble, J. E., & Olmedo, E. L. (1986). Assessment of acculturation. In W. L. Lonner & J. W. Berry (Eds.) *Field methods in cross-cultural research* (pp. 291-324). Beverly Hills, CA: Sage.

Bond, S., & Cash, T.F. (1992). Black beauty: Skin color and body images among African-American college women. *Journal of Applied Social Psychology, 22*, 874-888.

Brant, C. (1990). Native ethics and rules of behavior. *Canadian Journal of Psychiatry, 35*, 534-539.

Breland, A. M. (1998). A model for differential perceptions of competence based on skin tone among African Americans. *Journal of Multicultural Counseling and Development, 26*, 294-311.

Casas, J. M., & Pytluk, S. D. (1995). Hispanic identity development. In J.G. Ponterotto, J.M. Casas, L.A. Suzuki, & C.M. Alexander (Eds.), *Handbook of multicultural counseling* (pp. 155-180). Thousand Oaks, CA: Sage.

Choney, S. K., Berryhill-Paapke, E., & Robbins, R. R. (1995). The acculturation of American Indians. In J. G. Ponterotto, J. M. Casas, L. A. Suzuki, & C. M. Alexander (Eds.), *Handbook of multicultural counseling* (pp. 73-92). Thousand Oaks, CA: Sage.

Cohen, A. P. (1993). Culture as identity: An anthropologist's view. *New Literary History, 24*, 195-209.

Colón, F. (1998). The discovery of my multicultural identity. In M. McGoldrick (Ed.), *Re-visioning family therapy: Race, culture, and gender in clinical practice.* New York: Guilford Press.

Comas-Diaz, L. (1993). Hispanic Latino communities: Psychological implications. In D.R. Atkinson, G. Morten, & D.W. Sue (Eds.), *Counseling American minorities: A cross-cultural perspective* (pp. 245-264). Madison, WI: Brown & Benchmark.

Corsini, R. J. (1987). *Concise encyclopedia of psychology.* New York: Wiley.

Cross, W. E., Jr. (1971). The Negro to Black conversion experience. *Black World, 20*(9), 13-27.

Cross, W. E., Jr. (1995). The psychology of Nigrescence: Revising the Cross model. In J.G. Ponterotto, J.M. Casas, L.A. Suzuki, & C.M. Alexander (Eds.), *Handbook of multicultural counseling* (pp. 93-122). Thousand Oaks, CA: Sage.

Cuellar, I. (1998). Cross-cultural clinical psychological assessment of Hispanic Americans. *Journal of Personality Assessment, 70*, 71-86.

Dana, R. H. (1993). *Multicultural assessment perspective for professional psychology.* Boston: Allyn & Bacon.

Davis, F. J. (1991). *Who is Black? One nations' definition.* University Park, PA: Pennsylvania State University Press.

Deyhle, D. (1998). From break dancing to heavy metal: Navajo youth, resistance, and identity. *Youth and Society, 30*(1), 3-31.

Egan, G. (1998). *The skilled helper: A problem-management approach to helping.* Pacific Grove, CA: Brooks/Cole.

Erikson, E. H. (1963). *Childhood and society.* New York: W. W. Norton.

Ethier, K. A., & Deaux, K. (1994). Negotiating social identity when contexts change: Maintaining identification and responding to threat. *Journal of Personality and Social Psychology, 67,* 243-251.

Field, L. D. (1996). Piecing together the puzzle: Self-concept and group identity in Biracial Black/White youth. In M. P. P. Root (Ed.), *The multiracial experience: Racial borders as the new frontier* (pp. 211-226). Thousand Oaks, CA: Sage.

Frable, D. E. S. (1997). Gender, racial, ethnic, sexual, and class identities. *Annual Review of Psychology, 48,* 139-163.

Gao, G., Schmidt, K.L., & Gudykunst, W. B. (1994). Strength of ethnic identity and perceptions of ethnolinguistic vitality among Mexican Americans. *Hispanic Journal of Behavioral Sciences, 16,* 332-341.

Gaines, S. O., Jr., Marelich, W. D., Bledsoe, K. L., Steers, W. N., Henderson, M. C., Granrose, C. S., Barajas, L., Hicks, D., Lyde, M., Takahashi, Y., Yum, N., Rios, D. I., Garcia, B. F., Farris, K. R., & Page, M. S. (1997). Links between race/ethnicity and cultural values as mediated by racial/ethnic identity and moderated by gender. *Journal of Personality and Social Psychology, 72*(6), 1460-1476.

Gale, N. (1991). *Fighting alcohol and substance abuse among American Indian and Alaskan Native youth.* Charleston, WV: Eric Clearinghouse on Rural Education and Small Schools. (Eric Documentation Reproduction Service No. ED 335 207)

Garrett, M. T. (1999). Soaring on the wings of the eagle: Wellness of Native American high school students. *Professional School Counseling, 3,* 57-64.

Gibbs, J. T. (1987). Identity and marginality: Issues in the treatment of Biracial adolescents. *American Journal of Orthopsychiatry, 57,* 265-278.

Gibbs, J. T., & Moskowitz-Sweet, G. (1991). Clinical and cultural issues in the treatment of Biracial and bicultural adolescents. *Families in Society: The Journal of Contemporary Human Services, 72,* 579-592.

Giles, H., Bourhis, R.Y., & Taylor, D.M. (1977). Towards a theory of language in ethnic group relations. In H. Giles (Ed.), *Language, ethnicity and intergroup relations* (pp. 307-348). London: Academic Press.

Hardiman, R. (1982). White identity development: A process oriented model for describing the racial consciousness of White Americans. *Dissertations Abstracts International, 43,* 104A. (University Microfilms No. 82-10330)

Haymes, S. (1996). Race, repression, and the politics of crime and punishment in the bell curve. In J. Kincheloe, S. Steinberg, A. Greeson (Eds.), *Measured lies, the bell curve examined.* New York: St. Martin's Press.

Helms, J. E. (1984). Toward a theoretical model of the effects of race on counseling: A Black and White model. *Counseling Psychologist, 12* (4), 153-165.

Helms, J. (1990). *Black and White racial identity: Theory, research, and practice.* Westport, CT: Greenwood Press.

Helms, J. E. (1992). *A race is a nice thing to have: A guide to being a White person or understanding the White persons in your life.* Topeka, KA: Content Communications.

Henriksen, R. C., Jr. (2001). Black/White Biracial identity development: A grounded theory study. *Dissertation Abstracts International, 67,* 2605.

Henriksen, R. C., Jr., & Watts, R. E. (1999). Cultural self-exploration questionnaire. *TCA Journal, 27*(2), 65-70.

Herring, R.D. (1997). *Counseling diverse ethnic youth.* Fort Worth, TX: Harcourt Brace.

Hunt, L.L. (1998). The spirit of Hispanic Protestantism in the United States: National survey comparisons of Catholics and non-Catholics. *Social Science Quarterly, 79,* 828-845.

Ibrahim, F., Ohnishi, H., & Sandhu, D. S. (1997). Asian American identity development: A culture specific model for South Asian Americans. *Journal of Multicultural Counseling and Development, 25,* 34-50.

Ivey, A. E. (2000). *Developmental therapy: Theory into practice.* North Amherst, MA: Microtraining Associates.

Jacobs, J. H. (1992). Identity development in Biracial children. In P.P. Root (Ed.), *Racially mixed people in America* (pp. 190-206). Newbury Park, CA: Sage.

Jane Doe v. State of Louisiana, *479 So. 2d,* 1986.

Johnson, M. J., Swartz, J. L., & Martin, W. E., Jr. (1995). Applications of psychological theories for career development with Native Americans. In F. T. L. Leong (Ed.), *Career development and vocational behavior of racial and ethnic minorities,* (pp. 103-133). Mahwah, NJ: Lawrence Erlbaum Associates.

Jones-Correa, M., & Leal, D. L. (1996). Becoming "Hispanic": Secondary panethnic identification among Latin American-origin populations in the United States. *Hispanic Journal of Behavioral Sciences, 18,* 214-254.

Kerwin, C., & Ponterotto, J. G. (1995). Biracial identity development: Theory and research. In J.G. Ponterotto, J.M. Casas, L.A. Suzuki, & C.M. Alexander (Eds.), *Handbook of multicultural counseling* (pp. 199-217). Thousand Oaks, CA: Sage.

Kim, J. (1981). The process of Asian American identity development: A study of Japanese-American women's perceptions of their struggle to achieve personal identities as Americans of Asian ancestry. *Dissertation Abstracts International, 42,* 1551A. (University Microfilms No. 81-18080).

Kincheloe, J. L. (1999). The struggle to define and reinvent Whiteness: A pedagogical analysis. *College Literature, 26*(i3), 162-194.

Knight, G. P., Cota, M. K., & Bernal, M. E. (1993). The socialization of cooperative, competitive, and individualistic preferences among Mexican American children: The mediating role of ethnic identity. *Hispanic Journal of Behavioral Sciences, 15,* 291-309.

Krogman, W. M. (1945). The concept of race. In R. Linton (Ed.), *The science of man in the world crisis* (pp. 38-62). New York: Columbia University Press.

Kwan K. K., & Sodowsky, G. R. (1997). Internal and external ethnic identity and their correlates: A study of Chinese American immigrants. *Journal of Multicultural Counseling and Development, 25,* 51-67.

LaFromboise, T., Coleman, H. L. K., & Gerton, J. (1993). Psychological impact of biculturalism: Evidence and theory. *Psychological Bulletin, 144,* 395-412.

Liu, W. M., Pope-Davis, D. B., Nevitt, J., & Toporek, R. L. (1999). Understanding the function of acculturation and prejudicial attitudes among Asian Americans. *Cultural Diversity and Ethnic Minority Psychology, 5,* 317-328.

Marcel, A. V. (1994). Understanding ethnicity, identity formation, and risk behavior among adolescents of Mexican descent. *Journal of School Health, 64,* 323-328.

Marcia, J. (1966). Development and validation of ego-identity status. *Journal of Personality and Social Psychology, 3*, 551-558.

Marcia, J. (1980). Identity in adolescence. In J. Adelson (Ed.), *Handbook of adolescent psychology* (pp. 159-187). New York: Wiley.

McDonough, K. (1998). Can the liberal state support cultural identity schools? *American Journal of Education, 106*, 463-499.

Morrison, J. W., & Rodgers, L. S. (1996). Being responsive to the needs of children from dual heritage backgrounds. *Young Children, 52*, 29-33.

Morten, G., & Atkinson, D. R. (1983). Minority identity development and preference for counselor race. *Journal of Negro Education, 52*, 156-161.

Nagel, J. (1995). American Indian ethnic renewal: Politics and the resurgence of identity. *American Sociological Review, 60*, 947-965.

Nieto, S. (2000). *Affirming diversity: The sociopolitical context of multicultural education.* New York: Longman.

Okagaki, L., & Moore, D. K. (2000). Ethnic identity beliefs of young adults and their parents in families of Mexican descent. *Hispanic Journal of Behavioral Sciences, 22*, 139-162.

Parham, T. A., & McDavis, R. J. (1993). Black men, an endangered species: Who's really pulling the trigger. In D.R. Atkinson, G. Morten, & D.W. Sue (pp.89-99), *Counseling American minorities: A cross-cultural perspective.* Madison, WI: Brown & Benchmark.

Parks, R. E. (1931). Mentality of racial hybrids. *American Journal of Sociology, 36*, 534-551.

Peroff, N. C. (1997). Indian identity. *The Social Science Journal, 34*, 485-496.

Phinney, J. S. (1988). Ethnic identity search and commitment in Black and White eighth graders. *Journal of Early Adolescence, 8*, 265-277.

Phinney, J. S. (1989). Stages of ethnic identity development in minority group adolescents. *Journal of Early Adolescence, 9*, 34-39.

Phinney, J. S. (1990). Ethnic identity in adolescents and adults: Review of research. *Psychological Bulletin, 108*, 499-514.

Phinney, J. S. (1993). A three-stage model of ethnic identity development in adolescence. In M. Bernal & G. Knight (Eds.), *Ethnic identity: Formation and transmission among Hispanics and other minorities* (pp. 61-79). Albany, NY: State University of New York Press.

Phinney, J. S. (1996a). Understanding ethnic diversity. *American Behavioral Scientist, 40*, 143-152.

Phinney, J. S. (1996b). When we talk about American ethnic groups, what do we mean? *American Psychologist, 51*, 918-927.

Phinney, J. S., & Alipuria, L. (1990). Ethnic identity in college students from four ethnic groups. *Journal of Adolescents Research, 13*, 171-183.

Phinney, J. S., & Chavira, V. (1992). Ethnic identity and self-esteem: An exploratory longitudinal study. *Journal of Adolescence, 15*, 271-281.

Phinney, J. S., & Onwughalu, M. (1996). Racial identity and perception of American ideals among African American and African students in the United States. *International Journal of Intercultural Relations, 20*, 127-140.

Pomales, J., Claiborn, C. D., & LaFromboise, T.D. (1986). Effects of Black student's racial identity on perceptions of White counselors varying in cultural sensitivity. *Journal of Counseling Psychology, 34*, 123-131.

Ponterotto, J. G. (1988). Racial consciousness development and White counselor trainees: A stage model. *Journal of Multicultural Counseling and Development, 16,* 146-156.

Pope-Davis, D. B., & Ottavi, T. M. (1994). The relationship between racism and racial identity among White Americans: A replication and extension. *Journal of Counseling & Development, 72,* 293-297.

Poston, W. S. C. (1990). The Biracial identity development model: A needed addition. *Journal of Counseling & Development, 69,* 152-155.

Quintana, S. M., & Vera, E. M. (1999). Mexican American children's ethnic identity, understanding of ethnic prejudice, and parental ethnic socialization. *Hispanic Journal of Behavioral Sciences, 21,* 387-404.

Ramirez, M., III (1991). *Psychotherapy and counseling with minorities: A cognitive approach to individual and cultural differences.* New York: Pergamon Press.

Ramirez, M., III (1999). *Multicultural psychotherapy: An approach to individual and cultural differences* (2nd ed.). Boston: Allyn and Bacon.

Rinpoche, S. (1994). *The Tibetan book of living and dying.* New York: HarperCollins.

Root, M. P. P. (1990). Resolving "other" status: Identity development of biracial individuals. In L. Brown, & M. P. P. Root (Eds.), *Diversity and complexity in feminist therapy.* New York: Harrington Park Press.

Root, M. P. P. (1993). Guidelines for facilitating therapy with Asian American clients. In D. R. Atkinson, G. Morten, & D. W. Sue (Eds.) *Counseling American minorities: A cross-cultural perspective* (4th ed., pp. 211-224). Madison, WI: Brown & Benchmark.

Root, M. P. P. (1996). *The multiracial experience.* Thousand Oaks, CA: Sage.

Rose, P. I. (1997). *They and we: Racial and ethnic relations in the United States.* New York: McGraw-Hill.

Ross, L. E. (1997). Mate selection preferences among African American college students. *Journal of Black Studies, 27,* 554-569.

Ruiz, A. S. (1990). Ethnic identity: Crisis and resolution. *Journal of Multicultural Counseling & Development, 18,* 29-40.

Sabnani, H. B., Ponterotto, J. G., & Borodovsky, L. G. (1991). White racial identity development and cross-cultural counselor training: A stage model. *Counseling Psychologist, 19,* 76-102.

Salgado de Snyder, N., Lopez, C. M., & Padilla, A. M. (1982). Ethnic identity and cultural awareness among the offspring of Mexican interethnic marriages. *Journal of Early Adolescence, 2,* 277-282.

Sandhu, D. S. (1997). Psychocultural profiles of Asian and Pacific Islander Americans: Implication for counseling and psychotherapy. *Journal of Multicultural Counseling and Development, 25,* 7-22.

Smart, J. F., & Smart, D. W. (1995). Acculturative stress of Hispanics: Loss and challenge. *Journal of Counseling & Development, 73,* 390-396.

Sodowsky, G. R., Kwan, K. K., & Pannu, R. (1995). Ethnic identity of Asians in the United States. In J. G. Ponterotto, J. M. Casas, L. A. Suzuki, & C. M. Alexander (Eds.), *Handbook of multicultural counseling* (pp. 123-115). Thousand Oaks, CA: Sage.

Stonequist, E. V. (1937). *The marginal man: A study in personality and culture conflict.* New York: Charles Scribner's Sons.

Sue, D., & Sue, D. W. (1993). Ethnic identity: Cultural factors in the psychological development of Asians in America. In D. R. Atkinson, G. Morten, & D. W. Sue (Eds.)

*Counseling American minorities: A cross-cultural perspective* (4th ed., pp. 199-210). Madison, WI: Brown & Benchmark.

Sue, D. W., Arredondo, P, & McDavis, R. J. (1992). Multicultural counseling competencies and standards: A call to the profession. *Journal of Counseling & Development, 70,* 484-486.

Sue, D.W., & Sue, D. (1990). *Counseling the culturally different: Theory and practice.* New York: John Wiley & Sons.

Sue, D. W. & Sue, D. (1999). *Counseling the culturally different: Theory and practice* (3rd ed.). New York: John Wiley & Sons.

Sue, S., & Sue, D. W. (1971). Chinese-American personality and mental health. *Amerasia Journal, 1,* 36-49.

Szapocznik, J., Santisteban, D., Kurtines, W. M., Hervis, O. E., & Spencer, F. (1982). Life enhancements counseling: A psychosocial model of services for Cuban elders. In E.E. Jones & S.J. Korchin (Eds.), *Minority mental health* (pp. 296-329). New York: Praeger.

Teicher, J. D. (1968). Some observations on identity problems in children of Negro-White marriages. *Journal of Nervous and Mental Disease, 146,* 249-256.

Thomas, C. W. (1971). *Boys no more.* Beverly Hills, CA: Glencoe Press.

Thompson, C. E. (1994). Helms' White racial identity development (WRID) theory: Another look. *The Counseling Psychologist, 22,* 645-649.

Tizard, B., & Phoenix, A. (1995). The identity of mixed parentage adolescents. *Journal of Child Psychology and Psychiatry, 36,* 1399-1410.

Tokar, D. M., & Swanson, J. L. (1991). An investigation of the validity of Helm's (1984) model of White racial identity development. *Journal of Counseling Psychology, 38,* 296-301.

Trusty, J. (1996). Counseling for dropout prevention: Applications from multicultural counseling. *Journal of Multicultural Counseling and Development, 24,* 105-117.

Tse, L. (1999). Finding a place to be: Ethnic identity exploration of Asian Americans. *Adolescence, 34,* 121-138.

U.S. Bureau of Indian Affairs. (1988). *American Indians today.* Washington, DC: Author.

U.S. Bureau of the Census. (1991). *1990 census count of American Indians, Eskimos, or Aluets and American Indian and Alaska Native areas.* Washington, DC: Bureau of the Census, Racial Statistics Branch, Population Division.

Vance, P. R. (1995). *Career counseling with Native clients: Understanding the context.* Greensboro, NC: Eric Clearinghouse on Counseling and Student Services. (ERIC Document Reproduction Service No. ED 399 485)

Vontress, C. E. (1971). *Racial differences: Impediments to rapport. Journal of Counseling Psychology, 18,* 7-13.

Wardle, F. (1992). *Biracial identity: An ecological and developmental perspective.* Denver, CO: Center for the Study of Biracial Children. (ERIC Document Reproduction Service No. ED 385 376).

Wilson, A. (1996). How we find ourselves: Identity development for two-spirit people. *Harvard Educational Review, 66*(2), 303-317.

Yeh, C. J., & Huang, K. (1996). The collectivistic nature of ethnic identity development among Asian-American college students. *Adolescence, 31,* 645-661.

Ying, Y., & Lee, P. A. (1999). The development of ethnic identity in Asian American Adolescents: Status and outcome. *American Journal of Orthopsychiatry, 69,* 194-208.

Young, C. (1993). Psychodynamics of coping and survival of the African American female in a changing world. In D.R. Atkinson, G. Morten, & D.W. Sue (Eds.), *Counseling American minorities: A cross-cultural perspective*. Madison, WI: WCB.

Zitzow, D., & Estes, G. (1981). *Heritage consistency as a consideration in counseling Native Americans*. Aberdeen, SD. (ERIC Document Reproduction Service No. ED 209 035)

*Chapter 4*

# MULTICULTURAL COUNSELING IN SPIRITUAL AND RELIGIOUS CONTEXTS

*Timothy B. Smith and P. Scott Richards*[*]
Brigham Young University

Until the past century, religious and spiritual leaders provided most of the counseling and mental health treatment in North America and Europe. Even today, mental health counseling in the majority of the world is performed in religious or spiritual contexts. For many cultures, spiritual health and mental health are closely intertwined. Yet contemporary Western approaches and conceptualizations of health and healing typically do not mention spirituality. In fact, for many readers this chapter may be their first exposure to spiritual and religious concerns as they relate to counseling and personal development.

Spiritual and religious issues should be addressed in effective multicultural counseling (Fukuyama & Sevig, 1999; Richards & Bergin, 2000; Sue, Bingham, Porche-Burke, & Vasquez, 1999). Professional standards explicitly include spiritual and religious beliefs as aspects of multiculturalism that the counselor must understand and respect (ACA, 1995; CACREP, 2001). Regardless of their own personal beliefs, counselors have an ethical obligation to become competent in addressing the spiritual and religious beliefs of their clients (Richards & Bergin, 1997). This chapter will serve as an introduction to the topic.

In addressing the topic, we will first define what we mean by the terms *spirituality* and *religion*. Then we will review the relevance of spirituality and religion to multicultural counseling and briefly describe common spiritual issues faced by four racial-ethnic groups in North America. We describe a model of spiritual identity development, and we provide suggestions for integrating spirituality and religion into effective multicultural counseling.

[*] Address for correspondence: Timothy B. Smith and P. Scott Richards, Department of Counseling Psychology, Brigham Young University, 328 MCKB, Provo, Utah 84602, Phone: 801-378-1311, Fax: 801-378-3961, Tim_Smith@byu.edu, Scott_Richards@byu.edu

## DEFINITIONS OF TERMS

The term *spirit* refers to the life force within us (Kelly, 1995). Many believe that this life force fills the universe, and we are part of it. The spiritual nature of life is said to be *transcendent*, meaning that we do not observe it directly, but it is nonetheless present and universal (e.g., Fukuyama & Sevig, 1999). *Spirituality* is the recognition of transcendent experience and the subsequent internalization of the transcendent. Thus, spirituality is sensitivity to influences than are not ordinarily experienced via the five senses but are nevertheless felt to be real and certain. Spirituality is the degree to which one aligns with spiritual influences and incorporates them into daily living.

The term *religion* refers to an organized community of believers following a system of doctrines, faith, and practices that purport to enhance spirituality (Richards & Bergin, 1997). Therefore, *religiosity*, or the degree to which one adheres to the teachings of a certain religion, is one expression of spirituality. A useful metaphor is to think of spirituality as the substance and religion as the container. Alternatively, spirituality may be considered the essence of life, and religion may be considered the communal perspective on and expression of that essence.

## INTERCONNECTEDNESS OF SPIRITUALITY AND RELIGION

Contemporary society tends to separate religiosity from spirituality, and many people feel more comfortable discussing spirituality than religion. However, the two are often intricately intertwined. For example, religious practices or rituals are frequently performed in private as expressions of a person's spirituality. Within some cultures, the spiritual and the religious are very difficult to separate. Therefore, to be sensitive to cultural values, counselors should be open to both religious and spiritual issues and should consider them in the context they are presented by the client (Kelly, 1995).

## SPIRITUAL AND RELIGIOUS DIVERSITY AND EFFECTIVE MULTICULTURAL COUNSELING

In North America, 97% of people profess having some form of spiritual beliefs, and 65% report that those beliefs are central to their life (Gallup, 1995). Because of the high prevalence and salience of spiritual beliefs in the general population, counselors should remember that spirituality is a fundamental issue in their work with clients.

### Rationale for Addressing Spiritual and Religious Issues in Counseling

Several authors (e.g., Fukuyama & Sevig, 1999; Miller, 1999; Schwartz, 1999) maintain that professional counselors are becoming more interested in the spiritual lives of their clients, recognizing the importance of addressing spirituality in their work. The potential benefits of addressing spiritual and religious issues in counseling are significant (Richards & Bergin, 1997, 2000).

### Respect of Spiritual/Religious Values Enhances Trust

During the past century some counseling professionals have advocated relativism, social constructivism, hedonism, and even atheism in counseling practices, in direct conflict with many spiritual and religious values (Jones, 1994; Richards & Bergin, 1997). Many religious and spiritual people distrust counseling because they fear that secular counselors will misunderstand or seek to undermine their beliefs; they often seek out counselors who share or at least openly respect their values (e.g., Worthington, 1986; Worthington, Kurusu, McCullough, & Sanders, 1996). Counselors who demonstrate respect for the beliefs and practices of a client can increase the level of trust in the counseling relationship.

### Faith Enhances Well-Being

Authors (Benson, 1996; Koenig, 1997; Pargament, 1997) point to a growing body of evidence demonstrating that religious and spiritual beliefs, practices, and influences can both prevent problems and promote coping and healing where problems have occurred. Counselors who address spiritual and religious issues permit the salutary effects of religion and spirituality to enhance their clients' growth and well-being (Bergin, 1991; Miller & Martin, 1988; Richards & Potts, 1995; Shafranske, 1996).

### External Resources Facilitate Healing

According to Sue and Sue (1999), counseling that fails to account for the external resources available to clients will only be partially effective. For religious and spiritual clients, external resources may include group meetings, opportunities to give and receive meaningful service, consultation with spiritual leaders, spiritual bibliotherapy, and specific rituals or practices designed to promote healing (Fukuyama & Sevig, 1999). Counselors who recognize the availability of these resources may facilitate their clients' progress.

### Knowledge of Spiritual/Religious Contexts Improves Conceptualization

A goal of multicultural counseling is to accurately understand individuals within their cultural context (Sue & Sue, 1999). Understanding clients' religious and spiritual background is central to understanding their context. Fukuyama and Sevig (1999) noted that clients' religious and spiritual beliefs often directly influence their perceptions and attitudes about mental health and wellness. For this and other reasons, some research has suggested that certain clients may be effectively treated only when counselors directly address their spiritual and religious issues (Bergin, 1991; Kelly, 1995; Richards & Bergin, 1997; Shafranske, 1996; Worthington et al., 1996). Like other aspects of diversity covered in this book, religious and spiritual diversity need to be acknowledged and addressed through principles of effective multicultural counseling.

## Spiritual and Religious Diversity and Multicultural Counseling

Just as cultural beliefs and practices can differ greatly across groups and across individuals within groups, religious and spiritual beliefs and practice vary greatly from one group to another and from one client to another. In North America, there are literally hundreds of unique spiritual and religious groups. Catholics, Protestants, Jews, and Muslims are some of the more easily recognized, but these groups contain many subgroups such as Greek Orthodox, Pentecostal, Conservative, and Shiite. Moreover, there are many unique groups such as Unitarians, Sikhs, Mormons, and B'hais. Counselors must recognize religious diversity particularly because demographic trends show that religious diversity is increasing (Richards & Bergin, 2000; Shafranske, 1996). During their professional careers, counselors will work with individuals from many faith backgrounds.

A foundation in multicultural counseling facilitates work with clients from diverse religious and spiritual cultures (Richards & Bergin, 1997). The principles taught in other sections of this book are frequently applicable with such clients. However, general multicultural awareness, knowledge, and skills provide only a basic foundation. As in work with any specific population, such as international students, additional knowledge is acquired through further reading, training, and practice. Understanding the specific beliefs and practices of a religious or spiritual community is a necessary condition for effective counseling with members of those groups.

Often spiritual and religious diversity will overlap other aspects of diversity. Indeed, it is sometimes difficult to distinguish spiritual from cultural influences because religious traditions and spiritual beliefs have shaped many aspects of culture across the globe (Inglehart & Baker, 2000). Furthermore, many world cultures integrate religion across most aspects of their society, including politics, education, and health treatment. Such intersection of cultural values with religious and spiritual influences represents a new area of diversity for counselors to consider as they develop multicultural competence. To illustrate these intersections, the following section will review some of the spiritual and religious issues of four major racial-ethnic groups in the U.S.: African Americans, Hispanic Americans, Asian Americans,, and Native Americans Indians.

## SPIRITUAL AND RELIGIOUS CONTEXTS OF FOUR RACIAL-ETHNIC GROUPS

Because of the dangers in making generalizations about members of a group, a counselor working with an individual from a specific group should assess rather than assume certain characteristics, perceptions, or experiences (Sue & Sue, 1999). The following generalizations of religious and spiritual contexts across racial-ethnic groups will not apply to all individuals in theses groups; however these generalizations may be useful in beginning to understand the unique influences of each group's religion and spirituality upon its history, social roles, traditions, and beliefs.

### African Americans

Mbiti (1990) noted that spirituality and religion are central to most African cultures. For the Africans brought to the American continents as slaves from the 1500s to 1800s, spirituality was the only thing they were able to bring with them. Although they were forbidden to practice their own religions in the new land, they retained beliefs and strong inclinations toward spirituality that have been passed down through successive generations. Over time, their spiritual beliefs mixed with those of other African peoples and with Christianity. Although they were forced to profess Christianity, they used religious services for collective healing, gathering strength, and strengthening hope for a better life (Moore,

1991). For a people oppressed, the metaphors in their new faith of deliverance and salvation proved particularly compelling.

Christianity in African American communities retains some African influences. Music plays a central role in worship. Interactions between the pastor and the congregation, call and response patterns, public exclamations, and physical movement all represent aspects of African traditions blended in devotional services (Mitchell & Mitchell, 1989). Moreover, religion is often a community endeavor, with the church being a center for community activity and socialization. Individuals come to develop and increase their sense of identity through a collective, communal perspective. Often the metaphor that fits best is that of an extended family, with *sisters* and *brothers* looking out for one another. In that sense, religion still serves as a buffer against the harmful influences and the oppression evident in contemporary society (McRae, Thompson, & Cooper, 1999).

For these and other reasons, African American churches have been among the leaders in the Civil Rights Movement (Moore, 1991). In earlier decades, continual discrimination against African Americans in Christian churches had led to the formation of independent African American denominations, such as the Christian Methodist Episcopal (C.M.E.). Freed from the restraints of their parent organizations, these churches actively sought ways to benefit the lives of their members. Rallies, marches, and demonstrations of civil disobedience often began or ended at the local place of worship. Although not as publicized, churches and mosques are still centers for community activism, often sponsoring local charity and relief initiatives, such as homeless shelters, and providing community service through efforts to reduce violence among youth and to treat drug and alcohol addictions, for example (see also Moore, 1991).

Although in the U.S. and North America most African Americans are Christian, during recent years an exponential growth has occurred in conversions to Islam and in rediscovery of African spiritual traditions (Cook & Wiley, 2000). There is a notable tendency among younger generations to no longer claim affiliation with a specific organized religion. Nevertheless, many African Americans appreciate their spiritual heritage and acknowledge the role of religion in shaping their collective experience.

## Hispanic Americans

Spain and Portugal were for many centuries important centers of power for the Roman Catholic Church. Conquistadors bought with them the *padres* to spread the Catholic faith throughout the lands they invaded: altogether a massive area from southern Chile to northern California. Often violence enforced conversion. Indigenous religious traditions were modified or lost as Catholicism remained the only sanctioned religion over several centuries (Zea, Mason, & Murguia, 2000). In time, immigrants and native peoples of the Americas intermingled and developed a flourishing culture of their own, a unique combination of indigenous and European societies. Thus the Catholicism of Latin America has retained notable influences on the beliefs and practices of native peoples, particularly in rural areas where acculturation to European values is lower than in urban areas (Ramirez, 1983). In some regions, spiritual traditions such as *Santería*, *Espiritismo*, *Santerismo*, *Umbanda*, and *Candomblé* are more widespread than Christianity (Zea et al., 2000); and even in urban areas the *curandero* (traditional healer) is sought more often than the *cura* (priest). For a detailed discussion of traditional native spiritual traditions that continue to influence contemporary Hispanic cultures and perceptions of mental health, we refer the reader to Zea et al. (2000).

Ramirez (1983) pointed out that after Latin American countries gained independence from Spain and Portugal, Protestant influences from other European nations became more notable. For example, the people residing in present-day California, Arizona, New Mexico, and Texas began to encounter settlers from the eastern states of the U.S., who brought with them Protestant religion, along with a new government--following the loss of the Mexican-American war. The residents of these states acquired through war became second-class citizens; and although they were somewhat able to integrate with and influence the settlers over time (Ramirez, 1983), their affiliation with the Catholic Church was a source of distinction. Often this distinction was a source of ethnic pride, with their religion serving to buffer some of the painful effects of discrimination they experienced. Nevertheless, over time a sizeable minority (25%) of Americans of Hispanic heritage have converted to Protestant denominations (Diaz-Stevens & Stevens-Arroyo, 1998).

During the past century, immigrants from Caribbean nations such as Puerto Rico and Cuba, and more recently from Central and South American nations such as Honduras and Brazil, have experienced similar acculturation patterns. However, many ethnic and spiritual differences exist across nationalities, with the religious traditions and practices of each nation reflecting the unique influences of its indigenous peoples, its economy, and its history (e.g., Ramirez, 1983). These national and ethnic differences should be taken into account whenever working with a client of Latin American ancestry.

Across all Hispanic cultures, many religious influences are still notable. For example, the perception of mental health highly overlaps with notions of spiritual health, with some believing in evil spirits or curses that lead to distress and mental illness (Zea et al., 2000). Similarly, adoration of the Virgin Mary and female saints has reinforced *Marianismo*, the tendency for virgin women and mothers to be idealized, and for sexually active unmarried women to be demonized (e.g., Perez, 2000). In addition, "reverence for elders and the practice of *compadrazgo* . . . the warmth of emotion, the love of *fiesta*, the sense of destiny and a host of other 'Latino cultural characteristics' are derived from a religious worldview" (Stevens-Arroyo, 1995, p. 33). In sum, historical religious legacies continue to influence contemporary Hispanic American cultures.

## Asian Americans

Asian Americans comprise a diverse group of peoples whose origins range from Japan to India, from Mongolia to Indonesia (Uba, 1994). Across groups, a wide variety of religions are practiced, most notably Buddhism, Hinduism, Confucianism, Shintoism, Toaism, animism, ancestor worship, Islam, and Christianity (Bergin & Richards, 2000). The influences of these beliefs are often quite notable in Asian cultures. According to Tan and Dong (2000), Confucian principles often form the basis for the emphasis on filial piety, which manifests itself in an emphasis on submission of the self to the family, youth to elders, and wife to husband. Principles of Taoism that emphasize the importance of living in harmony with nature and with others have influenced the cultural emphasis on harmonious interpersonal relationships, family cohesion, and avoidance of direct confrontation. Buddhist principles concerning the role of fate and suffering have influenced cultural value on the passive acceptance of injustice or pain. In sum, a variety of spiritual values have shaped contemporary Asian American cultures, including emphasis of the patriarchal order, duty and respect, deference to authority, and self-control (Uba, 1994). However, it should be kept in mind that these values sometimes directly conflict with Western values, including principles of mental health taught in counseling programs (Sue & Sue, 1999).

Historically, many Asian Americans converted to Christianity when they could not publicly worship in their traditional ways. Influencing the trend toward conversion was the fact that amidst a climate of persecution, Protestant Christian missionaries often provided a source for community empowerment through educational and social development opportunities denied them elsewhere (Tseng, 1996). Even today, immigrants from Asia often find that local Christian churches with congregations specific to their own ethnicity are centers for group socialization.

Reflecting cultural dynamics, contemporary Asian American Christian churches tend to be divided by age as well as by ethnic group. Older congregations tend to prefer services in their native language, and they also tend to be more theologically conservative compared to the more charismatic evangelical influences often noted in younger congregations (Tan & Dong, 2000).

Even when individuals convert to Christianity, traditional cultural values and practices rooted in religious beliefs often continue to influence individuals' beliefs and practices. These influences can sometimes produce varying degrees of conflict, particularly when younger generations differ in their religious beliefs from their parents and grandparents. Many Asian Americans have therefore found it necessary to become bicultural, practicing more Western values and communication styles in public, while maintaining more traditional orientations at home (Uba, 1994). But with tolerance for differences increasing in American society, more and more Asian Americans are retaining their traditional religious beliefs and practices.

## Native American Indians

A common misconception is that there is a single, unified form of Native American Indian spirituality. Far from being unified, spiritual beliefs and religious practices differ dramatically among Native American people. In the U.S., there are over 500 distinct tribes, with many having unique histories, languages, traditions, familial and social roles, and so forth (Choney, Berryhill-Paapke, & Robbins, 1996). Each tribe has spiritual traditions and beliefs corresponding with their unique history and culture. From the sweat lodge ceremonies of the Lakota to the traditional dances of the Hopi, a wide variety of religious rituals and spiritual expressions represent a rich and varied tapestry of diversity (Trujillo, 2000).

Despite the many differences among tribes, there are some fundamental commonalities in traditional Native American spiritual beliefs and religious practices. According to Beck and Walters (1977) Native American Indian spirituality has the following characteristics: (a) belief in unseen powers; (b) a perception that all things in the universe are dependent on each other, denoting a need for balance and harmony; (c) personal worship that bonds the individual, tribal members, and the great powers; (c) responsibility of spiritual leaders to teach in the Native American Indian way of life and to pass on specialized, even secret Sacred knowledge from generation to generation; and (d) a belief that to be human is to be a necessary part of the Sacred.

A major factor influencing contemporary Native American Indian spirituality is the history of oppression of their traditional religious practices by European Americans. Similar to earlier colonization by Spain and Portugal, the British and French taught and imposed Christianity from the time of their first arrival in North America. During times of conflict, Native American Indians were stripped of their traditional religious artifacts, forbidden to practice their own beliefs, and forced to accept Christianity as their professed religion. During times of relative peace they were proselytized by missionaries, with converts often receiving special privileges. Differentiation between Christian converts and others sometimes created conflict within tribes, as families were split apart and discrimination arose between groups (Choney et al., 1996). This dynamic sometimes continues to the present day; but more and more often, contemporary Native American Indians are affirming or rediscovering the ways of their ancestors, sometimes simultaneously practicing Christianity and traditional religious customs (Trujillo, 2000).

Many European Americans are also discovering the wisdom of traditional Native American beliefs and practices. The so-called *New Age* religious movement draws heavily from Native American legends and teachings. However, Kasee (1995) noted that to many Native American Indians, the mass marketing of their beliefs and traditions represents yet one more form of exploitation, where what they have is taken from them and sold. Moreover, because the New Age movement extracts spiritual principles from many cultures across the world, some Native American Indians feel that the sanctity of their own traditions is minimized and that the beliefs themselves are distorted when they are presented in a form mixed with Celtic or Hindu traditions, for example. For others, however, the fact that European Americans are leaving Christianity to embrace Native American Indian traditions and beliefs represents an area for increasing mutual respect, even if their ancestors would not believe it to be true.

## Intersections of Multicultural Identities

As demonstrated in the descriptions just provided, all aspects of diversity intersect with one another. Culture and religious and spiritual influences clearly interact with one another; but they also interact with gender, sexual orientation, age, physical appearance and ability, and language to create for each individual a unique context that must be understood and respected in counseling. For each individual, different aspects of identity will have primary salience, some favoring an identity that emphasizes gender or culture, some an identity that emphasizes religious heritage or spiritual beliefs (McQuillen, Licht, & Licht, 2001). In every case, the counselor can assess the client's multicultural framework, provide assistance toward integration of their multiple identities, and strengthen the identities that best help the individual to cope with challenges and enhance their sense of well-being. Some even suggest that spirituality, or spiritual identity, integrates and gives meaning to other identities (e.g., Emmons, 1999).

# SPIRITUAL IDENTITY DEVELOPMENT

Research (Brandtstadter & Greve, 1994; Pulkkinen, & Roenkae, 1994; Sheldon & Kasser, 2001) has emphasized the importance of identity development in maintaining and enhancing mental health. Development of a spiritual identity, a pervasive awareness that an individual is an eternal being connected to God, is similarly purported to enhance well-being (Ganzevoort, 1998). A theistic perspective of counseling (Richards & Bergin, 1997) affirms that counselors can benefit their clients by assessing the level of clients' spiritual identity and then supporting them in their ongoing development toward higher stages of identity.

By integrating insights from existing psychological theories with theistic assumptions that God exists and that individuals can communicate with God through spiritual means, a tentative model of spiritual identity development has been proposed by Poll and Smith (in press). In the proposed model, individuals develop a sense of their own spirituality by interacting with a Higher Power and recognizing spiritual influences. William James (1902) called these interactions and recognitions *mystical experiences*, or more simply *spiritual experiences*. By remembering spiritual experiences from the past, recognizing them in the present, and projecting their occurrence into the future, individuals begin to feel continuity in their spiritual identity. That is, they begin to internalize spiritual experiences and to see themselves as spiritual beings with an eternal nature.

Because individuals' ideas about a Higher Power differ greatly, the content of spiritual identity varies from person to person (Poll & Smith, in press). But in general, people form a spiritual identity based on the specific attributes they ascribe to a Higher Power, God, or gods (Stark, 2000). Thus, if individuals fully believe that God loves them personally, their spiritual identity will reflect internalized values of kindness and charity toward others. If they believe in gods that are capricious and punishing, their spiritual identity will reflect mistrust and fear. If they believe there is no Higher Power or spiritual reality, they will not have a spiritual identity.

## Stages of Spiritual Identity Development

According to the proposed model (Poll & Smith, in press), a developmental sequence for spiritual identity development consists of four stages. The first stage of *Pre-awareness* characterizes individuals who do not consciously perceive themselves in spiritual terms. Usually these individuals have not had experiences perceived as spiritual in nature or else their past spiritual experiences have been forgotten or minimized.

The second stage involves a period of learning, conflict, or crisis that leads to an *Awakening* of awareness of the self in relation to God. Individuals at this stage begin to recognize events or interactions in spiritual terms, but the quality of spiritual awareness will tend to be inconsistent and specific to the crisis or situation at hand (such as only thinking of God when attending a worship service or when grieving the loss of a loved one).

The third stage entails a *Recognition* and recollection of other spiritual experiences, such that consistent spiritual themes emerge across multiple settings. Thus, individuals at this stage see themselves in spiritual terms, although their spiritual identity tends to be predominantly cognitive or emotional in nature.

The final stage denotes an *Integration* of spiritual experiences with self-concept. Individuals at this stage not only recognize their own spiritual nature, but they also interact with others accordingly. Spiritual experiences have been internalized through the development of consistent spiritual relationships with others and with a Higher Power. Spontaneously taking in and seeking out spiritual experiences has become for them a way of life.

It should be kept in mind that this developmental sequence of spiritual identity is not necessarily linear. For example, a person not ordinarily inclined to be spiritual might feel strongly the support of a Higher Power during the months surrounding the birth of a child (Awakening), begin consistently meditating, reading sacred literature, and attending worship services *(Recognition)*, but then over time losing all interest as other concerns arise and as continued opportunities for spiritual experiences are overlooked (Pre-awareness).

## Assessing Spiritual Identity Development in Counseling

As is the case with other aspects of identity (racial, gender, etc.), a brief assessment of a client's spiritual identity and religious context can improve a counselor's understanding of the client's presenting concern (Standard, Sandhu, & Painter, 2000; Richards & Bergin, 1997). Without such information, the counselor may incorrectly assume that spirituality is not relevant to the client's worldview and current condition. And, unless a counselor specifically asks about a client's spiritual or religious context, the client may assume that such topics are not appropriate for discussion in counseling. Simply broaching the topic implicitly sends the message that a counselor is interested in the client's experiences and perceptions, including those normally not discussed in public settings.

To illustrate, we present a practical example:

> Shilana asks her clients in the first session to list the resources they typically draw upon in resolving their life's challenges. She includes religious and spiritual resources as part of a list provided for the client to review and discuss. On one occasion, an agnostic client at first expressed surprise to see those items on the list. However, by following the client's lead, Shilana learned that the client spent a great deal of time in his garden, which he viewed as a relaxing place for meditation and attunement with nature. Throughout their work together, the client reported insights gleaned while gardening, and metaphors of growth, seasons, and death were used effectively in sessions together. Upon termination the client commented that he had never shared such personal experiences with friends or family members who did not seem to understand how his hobby could be so meaningful to him.

Based on the client's responses to a survey, checklist, or initial interview question, a counselor can then ask more specific questions as needed. Specific topics that may be useful in understanding a client's spiritual identity and religious context include not only their affiliation or major beliefs but also their degree of orthodoxy, their level of experience and knowledge, their congruence between professed beliefs and actual behaviors, and their perceptions of benefits or limitations of spiritual or religious resources in coping with their presenting concerns (Richards & Bergin, 1997). On occasion, it may be that clients' spiritual beliefs relate directly to their reason for seeking counseling. In such cases, it is important to assess how their perceptions interact with their concerns. Even when spiritual or religious beliefs and practices are not directly related to the client's concern they can still serve as a supplemental resource for client growth and progress.

## Facilitating Spiritual Identity Development in Counseling

A theistic perspective of counseling affirms that counselors should assist clients in their spiritual identity development (Richards & Bergin, 1997). Specifically, counselors can use the model presented above in assessing a client's stage of spiritual identity and then in supporting progression toward the next stage.

Because clients at a Pre-awareness stage have limited recognition of spirituality, the most relevant intervention would be guidance toward opportunities to have spiritual experiences. For example, counselors can attempt to connect with clients at a spiritual level without overtly mentioning religion or spirituality, a process termed *meta-empathy* (Richards & Bergin, 1997). Once clients have had experiences outside of counseling or connections with a counselor that could be considered spiritual, the secondary goal is to implicitly or explicitly label the experiences as spiritual in such a way that the clients can recognize them as such. Labeling spiritual experiences normalizes the topic and potentially differentiates spirituality from negative religious experiences the client may have had previously. Moreover, it provides the clients with an understanding and awareness that can advance them to the next stage of identity development.

Many clients are likely to have experienced life events that encourage reflection upon who they are and how they fit in the world. However, clients in the Awakening stage typically have minimal resources, understanding, or motivation to draw from to further their spiritual identity development, particularly when current difficulties are so prominent. Therefore, the most useful intervention with clients at this stage is to increase their trust in the availability and salience of spiritual guidance and strength. Counselors can assist clients at this stage by asking questions, posing paradoxes, and using metaphors and analogies designed to raise client awareness of spiritual influences and the potential additional strength they can provide.

Clients in the Recognition stage have already begun the cognitive and emotional process of generalizing spiritual awareness across situations and relationships. Therefore, the most pertinent intervention when working with clients at this stage is to assist them to put their awareness into practice, helping them to better align their actions with their beliefs about the attributes of a Higher Power.

Similarly, clients at an Integration stage already see themselves as spiritual beings, and they typically relate with others accordingly. The primary goal for clients at this stage is to refine their understanding of and establish an intimate relationship with a Higher Power. The section that follows presents a detailed discussion of practices and techniques that may be useful in strengthening the spiritual identity of clients at the Recognition or Integration stage.

# Incorporating Spiritual and Religious Interventions in Counseling

Many principles of counseling theory and mental health provide solutions for healthy living that are quite similar to those espoused in religious and spiritual traditions (Fukuyama & Sevig, 1999; Kelly, 1995). This section reviews some of the more common spiritual or religious interventions that can be appropriate at times in counseling with clients at the later stages of spiritual identity development (see Richards & Bergin, 1997 for a more detailed discussion of the techniques that follow).

## Sacred Texts and Spiritual Writings

Most religious and spiritual traditions have been passed on from one generation to another through the transmission of texts deemed sacred or profound. Often, these writings are not only central to an accurate understanding of the historical and cultural background of a particular group, they also frequently play a large role in the group's contemporary identity and practices. For some traditions, there is one central writing of greatest importance (e.g., for Muslims, the Qur'an), but for others, multiple texts inform the tradition (e.g., for members of the Church of Jesus Christ of Latter-day Saints, the Bible, Book of Mormon, Doctrine and Covenants, and Pearl of Great Price). Some traditions rely more heavily on current teachings of prophets, shamans, or other leaders.

Regardless of the format, these writings nearly always provide insights for healthful living or encouragement in overcoming or transcending personal difficulties. Members of a certain tradition may find such readings helpful and even inspiring. Counselors familiar with a particular tradition's writings may suggest passages relevant to the clients' concerns, or counselors may make reference to stories or principles found in the writings to support clients' progress or to reframe difficult situations. Counselors not familiar with such writings may have clients study on their own or in reading groups and then share passages that they found helpful.

Of course, individuals read spiritual texts with different levels of familiarity and with different purposes. For some, intellectual study may be more important than internalization of the principles taught. For others, archaic language or stories about another age and people may present difficulties. Counselors should consider these differences with clients as they include spiritual texts in their work.

## Consultation with Religious Leaders

Counselors can greatly improve their own understanding of a particular client by consulting with leaders of that client's spiritual tradition. Moreover, clients can benefit greatly from seeking spiritual guidance directly from these leaders. Even when religious and spiritual leaders have not received formal training in mental health, their role typically involves mentoring and advising others on a variety of concerns, oftentimes related to emotional health and relationships. Such leaders can provide social support and validation, insight and advice, absolution from wrongdoing, and sometimes financial support.

Consultation with religious leaders may not always be helpful. Occasionally they may provide superficial or uninformed advice, or they may shame the client or take advantage of the client's problems to further their own ends. Counselors should therefore be cautious and preferably establish a working relationship with the leader with the client's explicit consent.

## Service

Focusing on the needs of others may provide clients with the opportunity to exercise their talents, regain perspective on their own difficulties, establish or strengthen relationships, and increase their own self-esteem. Although many religious congregations offer opportunities for their members to aid others through financial donations, some provide opportunities for personal meaningful service. Counselors can facilitate meaningful involvement through consultation with religious leaders who can assist to match the area of service to the client's aptitudes.

## Ritual and Music

From birth to burial, religious and spiritual traditions often involve multiple rituals, both public and private. Often, these rituals are designed to enhance well-being, connection with the numinous, or communal interaction. From pouring libations to partaking of ritualistic meals, the rituals are often laden with symbolism and positive messages. Frequently, music plays a central role in ritual, with either singing or instrumental performance accompanying physical movement. More often, music serves as a kind of ritual in and of itself, with members of a group sharing in the performance of a certain song or group of songs specified for a certain occasion or more commonly, selecting from a common repertoire of songs for purposes of worship or celebration. Counselors can facilitate client exploration of ritual and use of sacred music outside of sessions and discuss the feeling, meaning, and symbolism they may contain. They can occasionally introduce clients to external sources to assist them in the performance of rituals perceived as potentially helpful that are grounded in clients' worldview (offerings to ancestors, healing or grieving ceremonies, baptism, chants, etc.), but typically counselors should not engage in such rituals during sessions.

## Repentance

From within several religious traditions, and particularly Christianity, the notion of sin is considered real. Whether or not the counselor agrees with such a perspective, it is important to recognize that the perception may be real for the client. Therefore, rather than minimizing the religious belief or minimizing the severity of the act considered sinful, a counselor can facilitate a client's resolution of the perceived misdeed through the process of obtaining forgiveness. The methods and practices for so doing will differ from one tradition to another, but the counselor can consult with religious leaders, utilize the client's perceptions, and study relevant literature on the topic in determining if and how they can facilitate the process of a client obtaining forgiveness for a perceived transgression. Clients who work through difficulties to realize a sense of forgiveness typically report an accompanying sense of inner peace and well-being.

An exception to the normal helpful repentance process is the issue of scrupulosity, an excessive and distorted perception of unworthiness (Ciarrocchi, 1998; 1995). If the counselor believes that clients' scrupulosity negatively affects their well-being, the counselor may consult with religious leaders and assist the client in reinterpreting their perception of the severity of their own misdeeds or in emphasizing the positive messages of love and forgiveness found in the religious tradition. Often, deeper psychological issues will have to be addressed before clients can see themselves as worthy of genuine affection and forgiveness.

## Forgiving Others

Individuals who have been hurt by others often carry intensely negative feelings about that person, which can in turn negatively impact their own mental health. The healing power of forgiving others has been well documented in recent research (McCullough, 2000; McCullough & Worthington, 1999; Wivlieit, Ludwig, & Vander-Laan, 2001). Although forgiving others does not necessarily include religious or spiritual components, oftentimes, clients may perceive the process as spiritual or as informed by messages they have received through their religious backgrounds (Wuthnow, 2000). That is, clients will often attempt to go about forgiving others in ways taught by their religion. Thus, before encouraging a client to forgive another person, a counselor should become informed of how the client views the process of forgiveness. In some cases, clients' spiritual or religious beliefs can aid them to return to a sense of peace. In other cases, clients' notions of forgiveness may not be optimal for a particular context. For example, if a client feels it is necessary to speak face to face with someone to offer them their forgiveness, a client who was abused may put themselves at risk by meeting with the perpetrator, who may perceive the client as being vulnerable or deserving of the abuse or of continued abuse. Thus, whereas counselors are strongly encouraged to assist clients in working through past offenses that can continue to hamper the clients' own progress, they are strongly cautioned to ensure that clients are not potentially increasing the depth of their own problems by offering premature forgiveness or by placing themselves in potentially harmful situations.

## Prayer, Meditation

Most religious and spiritual traditions emphasize either prayer or meditation as a beneficial practice for their members. Prayer may be any form of expression that denotes a relationship with God or a spiritual power. It can be formal or informal, public or private, verbal or nonverbal. Meditation refers to contemplation or introspection with or without reference to a spiritual power or deity. It too can take many forms. And although the format and content of prayer and meditation can differ markedly across traditions, the fundamental benefits are similar. Both tend to facilitate relaxation, increase insight, and enhance perceptions of support and well-being (Benson, 1996; Dossey, 1993; Emavardhana & Tori, 1997; McCullough, 1995).

On rare occasions, prayer or meditation may be used in sessions. For example, if a client expresses a strong desire to pray in session, the counselor may respectfully listen and then be open to discuss the meaning of the prayer for the client. Usually, however, the counselor will simply facilitate a client's experiences with prayer and meditation outside of the session. Counselors can learn about the prayerful or meditative practices of their clients, encouraging clients to use those practices that have previously been beneficial. Occasionally, a counselor can discuss ways in which meditation or prayer could potentially enhance the client's sense of well-being and provide referrals to appropriate leaders in the client's spiritual tradition. Outside of sessions, the counselor can meditate in private on their experiences with their clients or pray in behalf of their clients.

## Summary

Clients will often discuss relevant spiritual or religious issues if their counselor invites them to do so. Ongoing assessment of the relevance of a client's spiritual or religious perspective can inform a counselor's conceptualization and treatment approach. Whenever a client identifies spiritual or religious issues, they can be addressed with respect and sensitivity. There are multiple ways in which a counselor may facilitate a client's well-being through methods that implicitly or explicitly address a client's spiritual or religious experiences.

## ETHICAL ISSUES

Contemporary society is sensitive to religious and spiritual differences. Many individuals strongly feel that religious issues are best kept personal. Some fear that bringing up the topic in secular settings conflicts with the principle of separation of church and state, over which many legal battles have been fought in the past century. Others are concerned about having their own values imposed upon by others, about abuses of religious power, or about potential professional and clerical dual relationships. All of these concerns warrant attention. Therefore, the assertions made in this chapter about the multiple benefits of addressing client spirituality need to be understood within the context of professional ethical guidelines. The following discussion regarding the application of ethical guidelines to religious and spiritual issues in counseling is based in part on Richards and Bergin (1997). We refer readers who would like to read more about the issues below to their book and to articles by Tan (1994) and Younggren (1993).

## Church-State Boundary Violations

The assumption of most North Americans is that religion and politics should not mix, although this purposeful separation does not occur in many countries throughout the world. Thus, even though non-denominational theistic assumptions sometimes characterize North American society and government (e.g., *in God we trust*), advocacy of spiritual or religious content in civic settings is often prohibited by law. Counselors who represent the government in their work (e.g., state welfare agencies, public schools) should obey local and national regulations. Counselors not employed by the state but who find themselves in civic roles should identify potential violations of church-state boundaries and obtain consent from the clients and the authorities involved before integrating religious issues in their work.

## Dual Relationships and Confidentiality

The following example demonstrates the dilemma of dual relationships:

> Ricardo, a counselor, attended weekly services at a large religious congregation. He was friendly with the clergy, whom he admired greatly for their service to the community. Because she knew Ricardo was a counselor, one of the church leaders often asked him for advice on mental health issues. Sometimes she would even name the members of the congregation who were in need of assistance and ask Ricardo if he could work with them in his practice. Ricardo did end up working with one of the church members, but he found it awkward when he saw the client at church functions and particularly difficult when the clergy member repeatedly asked about the client's progress.

Professional ethical codes caution against dual relationships and provide explicit directives about client confidentiality (ACA, 1995). Counselors may often refer clients to leaders of spiritual traditions and in turn receive referrals from them. They may also consult with such leaders on mental health issues. However, such referrals and consultation should not occur within a local group attended by the counselor. There are multiple potential conflicts of interest that may develop when this occurs. For example, the counselor may become implicitly manipulative when they befriend their own spiritual leaders out of a desire to channel referrals to their own practice. Counselors may mistakenly reveal information about a client in a religious setting that they learned in counseling, or clients may bring up counseling issues in the religious setting. Clients may be less willing to trust the counselor with personal issues when they see each other regularly outside of session and have mutual acquaintances. Additional difficulties may arise if the client or counselor later become involved in service work (e.g., Habitat for Humanity) or religious functions (e.g., leading a group or class, potentially for one another's family members) where their roles require additional interaction and potentially even authority over one another. In particular, counselors in rural, isolated areas encounter dual relationship dilemmas. A counselor may be the only mental health resource for the community. In such cases, counselors must be diligent in balancing the need for counseling services with the need to avoid dual relationships; and counselors must take care in setting and maintaining appropriate professional boundaries.

## Assuming and Discrediting Religious Authority

Another area for potential boundary violations concerns the different roles of mental health professionals and religious-spiritual leadership. Counselors may err in assuming too much responsibility for the spiritual welfare of their clients, blurring their role with that of a spiritual leader, and/or undermining the authority of religious-spiritual leaders. Counselors are in an ideal position to assist clients with their spiritual concerns; however, spiritual concerns should not be the sole focus of counseling. Referrals to or collaboration with spiritual advisors and religious leaders should be initiated when spiritual issues become prominent. Similarly, counselors should rely upon the client's perceptions of their own religious and spiritual communities and leaders. They should not criticize such leaders even and especially when their actions contradict counselors' own values. Rare exceptions can be made in the case of cults that clearly endanger the safety of their members.

## Professional Competence

A related ethical issue is that counselors should always practice within their bounds of competence (ACA, 1995). More and more professional resources are becoming available to assist counselors develop their abilities to address spiritual and religious issues in counseling (e.g., Richards & Bergin, 1997). Some universities offer specific courses on the topic, and many are beginning to integrate relevant content in other courses, such as multicultural counseling. As with any new counseling skill, counselors learning a spiritual approach or technique should make opportunities to practice in simulation role-plays, seek out external consultation, and receive close supervision.

The following vignette provides and example of how competence is built:

> Janie decided that her client's emotional concerns were related to several blatant contradictions within his newly found spiritual beliefs. She sought out readings specific to that spiritual tradition, and she consulted with her supervisor and with a spiritual leader in that tradition. She learned that the apparent discrepancies were not actually contradictions, and she was further able to see that her client's difficulties were more related to beliefs he still retained about his previous spiritual tradition.

There is no substitute for learning through experience. As with all multicultural counseling, competence in addressing spiritual and religious diversity requires additional reading beyond what is provided in a basic textbook. But most importantly, competence entails working on the issues directly. Just as working with clients from diverse racial backgrounds is essential to become more multiculturally competent, working with clients from diverse spiritual and religious backgrounds is the best way to enhance skills in the area.

## Imposition of Values

Professional ethics affirm that counselors should not impose their own values on clients (ACA, 1995). This is particularly true with spiritual and religious values. The obvious ethical violations are when a counselor (a) asserts that a client's behavior is spiritually wrong or immoral, (b) attempts to persuade clients to alter their religious or spiritual beliefs, or (c) uses spiritual or religious interventions without the explicit consent of the client. Although religious organizations may openly practice such activities, counseling is never an appropriate forum for proselytizing.

Although counselors can facilitate the client's spiritual exploration through acknowledging their concerns or insights, even providing referrals to external sources for clients who request such information, their work should focus on the experiences and perceptions of the client--not their own experiences and convictions. When clients ask for information or clearly expresses interest in counselors' experiences, appropriate information can be provided in the interest of client progress and strengthening the counselor-client relationship. However, counselors should not self-disclose information intended to influence the client toward their own beliefs or use means that benefit themselves more than the client. To demonstrate:

> Keith attended several sessions of group therapy to enhance male intimacy. When the counselor encouraged the members to openly discuss masturbation experiences, Keith indicated that his religious beliefs were opposed to masturbation and that he felt uncomfortable talking about the issue in public. The counselor questioned the group about issues related to religious guilt. When Keith admitted that he had not masturbated since he was a teen, the counselor began a discussion of sexual repression.

Implicitly anti-religious or anti-spiritual values can sometimes be imposed on clients. Also, value imposition is more often indirect than direct. In the case above, the counselor proceeded with interventions before understanding Keith's perceptions and before knowing how the other group members (some of whom may have felt similarly) really felt about the issue. The decision to intervene immediately reflected the personal values of the counselor. The same dilemma would occur if Keith were the counselor and he had switched the topic when a client advocated masturbation. Awareness of one's own religious-spiritual values and close monitoring of their expression is a necessary therapeutic skill.

> Betty sought treatment from a counselor who shared her cultural background. However, when the counselor began the session with a prayer to their ancestors, Betty felt uneasy and reluctant to share her own unique spiritual beliefs with the counselor.

Assuming that a client shares the exact same spiritual beliefs as the counselor after the client acknowledges having similar beliefs to the counselor can lead to potentially unethical missteps. Even if clients indicate belonging to the same religious organization or spiritual tradition as the counselor, it is best to first assess their own beliefs and orthodoxy before assuming too much. A self-described devout Catholic, Orthodox Jew, born-again Christian, or Brahmin Hindu may vary greatly from stereotypes in their personal beliefs and actions. Sensitivity to individual differences within religious or spiritual traditions can strengthen the therapeutic relationship and improve counseling outcomes.

## CONCLUSION

Faith, or belief in things not proven, is central to human experience (e.g., Emmons, 1999). Faith is not specific to religion or to spiritual perspectives. Everyone must go through life believing in many things that they cannot prove to be true. Such beliefs provide a framework for individuals and cultures to make sense of their world and to maintain hope amid difficult circumstances.

This chapter has demonstrated that although individuals and groups rely on many different beliefs to help them cope and thrive, the processes of trusting the unknown is fundamental to the human experience. Spirituality and religion typically embody that faith for many people throughout the world. Many counselors and scholars have therefore recognized that religious and spiritual diversity are fundamental to effective multicultural counseling (e.g., Fukuyama & Sevig, 1999; Sue et al., 1999). However, some readers may question the assertions in this chapter for counselors to integrate spiritual interventions in counseling or to facilitate client spiritual identity development. Some may feel that counselors should not address spiritual issues at all.

Oftentimes, and particularly across cultures, what one person firmly believes will seem unusual, impractical, or unhealthy to an outsider. Attempts to understand a culture or a belief system from the "outside" often fail to consider the previous experiences of the believer and other influences of which the observer is unaware. Multiculturalism teaches that counselors should withhold judgment of others and instead seek more earnestly to understand and to respect differences in experiences and worldviews (Sue & Sue, 1999). To do so requires faith.

## DISCUSSION QUESTIONS

1. What are your experiences with spirituality and religion?
2. How have spiritual and religious values influenced your culture?
3. How do you explain research that suggests a positive relationship between spirituality and mental health?
4. How can an assessment of a client's religious and spiritual background facilitate counseling?
5. Why might counselors be more comfortable discussing spirituality than religion with clients?
6. What might be some limitations of only addressing spirituality and not religion in counseling?
7. What aspects of spirituality or religiosity might be harmful to a person's growth and development?
8. What ethical issues need to be considered when discussing spiritual or religious issues with clients?
9. In what ways can spiritual interventions facilitate counseling?
10. What reservations do you have about discussing spiritual or religious issues with clients?
11. How do spirituality and religion fit into your conceptualization of multicultural counseling?

## EXPERIENTIAL ACTIVITIES

A. Begin recording experiences that you consider spiritual. After several weeks, devote a portion of a class to discuss these events. Use the discussion as an opportunity to practice effective multicultural listening and facilitation of differing viewpoints.
B. Divide into small groups or pairs, then attend different religious services. Meet again as a class to discuss your observations and experiences.
C. Read passages from a sacred religious text as a class. Discuss reactions and implications of written traditions for counseling.

D. Start a "Worldviews" discussion group on your campus. Use the group as an opportunity to practice effective multicultural listening and facilitation of differing viewpoints.

E. Ask your family members, particularly those over age 60, about their spiritual beliefs and experiences. Bring your findings to class and discuss insights you may have gained about the values in your own family.

F. Interview a religious leader in depth about their perceptions of how their culture influences their work, or have representatives from several different religions briefly present ways they believe their culture interacts with their faith.

G. With the same religious representatives, you may ask regarding their perceptions of counseling and mental health. Find out ways in which they facilitate growth and development within their communities, and discuss ways to facilitate effective referrals between one another.

# REFERENCES

American Counseling Association (ACA) (1995). *Code of ethics and standards of practice.* Alexandria, VA: Author.

Beck, P. V. & Walters, A. L. (1977). *The Sacred Ways of knowledge Sources of life.* Tsaile (Navajo Nation), AZ: Navajo Community College Press.

Benson, H. (1996). *Timeless healing: The power and biology of belief.* New York: Scribner.

Bergin, A. E. (1991). Values and religious issues in psychotherapy and mental health. *American Psychologist, 46,* 394-403.

Brandtstadter, J., & Greve, W. (1994). The aging self: Stabilizing and protective processes. *Developmental Review, 14,* 52-80.

Choney, S. K., Berryhill-Paapke, E., & Robbins, R. (1996). The acculturation of American Indians: Developing frameworks for research and practice. In J. Ponterotto, J. M. Casas, L. A. Suzuki, and C. M. Alexander (Eds.) *Handbook of multicultural counseling* (pp. 73-92). Thousand Oaks, CA: Sage.

Ciarrocchi, J. W. (1998). Religion, scrupulosity, and obsessive-compulsive disorder. In M. A. Jenike, L. Baer, & W. E. Minichiello (Eds.), *Obsessive-compulsive disorder: Practical management* (pp. 555-569). St. Louis, MO: Mosby.

Ciarrocchi, J. W. (1995). *The doubting disease.* New York: Paulist Press.

Cook, D., & Wiley, C. (2000). Psychotherapy with members of African American churches and spiritual traditions. In P. S. Richards and A. E. Bergin (Eds.) *Handbook of psychotherapy and religious diversity* (pp. 369-396). Washington, D.C.: American Psychological Association.

Council for Accreditation of Counseling and Related Educational Programs (CACREP) (2001). *CACREP accreditation manual: 2001 standards.* Alexandria, VA: Author.

Diaz-Stevens, A. M. & Stevens-Arroyo, A. M. (1998). *Recognizing the Latino resurgence in U.S. religion: The Emmaus paradigm.* Boulder, CO: Westview Press.

Dossey, L. (1993). *Healing words: The power of prayer and the practice of medicine.* San Francisco: HarperCollins.

Emavarhana, T., & Tori, C. D. (1997). Changes in self-concept, ego defense mechanisms, and religiosity following seven-day Vipassana meditation retreats. *Journal for the Scientific Study of Religion, 36,* 194-206.

Emmons, R. A. (1999). *The psychology of ultimate concerns: Motivation and spirituality in personality.* New York: The Guilford Press.

Fukuyama, M., & Sevig, T. (1999). *Integrating spirituality into multicultural counseling.* Thousand Oaks, CA: Sage.

Gallup, G. (1995). *The Gallup poll: Public opinion in 1995.* Wilmington, DE: Scholarly Resources.

Ganzevoort, R. R. (1998). Religious coping reconsidered, part one: An integrated approach. *Journal of Psychology and Theology, 26,* 260-275.

Inglehart, R., & Baker, W. E. (2000). Modernization, cultural change, and the persistence of traditional values. *American Sociological Review, 65,* 19-51.

James, W. (1902). *The varieties of religious experience: A study of human nature.* New York: The Modern Library.

Jones, S. L. (1994). A constructive relationship for religion with the science and profession of psychology: Perhaps the boldest model yet. *American Psychologist, 49,* 184-199.

Kasee, C. (1995). Identity, recovery, and religious imperialism: Native American women and the new age. *Women and Therapy, 16,* 83-93.

Kelly, E. W. (1995). *Religion and spirituality in counseling and psychotherapy.* Alexandria, VA: American Counseling Association.

Koenig, H. G. (1997). *Is religion good for your health? The effects of religion on physical and mental health.* New York: Haworth Press.

Mbiti, J. S. (1990). *African religions and philosophies* (2nd ed.). Portsmouth, NH: Heinemann.

McCullough, M. E. (2000). Forgiveness as human strength: Theory, measurement, ad links to well-being. *Journal of Social and Clinical Psychology, 19,* 43-55.

McCullough, M. E. (1995). Prayer and health: Conceptual issues, research review, and research agenda. *Journal of Psychology and Theology, 23,* 15-29.

McCullough, M. E., & Worthington, E. L. JR. (1999). Religion and the forgiving personality. *Journal of Personality, 67,* 1141-1164.

McQullen, A. D., Licht, M. H., & Licht, B. G. (2001). Identity structure and life satisfaction in later life. *Basic and Applied Social Psychology, 23,* 65-72.

McRae, M. B., Thompson, D. A., & Cooper, S. (1999). Black churches as therapeutic groups. *Journal of Multicultural Counseling and Development, 27,* 207-220.

Miller, G. (1999). The development of the spiritual focus in counseling and counselor education. *Journal of Counseling & Development, 77,* 498-501.

Miller, W. R., & Martin, J. E. (Eds.). (1988). *Behavior therapy and religion: Integrating spiritual and behavioral approaches to change.* Newbury Park, CA: Sage.

Mitchell, E. P. & Mitchell, H. H. (1989). Black spirituality: The values of the "Ol' time religion." *The Journal of the Interdenominational Theological Center, 17,* 102-109.

Moore, T. (1991). The African-American church: A source of empowerment, mutual help, and social change. *Prevention in Human Services, 10,* 147-167.

Pargament, K. (1997). *The psychology of religion and coping: Theory, research, practice.* New York: The Guilford Press.

Perez, R. L. (2000). Fiesta as tradition, fiesta as change: Ritual, alcohol, and violence in a Mexican community. *Addiction, 95*, 365-373.

Poll, J., & Smith, T. B. (in press). The spiritual self: Toward a conceptualization of spiritual identity development. *Journal of Psychology and Theology.*

Pulkkinen, L., & Roenkae, A. (1994). Personal control over development, identity formation, and future orientation as components of life orientation: A developmental approach. *Developmental Psychology, 30*, 260-271.

Ramirez, M. (1983). *Psychology of the Americas: Mestizo perspectives on personality and mental health.* New York: Pergamon Press.

Richards, P. S., & Bergin, A. E. (Eds). (2000). *Handbook of psychotherapy and religious diversity.* Washington, D.C.: American Psychological Association.

Richards, P. S., & Bergin, A. E. (1997). *A spiritual strategy for counseling and psychotherapy.* Washington, D.C.: American Psychological Association.

Richards, P. S., & Potts, R. W. (1995). Using spiritual interventions in psychotherapy: Practices, successes, failures, and ethical concerns of Mormon psychotherapists. *Professional Psychology: Research and Practice, 26*, 163-170.

Schwartz, R. C. (1999). Releasing the soul: Psychotherapy as a spiritual practice. In F. Walsh (Ed.), *Spiritual resources in family therapy* (pp. 223-239). New York: Guilford Publications.

Shafranske, E. P. (Ed.). (1996). *Religion and the clinical practice of psychology.* Washington, D.C.: American Psychological Association.

Sheldon, K. M., & Kasser, T. (2001). Getting older, getting better? Personal strivings and psychological maturity across the life span. *Developmental Psychology, 37*, 491-501.

Standard, R. P., Sandhu, D. S., & Painter, L. C. (2000). Assessment of spirituality in counseling. *Journal of Counseling & Development, 78*, 204-210.

Stark, R. (2000). Religious effects: In praise of "idealistic humbug." *Review of Religious Research, 41*, 289-310.

Stevens-Arroyo, A. M. (Ed.). (1995). *Discovering Latino religion: A comprehensive social science bibliography.* New York: Bildner Center for Western Hemisphere Studies.

Sue, D. W., Bingham, R., Porche-Burke, L., & Vasquez, M. (1999). The diversification of psychology: A multicultural revolution. *American Psychologist, 54*, 1061-1069.

Sue, D. W. & Sue, D. (1999). *Counseling the culturally different: Theory and practice* (3rd ed.). New York: Wiley.

Tan, S. (1994). Ethical considerations in religious psychotherapy: Potential pitfalls and unique resources. *Journal of Psychology and Theology, 22*, 389-394).

Tan, S., & Dong, N. (2000). Psychotherapy with members of Asian American churches and spiritual traditions. In P. S. Richards and A. E. Bergin (Eds.) *Handbook of psychotherapy and religious diversity* (pp. 421-444). Washington, D.C.: American Psychological Association.

Trujillo, A. (2000). Psychotherapy with Native Americans: A view into the role of religion and spirituality. In P. S. Richards and A. E. Bergin (Eds.) *Handbook of psychotherapy and religious diversity* (pp. 445-466). Washington, D.C.: American Psychological Association.

Tseng, T. (1996). Chinese Protestant nationalism in the United States. *Amerasia Journal, 22*, 31-56.

Uba, L. (1994). *Asian Americans: Personality patterns, identity, and mental health.* New York: Guilford.

Witvliet, C. V., Ludwig, T. E., & Vander-Laan, K. L. (2001). Granting forgiveness or harboring grudges: Implications for emotion, physiology, and health. *Psychological Science, 121,* 117-123.

Worthington, E. L., Jr., Kurusu, T. A., McCullough, M. E., & Sanders, S. J. (1996). Empirical research on religion and psychotherapeutic processes and outcomes: A ten-year review and research prospectus. *Psychological Bulletin, 119,* 448-487.

Worthington, E. L. (1986). Religious counseling: A review of published empirical research. *Journal of Counseling & Development, 64,* 421-431.

Wuthnow, R. (2000). How religious groups promote forgiving: A national study. *Journal for the Scientific Study of Religion, 39,* 125-139.

Younggren, J. N. (1993). Ethical issues in religious psychotherapy. *Register Report, 19,* 7-8.

Zea, M. C., Mason, M., & Murguia, A. (2000). Psychotherapy with members of Latino/Latina churches and spiritual traditions. In P. S. Richards and A.E. Bergin (Eds.) *Handbook of psychotherapy and religious diversity* (pp. 397-420). Washington, D.C.: American Psychological Association.

# Chapter 5

# MULTICULTURAL COUNSELING THEORIES

*Sheilah M. Wilson*
Northern Arizona University Center for Excellence in Education
*Daya Singh Sandhu*
University of Louisville, KY

Multicultural counseling theories continue to evolve as effective counseling remains challenged in cross-cultural situations. It is puzzling that studies continue to reveal that most clients of color tend to under utilize traditional outpatient mental health services and that minority clients tend to terminate counseling at a rate of more than 50% after only one contact with a therapist (Sue & Sue, 1999). Additionally, an alarming percentage of culturally diverse older adults suffer with depression. Even though it is one of the most common and treatable mental disorders across all cultures, older adults do not seek counseling for assistance (Cavanaugh, 1997). Practitioners and the counseling profession are striving to find methods, concepts, and practices based upon applicable theories that address the inequities of treatment availability and promote success across all cultures and distinct populations.

In addition to the focus on multicultural counseling, there is extensive economic pressure from the managed health care environment for greater efficiency in treatment. With the American social preponderance for a "quick-fix," many researchers and practitioners seem to be searching for the single best approach that will be applicable to all clients from all cultures with any problem working with any counselor and in any multicultural context. In comparison, other mental health professionals believe that every therapeutic relationship is a cross-cultural experience and therefore, each situation requires careful and deliberate assessment as to its unique qualities and requirements for successful counseling outcomes (Ho, 1995; Sue, Ivey, & Pedersen, 1996; Sue & Sue, 1999).

This chapter is limited to discussing and reviewing theoretical thought having the potential to inform practice and research in multicultural counseling. Other chapters in this book focus on related topics, perspectives, and trends of social and cultural diversity that incorporate all the elements and 2001 standards of the Council for Accreditation of Counseling and Related Educational Programs (CACREP). The theories selected in this chapter are representative only and are not meant to be exhaustive of all models and approaches presently being offered in the multicultural literature.

# Theories, Models, and Perspectives - An Overview

Some of the dissension in integrating multicultural counseling thought today is in the use of definitions. For example, theorists argue and challenge what defines culture, racism, culture-bound, ethnocentrism, enculturation, acculturation, and alternation (Fuertes & Gretchen, 2001). It is even unclear as to how researchers are using the term theory. *Merriam Webster's Collegiate Dictionary Tenth Edition* (1994) defines theory with six distinct definitions and multiple subsets in each ranging from "a set of facts," "speculation," "plausible or scientifically acceptable general principle or body of principles," to "an unproved assumption" (p. 1223). Perhaps the most applicable definition for our purposes is "a body of theorems presenting a concise, systematic view of a subject", where a theorem is defined as "an idea accepted or proposed as a demonstrable truth often as a part of a general theory" (p. 1223). In addition, terms like theory, model, approach, and concepts appear to be used interchangeably throughout the multicultural literature. Without overly focusing on whether a proposed multicultural counseling approach is a theory, model, philosophy, or simply a meaningful link of related concepts, we can accept the fact that the value and goal of effective multicultural counseling includes an ongoing evolution of theoretical thought and development, research and empirical study, and practice and skills.

Much of the difficulty in comparing multicultural counseling theories is that most models assert different approaches, orientations, and structure; may be more or less comprehensive and explicit in assumptions and techniques; and are based on a diverse collection of assumptions. Fuertes and Gretchen (2001) present eight observations in analyzing selected emerging models that summarize the state of current thought and provide general themes and trends:

1. Emerging theories of multicultural counseling are at various stages of theoretical and empirical development.
2. There is more that one way to conceptualize and deliver multicultural counseling.
3. There is an emphasis on exploring multicultural constructs that inform all counseling.
4. Effective counselors understand the complex, idiographic nature of client identity and skills.
5. These theories supplement, rather than supplant, other counseling techniques and skills.
6. These theories focus on the sociopolitical and environmental context of clients' presenting complaints.
7. Counselor sociopolitical and racial/cultural self-awareness are important.
8. These theories provide mixed views of the "matching hypothesis" (p. 529).

Whereas some theories and models take a systemic orientation, others present a meta - theoretical approach. Still others incorporate a social constructionist orientation, a cross-disciplinary approach, a cognitive-behavioral model, a new paradigm, a synergistic foundation, a multicontextual model, a prescriptive structure, or an ecosystemic perspective.

Individual practitioner orientation and overall theoretical foundation, along with communication style and comfort will tend to direct counselors toward particular multicultural counseling models.

There is no single multicultural theory that is better than another, and each theory has value (Ivey, Ivey & Simek-Morgan, 1997). Each provides unique and important contributions to the literature. According to Thomas (2000), "no theory is designed to explain all aspects of development or all types of influence that affect development" (p. 12). Examining an array of human development theories can serve as an effective lens through which cultures can be viewed, thereby casting light on the difficulties people may experience in coping with cultures, either with their own or with other cultures they encounter. Multicultural theories based upon human development then can be designed and applied to explain or address (a) particular aspects of individuals' lives, (b) a particular category or group of people, and (c) a particular form of influence. Each theory identifies certain components of culture that affect the lives of individuals and their well-being.

## Theory versus Competence

Some respected professionals and researchers in the fields of counseling and psychotherapy see that multicultural theory may not be as important in cross-cultural therapeutic relationships as understanding limitations, barriers, and realistic cautions associated with applying specific philosophies, strategies, or treatments to individuals of various cultural groups. Sue and Sue (1999) propose a crisp, conceptual model identifying the processes (approaches, strategies, techniques, etc.) and goals (desired outcomes) of counseling that are to be examined for appropriateness (consistent) versus inappropriateness (antagonistic) after the counselor thoroughly evaluates those distinct factors forming the client's cultural identity and worldview. This schema can also be used for examining the appropriateness of alternative theoretical models of counseling and therapy for different individuals within a single culture. In these instances, it is the emphasis on professional multicultural competence that is the critical factor leading toward proficient treatment because the task of systematically determining the appropriateness of intervention approaches rests solely with the counselor.

Professionals "must take major responsibility to examine and evaluate the relevance of their particular theoretical framework with respect to the client's needs and values" (Sue & Sue, 1999, p. 220). Becoming a multiculturally competent mental health professional demands a constant and ongoing commitment to change in personal awareness, knowledge, beliefs, and skills (Fischer, Jome, & Atkinson, 1998; Ivey et al., 1997; D.W. Sue, Arredondo, & McDavis, 1992). D.W. Sue, Carter, Casas, Fouad, Ivey, Jensen, LaFromboise, Manese, Ponterotto, and Vasquez-Nuttall (1998) identify several vital variables that must be addressed. For instance, multiculturally competent counselors must be aware of the sociopolitical forces that have impacted the minority client. They must understand that culture, class, and language factors can act as barriers to effective, multicultural counseling, and should be able to point out how expertness, trustworthiness, and lack of similarity influence the minority client's receptivity to change and influence. In addition, multiculturally competent mental health professionals emphasize the importance of worldviews and cultural identity in the helping process, understand culture-bound and communication style differences among various racial groups, and become aware of their own racial biases and attitudes.

Sue and Sue (1999) take these notions a step further toward a focus of a subtler, yet powerful factor when they assert,

> There is an assumption that multicultural counseling/therapy simply requires the acquisition of knowledge, and that good intentions are all that is needed. This statement represents one of the major obstacles to self-awareness and dealing with one's own biases and prejudices. While we tend to view prejudice, discrimination, racism, and sexism as overt and intentional acts of unfairness and violence, it is the unintentional and covert forms of bias that may be the greater enemy because they are unseen and more pervasive (p. 30).

The well-intentioned therapist experiences himself or herself as moral, just, fair-minded, and decent. Thus, it is difficult to realize if what is said or done in the course of counseling may cause harm to their minority clients.

Sue and Sue (1999) contend that "multicultural helping cannot be approached through any one theory of counseling based upon the fact that theories of counseling are composed of philosophical assumptions regarding the nature of man and a theory of personality" (p. 39). Because these characteristics are highly culture-bound, what constitutes the healthy and unhealthy personality is debatable and varies from culture to culture, class to class. Adherence to defined and rigid techniques and strategies espoused by a particular theory may be an imposition to minority clients without basing therapeutic decisions on clients' needs and values. "Rather than stretching the client to fit the dimensions of a single theory, practitioners must make their theory and practice fit the unique needs of the client" (Corey, 2001, p. 460). Therapists who hope to be effective with a wide range of problems and with different client populations must be flexible, versatile, and familiar with the skills, competencies, and knowledge base of multiple theories (Ivey et al., 1997).

## CONDITIONS FOR SUCCESSFUL CROSS-CULTURAL COUNSELING

### Common Factors among Multiple Theories

Thomas (2000) describes the continuing professional counseling community debate over the issue of whether "(a) there are universal principles and techniques of counseling equally suitable for all cultures (common factors theory) or (b) distinct principles and techniques designed for each culture in order to be effective (culture specific theory)" (p. 25). Fischer et al. (1998) conducted a detailed analysis of multicultural counseling theories and empirical studies. They concluded that there are, indeed, general principles or factors that apply across all counseling styles and all cultures, but successfully applying the principles requires considerable understanding of the culture of each client. "In general, common factors theorists propose that the curative properties of a given psychotherapy lie not in its theoretically unique components. . . but in components common to all psychotherapies" (Fischer et al., 1998, p. 529).

The four common factors identified by Fischer et al. (1998) concern (a) the intellectual and emotional relationship between client and counselor, (b) the extent to which client and counselor share a common worldview, (c) the degree to which the client expects positive change to result from counseling, and (d) the nature of rituals or interventions that counseling provides.

These aspects form a sequence in which each successive factor builds on the previous ones. Because there is and has been so much tension between generic and culture-specific approaches to counseling, a common factors framework can be used as a unifying interpretative tool to assist the student and practitioner in managing, organizing, and making sense of the extensive, sometimes overwhelming amount of multicultural counseling literature. Fischer et al. (1998) believe that common factors may be used to frame (not to supplant) many of the seemingly disjointed clinical guidelines and systematic models that have appeared in the multicultural and counseling psychology literature.

Whereas the simplicity of a common factors approach may appear to minimize or devalue the inherent complexity of cultures and people, it is offered as an effective structural tool to integrate knowledge at a conceptual level across contributions to the clinical and empirical literature. Indeed, by the nature of its design from a big-picture perspective, it requires acquisition of a great deal of specific information, in this case, culturally specific knowledge, skills, and techniques.

The most fundamental therapeutic condition is a positive healing relationship in which the client feels comfortable, safe, understood, and trusting of the counselor. Counselor characteristics that encourage such a relationship include warmth, genuineness, and empathy. It is not necessary for the counselor to subscribe to a client's worldview in the sense of believing that the client's conception of reality is accurate; what is important is that the counselor understands and respects the client's beliefs. Similarly, through effective development of the first two factors, expectations for success in therapy may be raised by working to become a credible resource for help and assistance to the client. For example, cultural considerations may lead the counselor to appropriately conduct therapy outside the confines of the "50-minute hour," with the client's extended family, or within the client's home. The first three factors "set the stage for client and counselor to engage successfully in the application of a relevant intervention" (Fischer et al., 1998, p. 556). The common factors framework allows for appropriate treatment strategies and techniques to be employed in the context of the interdependence of an established and shared worldview, good relationship, and positive client expectation for change. A variety of excellent books and journal articles addressing culturally related specific interventions are widely available and continue to be written.

Fischer et al. (1998) caution that regardless of worldviews and whether the counselor's racial or ethnic background is similar to the client's, counselors will need to reflect on the client's cultural affiliation, orientation, and experience and ask themselves throughout the counseling process:

> What do I know or need to know about this individual, about his or her culture(s), and about people in general that will likely help me (a) to develop a good therapeutic relationship with him or her; (b) to discover or construct with the client a shared worldview or plausible rationale for distress; (c) to create an environment in which the client's expectations will be raised; and (d) to plan a healing procedure in which my client(s) and I both have confidence (p. 542)?

Again, no single theory can be all-inclusive to every counseling situation. The authors conclude with several caveats on the limitations of a common factors perspective. To begin with, they explain, "a general goal of working within the client's current belief system is far from consensual" (Fischer et al., 1998, p. 577). Helping clients consider the realities of oppression by examining political, historical, and social factors which impact their psychological functioning may be helpful as well. Practitioners can also encourage clients toward greater awareness of their capacities to transform those realities. Seeking the delicate balance of accepting and affirming the client's worldview without condoning destructive behavior or relinquishing clinical responsibility is a constant practical and ethical challenge for counselors.

Similarly, therapists are advised to remain ethically astute to issues that arise in an influence process such as counseling. In an attempt to develop shared worldviews, counselors are cautioned when it comes to bending, directing, or changing the client's beliefs, attitudes, values, or cultural patterns toward therapeutic ends. It is recommended that the greater modification come from the therapist.

Finally, Fischer et al. (1998) emphasize, "counseling psychologists should be aware that acquisition of cultural knowledge is an ongoing process" (p. 578). As always, counselors need to consider seeking consultation and supervision from knowledgeable colleagues whenever necessary.

## Bridges to Traditional Theories and Therapies

Many practitioners believe that long-standing, traditional theories currently implemented can and need to be augmented to incorporate multicultural applicability (Corey, 2001). There is a large contribution in the literature of multiculturalism that redefines traditional theories into cross-cultural practice. *Counseling and Psychotherapy, A Multicultural Perspective* (1997) by Ivey et al. incorporates the writings and studies of many scientist-practitioners advancing the field of cross-cultural efficacy, and it is an excellent source for studying and understanding how traditional theories can be evolved to effectively apply to multicultural therapeutic counseling. Ivey et al. (1997), with an emphasis on worldview and multiple perspectives with cultural sensitivity, present five general principles that can help guide the adaptation of traditional psychotherapeutic theories and practices to issues of diversity:

1. The general principles of Rogerian respect and empathy for the client seem to hold broadly across cultural groups while considering the balance of a more directive approach versus the contribution of silence.
2. It is important to be willing to move out of the office and work in the community, both professionally and personally.
3. Concrete approaches with an action orientation often seem to be accepted better than abstract talk.
4. Family approaches are often suitable, recognizing the value, influence, and importance of the family in diverse cultures. Social context considerations need to be extended to traditional therapies.
5. Counselors must continually educate themselves on new thinking about traditional practices as well as about multicultural counseling and therapy.

Those theories that focus on traditional orientations can be best applied to multicultural counseling situations through conscious and intentional consideration of differences among cultures. To this end, some professionals in the field view multicultural counseling theory as the "fourth force" (Ivey et al., 1997; Pedersen, 1990). Theories categorized in this group approach the issues of multicultural counseling from different perspectives not unlike the varied orientations of psychological thought provided us from the "first three forces" respectively known as Psychodynamic, Existential-Humanistic, and Cognitive-Behavioral theories. "Counseling psychologists need not discard all conventional approaches to counseling but must apply what they know in a culturally sensitive way" (Fischer et al., 1998, p. 551).

# CULTURAL DIVERSE PERSPECTIVES FROM HUMAN DEVELOPMENT THEORIES

## An Example Combining Eastern and Western Frameworks

Tamase's (1991) theory of Introspective Developmental Counseling (IDC) has been generated from a multicultural framework by integrating the Japanese Naikan therapy, Erikson's (1963) life-span theory and developmental counseling and therapy theory (DCT, Ivey et al., 1997). This theory (IDC) focuses on understanding how life histories of clients impact their present experiences and life situations.

Naikan therapy is aimed at assisting clients to discover meaning in their lives and to repair damaged relationships with others (Reynolds, 1990). This is a focus on the self in relation to others and involves alternating sessions of silent meditation on how the individual depends on others throughout the life span with debriefing discussions with the therapist. Naikan therapy usually is conducted in residential week-long sessions in which clients review their experiences of the past. Generally speaking in this therapy, clients focus on three main things: what they have done for others, what others have done for them, and what difficulties or problems clients might have caused others. Naiken Therapy is deeply rooted in Buddhist practices of intensive reflections on the past behaviors (Walsh, 1995).

One of the most interesting realizations in examining counseling theory that is non-Western in thought is that much of what we as Westerners consider foundational convention in psychology is virtually antithetical to Naikan. For example, humanistic and psychodynamic self-examination would be considered selfish from the Naikan perspective, and assertiveness training is not an intervention option under any circumstance.

## Examples of Western Developmental Theories

Thomas (2000) offers 25 theories selected from hundreds to illustrate "the value of using theories of development as lenses through which to interpret people's personal-social problems and to generate implications for counseling such individuals" (p. 30). Each theory presents an alternative vantage point through which to view a particular aspect of development, cultural diversity, cross-cultural difficulties, and counseling activities. The theories are categorized in four groups (sense of self or identity, family influences, social relations, and various personal characteristics that cause people to be regarded as extraordinary) that represent aspects of development that are often linked to the problems that bring clients to counseling. The counseling model Thomas (2000) uses in discussing each theory is founded on three propositions:

> (a) that the four factors proposed by Fisher, Jome, and Atkinson (1998) apply in all multicultural counseling situations, (b) that it is important for counselors to recognize how the cultural features implied in the four factors contribute to successful counseling sessions, and (c) that a knowledge of theories of human development can make a positive contribution to those sessions (p. 28).

Each theory draws attention to a particular facet of individuals' lives and identifies factors that are assumed to determine why development in the selected facet of life occurs as it does. These factors are causal variables whose interactions account for developmental outcomes. Whenever the outcomes are amiss, indicating that development has gone awry, the theory's causal factors can be analyzed to identify which of them may have been responsible for the undesired results and why. A theory's causal factors often include such cultural components as ideals, moral values, beliefs about reality, standards of behavior, types of knowledge, and conceptions of self. Treatment can then focus on altering those conditions in ways that foster positive development.

Thomas (2000) refers to counseling and allied treatments, defining the former as a process of providing aid or guidance through the use of language, including both verbal and nonverbal expressions; and the latter term refers to non-language activities designed to improve people's ability to achieve their goals and to adjust constructively to their social and physical settings. Allied treatments may include physical exercise, relaxation practices, meditation routines, medicines, dietary supplements, surgery, and a change of environments.

Good adjustment, normal development, reasonable progress, and continual improvement are terms to signify that a person's life is advancing satisfactorily. The way counselors specify the meaning of proper growth influences their diagnoses of clients' problems and affects the therapists' decisions about what the counseling process can successfully include. Thomas (2000) stresses the importance of defining desirable development especially in the multicultural counseling milieu and offers the following definition:

> People's development is satisfactory when: (1) they feel they are fulfilling their needs at least moderately well, (2) their behavior does not unduly encroach on others' rights and opportunities, (3) they carry out the responsibilities that are considered reasonable for people of their ability (physical and mental) and their social environment, and (4) their personal characteristics do not cause other people to treat them in ways that harm them physically, psychologically, or socially or that deny them opportunities (available to their peers of the same age and gender) to pursue their ambitions (p. 13-14).

Thomas (2000) identifies the following components used as the foundational multicultural model in discussing the various developmental theories selected:

1.  Aspects of culture can influence people's well-being. Differences among cultures, and differences between cultural expectations and an individual's needs, are significant causes of people's problems. Among the most prominent characteristics that contribute to people's personal-social problems are multiple cultural

membership, cultural homogeneity, cultural compatibility, cultural components (similarities and differences), salience and power, strength of commitment, and cultural change.

2.  Knowledge of theories of human development can serve as lenses for viewing cultures and thereby cast light on the difficulties people may experience in coping with cultures - either with their own culture or with other cultures they encounter.

3.  Helping people to alleviate their problems is accomplished through counseling and allied treatments. Helping people manage their personal-social problems often involves some combination of counseling and allied treatments.

4.  The way counselors define desired development and specify the meaning of proper growth influences their diagnoses of clients' problems and affects the therapists' decisions about what the counseling process can successfully include.

5.  Functions and procedures that counseling and allied treatments perform can help people solve problems related to cultural conditions. These functions include but are not limited to (a) achieving emotional catharsis, (b) profiting from a catalytic setting, (c) recognizing the frequency of one's problem, (d) learning from other's experiences, (e) confronting and analyzing reality, (f) revealing hidden personality contents, (g) enduring difficult circumstances, (h) gaining hope and assurance, (i) recognizing and esteeming one's virtues, (j) acquiring information, (k) altering reciprocal relations, (l) constructively reliving the past, (m) rearranging consequences to produce new habits, (n) developing skills, (o) revising values, (p) creating goals, (q) selecting constructive models, (r) adopting others' viewpoints, (s) integrating one's personality, (t) changing social environments, and (u) altering body chemistry.

6.  The four common factors (Fischer et al., 1998) for successful cross-cultural counseling underlying considerable understanding of the culture of each client are (1) the intellectual and emotional relationship between client and counselor (warmth, genuineness, and empathy), (2) the extent to which the client and counselor come to share (understand with respect) a common worldview (not necessarily subscribe to the same worldview), (3) the degree to which the client expects positive change to result from counseling, and (4) the nature of interventions that counseling provides (culturally compatible).

Thomas (2000) presents four propositions about relationships among the theories, cultures, and counseling:

1.  Some theories offer more direct guidance for counseling than do others.

2.  Some theories are more distinctly applicable to multicultural counseling than others.

3.  Different counseling styles or practices are implied by different theories, so that all human development models imply no single style of counseling.

4.  A client's presenting problem calls for different counseling methods and functions when viewed from the perspectives of different human development theories.

# TWO DIVERGENT APPROACHES TO
# MULTICULTURAL COUNSELING THEORIES

Whereas Fischer et al. (1998) present a framework designed to integrate and support both the etic (culturally universal) and emic (culturally specific) approaches to multicultural counseling theories, it is worthwhile to examine various models that fall into each of the two categories. To better understand and appreciate the direction of multicultural counseling it is important to become familiar with the prominent and varied approaches currently available for study and application.

## Generic Cultural Counseling Theories

Fuertes and Gretchen (2001) provide an analysis of nine emergent theories (those published within the past seven years) by evaluating each theory based upon comprehensiveness as a counseling model, operationalization for testing, and operationalization for clinical utility. Whereas these theories are recognized as having great potential to inform research and practice in multicultural counseling, various criticisms and shortcomings have been delineated for each emergent theory. Continued research and empirical studies will be needed to refine or dismiss the validity or applicability to the context for which each theory has been defined.

Due to space limitations, it is difficult to describe each theory of multicultural counseling here. However, a brief introduction to some of these evolving theories follows.

### Theory of Multicultural Counseling
Sue, Ivey, and Pedersen (1996) introduced this theory to stress differences in Western and non-western theories as they represent different worldviews. They also explain how cultural differences influence the counseling processes. Emphasis is also placed on the effects of various sociopolitical realities such as sexism and racism.

### Internalized Culture
The central theme of this theory is *internalized culture.* Ho (1995), the proponent of this theory, emphasizes the role of this internalized culture plays in the formation of clients' worldviews. To become effective, a counselor must be able to transcend their own cultural egocentrism. Self-understanding is considered crucial in multicultural training (Fuertes & Gretchen, 2001).

### Ramirez' (1999) Multicultural Model of Psychotherapy
We particularly liked Ramirez' model as it is based on cognitive–behavioral approaches to develop much needed flexibility in clients to adjust to diverse environments. Ramirez also encourages clients to become change agents to develop and promote a multicultural environment that is responsive to the special needs of the diverse individuals and populations.

These are just a few examples to demonstrate how new multicultural theories are evolving. These multicultural approaches represent a clear departure from the traditional Eurocentric approaches to counseling and psychotherapy. There appear to be many emerging roads to counseling goals and client goals. However, it remains to be seen whether or not these new roads will merge at some theoretical juncture. The field of multicultural counseling theoretical development remains a very complex area in the ongoing evolution of psychological thought and practice.

## Specific Cultural Counseling Theories

Rogers (1996) presents over three-dozen papers addressing multicultural theory through experiential perspectives foundationally supporting the need for "multiple theories emerging from diverse perspectives in a variety of styles" (Hooks, 1996, p. 58). The traditional concept of theory as a view, construction, or description of reality is purposefully ignored to present a rich variety of personal experiences, ideas, and perceptions. This approach may well constitute original, fresh models of appreciation for authentic thinking and understanding from culturally explicit writers, educators, scholars, psychologists, and scientists. Topics addressed that offer intense, conscious raising and thought-provoking positions cutting across political-socio-economic strata set on an historical backdrop include the following: Feminism, Black feminist thought, Afrocentric Metatheory, Queer theory, Native American response to "white shamanism," redefining "taking control" for rape victims, mathematics as cultural imperialism, survival in response to the matrix of domination, cultural equity and integrity, marginalization, gender, biology, sexuality, battered women, heterosexual coercion, sexuality as socially constructed, institutionalized violence, the culture of color, wives and mothers of color - the "double-bind situation," politics of "family values," economics of women working in the home, American Indian lesbians, Asian American heritage, dualistic/hierarchical thinking, Chicana feminist discourse, and masculinity politics.

## CONCLUSION

The need for multicultural counseling can be expected to increase in the 21st century as implied by several demographic trends of recent decades (Sue & Sue, 1999). The latter half of the 20th century witnessed an accelerating rate of migration throughout the world. As a result, many societies have become increasingly multicultural, obliged to entertain an ever-widening variety of peoples (Thomas, 2000). At the same time, previously silent ethnic, religious, feminist, and sexual-oriented groups within societies have acquired expanding organizational and social-action skills equipping them to challenge the hegemony of groups that traditionally wielded political control and enjoyed cultural dominance without consequence. With rapid population growth accelerated among many groups of color in countries around the world, increased conflicts among inhabitants of crowded regions have quickened the rate of migration. Political refugees and poverty-stricken individuals are motivated to flee from their homelands seeking opportunity and the hope of a better life for themselves and their families. "The increase in multicultural interactions accompanying such trends has resulted in a growing quantity of individuals seeking counseling in order to cope with the problems generated by their cross-cultural encounters" (Thomas, 2000, p. 214).

# REFERENCES

American Counseling Association, Standards for community counseling programs. [On-line]. Available*: http://www.counseling.org/cacrep/2001standards700.html.*

Cavanaugh, J.C. (1997). *Adult development and aging* (3rd ed.). Pacific Grove, CA: Brooks/Cole.

Corey, G. (2001). *Theory and practice of counseling and psychotherapy* (6th ed.). Belmont, CA: Wadsworth/Thomason.

Erikson, E. (1963). *Childhood and society* (2nd ed.). New York: Norton.

Fischer, A.R., Jome, L.M., & Atkinson, D.R. (1998). Reconceptualizing multicultural counseling: Universal healing conditions in a culturally specific context. *The Counseling Psychologist, 26*(4), 525-588.

Fuertes, J.N., & Gretchen, D. (2001). Emerging theories of multicultural counseling. In J. G. Ponterotto, J.M. Casas, L.A. Suzuki, and C.M. Alexander (Eds.), *Handbook of multicultural counseling* (2nd ed.) (pp. 509-541). Thousand Oaks: CA: Sage.

Ho, D.Y.E. (1995). Internalized culture, culturo-centrism, and transcendence. *The Counseling Psychologist, 23*(1), 4-24.

Hooks, B. (1996). Feminist theory: A radical agenda. In M.F. Rogers (Ed.), *Multicultural experiences, multicultural theories* (pp. 56-61). New York: McGraw-Hill.

Ivey, A.E., Ivey, M.B., & Simek-Morgan, L. (1997). *Counseling and psychotherapy: A multicultural perspective* (4th ed.). Boston: Allyn and Bacon.

Merriam Webster's Collegiate Dictionary (10th ed.). (1994). *Merriam Webster's Collegiate Dictionary*. Springfield, MA: Author.

Pedersen, P. (1990).The multicultural perspective as a fourth force in counseling. *Journal of Mental Health Counseling, 12* (1), 93-95.

Ramirez, M., III (1999). *Multicultural psychotherapy: An approach to individual and cultural differences* (2nd ed.). Boston, MA: Allyn & Bacon.

Reynolds, D. (1990). Morita and Naiken therapies--- Similarities. *Journal of Morita Therapy,1,* 159-163.

Rogers, M.F. (Ed.). (1996). *Multicultural experiences, multicultural theories*. New York: McGraw-Hill.

Sue, D.W., Arredondo, P., & McDavis, R.J. (1992). Multicultural counseling competencies and standards: A call to the profession. *Journal of Counseling and Development, 70*(4), 477-486.

Sue, D.W., Carter, R.T., Casas, J.M., Fouad, N.A., Ivey, A.E., Jensen, M., LaFromboise, T., Manese, J.E., Ponterotto, J.G., & Vasquez-Nuttall, E. (1998). *Multicultural counseling competencies: Individual and organizational development*. Thousand Oaks, CA: Sage.

Sue, D.W., Ivey, A.E., & Pedersen, P.B. (Eds.). (1996). *A theory of multicultural counseling and therapy*. Pacific Grove, CA: Brooks/Cole.

Sue, D.W. & Sue, D. (1999). *Counseling the culturally different: Theory and practice* (3rd ed.). New York: John Wiley & Sons.

Tamase, K (1991, April). *The effects of introspective-developmental counseling*. Paper presented at the American Counseling Association and Development, Reno, NV.

Thomas, R.M. (2000). *Multicultural counseling and human development theories: 25 theoretical perspectives*. Springfield, IL: Charles C. Thomas.

Walsh, R. (1995). Asian psychotherapies. In R.J. Corsini and D. Wedding (Eds.), *Current psychotherapies* (5$^{th}$ ed.). Itasca, IL: F.E. Peacock.

*Chapter 6*

# COUNSELING ETHNICALLY DIVERSE FAMILIES

*Eugenie Joan Looby*
*Tammy Webb*
Mississippi State University

## INTRODUCTION

For many ethnic groups, the most revered institution in their lives is the family, possessing its own set of unique cultural values, beliefs, mores, and socialization practices, which may be different from those of the dominant culture. These groups function within an interdependent, extended, family structure that helps to reinforce their collective selfhood and identity and protects them from a seemingly hostile world. In order to provide effective family counseling, it is important for practitioners to understand ethnically diverse families in their sociocultural context, the systems that impact their functioning and development, their world views and value orientations, and the culture-bound nature of family counseling. This chapter's focus is on the four, largest, non-White racial-ethnic groups in the United States: African Americans, Hispanic Americans, Asian/Pacific Islander Americans, and Native American Indians/Eskimos/Aleuts. It delineates information on demographic characteristics, sociocultural issues, cultural values, and family structure of these groups. The chapter also enumerates guidelines for facilitating family therapy, delineates family therapy models that have utility for these populations, and provides practice implications.

## ETHNICALLY DIVERSE POPULATIONS: DEMOGRAPHICS, VALUES, AND FAMILY STRUCTURE

This section provides information on ethnic group population characteristics, sociocultural issues and values, and variant family configurations of the four ethnic groups discussed. Hopefully, what will be gleaned is an understanding of factors that affect ethnically diverse families and how these factors impact the family therapy process.

## African American Demographic Characteristics

African Americans are bound together by ancestral heritage and by their experiences with slavery, racism, discrimination, and oppression (Atkinson, Morten & Sue, 1998; Fleming, 1992). African Americans comprise the largest non-White racial-ethnic group in the United States, constituting an estimated 12.8% of the total population (U.S. Census Bureau, 2001). However, recent estimates (i.e., The Learning Network, 2001) suggest that the Hispanic American group may be larger. African Americans as a racial group represent diverse ethnic and cultural heritages, including but not limited to Spanish-speaking populations from Cuba, Puerto Rico and Panama, groups from the Caribbean Islands and Northern Europe, Native Americans, immigrants from Africa, ancestors (freed Blacks) of African slaves who were brought to this country involuntarily, and free Blacks (Axelson, 1999; Dana, 1993; Lee, 1999; Ponterotto & Casas, 1991; Wehrly, 1991). Although most of the research has been done on African Americans who trace their ancestral roots to slavery, practitioners should not overlook individual differences. Whereas skin color may readily identify African Americans, many prefer to be recognized by their country of birth.

According to the U.S. Census Bureau (2001), African Americans are a young ethnic group, with a median age of 30.4 years. Most African Americans reside in the South, with about 10% living in the West, and 37% between the Midwest and Northeast (U.S. Department of Commerce, 1997). Domiciles include metropolitan, suburban, and rural areas. Major cities such as Atlanta, Baltimore, Birmingham, Detroit, Memphis, New Orleans, Newark, and Washington claim more than 50% African American populations (O'Hare, Pollard, Mann, & Kent, 1991). Racism, discrimination, prejudice, poverty, and little access to opportunities have been cited as contributing to some of the conditions in which African Americans find themselves (Lee, 1999; Sue & Sue, 1999). These include high birth, teenage pregnancy, mortality, unemployment, poverty, drug addiction, homicide, and incarceration rates; poor access to health care; lack of suitable male role models; lags in occupational status and opportunities, income levels, and educational attainment; and a large underclass with little hope for an improved life (Aponte & Crouch, 2000; Axelson, 1999; De Vita, 1996; Hoyt, 1989; O' Hare & Felt, 1991; Sue & Sue, 1999; U.S. Census Bureau, 1996b, 1996b).

Ford (1997) and Sue and Sue (1999), have expressed concern that much of the available literature on African Americans is derived from the underclass and not from other segments of the African American population. A substantial number of African Americans have been assimilated into the middle and upper classes. Sue and Sue (1999) report that more than 1/3 of African Americans constitutes the middle class. Further, Aponte and Crouch (2000), point out that the median income for African American families jumped by 4.3% from 1996-1997. Edwards and Polite (1992) indicate that between 1970-1989, the numbers of Blacks who had annual incomes more than $50.000 increased by 182%. Although there exists much diversity among African Americans, research continues to perpetuate misleading images suggesting a homogeneity which does not exist (Ford, 1997).

## African American Cultural Values

The great variation among African Americans makes it difficult to present descriptors applicable to all members. Thus, this section will present general characteristics most frequently cited in the literature (Boyd-Franklin, 1989; Congress, 1997; Dana, 1993; Gibbs, 1980; Lee, 1999; McAdoo, 1999; Sue & Sue, 1999; Taylor, Jackson, & Chatters, 1997; White & Parham, 1990 ). They include the following: (a) Deep abiding spirituality consisting of practice dimensions and faith in a superior power who will "solve all problems"(Dana, 1993, p. 40); (b) strong kinship bonds, and family as a referent point for mutual support and survival; (c) cooperation, interdependence, harmonious interpersonal relationships, and consideration for the welfare of others; (d) present time orientation; (e) animated emotional expression; (f) Afro-centric perception of the world emphasizing validating self in regard to others (Asante, 1987; Cheatham, 1990); (g) a holistic focus on harmony with self, others, nature, the spirit world, and the universe; (h) strong work ethic, occupational, and achievement orientation; and (i) flexibility of roles and adaptability to changing life circumstances.

## African American Families

Variations in African American family functioning are often labeled as deficits, and the assessment, reaction, and evaluation of African American families are outgrowths of the dominant culture's nuclear family orientation. Whereas changing social and population trends have expanded the traditional definition of the family, knowledge about African American families is derived from families of lower socioeconomic status. This gap in the literature ignores growing numbers of African American families who are economically and socially successful, who reside in "healthy" family systems, who participate in the economic, social, and educational successes enjoyed by the dominant culture, that is, families who have achieved the American dream. Middle class African American families are not immune from prejudice, discrimination and racism; however, they may possess the resources necessary to minimize the quality and quantity of problems experienced, and the type and extent of the problems may be different (Ford, 1997). Practitioners should be aware of the uniqueness and heterogeneity of African American families. Structurally, African American families model many alternate types of domestic arrangements that have been adopted "in the face of the demographic, economic, political, and social of Black life in America" (Sudarkasa, 1999, p. 196).

The perception, however, that an increasing number of African American families are female headed is reinforced by data which indicate the following: more than 55% of African American families consist of a single parent; over 64% of African American children reside in households with one parent--usually the mother; out of wedlock births represent two out of three first births to African American women under 35; about 42% of African American females have never married; African American single parent families, which number approximately 2.4 million, have surpassed two parent families, which number approximately 1.8 million; close to 70% of lower- class African American families are female headed; and unmarried African American females, including many teenagers, account for approximately 60% of births (Ingrassia, 1993; Sue & Sue, 1999; U.S. Census Bureau, 1992a, 1992b; U.S. Department of Commerce, 1997). Jayakody and Chatters (1997), reiterate that single parenthood among African American females is not a novel phenomenon. For example, at the beginning of the 20th Century, African Americans were three times more likely than Whites to live in a singe parent family, and more African American, single-mother families resided in extended families than did White single mothers (Morgan, McDaniel, Miller, & Preston, 1993).

What do these data portend for African American families? The social science literature is replete with disturbing, sometimes misleading portrayals of single parent families. These families are often depicted as economically unstable, living in poverty, pathological, dysfunctional, unhealthy, and lacking in role models. Offspring of these arrangements are said to be less likely to graduate, have lower levels of educational attainment, are less successful in adulthood, experience higher rates of teenage and single motherhood, participate in the labor force infrequently, and engage in delinquent and criminal behaviors (McLanahan & Casper, 1995). African American single mothers unfortunately comprise a large segment of this population. Whereas some experience the harsh economic and social realities that are a consequence of these circumstances; one is led to believe the homogeneity of these conditions, thereby ignoring within group variability. Single parent families have always been an acceptable form of organization in the African American community, and different unique dynamics underlie the formation and functioning of these households. Households may be headed by single-never married women, young teenage mothers, widows, women separated from their husbands, divorced women, mature women raising children by themselves and other complex configurations (Jayakody & Chatters, 1997). Consequently, it is critical to explore additional factors that may provide a more comprehensive understanding of the functional nature of single parent, African American families.

Often underemphasized is the resiliency and strength of African American families. Recent research (e.g., Connell, Spencer, & Aber, 1994; Trusty, in press; Trusty & Harris, 1999) points toward a high level of resilience in African American families and young people. This suggests that the traditional theoretical deficiency view of African Americans is not accurate. As a consequence of slavery, the African American family has a strong legacy of well-defined, close, kinship bonds, where authority and responsibility have been clearly delegated and the group--rather than the individual--remains paramount. In African American families, there exists an ethos of collective responsibility where children belong to and are raised by extended, elastic, kinship networks that include parents, uncles, aunts, cousins, grandparents, siblings, and other individuals who are not blood relatives, but maintain significant relationships with the family. This extended family is charged with the rearing of the children. This task may include teaching appropriate values, survival skills, and role responsibilities, providing economic, social, and emotional support and protection from what is viewed as a cruel world, and transmitting appropriate cultural values and traditions to posterity.

Many alternate living arrangements and fluidity of household boundaries exist, with relatives informally adopting children whose parents cannot take care of them, grandparents raising their grandchildren, and multigenerational households which arise as a consequence of economic conditions (Lee, 1999; Lum, 1992). Family members may live in close proximity to each other; children born out of wedlock are not shunned; there exist flexible, interchangeable, egalitarian gender roles and relationships; strong work, achievement, and religious orientations are evident, and there is less of a tendency to blame the family as a cause of problems (Billingsley, 1992; Boyd-Franklin, 1989; Hines & Boyd-Franklin, 1996; Lee, 1999; Taylor, Jackson, & Chatters, 1997).

According to Lum (1992), the mother-child-sibling relationship is considered the most important in the family. The mother is "often considered the family's strength and emotional center, acting as a stabilizing influence if the father does not have the level of education or employment needed to protect or provide for the family" (Pinderhughes, 1982, as cited in Lee, 1999, p. 78). Lee (1999) contended that African American men may be recognized as heads of households depending on their level of involvement and ability to provide for the family financially. Wilson (1986) claimed that African American mothers socialize their daughters to be strong, economically independent, responsible (especially to family), and accountable for their actions. Traits ascribed to African American women such as fortitude, inner strength, resiliency, ability to cope with adversity, and the survival instinct may be a consequence of the inculcation of such values. The reality is that absentee African American fathers are common, that many African American females are single parents, and that socialization practices help prepare African American women to adopt dual parental roles, something which they have historically done.

Homogeneous African American families do not exist. Some African American families identify with the values of the dominant culture; others do not maintain close relationships with their families; and others remain ensconced in their families, using them as referent points for social, economic, financial, and emotional support. Suffice to say that family counselors should be aware that there are almost as many variations among African American families as there are among African American individuals

## Hispanic American Demographic Characteristics

The term *Hispanic* is the official, sanctioned designation by the federal government to encompass individuals of Spanish ancestry living in the United States (U.S. Census Bureau, 1990b). The term is not embraced by all Hispanic groups, many of whom prefer to identify themselves by their birthplace. *Chicano, Mexican American, Mexican, Mexicano, Spanish American, Tejano, Puerto Riqueno, Newyorican, La Raza,* and *Latino*, are additional descriptors used by Hispanic Americans (Dana, 1993; Lee, 1999; Sue & Sue, 1999). The Hispanic American population in the United States originated from a variety of ethnic groups who arrived in this country at different periods of time. The Hispanic population is difficult to estimate due to the undocumented status of many Hispanic Americans. According to the U.S. Census Bureau (2001), they are the second largest group in the U.S.; however some recent estimates (i.e., The Learning Network, 2001) suggest that Hispanics may now outnumber African Americans. The U.S. Census Bureau (2001) estimated that Hispanics comprised 11.9% of the nation's population in the year 2000. As indicated by del Pinal and Singer (1997), Hispanics of Mexican ancestry represent more than 61% of the Hispanic population, Puerto Ricans (12.1%), Central and South Americans (10.7%), Cubans (4.8 %), and the remaining 12% from other Spanish speaking countries. Recent estimates (i.e., The Learning Network, 2001) suggest that Central and South Americans have replaced Puerto Ricans as the second largest Hispanic Group in the U.S. Close to 85% of Hispanics are concentrated in nine states: California, New York, Texas, Florida, Illinois, New Jersey, Arizona, New Mexico, and Colorado (del Pinal & Singer, 1997).

The Hispanic American population is a young one with a median age of 26.6 (U.S. Census Bureau, 2001). They have high birth rates, live in large, extended households, intermarry, and have very low divorce rates although there has been a recent increase in female headed households (Axelson, 1999; Sue & Sue, 1999; U.S. Census Bureau, 1996b).

Although gains have been made in occupational status, income, and education, Hispanic Americans still lag behind Whites and other ethnic groups in these areas (De Vita, 1996; O'Hare & Felt, 1991). The Hispanic American population is a diverse group in regard to factors such as ethnicity, racial and cultural backgrounds, income, social status, levels of acculturation, education, experiences with the dominant culture, immigration history, values, and language facility.

The largest Hispanic group, Mexican Americans, reside mostly in California and Texas (Sue & Sue, 1999). They are of Mestizo (Aztec Indian and Southern European) ancestry (Avila & Avila, 1995). Mexican Americans identify strongly with their cultural heritage and see little necessity in learning English. Many are documented and undocumented workers who represent a source of cheap labor, many times working as migrant farmers, in sweat shops, in service and blue collar jobs, and in occupations which are hazardous and provide little or no benefits (Dana, 1993; Sue & Sue, 1999). They are readily exploited and treated inhumanely. Economic stability is variable, and many live below the poverty level. Poor educational preparation and limited English facility in this group are evidenced by high illiteracy, school dropout, and poor college completion rates (Dana, 1993; Sue & Sue, 1999).

Puerto Ricans represent the second largest Hispanic American population, with most residing in the Northeastern areas of the country, especially in New York. Puerto Ricans trace their ancestry to North American Indians, African Americans, Spanish Explorers, and many other ethnic groups (Baruth & Manning, 1999; Dana, 1993; Sue & Sue, 1999). Puerto Rican culture combines European, African, Taino Indian, Spanish, and American influences. Puerto Ricans hold United States citizenship, but maintain strong allegiance to their culture including its language, religious and other customs, food, and reverence for family. Many Puerto Ricans come to the mainland with hopes of improving their economic base and eventually returning home. However, most remain clustered into secondary, unskilled, seasonal, and clerical occupations. Although statistics indicate more Puerto Ricans than Mexican Americans complete high school and college, this population continues to evidence high school dropout and employment rates, and poor economic living conditions ( Lee, 1999; Sue & Sue, 1999; Zapata, 1995).

Cubans represent the third largest Hispanic American population in the United States, with most residing in South Florida. The majority of Cubans are listed as White and of Spanish descent, but other representations include Black, Mulatto, Native American and other mixed ancestry (Axelson, 1999). Cuban migration history began shortly after the 1959 Cuban revolution (Dana, 1993). According to Dana (1993, p.68), "Many of the Cubans who arrived soon after the 1959 revolution were older, well educated, relatively affluent members of ruling or middle class. They expected to return to Cuba after the demise of the Castro government." The second migratory wave occurred in the 1980s and brought semiskilled and skilled workers, prison inmates, individuals with mental illnesses, and other "undesirables" that Castro wanted to purge from Cuba (Axelson, 1999). In aggregate, Cubans possess the most economic wealth of any Hispanic American group, and in Miami they have been able to establish thriving careers in business, banking, textiles, food, cigars, and trade (Dana, 1993; Zapata, 1995). Additionally, Cubans have exemplary graduation rates both from high school and college, few families meet the poverty criteria, and those born in this country have become highly acculturated (Lee, 1999; Valdivieso & Davis, 1988).

## Hispanic American Cultural Values

There is consistency and unity in some values that Hispanic Americans share. The following are most frequently cited in the research literature (Axelson, 1999; Baruth & Manning, 1999; Arciniega & Newlon, 1999; Dana, 1993; Gladding, 1995; Lee, 1999; Lum, 1992; Sue & Sue, 1999): (a) allegiance to immediate and extended family and commitment to family over self; (b) adherence to philosophies such as machismo (male as provider, family protector, honor and dignity for family ), *respeto* (deference to others in regard to their status, gender, age, etc.), *dignidad* (appropriate behaviors), *personalismo* (personal, informal, individualized, relationships), *platicando* (chatting to create ambience); (c) cooperation, collectivism, and close interpersonal relationships; (d) family as referent point for behavior, values, emotional, social, and economic support; (e) patriarchal, hierarchical, family structure in traditional families and clearly defined gender roles; (f) strong reliance on Catholicism and a fatalistic outlook on life; (g) unwavering love and respect for the mother who unifies family; and (h) focus on harmony with self and nature.

## Hispanic American Families

Hispanic culture is firmly rooted in the family, using it as a referent point for modeling behavior, garnering emotional, social and economic support, and identity of the self. Great emphasis is placed on interpersonal relationships, and much warmth, cohesiveness and personal closeness characterize Hispanic American families (Lum, 1992; Sue & Sue, 1999). Dana (1993) and Lum (1992) noted that this network includes the nuclear family, the extended family, significant individuals in the family's lives, and compadres or godparents who are pledged to stand in the parent's stead if such a need arises. There is a sense of collective responsibility and obligation to each other, and the family takes precedence over the individual.

Traditional Hispanic American families are described as very hierarchical and patriarchal, with special authority given to the elderly, parents, and males. Traditional sex roles are exemplified by the concept of machismo for men and marianismo for women. Dana (1993, p.70) says of machismo: "It includes the role of a provider who is responsible for the welfare, protection, honor and dignity of his family." And of marianismo: "Marianismo refers to the spiritual superiority of women and their capacity to endure all suffering with reference to the Virgin Mary" (p.70). Women are described as nurturing, submissive to the male, emotionally supportive, and self-sacrificing. Children are expected to be obedient to their parents and elders, and are responsible for the welfare of the family and younger siblings. Sons usually have more and earlier independence than daughters, and women are expected to remain chaste until they are married. Hispanics marry and have children early in life, and children are welcomed as a source of pride. Hispanics often choose to reside in close proximity to each other, to stay in contact with extended family, to fulfill familial obligations to the elder generation, and to guide and protect siblings or sons and daughters (Lum, 1992). There is considerable diversity, however, among Hispanic American families, and the desire to become acculturated has resulted in value shifts to a congruency with those of the dominant culture.

The predominant religion for Hispanic American families is Roman Catholicism (Lee, 1999). The church is the force that shapes the moral and ethical behaviors of the family, and many of those values remain deeply rooted for life (Lum, 1992). Religion is regarded as a source of comfort in times of crisis and turmoil. Going to Mass is an integral part of everyday life. The strong belief in prayer stems from several beliefs: Sacrifice brings salvation; Charity is a virtue, and everyone should endure wrongs committed against them (Yamamoto & Acosta, 1982). As a consequence of their strong religious faith, many Hispanics are fatalistic, and believe that life events cannot be changed (Sue & Sue, 1999).

Racial discrimination, poor English facility, prejudice, poverty, racial discrimination and differential access to opportunities have impeded some Hispanic American families that reside in this country. However, there is great variability in these families. As second and third generation Hispanic Americans acculturate, value shifts will occur, and will affect family dynamics. Family therapists must be aware of and continue to view these families as individual entities and derive treatment protocols that reflect diversity.

## Asian/Pacific Islander American Demographic Characteristics

Recent immigration, refugee resettlement, and political asylum have given Asian/Pacific Islander Americans the distinction of being the most diverse and fastest growing ethnic group in the United States (Aponte & Crouch, 2000; Axelson, 1999; Lee, 1999; Sue & Sue 1999). By 2050, it is expected that this population will exceed 32 million (Lee, 1998; U.S. Census Bureau, 1996a). It is estimated that there are between 30-50 different cultural subgroups of Asian/Pacific Islander Americans, with the largest being Chinese-24%, Filipinos-21%, Asian Indians-13%, Vietnamese- 11%, Japanese-10%, and Koreans-10% ( Lee, 1998; Lee, 1999). Some have resided in this country for many generations, whereas others such as Vietnamese, Cambodians, Khmer, Laotian, and Hmong are recent newcomers.

The Chinese, Japanese, and Filipinos were the earliest Asian ethnic group to begin immigrating to the United States to work on the railroads, in the gold mines, and provide agricultural and road-maintenance labor (Arciniega & Newlon, 1999; Baruth & Manning, 1999; Dana, 1993). A large group of-Southeast Asian refugees have entered this country since 1975, fleeing their homeland for political and economic reasons. They constitute a population who has suffered numerous traumatic experiences. Asian/Pacific Islander Americans, including the Chinese and Japanese, have had a history of negative experiences in this country including racism, discrimination, forced internment in prison camps during World War II, restrictive immigration practices, violence, and mistreatment. Because much of the existing literature on Asian/ Pacific Islander Americans focuses on Chinese and Japanese Americans, the information presented here pertains exclusively to these groups.

The largest concentrations of Asian/Pacific Islander Americans are in California (about 4 million), New York (approximately 953, 000), Hawaii (about 749,000), Texas (approximately 533, 000), and New Jersey (about 424,000), with most living in metropolitan areas (Aponte & Crouch, 2000). The median age of this group is 32.1 years (U.S. Census Bureau, 2001). Asian /Pacific Islander Americans have the lowest birth rates of the four ethnic groups, low rates of single parent households, live in extended family networks, evidence variations in occupational and income levels, and have the largest gains in educational achievement (Aponte & Crouch, 2000; Lee, 1998, U.S. Census Bureau, 1990a).

Sue and Sue (1999) negate the myth that Asian/Pacific Islander Americans are successful educationally and occupationally, and have few counseling needs. They acknowledge the following problems: (a) a large, undereducated underclass; (b) poverty and unemployment; (c) poor English facility; (d) Asian communities plagued with crime, juvenile delinquency, drug addiction, poverty, overcrowding, and Asian gangs; and (e) refugee populations with many mental health problems.

## Asian/Pacific Islander American Values

Asian/Pacific Islander Americans represent a diverse population; thus, it is difficult to enumerate values specific to each group. However, many Asian cultures are influenced by Confucianism, Buddhism, and Taoism (Dana, 1993; Lee, 1999), philosophies from which core cultural values and practices have developed. The following listing represents the most frequently cited cultural values in the literature (Axelson, 1999; Baruth & Manning, 1999; Dana, 1993; Homma-True, 1990; Huang, 1994; Kitano, 1989; Lee, 1998; Lum, 1992; Sue & Sue, 1999; Uba, 1994): (a) a great sense of obligation, duty, and dependence toward parents and family; (b) interpersonal harmony, emotional restraint, humility, and formality in interpersonal relationships; (c) hierarchical relationships; (d) respect and obedience to authority figures based on their role and status; (e) structure and adherence to role expectations; (f) internal means of control such as guilt, shame, obligation, and duty; (g) importance of the collective; (h) passive, conservative, conforming, inhibited style of interacting; and (i)reverence for past, present and future generations.

## Asian/Pacific Islander American Families

The family is highly valued in Asian/Pacific Islander American culture. Traditional Chinese and Japanese families are patrilineal, with hierarchical relationships existing within and outside the family (Dana, 1993; Kitano, 1989; Sue & Sue, 1999). Respect, adherence, and obedience to authority figures beginning with the males in the family are expected. The most important relationship is that of the father and son, and the father expects to play an active role in his son's education, arranging his marriage, and determining his inheritance (Axelson, 1999). The son owes his mother service, obedience, and respect, and divorce is considered highly shameful (Axelson, 1999).

Guilt, shame, duty, honor, and obligation to the family are used to maintain conformity; and responsibilities to the family take precedence over everything else (Dana, 1993). Significance of roles, birth order, and sex and gender roles are strongly emphasized (Huang, 1994). Individual achievement is undertaken to bring honor to the family; and in whatever behaviors one engages, it is a reflection on the family. As emphasized by Dana (1993, p. 55), "Negative behaviors such as delinquency, school failure, unemployment, or mental illness are considered family failures that disrupt the desired harmony of family life." Therefore, many Asian/Pacific Islander Americans practice a strong code of behavior designed to bring honor to the family.

Interdependent roles, strict adherence to traditional norms, and minimization of conflict by suppressing of overt emotions are additional codes of conduct in traditional Asian/Pacific

Islander American families. The nuclear and extended families are important, as are past and future generations (Lee, 1999).

Although the traditional structure of Asian/Pacific Islander American families may restrict freedom and individuality, they provide security, belonging, identity, and role definition (Axelson, 1999). However, second and third generation Chinese and Japanese may experience conflict and anxiety as they try to reconcile traditional cultural values with those of the dominant culture. Further, as generations assimilate, there is some question as to the degree to which these values are still practiced in Asian/Pacific Islander American families.

## American Indian/Eskimo/Aleut Demographic Characteristics

According to Axelson (1999, p. 73), "There are about 550 federally recognized nations, tribes, bands, clans or communities of American Indians living in the United States today," and an additional 365 state recognized Native American Indian tribes (Manson & Trimble, 1982). Between 200-2,200 tribal tongues are spoken by American Indians (Axelson, 1999; Baruth & Manning, 1999; LaFromboise, Berman & Sohi, 1994). Roughly 22% of Native American Indians occupy federal reservations which number 314 (Baruth & Manning, 1999; U.S. Census Bureau, 1993a,1996b); whereas others of mixed blood have chosen to take up a domicile in urban or metropolitan areas (Baruth & Manning, 1999). These individuals may be described as marginal persons and experience isolation, rejection, and alienation, unlike urban Indians who visit the reservation regularly to maintain their identity and sense of community (Sage 1997). Native American Indians have a legal definition formulated for them by Congress to include being registered as a member of a federally recognized Indian tribe or legally proving 25% Indian heritage (Lee, 1999; Sue & Sue, 1999).

More than 48% of Native American Indians are located in the West, almost 29% reside in the South, about 17% in the Midwest, and close to 6% in the Northeast (U.S. Census Bureau, 1996b). California, Oklahoma, Arizona, New Mexico, Alaska, Texas, New York, Michigan, North Carolina, Washington, and South Dakota contain populations of more than 50,000 American Indians, with Oklahoma, California, Arizona, and New Mexico having the largest numbers (Axelson, 1999; Baruth & Manning, 1999; Lieberg, 1996; U.S. Census Bureau, 1996b). American Indians are a young population, with a median age of 27.8 (U.S. Census Bureau, 2001). They experience the following: The highest birth rate of the four ethnic groups, including Whites; They maintain households of varying arrangements; There exists high poverty, unemployment, alcohol and other drug use, suicide, school dropout, and child abuse; and they are plagued by many cases of diabetes and kidney disease (Baruth & Manning, 1999; Herring, 1991; Lee, 1999; Shore, 1988; U.S. Census Bureau, 1993b, 1996b). Further, the coercive assimilation of Native American Indian children by placing them in federal boarding schools and into non-native foster homes has produced negative outcomes (Herring, 1999; Tafoya & DelVecchio, 1996).

Today, Native American Indians engage in a variety of occupations, including hunting, farming, raising livestock, fishing, timber production, making and selling crafts; and they have begun to parlay federal monies owed them into resorts, fishing ventures, auto mechanics, oil and gas, timber, bingo halls, lottery and casinos (Axelson, 1999). Whereas there is much variation in tribal cultures, Native American Indians have a common history of hardship, cultural trauma, ambivalence, and mistrust of outsiders (Lee, 1999), factors that may impact their relationships with non-Native family counselors.

## American Indian/Eskimo/Aleut Cultural Values

Authors (Attneve, 1982; Axelson, 1999; Baruth & Manning, 1999; Garret & Garret, 1994; Herring, 1997; Lafromboise, 1994; Lee, 1999; Sage, 1997; Sue & Sue, 1999; Trimble, 1981) have identified the following values as traditional for Native American Indians. They include: (a) respect and reverence for nature, living in harmony with nature and animate and inanimate objects; (b) a strong sense of spirituality and belief in the spirit world, reincarnation, and dreams; (c) no distinction between the mind, body, spirit world, and reality; (d) family and group more important than the individual; (e) the elderly valued for their wisdom and knowledge; (f) emphasis on doing things well instead of quickly; (g) cooperation; (h) praise must come from others and individual achievement abhorrent; (i) honor and respect gained by sharing, generosity, and gift giving; (j) present time orientation and living in harmony with the world important, not long term planning; (k) cultural traditions important and add value to the quality of life; (l) non interference in the lives of others; (m) self sufficiency valued; and (n) patience, control of one's emotions, honesty, and avoiding/withdrawing from confrontation/aggressive situations valued.

## American Indian/Eskimo/Aleut Families

Because Native American Indians are extremely heterogeneous, family structure often varies from tribe to tribe. There are some commonalities, however, that can be gleaned from the literature. The immediate or extended family is of critical importance to Native American Indians, particularly because they view themselves as appendages of their family ( Ho, 1987; Sue & Sue, 1999). The family serves as a referent point for identity development, inclusion, acceptance and security. American Indians view the family or tribe as central to their actions and derive honor, praise, status, rewards, and respect by adhering to tribal dictates. According to Baruth and Manning, (1999, p.325), the Native American Indian family "extends well beyond one's immediate relatives to extended family relatives through the second cousin, members of one's clan, members of the community, all other living creatures in this world, nature as a whole, and the universe itself."

Associated with of their young median age, Native American Indians evidence high fertility rates, frequent out of wedlock births, a large percentage of single parent households, and households below the poverty line. Children are considered as gifts that should be shared with others. Whereas it is common for children to live in many different households and be raised by various relatives, grandparents are responsible for their rearing; and parents provide economic support but seldom interfere (Lum, 1992). Grandparents raise the children because it is believed that American Indian parents are too young and not wise enough to fulfill such a serious responsibility ( Baruth & Manning, 1999). Children are trained to be self-sufficient and live in harmony with the world and their natural surroundings

The elderly are valued for their experience and wisdom; they teach the children customs, traditions and legends, and monitor their behavior (Lum, 1992). All family members seek social acceptance, wisdom and advice from the elders. Native American Indian families feel an obligation to care for the elderly because they are held in reverence and respect (Attneve, 1982; Lum, 1992). Other family characteristics include sharing of material goods and possessions, acquiring enough to satisfy immediate needs, respecting individuality, contributing to the maintenance of group identity by promoting a harmonious whole, patience and passivity in relationships with others inside and outside of the family, and noninterference and respecting individual rights to self determination (Axelson, 1999; Baruth & Manning, 1999; Garrett & Garrett, 1994; Herring, 1997; Lum, 1992; Sage, 1997; Sanders, 1987; Sue & Sue, 1999).

## COUNSELING WITH ETHNICALLY DIVERSE FAMILIES

Family counselors believe that personality development is strongly influenced by the family system and "relationships formed among family members are extremely powerful and account for a considerable amount of human behavior, emotions, values and attitudes" (Gladding, 1995, p.57). Because the family is an interconnected entity, the actions of each family member affect the other and moderate the family's psychological health. Family systems therapy is governed by several tenets: Treat the entire system; the presenting problem is a symptom of the family's health; all behaviors serve a purpose; the family is always the client; the behaviors of family members are reciprocal in nature, and the counselor's role is to restructure relationships to restore family equilibrium (Arciniega & Newlon,1999; Gladding, 1995; McGoldrick & Giordano, 1996; Sue & Sue, 1999).

Several elements of family systems therapy are compatible and congruent with the experiences and values of ethnically diverse populations. Among others, they include: (a) the emphasis on family as the basic social system; (b) understanding the family in its sociocultural context (social, cultural, psychological, environmental); (c) examining multisystems which impact the family; (d) the focus on extended family networks, multigenerational conflicts, and family patterns; (e) the emphasis on immediate, concrete, goal oriented, short term resolution of problems; (f) the therapist as expert; and (g) the focus on family configuration and interaction (boundaries, hierarchies, alliances, roles, enmeshment, dysfunction, etc.).

Additionally, to provide effective family counseling with ethnically diverse populations it is important that a complete assessment of the family be attempted before engaging in the counseling process. Some important considerations include but are not limited to the following: (a) language facility; (b) age and generational status; (c) cultural and indigenous heritage; (d) acculturation levels; (e) religious background; (f) social status; (g) gender socialization patterns; (h) kinship bonds; (i) psychohistory; and (j) experience in therapy (Arciniega & Newlon, 1999; Baruth & Manning, 1999; Gladding, 1995; Hays, 1996). The next section presents guidelines for working with African American, Hispanic, Asian/Pacific Islander, and American Indian families in counseling.

### Counseling with African American Families

The communal nature of the African American family makes it very conducive to family therapy (Baruth & Manning, 1999; Sue & Sue, 1999; Wilson & Stith, 1993). Counselors who work with African American families must not only recognize the uniqueness of each family but also gain familiarity with their world views (Montague, 1996). African American families may ostensibly seek counseling because a child has been referred for behavioral problems. In this situation, the counselor should arrange to meet with all affected and influential individuals who have an impact on the child (Hines & Boyd-Franklin, 1996; Wilson & Stith, 1993). Each participant may define the problem differently or may not be aware that a problem exists. Wilson and Stith (1993) noted that excluding important subsystems may reduce therapeutic effectiveness. Understanding varying perspectives facilitates quick identification and resolution of the problem.

To continue, a key element in engaging African American families in counseling is communicating respect and acknowledging the family's strengths (Boyd-Franklin, 1989; Montague, 1996). Participating in therapy is a last resort to African American families who utilize extended family systems, church, important social institutions, and significant individuals in time of stress (Richardson & Lee, 1997; Sue & Sue, 1999). Hines and Boyd-Franklin (1996) pointed out that acknowledging intimate problems to strangers may mean an admission of failure, powerlessness, and a betrayal of family confidence. Therefore, it is important for counselors to praise the family for seeking help, and relate to them in a direct and supportive manner. Blaming the family for the difficulty will not encourage a second visit.

Another point is that family counselors should be cognizant about making negative or disparaging remarks about the behavior(s) of family members. Hines, Garcia-Preto, McGoldrick, Almeida, and Weltman (1999, p. 73), caution that when working with African American families, "Therapists are likely to encounter difficulty if they label any family member as a "villain" or "bad" regardless of how angry, disappointed, or rejecting family members may be because of that person's behavior." Family therapists should always remain neutral; taking sides and making negative judgments will not facilitate personal information sharing. The authors contend that if this occurs early in the counseling session when trust has not been established, the family may perceive the counselor as judgmental, insensitive, disrespectful, overstepping boundaries, and not trustworthy. Consequently, they may regard the family counseling experience as negative and forego any further involvement in the process.

Hines and Boyd-Franklin (1996) offer further suggestions for working with African American families. Counselors who address family members by their first names without asking permission are assuming a familiarity that may not exist; and this could communicate disrespect for the family. Similarly, in order to build rapport, therapists should avoid using jargon, Ebonics, or pretending a superficial familiarity with the African American culture. African American families may interpret these behaviors as ingratiating, patronizing, and condescending. This erodes trust and damages rapport.

If family therapy is focused upon a child, counselors should involve all individuals who share care-taking roles because of the multigenerational, multidimensional structure of African American families (Hines et al., 1999). These caretakers may not necessarily be the child's biological parent(s), but an aunt, grandmother, brother, cousin, sister, niece, or other individual. Consequently, family counselors should incorporate and support these systems in therapy because they simulate the family structure (Boyd-Franklin, 1989; Hines & Boyd-Franklin, 1996). Frequently, support from other family members can result in positive behavioral changes and improved family relationships.

Additionally, Hines and Boyd-Franklin(1996) mention that role flexibility evident in many African American families may preclude male children from developing clear definitions and perceptions of gender roles, particularly because there may not be a male role model in the home. The authors suggest that family counselors seek the father's participation in counseling, but acknowledge that this may be problematic. Fathers may not be present, and those who are may not be able to take time from work for sessions. Family therapists can devise alternatives to accomplish this goal. For example, some strategies may include utilizing the resources of other significant male adults such as grandfathers, uncles, cousins, nephews, other male relatives, or significant family friends; pairing them with male mentors from the church or community; referring them to African American all male groups; encouraging them to attend boys clubs; and helping them to establish and access linkages to other valuable community resources designed to work with African American males.

A further point is that family counselors must understand and assess the impact of environmental conditions such as racism, poverty, family configuration, unemployment, discrimination, and other stressors on African American families (Baruth & Manning, 1999; Montague, 1996; Sue & Sue, 1999). These factors will affect the family's world view and perceptions of problems. Further, family counselors should allow African American families to frame the problem congruent with their perceptions, not the counselor's. The more families are involved in the therapeutic process, the more invested they become in determining solutions. Additionally, Montague (1996) noted that counselors who hold middle class values--especially those acknowledging the nuclear family as the most viable family structure--will have difficulty working with the variant African American family configurations. Family counselors empower African American families when they recognize their uniqueness, acknowledge and value the appropriateness of variant family structures, and allow families to be active participants in problem resolution. In this manner, African American families feel valued, understood, and respected.

Hines and colleagues (1999) presented a particular difficulty in counseling African American families. That is, the close-knit relationships evidenced in African American families may preclude family members from discussing sensitive issues; and this may lead to disharmony and negative feelings. Family counselors have to maintain a delicate balance with this issue. Their credibility is enhanced if they acknowledge and honor the individual's concern and desire to protect the family and maintain positive relationships; then they can reiterate that the individual can show leadership in the family by communicating information that will improve family relationships. This should be done in ways that acknowledge the family member's efforts and emphasize the benefits and rewards to the family.

Finally, family counseling with African Americans is a recent development (Willis, 1988). Therapies that seem to work for African American families are ones which adopt active, intervention oriented strategies, emphasizing social functioning over inner feelings, and are problem focused, multisystemic, and time limited ( Boyd-Franklin, 1987, 1989; Hines & Boyd Franklin, 1996; Lee, 1999). Three family therapy theories--structural, strategic, and Bowenian, have shown utility with African American families (Boyd-Franklin, 1987, 1989; Lee, 1999; Minuchin, 1984). Family counselors should employ outside resources such as significant family members, important social institutions, and the church ( Boyd-Franklin, 1989; Cheatham, 1990; Richardson & Lee, 1997; Wilson & Stith, 1993). Because of the high regard in which these institutions and individuals are held in the African American community, families attend therapy if the minister, an elderly relative, or a family member of significant influence recommends their involvement. Maintaining alliances with these resources can be very effective in facilitating family counseling with African Americans.

## Counseling with Hispanic American Families

Hispanic American families underutilize therapeutic services for a variety of reasons, including language barriers, value differences between clients and counselors, counselors' insensitivity and lack of understanding, a small number of Hispanic professionals, and clients' lack of familiarity with the therapeutic process (Baruth & Manning, 1999; Lee, 1999; Sue & Sue, 1999). Further, because of the close-knit nature of Hispanic American families, problems are usually kept in the family because there is a distrust of outsiders. Therefore, when these families do engage in counseling, family counselors must utilize considerable skill to get them to return for a second visit. In addition to counselors having some familiarity with the culture, language, family acculturation patterns, stressors, and developmental conflicts, family counseling with Hispanic Americans merits several considerations.

First, because of the complex hierarchy of Hispanic American families, all family members who are connected to the problem should be involved, particularly if the problem is presented as a child's problem (Baruth & Manning, 1999). Family members can provide assistance, support and guidance (Christensen, 1989). Because, it may not be possible to meet with the entire family, arrangements should be made to consult with significant family members (Christensen, 1989) preferably a male relative. Because of the patriarchal nature of the Hispanic culture (Sue & Sue, 1999), relying on a female family member may be deemed an affront

Second, Hispanic American families are also hampered by obstacles that prevent them from attending therapy sessions. Nieves and Valle (1989) encouraged family counselors to consider making home visits. Observing families in their natural setting often present counselors with a clearer picture of family configurations, imbalances in the family hierarchy, boundaries, alliances, triangulations, and subsystems, elements which may not be readily evident in counselors' offices.

Third, Aponte (1991) addressed the importance of understanding the roles of family members and the Hispanic family structure. Questions should be directed at the parents if it is a child's problem, and the father addressed first in deference to his position as head of the household (Falicov, 1996; Garcia- Preto, 1996). In most cases, the father will be the only person who speaks. If the father is not available and another adult male is present, he should be addressed first, then other family members as permitted.

Fourth, a bilingual therapist may serve as a valuable addition to the family therapy process with Hispanic American families (Baruth & Manning, 1998, Garcia-Preto, 1996; Sue & Sue, 1999). Language difficulty between Spanish-speaking clients and English-speaking counselors can lead to misunderstandings, misinterpretation of what is being said, and frustration for both the counselor and family (Garcia-Preto, 1996, Sue & Sue, 1999). In some cases, the family therapist may assign the role of interpreter to children in the family who can speak English. This may be problematic, particularly if the subject matter is of a sensitive nature. Further, this practice usurps the parental role, and disrupts the family's hierarchical structure. Whereas interpreters can help to facilitate the communication process, issues of confidentiality and accuracy of translation may arise.

Fifth, Hispanic men may not embrace family counseling; it may cast doubt on their ability to fulfill their role as family protectors (Garcia-Preto, 1996). It may also be difficult for men to discuss sensitive issues (e.g., sexual concerns) in the presence of children, women, and female family counselors. Therefore, if male family counselors are available, Hispanic men may feel more comfortable in disclosing. Garcia-Preto (1996) suggested that diligent effort should be made to include Hispanic men in family counseling sessions because of their responsibilities and role as head of the family. Additionally, to reduce tension and anxiety, family counselors may want to schedule separate sessions for the husband and wife couple, and for the children. If it is a child's problem, children may feel more comfortable disclosing without the father or mother present.

To continue, Hispanic American families in therapy may be more concerned with survival issues (food, housing, bills, employment, parenting, learning particular skills, medical concerns, etc.), and less interested in participating in long term, introspective therapy. Thus, the family counselor should deal with these immediate issues. Providing guidance in these areas communicates to the family that their needs are important. If there are therapeutic issues, the family will trust the counselor enough to self-disclose because a trusting relationship has already been established. In many instances, family counsleors must have the flexibility to adopt roles such as resource persons, teachers, trainers, advocates, employment counselors, cheerleaders, and educators, among others. Further, philosophies such as respeto (respect because of gender, status, age), and personalismo (warm, friendly, interpersonal behavior) are integral components of Hispanic American culture (Christensen, 1989; Ho, 1987; Inclan, 1990; Sue & Sue, 1999). In the initial stages of counseling, family counselors should greet the family warmly, make small talk, build rapport, and create a warm, comfortable atmosphere. For Hispanic American families, a relationship has to be established before they are willing to trust strangers with personal issues. The relationship may also help to ease the anxiety of seeing a counselor. It is usual for adult family members to ask family counselors questions surrounding age, marital status, religious affiliation, children, and other issues. Counselors should not perceive these questions as intrusive, rather, the family's desire to feel comfortable with the counselor. Family counselors should also remain active, polite, friendly, open, formal, willing to give advice, and non-confrontational (Baruth & Manning, 1999; Ho, 1987; Sue & Sue, 1999). Respecting these philosophies and cultural values can engender trust, aid successful joining with the family, and increase chances for therapeutic success (Inclan, 1990).

Finally, the hierarchical nature of Hispanic American families makes them conducive to structural and behavioral family therapy and active, short term, behavioral approaches (Canino & Canino, 1982; Juarez, 1985; Ponterotto, 1987). Hispanic American families may also perceive therapists as medical doctors and expect to be diagnosed and treated (Gladding, 1995; Sue & Sue, 1999). They may look to the counselor as the expert (Ho, 1987), and find little necessity in long-term therapy. In order to achieve success with Hispanic families, family counselors should maintain an active yet respectful stance, remain warm, encouraging, and professional, be willing to adopt a variety of roles, and respect and honor Hispanic cultural values.

## Counseling with Asian/Pacific Islander American Families

For Asian/Pacific Islander American families, the decision to enter treatment is not easy, given their reluctance to disclose personal information, and that admitting problems brings shame and disgrace to the family (Baruth & Manning, 1999; Sue & Sue, 1999). Nonetheless when Asian/ Pacific Islander Americans seek counseling, the following guidelines may facilitate more effective outcomes.

A crucial point is that family therapists should honor the family hierarchy by addressing the father first. In many cases he will be the only one to speak, and he will not be likely to reveal personal information (Ho, 1987; Sue & Sue, 1999). As in the case of Hispanics, admitting to problems questions his ability to take care of his family. Further, other family members may also be reluctant to reveal information because disclosure of a problem is viewed as bringing shame and disgrace to the family (Baruth & Manning, 1999; Sue & Sue, 1999). The family will have to be encouraged to share information. Family therapists can do this by acknowledging how good the parents have been, and reframing the problem(s) such that the family can recognize that there may be positive benefits.

Sue and Sue (1999) suggested that family counselors be aware that asking Asian/Pacific Islander American family members to engage in behaviors which are counter to family expectations will be met with ambivalence, anxiety, and conflict. For example, some behaviors expected by counselors might include children confronting parents, expressing feelings, establishing independence, making decisions without seeking family advice (particularly the father's), and separating from parents and families. These behaviors may be acceptable goals for family members from the dominant culture. However, the collective nature of Asian cultures, the reverence in which families and parents are held, and the dependency and security promoted by family values place these behaviors at odds with Asian/Pacific Islander Americans' belief systems.

Additionally, Asian/ Pacific Islander American families may not understand the role of family counselors or family therapy (Baruth & Manning, 1999; Lum, 1992; Sue & Sue, 1999). According to Ho (1987), they may perceive counselors as competent, skilled, knowledgeable experts who will identify the problem and tell them what to do. They do not expect to be active participants in the therapeutic process; therefore, asking their opinions may be met with silence and resistance; they may feel that they are usurping the counselor's authority or that the counselor is incompetent; and as a result, they become even confused. Family counselors, therefore, must take an active role in explaining the counseling process, their roles, the family's roles, and the benefits of family therapy (Baruth & Manning, 1999). If these are not addressed, then Asian/Pacific Islander American families may not continue with therapy.

Further, Asian/Pacific Islander American families may go to family therapists for somatic symptoms experienced by a family member or family members (Baruth & Manning, 1999; Ho, 1987; Sue & Sue, 1999). It is important that family counselors help families with these concerns, and not assume problems that they may not want to address. Embarrassment and shame may prevent family members from admitting problems. When trust has been established, family members may feel comfortable discussing more serious issues. Skills such as patience, understanding cultural values, and recognizing the family's need to save face are critical for family counselors working with Asian/Pacific Islander Americans.

To continue, Baruth and Manning (1999, p.187) stated, "Ethical dilemmas might arise when family members who feel a sense of collectivism for the family and who do not understand confidentiality associated with the counseling professional asks the counselor what the family member revealed during sessions." This situation may be difficult for family counselors who have to adhere to the ethical principles of their profession, while honoring and respecting the cultural beliefs of Asian/ Pacific Islander American families. Ensuring that the objectives, procedures, and confidentiality of the therapeutic process have been clearly delineated and understood may discourage such misunderstandings.

Finally, Ho's (1989) Fundamental Interpersonal Relations Orientation theory, which focuses on structural and communicative interactions within the family, has produced success with Asian/Pacific Islander Americans. Structural family therapy with its focused, direct, concrete, problem solving approach is also well suited for Asian/ Pacific Islander American families (Lee, 1989), who may find little utility for introspective and insight oriented therapies (Sue & Sue, 1999). Other approaches that have been identified include a multigenerational approach which takes into account generational conflicts within the extended family environment (Ho, 1987) and brief, solution oriented approaches (Wang, 1994).

## Counseling with Native American Indian/Eskimo/Aleut Families

According to Sutton and Broken Nose (1996), Native American Indian family structure blends well with family therapy's systemic approach, given the emphasis on relationships and joint problem solving. However, the close-knit Native American Indian family, with their cultural traditions and their history in this country, may perceive little incentive for engaging in family therapy with counselors from the dominant culture. Thus, counselors working with Native American Indian families should be cognizant of several considerations.

Several authors (Attneve, 1982; Baruth & Manning, 1999; Herring, 1997; Ho, 1987) recognize that Native American Indian culture emphasizes harmony with nature, endurance of suffering, the importance of the family, and noninterference with others. Further, Native American Indians may lack familiarity with counseling, and may seek counseling as a last resort. In essence, counselors who lack flexibility may encounter many difficulties in working with Native American Indian families. It is critical that counselors become familiar with Native American Indian culture, the tribes, the value systems, the family patterns, the overlapping relationships, the communication patterns, and the behaviors associated with these (Attneve, 1982; Herring, 1997; Ho, 1987; Sage, 1997; Sutton & Broken Nose, 1996).

Family therapists should proceed cautiously when engaging Native American Indian families in counseling. Native American Indians move at their own pace, and because of cultural mistrust, it may take several sessions for family therapists to build rapport (Ho, 1987). To facilitate the process therapists may self-disclose, ask general questions about Native American Indian life and culture, remain genuine and sincere, and be respectful of Native American Indian culture and traditions (Attneve, 1982; Ho, 1987; Sage, 1997). According to Ho (1987), advice giving and asking many personal questions may be perceived as disrespectful and intrusive. Being patient and being a good listener communicates interest in and respect for Native American Indian families. Family counselors who are overbearing, who operate as the expert, and who are disrespectful of family traditions will be perceived negatively by Native American Indians.

To continue, Native American Indians perceive a problem as belonging to everyone. Consequently, it is important that interventions include the entire family (Attneve, 1982; Herring, 1997; Ho, 1987; Trimble & Fleming, 1989). Counselors must be aware of and respect the variety of Native American Indian families and the roles each family member plays. For example, the elderly are revered in American Indian culture (Axelson, 1999; Herring, 1997; Lum, 1992 ); therefore, this subsystem should be included in family counseling sessions. Elders speak for the family. If they are not supportive of counseling, counselors may have little luck engaging Native American Indian families. Additionally, the elders and other family members may not want to disclose personal information to a stranger (Attneve, 1982). Family counselors telling Native American Indian families what to do may be perceived as usurping the authority and advice of the elders, turning away from the teachings of the tribe, or interference (Ho, 1987). Therefore, family counselors must build alliances with significant individuals that Native American Indian families respect. Herring (1997) noted that such alliances generally enhance therapeutic effectiveness and behavior change.

Another consideration is that counselors should utilize techniques that respect and take into account Native American Indians' nonverbal and verbal communication styles (Attneve, 1982; Ho, 1987; Sutton & Broken Nose, 1996). Counseling in the dominant culture emphasizes verbalization, emotional expression, equality of roles between therapists and clients, gaining insight, and long term, introspective therapy (Sue & Sue, 1999). For Native American Indians, nonverbal expressions such as silence, moderation in speech, avoidance of direct eye-contact, a soft handshake, an impassive voice, and a calm manner are all cultural modes of communication (Attneve, 1982; Herring, 1997; Sanders, 1987). Attneve (1982) cautioned that family counselors should not interpret these behaviors as lack of interest. Native American Indians learn by observing, and patience and calmness may conceal deeper feelings.

Additionally, Native American Indians use of silence in family therapy can be frustrating to counselors from the dominant culture (Herring, 1997; Sage, 1997). Silence may be used as a safe response to defend against outsiders, as Native American Indians assess the therapist, or silence may be used for contemplation (Herring, 1997; Ho, 1987). Conversational exchanges may also be brief. How counselors react sets the stage for future sessions (Attneve, 1982). This mode of behavior fits the Native American Indian concept of living life with harmony and balance.

Many Native American Indians believe that mental health difficulties result from disobeying tribal dictates and living out of harmony with nature (Garrett & Garrett, 1994; Herring, 1997). Therefore, family counselors should not ask family members to engage in behaviors that dishonor the cultural beliefs of their group (e.g., moving off the reservation, adopting values of the dominant culture such as independence, developing autonomy, competition, challenging parents, etc.). These actions disrupt the natural harmony and balance that are an element of Native American Indian culture (Garrett & Garrett, 1994).

Time is conceptualized differently in Native American Indian culture, and tasks are undertaken based on the natural cycle of life (Garrett & Garrett, 1994; Herring, 1997; Sage, 1997). Punctuality is not highly valued, and plans for tomorrow are often left until tomorrow. Authors (Herring, 1997; Ho, 1987; Sage, 1997) suggest that family counselors should avoid asking families to adhere to strict appointment times or maintain rigid therapy schedules. Maintaining flexibility with appointments, frequency of therapy, and time will facilitate more frequent participation by Native American Indian families in the therapeutic process.

Another important point is that American Indians believe in living in and experiencing the present (Herring, 1997; Sue & Sue, 1999). Asking families to engage in long-term goal setting may be inappropriate, irrelevant, and have little consistency with the cultural belief that tomorrow will take care of itself. Such acts by counselors are seen as presumptuous, rejecting the dictates of the tribe, and disrupting the natural order of things. Practical, immediate solutions to problems will elicit more positive results than planning for a future that holds little attention.

In Native American Indian culture, group decisions takes precedence over individual choices (Herring, 1991; Ho, 1987; Sue & Sue, 1999). Family therapists should remain mindful of this when determining behavioral outcomes for family members. Individual decision-making is frowned upon, as is focusing on individuality. Therefore, asking a family member to choose a particular course of action without consulting with the rest of the family is inappropriate. Such group involvement might be interpreted as dependency. However, it is culturally acceptable and expected behavior, and is part of the supportive system within which Native American Indians function.

Finally, home-based therapy (Schatch, Tafoya & Mirabla, 1989) has been used with American Indian families. This approach dictates that family counselors spend time with the family in their natural setting before attempting to help the members. Network therapy has been used effectively with Native American Indian families because of its compatibility with their healing approaches and family systems (Attneve, 1982; LaFromboise, Trimble, & Mohatt, 1990). Network therapy utilizes the extended family and community as social networks that can provide support and encouragement during and after counseling. Traditional Native American Indian healing ceremonies performed in an extended family setting, and structural family therapy combined with traditional healing practices have proven effective (Gladding, 1995; LaFromboise et al., 1990).

# FAMILY THERAPY MODELS

Because of the diversity of ethnic families, no one therapeutic approach works for all families. The choice of a theory/model should ultimately depend on the presenting problem, therapists' knowledge of the culture, and the individual family configuration. In addition to the family therapy approaches previously discussed there are others cited in the literature which have utility with ethnically diverse families. The strengths of these models lie in their emphasis on blending therapeutic approaches with cultural values and traditions.

*Ecological therapy.* This approach integrates families and their cultural/ environmental context as one process, with each influencing the other (Aponte, 1991; Boyd-Franklin, 1987; Inclan, 1990). This works especially well with ethnically diverse families who often struggle with cultural and multigenerational issues.

*The structural approach.* This approach assesses family structure (especially three generational families), identifies areas of difficulty, and restructures the family to produce change (Boyd-Franklin, 1987; Minuchin, 1974). The focus is on problem solving, and concrete and direct resolution of problems is consistent with the therapeutic approach preferred by some ethnically diverse populations (Boyd-Franklin, 1987, 1989; Hines & Boyd-Franklin, 1996).

*Eco-structural therapy.* This model stresses engagement, problem solving, and examination of institutions that impact families in therapy (Aponte, 1991). The counselor is expected to include the family's environment and community when making diagnostic and treatment decisions (Inclan, 1990). This approach helps families' communication with institutions that affect their lives. This approach is particularly well suited for ethnically diverse families who are constantly negotiating the social, economic, emotional, and psychological systems which negatively impact their family life and mental health.

*Ecological systemic approach.* This approach (Ho, 1987) stresses respecting the family's values, understanding acculturation patterns, and working toward bicultural lifestyles. The focus is on understanding the ethnically diverse family and enhancing the counselor's repertoire of skills.

*Cultural* stories. Mc Gill's (1992) cultural stories, grew out of work with ethnically diverse families. The idea is that these families bring to therapy stories that reflect their and society's perceptions about issue such as gender roles, the family life cycle, ethnic orientation, social class, and racial identity. Therapists who utilize this approach must be familiar with the values and world views of several diverse groups.

*Cervantes' and Ramirez' (1995) model.* Cervantes and Ramirez have developed a model of family therapy based on the Mestizo worldview. This model draws from Mestizo spirituality and Mexican folk healing used with Latino families in Texas.

*The Bowenian model.* This model provides techniques for examining extended family dynamics and behavioral patterns, and provides techniques for generating extended ethnic family data (Boyd-Franklin, 1987, 1989; Hines & Boyd-Franklin, 1996). The multigenerational nature of ethnically diverse family structures is compatible with this approach which lends insight into family patterns and transmission of behaviors.

*Brief solution focused family therapy.* This approach (deShazer, 1985; Wang, 1994) focuses on solutions, problem solving skills, and changes in the here and now. The emphasis is on action, not growth and insight. This approach is also suited for ethnically diverse families who expect an active therapist, to be told what to do, are not interested in long term therapy, and who want immediate resolution of their problems.

*Indigenous approaches.* These approaches include incorporating culturally indigenous methods of healing, as well as healers into the therapeutic process (Attneave, 1982; Cervantes & Ramirez, 1995; LaFromboise et al., 1990). For ethnically diverse families who may lack familiarity with counseling and feel more comfortable with familiar, culturally specific approaches, these practices have utility. Also, incorporating indigenous treatment methods along with those from the dominant culture communicates respect for the family and its culture.

# IMPLICATIONS FOR WORKING WITH
# ETHNICALLY DIVERSE FAMILIES

Family therapists cannot be experts on all cultures, but can acquire general abilities that will help them to be successful in conducting therapy with ethnically diverse families. These practices include but are not limited to the following:

1. *Exercising cultural sensitivity*. The following aspects of cultural sensitivity help to foster respect, trust, communication, and counselors' openness and willingness to learn about families: (a) sensitivity toward the family's personal beliefs and values; (b) becoming aware of the family's cultural group history and experiences, (c) avoiding making stereotypical assumptions and generalizations, (d) understanding the family's world view, and (e) treating the family as unique members of their particular ethnic group.

2. *Acquiring appropriate attitudes, skills, and knowledge*. It is ethically irresponsible for counselors to practice beyond the scope of their expertise. Further, they should derive treatment objectives that address the individual, unique needs of the clients and families with whom they work, including those from diverse backgrounds. Therefore, it is incumbent upon family therapists to acquire the requisite knowledge, awareness, and skills necessary to provide effective therapy to ethnically diverse families. This can be done in a variety of ways: attending conferences, workshops, and symposiums; taking continuing education courses; keeping abreast of current literature in the field; inviting multi-cultural encounters with ethnically diverse family members; asking questions, listening carefully, and learning as much as possible about the culture; practicing creative counseling techniques; examining individual prejudices and biases, and appreciating diversity.

3. *Developing creative counseling strategies*. The counseling literature continues to document the reluctance of ethnically diverse families to participate in therapy. Family therapists must develop creative ways to draw and keep ethnically diverse families in therapy. There are several ways to accomplish this: draw on the strengths of the family, including important cultural rituals, practices and activities and incorporate them into therapy; be willing to conduct therapy outside of the office- in the home or other places where the family might feel more comfortable; practice flexibility with appointment times and frequency of therapy; utilize familiar sources of cultural support, for example preachers in the African American community, the Medicine Man on the Reservation, herbalists in the Hispanic community, and the elders in the Asian community; and devise treatment strategies congruent with the individual needs of ethnically diverse families.

4. *Engaging in constant examination of individual assumptions, values, biases and prejudices concerning ethnically diverse individuals*. It is important to identify the origin of these perceptions, determine their validity, and the impact of these beliefs on working with ethnically diverse families in therapy. If family therapists harbor negative attitudes about the populations with whom they work, they may end up harming the families.

5. *Managing conflicting value systems*. The counseling literature is replete with documentation of the poor participation of ethnically diverse individuals and families in therapy. Much of this resistance has been attributed to the middle class value orientations of counselors and a counseling orientation which is in direct conflict with the value systems, beliefs, and behaviors of families from ethnically diverse backgrounds. Counselors'

awareness of class and culture-bound values that can impede the counseling process will help to facilitate effective treatment for ethnically diverse families.

6. *Coping with the effects of sociopolitical and environmental stressors.* Ethnically diverse families continue to be plagued with conditions such as racism, poverty, discrimination, prejudice, and other destructive social ills which have had devastating consequences on family functioning. As a consequence, suspicion and distrust of counselors from the dominant culture often occur. Family therapists should realize that these behaviors represent survival mechanisms derived to protect ethnically diverse families from institutions in which they have little faith or trust. Culturally competent family counselors are able to understand the reasons for these behaviors, bridge differences, and work effectively with ethnically diverse families.

7. *Respecting family differences.* Family counselors should respect the variant family structures evident in ethnically diverse families, work within the extended family networks-hallmarks of ethnically diverse families, honor the family hierarchy, avoid applying universal models of family functioning, communicate acceptance by learning about the family, understand the family and their problems in a cultural context, and devise culturally relevant and appropriate treatment strategies.

## CONCLUSION

The philosophical underpinnings of family counseling are extremely compatible with the family structure of the four major ethnically diverse families discussed in this chapter. The mental health system, however, still continues to endorse the nuclear family structure as the ideal, thereby judging other families accordingly. The number of ethnically diverse families continues to increase, giving rise to the need for developing strategies to assist these families with their mental health needs.

Family counselors should possess a clear understanding and appreciation of cultural similarities and differences between majority and nonmajority families, between families from the many ethnic groups, and within-family differences. Family counselorss must also avoid falling victim to the notion of family homogeneity, and instead, treat ethnically diverse families in the context of their own culture, perceptions of the problem, values, behaviors, beliefs, and world views. Moreover, family therapists working with ethnically diverse families should recognize the impact of social and environmental realities on the family's psychological and behavioral functioning. Effective approaches for working with ethnically diverse families are holistic, multi-faceted, and culturally appropriate. Most important, however, the delivery of ethnically diverse family counseling cannot be effective without a basic understanding and recognition of cultural differences and the uniqueness of families.

## REFERENCES

Aponte, H. J. (1991). Training on the person of the therapist for work with the poor and minorities. *Journal of Independent Social Work, 5,* 23-29.

Aponte, J. F., & Crouch, R. T. (2000). The changing ethnic profile of the United States. In J. F. Aponte, R. Rivers, & J. Wohl (Eds.), *Psychological interventions and cultural diversity* (pp. 1-18). Boston: Allyn & Bacon.

Arciniega, G., & Newlon, B. (1999). Counseling and psychotherapy: Multicultural considerations. In D. Capuzzi & D. Gross (Eds.), *Counseling and psychotherapy: Theories and interventions* (pp.435-480). Upper Saddle River, NJ: Prentice-Hall.

Asante, M. K. (1987). *The Afrocentric idea*. Philadelphia: Temple University Press.

Atkinson, D. R., Morten, G., & Sue, D. W. (1998). *Counseling American minorities* (5th ed.). Boston: McGraw-Hill.

Attneave, C. (1982). American Indian and Alaskan Native families: Emigrants in their own homeland. In M. McGoldrick, J. Pearce, & J. Giordano (Eds.), *Ethnicity and family therapy* (pp. 55-83). New York: Guilford Press.

Avila, D. L., & Avila, A. L. (1995). Mexican-Americans. In N. Vacc, S. DeVaney, & J. Wittmer (Eds.), *Experiencing and counseling multicultural and diverse populations* (pp. 119-146). Bristol, PA: Accelerated Development.

Axelson, J. A. (1999). *Counseling and development in a multicultural society*. Pacific Grove, CA: Brooks/Cole.

Baruth, L. G., & Manning, M. L. (1999). *Multicultural counseling and psychotherapy: A lifespan perspective* (2nd ed.). Upper Saddle River, NJ: Prentice-Hall.

Billingsley, A. (1992). *Climbing Jacob's ladder*. New York: Simon & Schuster.

Boyd- Franklin, N. (1987). The contribution of family therapy models to the treatment of Black families. *Psychotherapy, 24*, 621-629.

Boyd-Franklin, N. (1989). *Black families in therapy*. New York: The Guilford Press

Canino, I. , & Canino, G. (1982). Cultural syntonic family therapy for migrant Puerto Ricans. *Hospital and Community Psychiatry, 33*, 299-303.

Cervantes, J. M., & Ramirez, O. (1995). Spirituality and family dynamics in psychotherapy with Latino children. In K. P. Montiero (Ed.), *Ethnicity and psychology*. Dubuque, IA: Kendal/Hunt.

Cheatham, H. (1990). Empowering Black families. In H. Cheatham & J. Stewart (Eds.), *Black families* (pp. 373-393). New Brunswick, NJ: Transaction Press.

Christensen, E. W. (1989). Counseling Puerto Ricans: Some cultural considerations. In D. R. Atkinson, G. Morten, & D. W. Sue (Eds.), *Counseling American minorities* (3rd ed., pp. 205-212). Dubuque, IA: Wm. C. Brown.

Congress, E. (1997). *Multicultural perspectives in working with families*. New York: Springer.

Connell, J. P., Spencer, M. B., & Aber, J. L. (1994). Educational risk and resilience in African-American youth: Context, self, action, and outcomes in school. *Child Development, 65*, 493-506.

Dana, R. (1993). *Multicultural assessment perspectives for professional psychology*. Boston: Allyn & Bacon.

deShazer, S. (1985). *Clues: Investigating solutions in brief therapy*. New York: Norton.

del Pinal, J., & Singer, A. (1997). Generations of diversity: Latinos in the United States. *Population Bulletin, 52*(3), 1-48.

DeVita, C. J. (1996). The United States at mid-decade. *Population Bulletin, 50*(4), 1-48.

Edwards, A., & Polite, C. K. (1992). *Children of the dream: The psychology of Black success*. New York: Doubleday.

Falicov, C. J. (1996). Mexican families. In M. McGoldrick, J. Giordano, & J. K. Pearce (Eds.), *Ethnicity and family therapy* (2nd ed., pp. 169-182). New York: Guilford Press.

Fleming, C. G. (1992). African Americans. In J. D. Buenker & L. A. Ratner (Eds.), *Multiculturalism in the United States: A comparative guide to acculturation and ethnicity* (pp. 9-29). New York: Greenwood.

Ford, D. Y. (1997). Counseling middle-class African Americans. In C. C. Lee (Ed.), *Multicultural issues in counseling* (2nd ed., pp. 81-108). Alexandria, VA: American Counseling Assoication.

Garcia-Preto, N. (1996). Puerto Rican families. In M. McGoldrick, J. Giordano, & J. K. Pearce (Eds.), *Ethnicity and family therapy* (2nd ed., pp. 183-199). New York: Guilford Press.

Garrett, J. T., & Garrett, M.W. (1994). The path of good medicine: Understanding and counseling Native American Indians. *Journal of Multicultural Counseling and Development, 22,* 134-144.

Gibbs, J. T. (1980). The interpersonal orientation in mental health consultation: Toward a model of ethnic variations in consultation. *American Journal of Orthopsychiatry,45,* 430-445.

Gladding, S. (1995). *Family therapy: History, theory, and practice.* New Jersey: Prentice-Hall, Inc.

Goldenberg, I., & Goldenberg, H. (1996). *Family therapy: An overview* (4th ed). Pacific Grove, CA: Brooks/Cole.

Hays, P. A. (1996). Addressing the complexities of culture and gender in counseling. *Journal of Counseling & Development, 74,* 332-338.

Herring, R. D. (1997). Counseling indigenous American youth. In C. C. Lee (Ed.), *Multicultural issues in counseling: New approaches to diversity* ( 2nd ed., pp. 53-70). Alexandria, VA: American Counseling Association.

Hines, P., & Boyd-Franklin, N. (1996). African American families. In M. McGoldrick, J. Pearce, & J. Giordano (Eds.), *Ethnicity and family therapy* ( 2nd ed., pp. 66-84). New York: Guilford Press.

Hines, P., Garcia-Preto, N., McGoldrick, M., Almeida, R., & Weltman, S. (1999). Culture and the family life cycle. In B. Carter & M. McGoldrick (Eds), *The expanded family life cycle: Individual, family, and social perspectives* (3rd ed., pp. 69-87). Boston: Allyn & Bacon.

Ho, M. K. (1987). *Family therapy with ethnic minorities.* Newbury Park, CA: Sage.

Ho, M. K. (1989). Applying family therapy theories to Asian/ Pacific Americans. *Contemporary Family Therapy: An International Journal, 11,* 61-70.

Homma-True, R. (1990). Psychotherapeutic issues with Asian American women. *Sex Roles, 22,* 477-486.

Hoyt, K. B. (1989). The career status of women and minority persons: A 20-year retrospective. *Career Development Quarterly, 37,* 202-212.

Huang, L. (1994). An integrative approach to clinical assessment and intervention with Asian American adolescents. *Journal of Clinical Child Psychology, 23* (1), 21-31.

Inclan, J. (1990). Understanding Hispanic families: A curriculum outline. *Journal of Strategic and Systemic Therapies, 9,* 64-82.

Ingrassia, M. (1993, August 30). Endangered family. *Newsweek* 17-27.

Jayakody, R., & Chatters, L. (1997). Differences among African -American single mothers. In R. J. Taylor, J. S. Jackson, & L. M. Chatters (Eds.), *Family life in Black America* (pp. 167-184). Thousand Oaks, CA: Sage.

Juarez, R. (1985). Core issues in psychotherapy with the Hispanic child. *Psychotherapy, 22,* 441-448.

Kitano, H. H. L. (1989). A model for counseling Asian Americans. In P. B. Pedersen, J. G. Draguns, W. J. Lonner, & J. E. Trimble (Eds.), *Counseling across cultures* (3rd ed., pp. 139-151). Honolulu: University of Hawaii Press.

LaFromboise, T. D., Trimble, J. E., & Mohatt, G. V. (1990). Counseling intervention and American Indian tradition: An integrative approach. *The Counseling Psychologist, 18,* 628-654.

LaFromboise, T. D., Berman, J. S., & Sohi, B. K. (1994). American Indian women. In L. Comas-Diaz & B. Greene (Eds.), *Women of color: Integrating ethnic and gender identities in psychotherapy* (pp. 30-71). New York: Guilford Press.

Lee, S. (1998). Asian Americans: Diverse and growing. *Population Bulletin, 53*(2), 1-40.

Lee, W. L. (1999). *An introduction to multicultural counseling.* USA: Taylor & Francis.

Lieberg, C. (1996). *Calling the Midwest home.* Berkeley, CA: Wildcat Canyon Press.

Lum, D. (1992). *Social work practice and people of color: A process-stage approach.* Monterey, CA; Brooks/Cole.

Manson, S.M., & Trimble, J. E. (1982). American Indian and Alaska Native communities: Past efforts, future inquiries. In R. L. Snowden (Ed.), *Reaching the underserved: Mental health needs of neglected populations* (pp, 143-163). Beverly Hills, CA: Sage.

McAdoo, H. (Ed.). (1999). *Family ethnicity: Strength in diversity,* (2nd ed.). Thousand Oaks, CA: Sage.

McGill, D. W. (1992, June). The cultural story in multicultural family therapy. *Families in Society: The Journal of Contemporary Human Services,* 339-349.

McGoldrick, M., & Giordano, J. (1996). Overview: Ethnicity and family therapy. In M. McGoldrick, J. Giordano, & J. K. Pearce ( Eds.), *Ethnicity and family therapy* (2nd ed., pp. 1-27). New York: Guilford Press.

McLanahan, S. S., & Casper, L. (1995). Growing diversity and inequality in the American family. In R. L. Farley (Ed.), *State of the union: America in the 1900's. Vol. 2: Social trends* (pp. L45). New York: Russell Sage.

Minuchin, S. (1974). *Families and family therapy.* Cambridge, MA: Harvard University Press.

Montague, J. (1996). Counseling families from diverse cultures. *Journal of Multicultural Counseling and Development, 24,* 37-41.

Morgan, S. P., McDaniel, A., Miller, A. T., & Preston, S. H. (1993). Racial differences in households and family structure at the turn of the century. *American Journal of Sociology, 98,* 798-828.

Nieves, W., & Valle, M. (1982). The Puerto Rican family: Conflicting roles for the Puerto Rican college student. *Journal of Non-White Concerns in Personnel and Guidance, 4,* 154-160.

O'Hare, W.P., & Felt, J.C. (1991). *Asian Americans: America's fastest growing minority group.* Washington, DC: Population Reference Bureau.

O'Hare, W. P., Pollard, K. M., Mann, T. L., & Kent, K. M. (1991). African Americans in the 1990's. *Population Bulletin, 46,* 1-40.

Pinderhughes, E. (1982). Afro-American families and the victim system. In M. McGoldrick, J. Pearce, & J. Giordano (Eds.), *Ethnicity and family therapy* (pp. 108-122). New York: Guilford Press.

Ponterotto, J. G., & Casas, J. M. (1991). *Handbook of racial/ethnic minority counseling research.* Springfield, IL: Charles C. Thomas.

Ponterotto, J. G. (1987). Counseling Mexican Americans: A multimodal approach. *Journal of Multicultural Counseling and Development, 65,* 308-312.

Richardson, B., & Lee, J. (1997). Utilizing and maximizing the resources of the African American church: Strategies and tools for counseling professionals. In C. C. Lee (Ed.), *Multicultural issues in counseling: New approaches to diversity* ( 2nd ed., pp.155-170). Alexandria, VA: American Counseling Association.

Sage, G. P. (1997). Counseling American Indian adults. In C. C. Lee (Ed.), *Multicultural issues in counseling: New approaches to diversity* (pp. 35-52). Alexandria, VA: American Counseling Association.

Sanders, D. (1987). Cultural conflicts: An important factor in the academic failures of American Indian students. *Journal of Multicultural Counseling and Development, 15,* 81-90.

Schacht, A. J., Tafoya, N., & Mirabla, K. (1989). Home based therapy with American Indian families. *American Indian and Alaska Native Mental Health Research, 3,* 27-42.

Shore, J. H. (1988). Introduction. *American Indian and Alaskan Native Mental Health Research, 1,* 3-4.

Sudarkasa, N. (1999). African American females as primary parents. In H. P. McAdoo (Ed.), *Family ethnicity: Strength in diversity* (2nd ed., pp. 191-202) Thousand Oaks, CA: Sage.

Sue, D. W., & Sue, D. (1999). *Counseling the culturally different: Theory and practice* (3rd ed.). New York: John Wiley & Sons.

Sutton, C., & Broken Nose, M. A. (1996). American Indian families. In M. McGoldrick, J. Giordano, & J. K. Pearce (Eds.), *Ethnicity and family therapy* (2nd ed., pp.31- 44). New York: Guilford Press.

Tafoya, N., & DelVecchio, A. D. (1996). Back to the future: An examination of the Native American holocaust experience. In M. McGoldrick, J. Giordano, & J. Pearce (Eds.), *Ethnicity and family therapy* (2nd ed.), New York: Guilford Press.

Taylor, R. J., Jackson, J. S., & Chatters, L. M. (Eds.). (1997). *Family life in Black America.* Thousand Oaks, CA: Sage.

The Learning Network (2001). *Population of the United States by race and Hispanic origin: 2000 census results.* Retrieved November 15, 2001, from *http://In.infoplease.com/ ipa/A0762156.html*

Trimble, J. E. (1981). Value differentials and their importance in counseling American Indians. In P. B. Pedersen, J. G. Draguns, W. J. Lonner, & J. E. Trimble (Eds.), *Counseling across cultures* (pp.203-243). Honolulu, HI: University of Hawaii Press.

Trimble, J. E., & Fleming, C. M. (1989). Providing counseling services for Native American Indians: Client, counselor and community characteristics. In P.B. Pedersen, J. G. Draguns, J. Lonner, & J. E. Trimble (Eds.), *Counseling across cultures* ( 3rd ed. , pp. 177-204). Honolulu, HI: University of Hawaii Press.

Trusty, J. (in press). African Americans' educational expectations: Longitudinal causal models for women and men. *Journal of Counseling & Development.*

Trusty, J., & Harris, M. B. C. (1999). Lost talent: Predictors of the stability of educational expectations across adolescence. *Journal of Adolescent Research, 14,* 359-382.

Uba, L. (1994). *Asian Americans: Personality patterns, identity, and mental health.* New York: Guilford Press.

U. S. Census Bureau. (1990a). *1990 Census of population and housing-summary tape file 3. Summary social, economic, and housing characteristics.* Washington, DC.

U. S. Census Bureau. (1990b). *Statistical abstract of the United States.* Washington, DC: U. S. Government Printing Office.

U. S. Census Bureau. (1992a). *1990 Census of population, 1990 CP-1-4, General population characteristics.* Washington, DC: U. S. Government Printing Offiice.

U. S. Census Bureau. (1992b). *Statistical abstract of the United States: The national data book* (112th ed.). Washington, DC: U. S. Government Printing Office.

U. S. Census Bureau. (1993a, September). *We the first Americans.* Washington, DC: U.S. Government Printing Office.

U.S. Census Bureau. (1993b). *We the first Americans.* Washington DC : Author.

U.S. Census Bureau. (1996a). *Current population reports: Population projections of the United States by age, race, and Hispanic origin: 1995 to 2050.* pp. 25-1130. Washington, DC: U.S. Government Printing Office.

U.S. Census Bureau. (1996b). *Statistical abstract of the United States* (116th ed.). Washington, DC: Author.

U.S. Census Bureau. (1998). *United States Department of Commerce news, CB 98-175.* Washington, DC.

U.S. Census Bureau (2001). Resident population estimates of the United States by sex, race, and Hispanic origin. U.S. Census Bureau, Population Estimates. Retrieved June 15, 2001, from *http://www.census.gov/population/estimates/nation/intfile3-1.txt*

U.S. Department of Commerce. (1997). *Statistical abstract of the United States: 1997.* Washington, DC: U.S. Government Printing Office.

Valdivieso, R., & Davis, C. (1988). *U. S. Hispanics: Challenging issues for the 1990s.* Washington, DC: Population Reference Bureau.

Wang, L. (1994). Marriage and family therapy with people from China. *Contemporary Family Therapy: An International Journal, 16,* 25-37.

Wehrly, B. (1991). Preparing multicultural counselors. *Counseling and Human Development 24*(3), 1-24.

White, J., & Parham, T. (1990). *The psychology of Blacks: An African American perspective* (2nd ed.). Englewood Cliffs, NJ: Prentice Hall.

Willis, J.T. (1988). An effective counseling model for treating the Black family. *Family Therapy, 15,* 185-194.

Wilson, L., & Stith, S. (1993). Culturally sensitive therapy with Black clients. In D. Atkinson, G. Morten, & D. Sue (Eds.), *Counseling American minorities* (4th ed., pp.101-111). Dubuque, IA: Wm. C. Brown.

Wilson, M. N. (1986). The Black extended family: An analytical review. *Developmental Psychology, 22,* 246-258.

Yamamoto, J., & Acosta, F. X. (1982). Treatment of Asian Americans and Hispanic Americans: Similarities and differences. *American Academy of Psychoanalysis,10,* 585-607.

Zapata, J. T. (1995). Counseling Hispanic children and youth. In C. C. Lee (Ed.), *Counseling for diversity: A guide for school counselors and related professionals* (pp. 85-108). Boston: Allyn & Bacon.

*Chapter 7*

# DISABILITY: AN EMERGING TOPIC IN MULTICULTURAL COUNSELING

## *Liza M. Conyers*
Pennsylvania State University

The emergence of disability culture as a distinctive cultural phenomenon that is germane to the practice of multicultural counseling has been largely unrecognized by mainstream counselors. In fact, inclusion of the topic of disability in the discourse of multicultural counseling has been virtually nonexistent despite the fact that there is a disproportionate representation of disability among ethnic minorities in America (Rehabilitation Services Administration, 1993). This lack of attention to disability culture among counselors is reflective of an overall lack of awareness about disability, the disability rights movement, and disability culture among the general population (Mitchell & Snyder, 2000). How can disability be a culture? Is it not an illness, medical problem, or some sort of pathology? These questions both highlight the tension that led to the emergence of the disability rights movement and serve as a challenge to understanding disability culture.

Whereas the conceptualization of disability as a minority or cultural group was unheard of only 20 years ago, it is a phenomenon that has rapidly achieved recognition and legitimacy (Brown, 1995a; Peters, 2000). In 1990, the United States Congress formally recognized people with disabilities as the largest minority group in America and noted that this group has experienced systematic neglect and oppression by the broader majority culture (Americans with Disabilities Act, 1990). Proponents of disability culture firmly believe that disability is a difference to be celebrated as part of the greater diversity of human experience, not a deficiency to be cured (Mackelprang & Salsgiver, 1999). The emergence of disability culture has resulted in the production of poetry, literature, comedy, history, and political leadership that promotes a more positive role for people with disabilities in society and challenges the more oppressive majority viewpoint (Fries, 1997; Gill, 1995; Mackelprang & Salsgiver, 1999). In academic circles, a new field of disability studies has also emerged (Mitchell & Snyder, 2000).

As more and more people with disabilities are able to gain access to education, technology, employment, positive role models, and political power, disability culture is likely to continue to grow (Mackelprang & Salsgiver, 1999). However, within all minority and cultural groups there are varied levels of acculturation and identification with the norms of the group. In light of the recent emergence of disability culture, this may be particularly true among individuals with disabilities. Awareness of the wide range of perspectives on how disability has been understood in our society and knowledge of the emerging disability culture will provide counselors with greater insight into the experience of disability and greater flexibility to respect individual world-views during counseling sessions.

If counselors continue to perceive disability exclusively as a medical problem, they are likely to lack cultural sensitivity to the issues and concerns of people with disabilities that are related to the sociopolitical consequences of their minority group status. The purpose of this chapter is to provide a foundation of the knowledge, skills, and awareness needed to work effectively with this population from a multicultural counseling perspective. To this end, the following topics are addressed (a) traditional sociocultural models of disability, (b) the disability rights movement, and (c) the minority-group model of disability and the emergence of disability culture.

# TRADITIONAL SOCIOCULTURAL MODELS OF DISABILITY

traditional sociocultural models of disability have fueled a vast array of negative stereotypes and intense stigma that eventually led to the disability rights movement. Review of these models can be instrumental in gaining a better cultural understanding of the source of disability stereotypes and stigma that continue to pervade our society today (Chelberg & Kroeger, 1995). Beliefs about disability, even if erroneous, have strong implications for how individuals with disabilities are treated (Bickenbach, 1993). Whereas there is some historic relevance of how traditional sociocultural models emerged and the degree to which they have been endorsed by the society as a whole, it is fair to say that elements of each of these models persist in modern society (Gilson & Depoy, 2000). This section will review four major models of disability (moral, eugenic, medical, functional) from a historical cultural perspective and then explore how these models have limited the cultural affiliation of people with disabilities. Each of these models has had a profound impact on our society and raises fundamental questions regarding counselors' personal and cultural values regarding disability.

## Moral Model

One of the earliest and most explicitly stigmatizing models of disability is the "moral model." From this perspective, disability is culturally equated with evil and is usually presumed to be the result of a curse from God, moral inferiority, or retribution for some sinful or amoral act committed by people with disabilities, their family members, or ancestors (Smart, 2001). Throughout history, many societies considered disabilities to be caused by sin. Historically, the belief that individuals with disabilities are morally responsible for their disability or are morally inferior because of their disability has led to cruel and inhuman treatment. The Spartans are known to have abandoned people with disabilities to die in the countryside and Plato, who had a tremendous impact on Western culture, argued that people with disabilities should be put away in mysterious, unknown places (Mackelprang & Salsgiver, 1999).

The Old and the New Testaments, each of which has been instrumental in the development of Judeo-Christian thought and Western cultural beliefs, are perhaps the most influential cultural documents referenced in modern society that perpetuate the moral model of disability. In Biblical times, physical disabilities such as blindness were thought to be indicators of inner evil (Bickenbach, 1993). In the Old Testament, disability is portrayed as an indicator of God's displeasure and in the New Testament people with disabilities are generally possessed or cursed with evil (Shapiro, 1993). Whereas Judeo-Christian philosophy does not advocate exterminating individuals with disabilities, the Old Testament did not permit people with physical disabilities to enter certain places (Wright, 1983).

Evidence of the moral model is noted in the United States' history of institutionalizing many people with disabilities who were then abused and neglected. In early American history, people with mental illness, mental retardation, and other impairments were institutionalized along with criminals, again highlighting the devastating consequences of the moral view of disability. In the 1840s, Dorthea Dix led social reforms of the institutions and cited cases of individuals being locked in closets and cages, being chained naked, and lashed into obedience with sticks (Stone, 1997). Whereas some efforts were made to address these conditions, significant problems remained which led to the development of the mental patient's liberation movement in the early 1970s. This movement consisted of a national network of ex-patient groups (e.g., the Mental Patient's Liberation Project, Patient's Liberation Front) that sponsored annual conferences on Human Rights and Psychiatric Oppression and fought to improve the treatment of individuals labeled with "mental illness" (Chamberlin, 1990).

The moral view of disability has been so widely accepted throughout history that using disability to symbolically represent evil or poor character is a common literary technique (e.g., Captain Ahab, Phantom of the Opera, Richard III) that has been encouraged by professional literary guidelines. The power of this rhetorical effect is based on the often ambiguous yet visceral responses that many able-bodied people experience when they encounter an actual person with a disability (Garland Thompson, 1997), a phenomenon identified in clinical terms as relationship strain (Smart, 2001).

Whereas modern society intellectually tends to reject this moral interpretation and provides more scientific explanations of the etiology of most disabilities, the cultural impact of the moral model continues to influence attitudes and social acceptance today (Chelberg & Kroeger, 1995). A recent example of the impact of the moral model on actual individuals with disabilities is noted in the initial lack of response to the AIDS epidemic. These attitudes and beliefs continue to impede the social acceptance of individuals with HIV/AIDS. Furthermore, cultural icons, such as James Bond movies, continue to use disfigurement to portray evil characters, or use disability as a rationale for evil behavior (e.g., the villain in the recent movie "Unbreakable"). Unfortunately, as these representations of physical disability do not factually represent the lived experience of disability, they do achieve some level of universal recognition (Mitchell & Snyder, 2000). As such, a great disparity exists between the identity, perceptions, and experiences of real people living with disabilities and their fictionalized representations in popular culture (Garland Thompson, 1997). Regrettably, the real life experience of disability is negated in exchange for a more dramatic, tragic, and moralized version. Repeated portrayal of evil as an inherent quality of disability has the capacity to augment counselors' stigmatized perceptions of disability, especially among those counselors who have little experience in this area.

## Eugenicist Model

The eugenicist model of disability is similar to the moral model in the extent to which disability is considered a direct threat to the broader society. However, rather than attributing disability to moral sin, eugenicists attribute it to inferior biological traits located in the genetic composition of the individual. Eugenics emerged out of Darwin's theory of evolution and resulted from the statistical analyses of biological traits among large segments of the population (Stone, 1997). These analyses helped lead to the construction of what was considered to be "normal" through the concept of normal distribution (Smart, 2001) and also fueled social initiatives to control or eradicate "defectives" who were often racial minorities and people with disabilities. As a cultural phenomenon, eugenics is grounded in the desire to protect the genetic stock of a society by preventing the over-production of less valued members of the society (Marks, 1999a). In the United States, many citizens became concerned that civilization was doomed unless "defectives" were kept under control and prevented from multiplying (Pfeifer, 1994).

Pfeifer (1994) provides examples of how the cultural climate of the eugenicist movement limited the basic civil rights of individuals with disabilities (e.g., right to marriage, parenting). For example, during the 19th and into the 20th century, many people with disabilities were sterilized involuntarily as a "remedy" for feeblemindedness. As of 1994, involuntary sterilization was still authorized in 14 states and in many other states, courts can compel individuals with disabilities to involuntary sterilization (Pfeifer, 1994). In the early 20th century, Connecticut, as well as four other states, had laws that prohibited the marriage of any man who was an "epileptic, imbecile, or was feeble minded" from marrying a woman under 45 years of age, the presumed limit of child-bearing (Pfeifer, 1994). Likewise, women who were considered feebleminded could not marry prior to age 45. This statute was not repealed until 1969.

The right to parent is considered a basic right by the Supreme Court and can only be revoked on the premise of the safety or health of the child. Parents who have disabilities must prove their parenting skills to a far greater degree than non-disabled parents, and they are at a much higher risk for having their parenting skills challenged in court (Pfeifer, 1994). Although higher courts now tend to overthrow lower court rulings that take away parental rights of people with disabilities, this does not change the heightened scrutiny and vulnerability that these parents experience (Kirshbaum, 1996; Zemenchuk, Rogosch, & Mowbray, 1995).

Even more drastic than limiting civil rights, eugenicist cultural beliefs laid the foundation for the Holocaust in which people with disabilities were the first to be used for "scientific" experimentation and then frequently starved to death (Smart, 2001). Hitler and the Nazi regime first targeted individuals with disabilities by referring to this group as "life unworthy of life" before moving onto other groups such as gays and lesbians and the Jewish population (Smart, 2001). The eugenicist debate continues in modern society as evidenced by the debates fuelled by publication of books such as *The Bell Curve* (Herrnstein & Murray, 1994) and *Measured Lies: The Bell Curve Examined* (Kincheloe, Steinberg, & Gresson, 1997).

Eugenicists reject support of social programs for individuals with disabilities primarily because they believe that people with disabilities are unworthy and should not be helped to survive (Pelka, 1997). These themes are at the forefront of current political debates regarding public policy and the use of tax-payers' dollars. Eugenicist cultural beliefs are also evident in the practice of prenatal screening in which many parents are advised to abort fetuses with any signs of severe disabilities. In the United Kingdom, abortion is legal up to 20 weeks into pregnancy for women with healthy fetuses, but is allowed up to 40 weeks for women with fetuses which have been diagnosed as impaired (Marks, 1999a). This practice would be unheard of for racial or other minority populations. Debates about euthanasia are also cited as eugenicist in nature, as many are quick to assume that it is best for people with disabilities to be put out of their presumed misery; and many question any costs associated with accommodating the disabled (Marks, 1999a).

## Medical Model

The medical approach within Western science emerged from the enlightenment period with the optimistic ideal that humans could be perfected (Mackelprang & Salsgiver, 1999). From the medical model, disability is viewed as an organic condition and the focus of intervention is on treatment or cure (Smart, 2001). In this context, disability is pathology within an individual who is the object of medical intervention. Medical experts, primarily physicians, use objective criteria and standards to define disability, its causes, prognosis, and treatment (Fowler & Wadsworth, 1991). The medical model remains the most widely recognized and applied conceptualization of disability in Western culture (Smart, 2001), and therefore many counselors do not stop to critically assess the negative cultural assumptions of disability that have emerged from this model.

Disability is a natural part of life and human experience, yet through the lens of the medical model it is primarily viewed as pathology and therefore something that needs to be cured and excised from society (Shakespeare, 1998). It is apparent how the emphasis on pathology over the acceptance of disability as a naturally occurring phenomenon can contribute to the cultural stigmatization of disability. The identification of disability with pathology automatically implies a negative nature of disability. This concept is not universally endorsed by all people with disabilities, many of whom resent the cultural assumption that disability in and of itself is negative.

A primary focus of the medical model is to categorize people by diagnosis. Culturally, this labeling process tends to promote an inaccurate perception of disability as a dichotomous state in which one is either normal or disabled. The label "disabled" is laden with heavy affectual content that often provokes many negative stereotypes (e.g., incompetent, pitiful, tragic, dependent, sick) (Stein, 1979). In actuality, illness and health are part of one continuous spectrum (Stein, 1979); and there is wide diversity among individuals with disabilities, even within specific disability groups (e.g., Deaf, blind, physical disability, psychiatric disability). Given the emphasis that the medical model places on medical interventions, disability is often confused with being sick. When people are sick, they are not expected to be productive and are usually taken care of until they recuperate. Many people with disabilities are perfectly healthy and have no need to see a doctor beyond routine care. Nonetheless, in the vast majority of cases, they are treated as though they are sick and restricted or excused from actively participating in many life roles. This "sick" stereotype can lead to unnecessary restrictions and an unhealthy level of passivity. Failure to participate in key life roles can hinder development and create delays in social and vocational skill development.

Because the medical model of disability places such a heavy emphasis on "expert" opinion, it has been criticized for being very paternalistic and fostering the stereotype that individuals with disabilities are incompetent or childlike (Mackelprang & Salsgiver, 1999; Swain, Finkelstein, French, & Oliver, 1994). This belief that individuals with disabilities are incompetent has a direct impact on their social interactions in the community as well as their employability. For example, many people with disabilities remark that others will pose questions to their companions and attendants rather than speak directly to them. Disability usually involves a complex interaction of medical and social phenomena (Davis, 1997). Nonetheless, the cultural perception of disability from the medical model perspective tends to focus exclusively on the organic limitations of the person with the disability (Shakespeare, 1998; Swain et al., 1994). When medical treatments fail, the disability remains an individual problem that one must strive to overcome, often with little assistance from medical professionals. As many people with disabilities lack access to needed medical and community resources, they often remain at home or institutionalized. Failure to respond to treatment or overcome disability often results in the implicit message that the person with a disability is a failure. This approach can undermine the self-concept of individuals with disabilities (Reeve, 2000) and completely negates the influence of environmental, cultural, and sociopolitical factors (e.g., lack of access to appropriate medical interventions and lack of comprehensive civil rights protection prior to the passage of the ADA in 1990).

## Functional Model

The functional model defines disability with respect to the degree that it interferes with a person's ability to complete life roles (Smart, 2001). Therefore, disability is relative to an individual's activities, goals, and desires. From a functional model perspective even an otherwise "minor" injury such as losing the tip of a pinky, would be considered a major disability for a professional violinist. Similarly, a spinal cord injury may not be perceived as a disability for people who can otherwise enjoy their life roles (Conyers, Koch, & Szymanski, 1998). Because of its primary focus on occupational roles and activities of daily living, the functional model is also referred to as the economic model of disability, and is the model that is frequently used in the legal assessment of disability, workers' compensation, and in the field of rehabilitation. Instead of trying to cure disability, the aim of interventions in the functional model is to first assess the impact of the impairment on the individual's life roles and then to implement methods to improve the individual's functioning to the greatest degree possible (e.g., rehabilitation services, assistive technology). In the case of legal disputes, the functional model is often used to measure economic loss associated with disability based on loss in earning capacity and other life roles.

The functional model of disability provides important insight to the cultural aspects of disability. Because the definition of disability in this model is closely related to life roles, any major shift in society has had a dramatic impact on who is considered disabled and how those individuals are treated (Higgins, 1992). The rise in industrialization is a prime example of this phenomenon (Hahn, 1997; Higgins, 1992). Prior to industrialization, many people with disabilities lived with their families, often working on the family farm. However, with the rise of industrialization, the nature of the American workforce changed dramatically. Many machines were designed based on the average human body and people were expected to work at a certain pace in order to maximize productivity. Those who could not meet those standards were weeded out and there was an increase in the categorization of disability as well as a concurrent increase in almshouses to place these individuals for residential services.

The functional model is the foundation of the rehabilitation profession and rehabilitation interventions. Rehabilitation has been defined as a "holistic and integrated program of medical, physical, psychosocial, and vocational interventions that empower a [person with a disability] to achieve a personally fulfilling, socially meaningful, and functionally effective interaction with the world" (Banja, 1990, p.615). Following World War II, there were major advances in rehabilitation as a result of the increased funding provided by the Vocational Rehabilitation Amendments of 1954 (PL 83-565) (Jenkins, Patterson, & Szymanski, 1992). During this time, the field of rehabilitation medicine was created by Dr. Howard Rusk who was a strong advocate for the community integration of people with disabilities. He founded The Rusk Institute for Rehabilitation Medicine in 1943 (Rusk, 1972). Rehabilitation medicine differed from traditional medicine in that it focused more on improving individual functioning and the quality of life of individuals with disabilities rather than searching for a cure.

Rehabilitation services are often provided in a team approach that typically includes physicians, nurses, occupational therapists, physical therapists, recreational therapists, psychologists, social workers, counselors, and vocational rehabilitation specialists (Rusk, 1972). Common methods used to improve functional ability include medical treatment to stabilize the impairment, physical-occupational therapy to regain maximum use of residual lower and upper body function, counseling to address emotional issues that may inhibit functioning, mobility training, vocational assessments, training and job modifications, and family counseling. Another key intervention that is used to improve individual functioning is the use of assistive technology. Assistive technology is designed to compensate for any loss in function so that people with disabilities can continue in their life roles (Smart, 2001). Examples of assistive technology include computer voice systems that can voice whatever is typed into them for people with speech impairments, wheelchairs for mobility, and telecommunication devices for the deaf (TDD) which allow deaf people to use the telephone system for communication. As a result of the many specific and individualized needs that people with disabilities have, a whole new field of assistive technology now exists to continue to develop technology that addresses the functional needs of people with disabilities.

Some critique the functional model in a similar way as they do the medical model for: (a) being too paternalistic, valuing the "experts" over the person with the disability, (b) trying to "normalize" rather than accept disability, and (c) focusing on individual change rather than societal change (Swain et al., 1994). Whereas rehabilitation medicine has tried to treat the whole individual, it has also dramatically increased the number of "experts" in the lives of individuals with disabilities and the number of professional assessments (Finkelstein, 1994). Although unintended, this approach can convey the message that the lives of individuals with disabilities are fraught with problems that they are incapable of solving on their own; and therefore they need professionals to solve their problems, again underscoring (or creating) the perception of incompetence (Mitchell & Snyder, 2000). Although several laws have been passed to support full participation of individuals with disabilities in the rehabilitation process, many still express concern that the voice of individuals with disabilities is not sufficiently heard.

## Sociocultural Barriers to Disability Culture

As early as the 1950s, Beatrice Wright and Roger Barker began to draw similarities between people with disabilities and other minority groups, and to emphasize the negative impact of their lowered social status on their behavior (Myerson, 1990). Despite these early initiatives, disability continued to be experienced and perceived as an individual problem based on the traditional sociocultural perspectives. Many barriers existed to prevent people with disabilities from developing a strong cross-disability group affiliation (Gill, 1995). These barriers included the disability-specific focus of disability policy, social isolation, and lack of education.

A review of early disability policy and legislation for individuals with disabilities sheds some light on the impediments to the development of cross-disability affiliation (Shapiro, 1993). Primary emphasis of early legislation was based on the functional model, a model not conducive to establishing a communal perspective on disability. Legislation was generally targeted to specific disability groups (physical, visual, developmental). This approach created a disability hierarchy and competition among groups for resources. For example, early vocational rehabilitation legislation (e.g., The Smith-Fess Act of 1920) only authorized services for individuals with physical disabilities. People who had visual impairments, mental retardation, or mental illness were not covered by vocational rehabilitation legislation until passage of the Bardon-LaFollette Act in 1943, 23 years later. Similarly, as early as 1936 special legislation was passed to support the employment of individuals with visual impairments but did not cover others. The Randolph -Sheppard Act of 1936 allowed people classified as legally blind to operate vending stands on Federal property. This was followed up with the Wagner-O'Day Act of 1938, which made it mandatory for the federal government to purchase designated products from workshops for persons who are blind (Jenkins et al., 1992), again privileging one disability group above others. In addition to type of disability, hierarchies in disability services were also influenced by how one became disabled, and this played a key role in access to treatment and resources (Smart, 2001). For example, veterans with disabilities receive the most extensive government disability benefits and services. Likewise, individuals who have participated in the workforce or are children of those in the workforce are eligible for better benefits (SSDI) than those who have never worked before (SSI).

Social isolation has also been a long-standing problem for people with disabilities, and has contributed to the delayed formation of a cultural disability affiliation (Gill, 1995). Many people with disabilities have had limited opportunities for interaction with mainstream culture, much less the ability to communicate and socialize with others who were equally isolated. Lack of adequate resources to support their physical needs (e.g. an attendant to help them out of bed) and inaccessible environments (e.g., lack of trained sign language interpreters) also contributed to social isolation. These restrictions inhibited the ability to work, leaving many people with disabilities in abject poverty with little time or energy to do anything besides basic self-care (Peters, 2000).

Gill (1995) noted that the lack of accessible public education was another factor that created social isolation and limited the ability to share cultural experiences. Children with disabilities did not have the right to a free and accessible public education until as recently as 1975 with the passage of the Individuals with Disabilities Education Act (IDEA, originally entitled, Education for All Handicapped Children Act). Prior to IDEA, many children with severe disabilities stayed at home all day rather than going to school with their peers. The ability to foster cultural development usually requires some intellectual and political leadership that was difficult to accomplish in the absence of an educated population.

## DISABILITY RIGHTS, DISABILITY CONSCIOUSNESS, AND CIVIL RIGHTS

An important multicultural competency counseling skill is to be knowledgeable about the sociopolitical influences that affect the lives of cultural groups and minorities. Despite its tremendous impact, the disability rights movement has been defined as a sleuth movement with no widely recognized defining points or leaders (Shapiro, 1993). Although the leaders of the disability rights movement have not been widely acclaimed by our society, the movement itself achieved a success similar to the civil rights movement by challenging negative disability stereotypes and fighting for enactment of the Americans with Disabilities Act of 1990 (Longmore & Umansky, 2001). This success was due, in part, to the foundation that the civil rights movement created by raising public consciousness about oppression and discrimination, topics with which many people with disabilities, regardless of type of disability, could identify (Gill, 1995; Middleton, Rollins, & Harley, 1999). Furthermore, the success of the disability rights movement lay in the ability to unify a diverse population of millions of individuals nationwide to create a powerful political force for social change. As more and more people with disabilities had the opportunity to share their personal experiences with each other, a powerful disability consciousness developed which created a burgeoning disability culture (Gill, 1995; Mackelprang & Salsgiver, 1999). This section will provide a broad overview of the development of a disability community, the disability rights movement, key factors that facilitated a shift in the cultural perception of disability in America, and disability civil rights legislation.

### Sociocultural Influences on the Development of a Disability Community

Several sociocultural phenomena (e.g., war, aging of baby boom generation) have increased the number of people with disabilities which has contributed to advancements in modern medicine. Medical advancements and the outcome of vocational rehabilitation legislation made considerable contributions to the development of a community that would unite behind the disability rights movement and redefine disability in America.

Shapiro (1993) documented advances in modern medicine that have contributed to the increased presence of disability consciousness in our society. Notably, many of these advancements came in response to major wars. For example, during World War I, 90% of the 400 men who had paralysis died before coming home. In contrast, during World War II, 2,000 men survived with paraplegia and 85 % of them were still alive 20 years later (Shapiro,

1993). With the vast array of veterans from World War II returning with disabilities, several university campuses established specific programs to begin to accommodate veterans and others with disabilities, which increased access to higher education as well as the number of college graduates. The development of antibiotic drugs during this time was extremely instrumental in sustaining life, reducing infections, and increasing the life-span of people with spinal cord injuries (Crewe, 1993) as well as those with other illnesses.

Additional war-related medical advancements include chemotherapy and emergency medicine. Chemotherapy was developed through WW II gas experiments and has expanded the lifespan of individuals with cancer although some residual disability often persists. Emergency medicine trauma centers were modeled after helicopter evacuation units from Vietnam. As a result of emergency medicine, many more people are able to make it to the hospital alive and survive. For example, in 1980 less than 10% of individuals with spinal cord injuries or traumatic brain injuries survived compared to a 90 % survival rate currently (Smart, 2001).

In addition to the increase of individuals with acquired physical disabilities, there has also been an increase in individuals with congenital-developmental disabilities as a result of advances in neonatal medical care (Smart, 2001). Advancements in medical practice have extended the life span of all Americans and created a need for the practice of geriatrics. Given that the rate of disability tends to increase with age, we see that the aging population also plays a significant role in the emerging numbers and cultural presence of disability in daily American life. As a result of the overall increase in people with disabilities in our society, many more people (parents, siblings, friends, children, coworkers) are gaining wider exposure and experience with disability than ever before and have a greater political, economic, and social investment in their lives

Although early disability legislation did not foster cross-disability affiliation, it did support advancing the vocational training and increased community interaction of people with disabilities through employment initiatives and funding for assistive technology. Assistive technology has been instrumental to cultural integration (Smart, 2001). One basic example of this is the transformation of the wheelchair. As wheelchairs were originally designed for individuals who were expected to remain at home or within an institutional setting, they were a major obstacle for people with mobility impairments who wanted to engage in more active lifestyles in the community (Shapiro, 1993). Today there are a wide variety of wheelchairs to meet almost any individual need, ranging from sport chairs that can collapse and be stored in the back seat of a car to motorized chairs that carry respirators and can be controlled with a nod of the head. Greater access to technology has had a tremendous impact on the ability of people with disabilities to become more involved in community activities and to alleviate much of the extreme social isolation. As people became more integrated into the community, they also had greater access to one another and could begin to see similarities in how the cultural experience of disability, regardless of type, had affected all their lives in common ways.

## Birth of the Disability Rights Movement

Whereas many people with disabilities have engaged in acts of civil disobedience and struggled to control their social identities at different points throughout history (Longmore & Umansky, 2001), the development of a widespread disability rights movement did not emerge until the 1960s. Because of the close relationship between the civil rights movement and disability rights, it is not surprising that the birth of the disability rights movement in 1962 has been noted as being the same year that James Meredith integrated the University of Mississippi for African Americans (Shapiro, 1993). During that same school year, Ed Roberts, a prominent leader in the disability rights movement, entered the University of California at Berkeley. What distinguished Ed Roberts was the fact that he had quadriplegia as a result of polio and, like James Meredith, gained his admission into UC Berkeley despite extensive opposition. Perhaps Robert's first success was the way in which he changed social perceptions about the capabilities of individuals with severe disabilities. Despite the fact that Roberts could only be away from his eight-hundred-pound iron lung for several hours at a time, he managed to complete his course work and become actively involved in political debates as well as other civil rights activities (Shapiro, 1993). Robert's success facilitated the admissions of others with severe disabilities and created an intellectual, social, and political hotbed that catapulted Roberts to the forefront of the disability rights movement. By 1967 there were 12 other students with disabilities living in the UC-Berkeley university hospital who developed a strong disability community, self-named the "Rolling Quads." These students rallied together to eliminate physical and social barriers to their full participation at Berkeley--and along with efforts of other university students (e.g., Illinois)--initiated the Independent living movement (Nosek, 1992).

## Independent Living Movement

The Independent Living Movement was a central force within the disability rights movement. Although it shared many of the same principles and ideals of disability rights, the focus of its efforts were on changing the service delivery system, not pursuing civil rights. Independent living has been defined as "control over one's life based on the choice of acceptable options that minimize reliance on others in making decisions and performing everyday activities" (Nosek, 1992, p. 103). The Rolling Quads developed many of the key principles of independent living in response to their frustrations with their living arrangements at Berkeley. They actively began to pursue self-governance when one of the state vocational rehabilitation professionals threatened to withdraw funding for students based on poor grade performance. The students resented this paternalism and argued that they should not be held up to higher matriculation standards than students who were not disabled. Based on skills developed in civil rights protests, Roberts contacted the media and appealed to the liberal student body for support and eventually the counselor was removed (Shapiro, 1993). Nonetheless, the Rolling Quads concluded that in the future, they wanted to be their own case managers as they no longer trusted the motives of state-federal employees (who seemed to place the government's financial investment at a higher priority than the interests of their clients with disabilities). The Rolling Quads resented the power differential in the counseling relationship and no longer wanted to be controlled by government bureaucrats who directed their funding (Shapiro, 1993). They argued that clients should be called consumers rather than clients and that they should be treated as consumers as well. The explicit message in this change of terminology was that it was the counselor's role to serve the consumer not the other way around.

Despite the success with the matriculation battle, many of the Rolling Quads had become anxious to leave the hospital dormitory to distance themselves from the sick role stereotype. These students felt that it was stigmatizing to be seen as patients even though they were perfectly healthy and they did not want to live in a "disability frat house" forever (Shapiro, 1993, p. 49). Additionally, students who were getting ready to graduate also needed community resources now that they would no longer be eligible for university services. However, community resources were scarce. Many people from the community had already been turned away from the Center for Physical Disabilities at Berkeley due to lack of resources. It was clear that more community resources were needed and, with a degree in community organization, Roberts had the experience and training to do something about it. In 1972, Roberts founded the Berkeley Center for Independent Living (Nosek, 1992) and incorporated many of the ideals promoted by the Rolling Quads. Foremost, the center was designed as a community-based self-help group managed primarily by individuals with disabilities. It is important to note that the term *independent* does not necessarily mean living by oneself or being able to dress without the assistance of others. Rather, independence was defined as having control over one's life and having the decision-making, advocacy, and assertiveness skills, as well as access to needed resources (attendant care, accessible apartments, affordable health insurance) to be able to thrive in a community setting. Therefore, the mission was to continue to broaden access to community services and to facilitate the development of the necessary personal skills for full community integration. The response to this form of service delivery was so strong across the nation that efforts to promote the centers around the country became known as the Independent Living Movement. This movement has helped to establish independent living as a national priority and the Berkeley program served as the model from which a network of over 200 independent living centers have been created. Each individual center created local communities where people with disabilities could come together and share their cultural experiences and wisdom with each other and thrive.

## Redefining Disability and Discrimination

As people with disabilities developed more of a cultural affiliation, they began to see themselves and their life circumstances from a new lens. Disability rights activists argued that the traditional definition of disability as a biological deficit in the individual limited the civil rights of people with disabilities by placing the primary responsibility for adaptation on the individual rather than changing societal barriers (Shapiro, 1993). To assert this concern, they began to challenge the traditional definition of disability (Mackelprang & Salsgiver, 1999). A key problem with the traditional definition was that it failed to make a distinction between impairment and disability. To help articulate this distinction a number of conceptual models (e.g. Nagi, 1976, 1977 ; World Health Organization, 1980) were developed to help clarify the role of the environment in disability. Review of one of the first models to break down the concept of disability to four components (Nagi, 1976), helps to illustrate this point. The four components are (a) active pathology (the initial disruption of normal bodily processes), (b) impairment (any abnormality or loss of physiological, psychological, or anatomical structure or function), (c) functional limitation (relates more specifically to a person's restriction to perform basic physical activities as a result of impairment), and (d) disability (inability to fulfill life roles). In this model, disability addresses disadvantages resulting from how society reacts to the individual with the impairment. For example, a woman may have a spinal cord injury (active pathology) which results in paralysis (impairment), which prevents her ability to walk (functional limitation). However, the degree to which disability exists (ability to go to work) would depend upon the accessibility of her environment. If her office is accessible, she can go to work and would not be considered disabled. Unlike more traditional models of disability, having an impairment does not automatically mean that one has a disability. This distinction is important because it highlights the fact that impairments only become salient and disabling in specific settings (Marks, 1999a). The cultural importance of this distinction lies in the conceptualization of who is responsible for the level and nature of disability that exists in society and how the concept of discrimination is defined. When there is no distinction between the concept of impairment and disability, then disability is viewed as an individual tragedy that the person must struggle to overcome (medical and functional model approach). By contrast, when the concept of impairment and disability are seen as two distinct phenomena, disability is not exclusively an individual problem. Rather, more consideration is given to the impact of the social and physical environment on imposing undue restrictions. Viewed from this perspective, society's failure to accommodate the person with the impairment is viewed as discriminatory and requires civil rights intervention.

## Development of Disability Rights Organizations

With the emergence of disability consciousness, the number and type of disability rights organizations began to increase all over the country. In some cases, organizations and their leaders seemed to emerge spontaneously in response to specific incidents of social injustice; and in others, organizations were carefully orchestrated through deliberate political strategy and extensive grassroots networking. Despite plans to become a teacher, Judy Heumann became one of the nation's leading disability rights activists based on the strong spontaneous nationwide support that she received when the New York Board of Education denied her a teaching license because she had polio (Shaw, 2000). Her story was featured in a New York Times editorial entitled, *You Can be President, Not Teacher, with Polio*, and on NBC's Today Show. Although her lawsuit was eventually settled out of court, her career path was forever altered as she felt compelled to challenge the depths of disability discrimination that many of her supporters shared with her. Her first step was to simply contact those who had written letters of support to see if they wanted to meet as a group to discuss their concerns. The result was *Disabled in Action*, a disability rights group that advocated for curb cuts, ramps, and demonstrated against the Jerry Lewis telethons and other disability causes, using "in your face tactics" when more tactful approaches were ignored (Shaw, 2000, p. 99). In contrast, the *American Coalition of Citizens with Disabilities* (ACCD) was created in 1975 as the brainchild of Eunice Fiorito who had a specific agenda for creating a national disability rights movement run by people with disabilities (McMahon, 2000). The focus of ACCD was to bring all disability-specific organizations together to accomplish cross-disability goals (e.g., enactment of national civil rights legislation). These and many similar organizations (e.g., MIGHT, ADAPT, DREDF) engaged in political activity throughout the 1970s and 80s and many continue to challenge discrimination and traditional perceptions of disability in local communities throughout the country. Like the civil rights initiatives, one of the goals of the disability rights activists was to help people with disabilities focus their anger and energy towards social change (Brannon, 1995). Increasingly, people with disabilities were less tolerant of bigotry and began to demand changes in the environment (Chamberlin, 1990; Swain et al., 1994). Modern disability groups that encourage a common identity not only reflect a growth of a unified front against medical and administrative dominance but also represent an historic leap in redefining disability in positive terms (Walmsley, 1994).

## Rehabilitation Act of 1973

The success of the early disability rights and independent living movement is noted in their impact on social policy. In the Rehabilitation Act of 1973, disability is not defined as a list of individual categories or pathologies. Rather, disability is defined as (a) having a major impairment that has a substantial impact on completing major life activities (e.g., walking, eating, breathing, writing, working), (b) having a history of such impairment, or (c) being regarded as having such impairment. This definition focuses on the shared characteristics of disability. Under this definition, people with a wide range of varied disabilities all qualify. This shift in definition from the individual type of disability to a broad social category of disability reflects the cultural changes in perception of disability that were occurring at that time. This Act also authorized independent living demonstration projects, required active participation of *consumers* in the rehabilitation planning process, and established the Architectural and Transportation Barriers Compliance Board (Jenkins et al. 1992). Another major success of this Act was Section 504, which introduced limited civil rights initiatives by prohibiting employment discrimination against people with disabilities who worked for the federal government or agencies funded by the federal government. For the first time in federal legislation, discrimination was defined as the failure to provide a reasonable accommodation to a qualified individual with a disability. This requirement clearly reflects a change in social policy that acknowledges the potential role of society in limiting the life roles of people with disabilities and defining that practice as discrimination. Most importantly, Section 504 provided the legal foundation for the subsequent civil rights legislation, the Americans with Disabilities Act of 1990.

Although enactment of the Rehabilitation Act of 1973 did not require major acts of civil disobedience, getting the regulations approved did. Shaw (2000) chronicled this event. As director of the ACCD, Frank Bowe organized a civil disobedience protest at the home of Joseph Califano, the Director of Health, Education, and Welfare (HEW), as well as at all eight of HEW's regional offices. Califano then refused to allow any food, medical supplies, or communication to the protestors forcing many to retreat. Despite Califano's orders, Judy Heumann's group in California received local support and, 25 days later, Califano, was forced to sign the regulations without watering down the content. This victory was very important for disability rights activists as it demonstrated their political power and encouraged them to continue to pursue their civil rights agenda (Shapiro, 1993).

## Americans with Disabilities Act of 1990

Following HEW protests many disability activists continued to mobilize the disability community to press for full civil rights legislation (West, 1991). In response to the emerging disability community, the first White House Conference on the Handicapped was held in 1977 (Shapiro, 1993). During the 1980s, Justin Dart became a key figure in the disability rights movement and was appointed to the National Council on Disability (NCD). In this role, he traveled to all 50 states and enlisted the help of disability rights organizations nationwide (including Judy Heumann and Ed Roberts at the World Institute on Disability and Frank Bowe at ACCD) to write a draft of major civil rights policy (Reid, 2000). In 1986, the National Council on Disability published *Towards Independence*, a Congressionally mandated examination of the status of people with disabilities in the United States, that contained a series of recommendations including one for civil rights legislation (Brannon, 1995). In 1988, Dart was named co-chair of the Congressional Task Force on the Rights and Empowerment of Americans with Disabilities which was established to make recommendations regarding the proposed Americans with Disabilities Act, introduced to Congress that same year. Despite the fact that this task force was not provided with any funding, Dart used his own money and contributions from disability rights organizations and chaired 63 public forums across the United States to gain support for the ADA (Reid, 2000). These efforts resulted in thousands of petitions regarding disability discrimination being filed with Congress, clearly demonstrating the political power of constituents with disabilities. Another demonstration of the increasing political strength of people with disabilities was reflected in the Deaf President Now movement, in which the students at Galluadet University protested the appointment of a hearing president. In effect, the students shut the University down and refused to attend classes until the Board of Trustees reversed its decision. This protest received national media attention and occurred four months prior to the second vote of the Americans with Disabilities Act. Several authors have argued that this demonstration was critical to raising the needed public awareness that helped to ensure the passage of the Americans with Disabilities Act (Barnartt, 1996; Shapiro, 1993). Whereas there was some initial resistance to this Act, no one wanted to endure the threat of offending a powerful constituency of 35 million people with disabilities (Reid, 2000).

The Americans with Disabilities Act of 1990 was instrumental in that it extended the civil rights protections introduced in the Rehabilitation Act of 1973 to all people with disabilities, not just those working for the federal government (West, 1991). Much of the ADA was based on the Rehabilitation Act of 1973, including the definition of disability and key constructs such as reasonable accommodation (West, 1991). Title I of the ADA describes discrimination against people with disabilities as failure to provide reasonable accommodation, which is defined as any alteration to a job, the environment, or the way that business is done that offers qualified individuals with disabilities an equal opportunity to perform their jobs (Equal Employment Opportunity Commission, 1992). Titles II through V address public services, public accommodations, telecommunications, and other miscellaneous aspects of the Act. In order to prevent discriminating against clients with disabilities, counselors need to make sure that their services are accessible and that any use of assessment instruments are evaluated for their appropriateness for a person with a disability (American Psychological Association, 1993).

# Minority-group Model of Disability and the Emergence of Disability Culture

The minority-group model of disability (Gliedman & Roth, 1980; Hahn, 1985) developed from the social movements of the 1960s and provides a theoretical framework for the emerging disability culture perspective (Brannon, 1995). This model of disability is a radical departure from the medical and functional models in that it is based on a sociopolitical definition of disability that focuses primarily on the social or attitudinal environment (Hahn, 1993). The minority-group model views all people with disabilities as sharing one common problem--living in a society that is riddled with inaccurate, negative stereotypes about disability and unnecessary physical and social barriers. Instead of examining the particular problems that arise from the state of not seeing, not walking, or other specific disability limitations (Marks, 1999b), this model looks at the ways in which the physical and cultural environment contribute to disability. Of note, this model specifies that all aspects of the environment are molded by public policy which reflects widespread social attitudes and values, not happenstance (Hahn, 1986).

Rather than focusing on impairments that distinguish people with disabilities from one another, the minority-group model of disability takes a cross-disability perspective that views individuals with disabilities as members of a distinct minority group within a dominant nondisabled majority society. From this perspective, disability is valued as a contribution to human diversity. Nonetheless, as a minority group, individuals with disabilities face daily oppression related to their marginalized cultural status. Proponents of this model believe that negative social attitudes about disability, which result in inaccessible environments, are far more limiting to an individual with a disability than the actual physical impairment (Davis, 1997; Shakespeare, 1998; Swain et al., 1994). They note that powerful social forces such as prejudice, discrimination, and stigma are not inherent qualities of disability (Balcazar, Bradford, & Fawcett, 1988). Rather, they are part of the environment that needs to be eradicated and replaced with civil rights, respect, and a valuing of life with disability.

## Minority-Group Status and Cultural Empowerment

Although impairments are universal, their significance is influenced by the broader cultural environment (Ingstad & Whyte, 1995). The minority-group model highlights this phenomena by stressing that disabling environments are created by the social attitudes of the nondisabled majority, a far more complex challenge (Hahn, 1993). In American culture, health, beauty, strength, and youth are highly valued (Buss, 1998), which reflects an inherent bias toward the able-bodied majority. Furthermore, the American cultural emphasis on independence and individualism also conflicts with the emphasis that disability culture places on interdependence (Chelberg & Kroeger, 1995). Culturally, people with disabilities often represent a threat to the American ideal and as such are often marginalized as cultural outcasts. Hahn (1993) explains this phenomenon as aesthetic anxiety in which the nondisabled individual avoids those with disabilities because of the tremendous cultural importance of physical appearance.

The civil and women rights movements placed a heavy emphasis on cultural empowerment of African Americans and women, particularly in the ability to transform devalued characteristics into positive sources of identity (Brannon, 1995). Likewise, it had a tremendous impact on how people with varied disabilities began to view themselves as sharing a common cultural experience related to their devalued disability status (Marks, 1999a). People with many different types of disabilities identified with the struggles of African Americans and women and they realized that they shared many similar experiences of discrimination and stigma (Chamberlin, 1990). For example, many people with disabilities rejected the idea that "anatomy was destiny," a slogan used in the women's rights' movement (Shapiro, 1993, p. 47), and began to question the ways in which disability status influenced social perceptions and access to power like race and gender had.

Culture often provides people with a meaning to life, and for minorities, it can also serve as a protective shield from the oppressive forces of the dominant culture (Mackelprang & Salsgiver, 1999). One of the benefits of the disability rights movement has been an appeal to cultural concepts to develop coalitions among disability groups and to foster disability empowerment (Brannon, 1995). As a result of the increased interactions among people with disabilities, many report a strong sense of cultural identification with one another and have begun to identify themselves as members of a disability culture.

## Language

According to Gilson (2000), people who share unique cultural meanings of signs and symbols can easily identify and exclude those who do not. Within disability culture, language is often used to establish in-group and out-group boundaries. For example, a TAB (temporarily able-bodied) is a term coined for people who are "not yet disabled." This term empowers individuals with disabilities because it undermines the assumption of difference between people with and without disabilities and serves as a reminder that anyone can become disabled at anytime. "Crip" is another term used to empower people with disabilities in the tradition of reclaiming one's identity by using otherwise derogatory terms as an indication of disability pride. However, it is a term that can only be used appropriately among people with disabilities themselves. In this sense, language plays an important role in creating and maintaining a bond among members of disability culture and assures the identification of those who do not belong (Shapiro, 1993). Likewise, members of Deaf culture use uppercase, Deaf, when they are referring to a member of the Deaf culture and lowercase, deaf, when they are referring to an audiological impairment. Furthermore, specific terms are used to convey the boundaries of Deaf culture. For example, the term Deaf culture is reserved specifically for people who use American Sign language as their primary language and embrace the cultural practices of Deaf culture. By contrast, the term deaf community is used to describe a broader community of hearing, deaf, and Deaf people who have common interests (Padden, 1989). Since the enactment of special education legislation in 1975, more Deaf children are attending public schools rather that the more traditional Deaf residential schools. This change in educational demographics has created a new phenomenon of bilingualism and biculturalism -- Deaf children who have gained cultural competency in both Deaf and hearing cultures (Lane, Hoffmeister, & Bahan, 1996).

According to Brzuzy (1997) language and labeling can play an important role in either reflecting or transforming the dominant cultural definitions of minority groups. During the years of the disability rights movement, there was a clear transformation in disability labels from *crippled* to *handicapped* to *person-with-a-disability*. As disability consciousness grew, Americans with disabilities wanted to transform their image from one of helplessness to a greater emphasis on the personhood of an individual with a disability, reducing objectification. This progression mirrors the transformation in labeling of African Americans from *negro* to *colored* to *African American*. The choices of language and labels that came from within the disability community helped to create bonds to counter the derogatory and oppressive language often used by those outside of their cultural group (Gilson & Depoy, 2000). Changes in self-labeling were also made within specific disability sub-cultures. For example, people with mental illness are no longer referred to as "the chronically mentally ill" and they reject many of the common social labels for mental illness (e.g., waco, crazy, nut, mental case). Like many, they asserted a preference for person first language (e.g., person with schizophrenia, person with spinal cord injury) (Finkelstein, 1994).

How individuals or groups choose to assert their cultural affiliation can vary. Although strongly emphasized by many disability groups in the United States, endorsement of person first language is not universal among all people with disabilities. In the United Kingdom, the disability social movement has taken the opposite position from Americans in which they prefer to be called *disabled people*. In this case, the emphasis is deliberately placed on disability first to display disability pride. Deaf people also reject person first language. This is related to the fact that many Deaf people do not consider themselves to be disabled. Rather, they identify themselves as a linguistic minority with a distinct cultural heritage including the use of sign language, which manifests itself in a unique Deaf culture. The commitment to Deaf culture is so strong that many Deaf people protested the use of technological devices (e.g., choclear implants) designed to improve Deaf children's hearing abilities. They argued that it was a violation of their cultural heritage to try to take away the Deaf identity of these children.

Disability identity can be viewed as internally derived or externally imposed depending upon the lens through which it is viewed (Gilson & Depoy, 2000). From an external lens, (Mitchell & Snyder, 2000) argue that many people with disabilities must contend with a *contamination of identity*, as their impairments are often viewed as being embedded in the very essence of their physical and moral personhood. In clinical terms, this phenomenon has been termed *Spread* and refers to the power of a single characteristic to invoke inferences about a person (Wright, 1983). Given that disability is often considered to be a negative trait, the inferences associated with disability are also negative, especially in the absence of further information about the person (Wright, 1983). People with disabilities have to integrate how they are perceived publicly with their views of themselves. As such, healthy disability identity development occurs within intrapsychic, interpersonal, and social domains, and needs to be accompanied by the integration of oneself as a valued member of a community (Gilson & Depoy, 2000).

The disability community's choice to increasingly assert the right to self- definition is an example of the growth in disability and political consciousness (Anspach, 1979; Fine & Asch, 1988; Oliver, 1996; Shakespeare, 1996; Shapiro, 1993). How people choose to label themselves can be a reflection of their disability worldview (Mackelprang & Salsgiver, 1999). Therefore it is important for counselors to be sensitive to this issue. In an attempt to reduce the stigma associated with mental illness, many members of the National Association for Mental Illness (NAMI) refer to mental illness as a brain disorder. This reflects their emphasis on viewing mental illness as a biological issue requiring medical care, rather than a moral problem or sign of evil. Others strictly refer to themselves as *consumers of mental health services*--rather than patients to avoid the stigma associated with labels for mental illness (Pratt, Gill, Barrett, & Roberts, 1999). The choice of language used to describe individuals with disabilities and their life circumstances is one of the most obvious ways to reveal abelist attitudes and to note internalized abelism. Counselors who work with individuals with disabilities should be familiar with the various cultural expressions of disability identity to both gain better insight into the cultural dynamics and worldview of their clients and to be able to use language appropriately themselves to build rapport and trust.

## Image and Cultural Representation

Black history, women's history, and the history of the gay rights movement have cultural as well as political components and can provide a broader intellectual and cultural framework to view disability culture (Brannon, 1995). Like members of other cultural minority groups, individuals with disabilities have become increasingly sensitive to how their image is portrayed by the majority culture and have begun to carefully critique the assumptions behind much of the language and images that are portrayed (Mitchell & Snyder, 2000). Language has been used as a powerful tool helping to articulate how people with disabilities are devalued by non-disabled dominant groups and in defining the parameters of disability culture (Gilson & Depoy, 2000). For example, *ableism* is a term used to describe the belief that people with disabilities are inferior to those who are not disabled and is similar to the many other "isms," such as sexism or racism (Mackelprang & Salsgiver, 1999). This terminology was deliberately chosen to raise consciousness about how "ableist" attitudes devalue individuals with disabilities and lead to social policies and practices that segregate, isolate, and limit their full participation in society. Like many other minority group members, individuals with disabilities have internalized negative societal stereotypes. This "internalized ableism" can have a devastating impact on healthy psychological functioning (Mackelprang & Salsgiver, 1999). Unfortunately, such attitudes and behaviors are so rarely questioned by the majority culture that it can be difficult for counselors to identify their own abelist tendencies (Reeve, 2000). The unconscious perpetuation of abelism may not only limit the development and depth of the counseling relationship, it may limit the counselor's ability to recognize and confront self-defeating patterns of internalized abelism.

As African Americans rejected negative stereotypes associated with afrocentric features by reclaiming them with pride, incorporating slogans such as *Black is Beautiful*, people with disabilities began to claim *Disability Pride*. In addition to fighting negative representations of disability in the media, many people with disabilities are beginning to make their own cultural statements by sharing their disability pride through art, literature, poetry, and film (Brannon, 1995; Fries, 1997; Mackelprang & Salsgiver, 1999). In contrast to the traditional disability stereotypes often created by the nondisabled majority, these newer artists transform negative representations of disability and infuse strength and power where tragedy and dependency have been (Brannon, 1995). As an example, the poem, *Hearing the Sunrise*, written by Nancy Scott, is dedicated to the light sensor (an instrument that senses light and transmits this information through auditory signals for people who are blind) on her kitchen windowsill.

> The sun rises in B major
> To sing one verse of "My Way."
> Pitch to remind, tempo to awaken,
> Twenty-three seconds of song
> Bordered by silence
> Serenade through any window I choose
> On any morning.
> No long gazes,
> No missed opportunities.
> Twenty-three seconds
> Is more than enough time
> When you hear the light.*

This poem playfully refutes dominant cultural views about the tragedy of blindness often conveyed through the popular perception of "I'd rather be dead than blind." The tragic view of blindness is based on assumptions of what people who are blind are not able to do without sight. Able-bodied people often assume that because a person with a disability can not do things the "normal" (i.e., dominant culture) way, they can not do it at all. The specific assumption that this poem belies is the assumption that because one can not *see* the sunrise, one can not *experience* it. Through this poem, the poet not only experiences the sunrise, but she does so with great pleasure, *her* way. The poem conveys the poet's sense of power and control over her life through its emphasis on personal choice (awakening to the song "My Way" and placing the sensor at "any window I choose") and therefore further negates traditional assumptions of helplessness. Finally, whereas dominant culture tends to globalize the losses associated with disability, this poet explicitly asserts her perception that there are no missed opportunities.

Gilson and Depoy (2000) noted that viewing disability as a culture has significant advantages over previous or alternative views in that culture places disability within the human experience, drawing parallels among disabled people and all others. In addition to the enactment of civil rights legislation, there has been a marked change in the cultural representation of disability over the past 20 years. Since the emergence of disability culture, there have been many more positive and realistic portrayals of people with disabilities on television (e.g., Marlee Matlin, Chris Burke), the movies (e.g., Coming Home, Children of a Lesser God, Passion Fish, Gaby, Waterdance), in photography (e.g., Gans, 1994; Hevey, 1992), and in literature (e.g., Brown, 1995b; Callahan, 1989; Dunn, 1989; Miller, 1985). A number of comics with disabilities have also gained prominence and provided a humorous, yet empowering, perspective on the disability experience (Callahan, 1990; Dougan, 1993). Increasingly, these images convey the message that there is no pity or tragedy in disability (Shapiro, 1993).

In addition, many more advertisements include people with disabilities and focus on the positive and unique contribution of this population. The inclusion of people with disabilities in advertisements is also significant in that it reflects the power that this group has obtained as an important consumer group that is now being recognized and taken into consideration (Shapiro, 1993). In light of the increasing contributions to disability culture, an Institute on Disability Culture has been established and an archive of disability culture resources is

---

* Poem *Hearing the Sunrise* by Nancy Scott.

published periodically (e.g., Brown, 1995a). It is important that counselors are familiar with these resources as a way of gaining exposure to the diverse range of opinions and manifestations of disability culture. Counselors may also want to become familiar with some of the key disability magazines (e.g., Disability Rag, Mainstream: Magazine of the Able-Disabled) as a way to keep informed of current events and perspectives from the disability community.

## Disability Studies

The emergence of disability culture has also led to the academic discipline of disability studies, a field in which the cultural aspects of disability are explored, debated, and critiqued. People with disabilities can most accurately be defined as an ignored population in academic and public discourses on civil rights, identity, and representation (Fine & Asch, 1988). As with most minority populations who have sought to break down the barriers of racial, class, and gendered discrimination, disability studies is an attempt to redress the social *voicelessness* and institutional neglect of disability (Mitchell & Snyder, 2000). The field of disability studies shares the perspective of the minority group model that disability is socially constructed within a range of disabling environments (Marks, 1999a). As such, the field of disability studies is similar to other cultural studies programs and disciplines such as African American Studies. In addition to expanding the cultural knowledge of disability, disability studies can inform understanding of American culture and enlarge the scope of historical inquiry into the experience of being American (Brannon, 1995). Before the participation of scholars with disabilities, academic research on disability was primarily conducted by practitioners in applied fields in which traditional constructs of disability were empirically tested (Marks, 1999a). Today, there are a range of disability studies textbooks and readers (Davis, 1997; Hales, 1996; Shakespeare, 1998; Swain et al., 1994) as well as two academic journals, *Disability and Society*, and the *Disability Studies Quarterly*. These are additional resources that may help counselors maintain their cultural competency with this group.

## Minorities with Disabilities

Like all other people, those with disabilities are multifaceted, and a number of characteristics (e.g., gender, class, race, sexuality) influence their personal identity (Reeve, 2000). Women and minorities with disabilities often must contend with dual or triple discrimination from the majority culture while they are also the target of many cultural myths and are marginalized among members from their own cultural group. Likewise, lesbians and gays with disabilities also report a sense of hopelessness, belonging to several separate communities, but rarely finding acceptance in any (Hunt, ; Peters, 2000). Although disability may be conceptualized as occurring in the environment, its impact on particular cultural groups can not be fully understood in the abstract. Rather, disability is shaped by people's particular social and cultural identity and their positions in society (Ingstad & Whyte, 1995). Therefore, it is essential that counselors consider how disability is understood and dealt with in different cultural groups. This is particularly important given the disproportionate amount of ethnic minorities with disabilities in America (Smart, 1997). Unfortunately, some evidence suggests that minorities with disabilities have not participated in vocational rehabilitation services at the same rates as their White counterparts and may not have been exposed to the same level of opportunities for employment and cultural integration (Wilson, Jackson, & Doughty, 1999).

Clearly, racism can have an impact on the experience of disability and the consequences for people with disabilities and racial minorities are similar (Marks, 1999a). It is not uncommon for individuals with disabilities to have to combat multiple levels of discrimination and to have to integrate many different cultural phenomena into their identity development. In fact, some people with disabilities speak of living multicultural lives (Peters, 2000). Thus, counselors who work with individuals with disabilities will need to develop a broad range of cultural competencies. In these cases, failure to understand the interaction of race, gender, ethnicity, sexual orientation, and disability across varied cultures can undermine the client-counselor relationship.

## Limitations of Minority-Group Model and Disability Culture

Although the minority-group perspective and adherence to disability culture has gained popularity among an increasing number of people with disabilities, this perspective is not universally acknowledged or endorsed by all who are disabled. It is important to note that because many people with disabilities live in abject poverty, cultural issues are secondary to basic economic survival (Peters, 2000). On the other hand, a number of people with disabilities live very privileged lives and do not identify with being oppressed. Furthermore, some have criticized disability culture as being too narrow and failing to take into consideration the multiple identities of people with disabilities (Peters, 2000; Vernon, 1999).

Many of the barriers that made it difficult for a disability community to develop continue to challenge disability groups today. Despite advancements in community integration, many people with disabilities remain socially isolated with limited opportunities to interact with each other. Despite the fact that, as a cohesive group, people with disabilities have tremendous political power, tension still remains among disability groups who continue to vie for political advantage. In part, this is because the needs and life circumstances of people with differing disabilities are so diverse (French, 1994). In fact, efforts to accommodate (e.g., automatic electronic door openers) people with one type of disability (e.g., mobility impairment) can be quite hazardous to those who have a different disability (e.g., blind). Thus, the competition for money, resources, and public perception continues today (Gilson & Depoy, 2000). Furthermore, many people with disabilities have been acculturated into dominant society, either by parents who were not disabled themselves or because of lack of exposure to disability culture prior to joining the "unexpected minority." This acculturation often leads to entrenched levels of internalized abelism in which even people with disabilities do not want to be associated with one another because of the associated stigma. Similarly, there are still many people with impairments that may not be visible who do not self-identify as disabled (Peters, 2000; Reeve, 2000). Some have associated the reluctance to self-identify with the stigma of disability itself (Mackelprang & Salsgiver, 1999).

Although some authors agree with the tenets of the minority group model, they also contend that some of the difficulties faced by people with certain impairments are practically impossible to solve exclusively thorough social manipulation (French, 1994). According to French (1994), some of the social difficulties encountered by individuals with disabilities are not the result of oppressive attitudes. Rather they can result from the challenges encountered in communicating about functional limitations that impact on interpersonal relationships (e.g. difficulty of a blind person picking up on non-verbal communication). Even with accommodations, many people with disabilities often struggle with time constraints, as alternative ways of achieving goals are often more time consuming and require effort and energy that may be limited, depending on the nature of the disability. To deny these realities can lead to further oppression (French, 1994). Thus, counselors must be aware of the impact of impairments on social interactions and pay attention to the individual perspectives and concerns of each client.

## CONCLUSION

Multicultural counseling has been defined as the preparation and practices that integrate multicultural and culture specific awareness, knowledge, and skills into counseling interactions (Arredondo et al., 1996). Having a disability culture perspective invites the topic of disability into the broader discourse of multiculturalism. This allows the theory, research, and social action of multiculturalism to shed light on understanding disability as an essential element of identity and on viewing the disability community relative to others (Gilson & Depoy, 2000). An increasing number of individuals with disabilities have developed a disability consciousness and identify with many of the basic premises of disability culture, if not directly with the culture itself. Therefore, it is imperative for counselors to be aware of this perspective as well as the range of cultural influences that can effect the development and worldview of their clients with disabilities. If counselors fail to receive training on the disability culture perspective, they may continue to view their clients with disabilities exclusively from the more traditional and restrictive medical model approach that negates the impact of the cultural, social, and political environment on the life circumstance of their clients.

As with different cultural groups, it is important that counselors are aware of the specific medical conditions that resulted in their client's disability. Moreover, counselors should understand the psychosocial and sociocultural impact of the disability. The integration of these three areas is essential to avoid the restrictive medicalization of disability and to actively challenge the social constructs of disability that lead to abelism, internalized abelism, and restrictive environments and social policies that further create or exacerbate disability. To disregard a person's disability all together would be the equivalent of disregarding one's race or gender and would result in negating a core part of a client's life experience. On the other hand, treating disability as the most central feature of clients' experience may over-emphasize one aspect of their lives at the expense of other core qualities (e.g., abilities, interests, relationships). Rather than imposing their own beliefs about disability onto their clients, counselors need to listen to and understand their clients' worldviews and how they experience disability within this context. Counselors need to be able to help their clients with disabilities develop positive self-identities and need to be able to seek out supervision when their personal attitudes about disability interfere with this process (Reeve, 2000). Language plays a critical role in this process and therefore counselors and supervisors must carefully consider the language that they use when discussing disability and relating to clients and others about disability issues. How counselors use language and label people with disabilities can have a strong impact on their ability to develop rapport with clients and to reframe negative disability stereotypes. Counselors who familiarize themselves with the language and labels that have been emerging from within the disability community will have greater awareness of the implications of different terms and greater skill in countering derogatory or oppressive language that frequently goes unquestioned in the broader culture (Gilson & Depoy, 2000; Reeve, 2000).

Although knowledge of specific disabilities is important, it is essential that counselors do not impose any unnecessary restrictions on their clients based upon uninformed assumptions about resulting limitations. For example, it is not uncommon for people to assume that people with quadriplegia can not engage in active sports such as sailing (how could they get on to the boat?) or triathlons. Nonetheless, people with quadriplegia have been trained through various athletic programs across the country (note: depending on the level of spinal cord injury some people with quadriplegia have some degree of use of their arms) to become skippers and to compete in triathlons (Ziegler, 2001). These programs have used hydraulic lifts to assist with transfers on to the boat and made other mechanical modifications (e.g., arm-powered bicycles), when necessary, to accommodate individual needs. Many of these programs have only been developed within the past 15 years, despite the fact that the technology to run them has been available much longer. These new opportunities reflect the critical role that social attitudes about disability play in defining disability and altering the environment to encourage active integration of people with "disabilities." Counselors need to constantly challenge their own assumptions about disability and stay informed of the advancements in technology and social attitudes so that they are informed of the many possibilities and opportunities and ensure that their counseling services are accessible to clients with disabilities (Enright, Conyers, & Szymanski, 1998; Reeve, 2000). One way of staying current is to contact local and national disability organizations and read their newsletters, magazines, and web sites and to attend the local and national conferences that they sponsor. Given that many counselor-training programs do not focus on disability issues in their programs, it is critical that counselors seek continuing education in this content area. The annual American Counseling Association Worldwide Conference routinely provides sessions addressing disability, and could offer a valuable opportunity for counselors to expand their knowledge and skills in this area.

Finally, it is important for counselors to recognize that many counseling theories have been developed on able-bodied assumptions and do not uniformly apply to people with disabilities (Mackelprang & Salsgiver, 1999). For example, many developmental theories do not account for the implications of disability on development and therefore fail to address developmentally appropriate counseling interventions for children with disabilities. As with women, ethnic minorities, and other cultural groups, more research is needed on the applicability of various counseling theories to the experiences of people with disabilities.

## CLASS ACTIVITY

**Divide the class into pairs. Have the students read "The Magic Wand" and respond to the questions below. Once the students have responded to the questions in their pairs, bring the class together as a whole to discuss the poem and the responses to the questions. At the end of the discussion, have each pair hand in their written responses.**

**The Magic Wand**
**By Lynn Manning**

Quick-change artist extraordinaire,
I whip out my folded cane
and change from black man to blind man
with a flick of my wrist.
It is a profound metamorphosis –
Form God-gifted wizard of roundball
Dominating backboards across America
To God-gifted idiot savant
pounding out chart busters on a cockeyed whim;
From sociopathic gangbanger with death for eyes
To all-seeing soul with saintly spirit;
From rape driven misogynist
To poor motherless child;
To welfare-rich pimp
To disability rich gimp;
And from "white man's burden"
To every man's burden.

It is always a profound metamorphosis
Whether from cursed by man to cursed by God;
Or from scripture-condemned to God-Ordained,
My final form is never of my own choosing;
I only wield the wand;
You are the magician.

1. **What disability stereotypes does this poem portray?**
2. **What racial stereotypes does this poem portray?**
3. **Who controls how the person in the poem is defined? Who is the magician?**
4. **How does this poem differ from "Hearing the Sunrise" (see page #) in terms of the poet's portrayal of the (a) personal control of the individual and (b) the impact of social attitudes on the identity of the person with a disability?**
5. **How does this poem increase the readers' awareness of the impact of social labeling and the readers' role in contributing to that process?**
6. **What does this poem convey about having a multiple cultural identity?**
7. **What role can poetry play in transmitting disability cultural perspectives?**

## REFERENCES

American Psychological Association, D. o. E. M. a. S. (1993). Psychometric and assessment issues raised by the Americans with Disabilities Act. *The Score, 15*(4), 1-2, 7-14.

Americans with Disabilities Act. (1990). *Americans with Disabilities Act* .

Anspach, R. P. (1979). From stigma to identity politics: Political activism among the physically disabled and former mental patients. *Social Science of Medicine, 13A*, 765-773.

Arredondo, P., Toporek, R., Brown, S. P., Locke, D. C., Sanchez, J., & Stadler, H. (1996). Operationalization of the multicultural counseling competencies. In *A. P. S. a. C. Committee* (Ed.) (pp. 1-3): Empowerment Workshops Inc.

Balcazar, Y., Bradford, B., & Fawcett, S. (1988). Common concerns of disabled Americans: Issues and options. In M. Nagler (Ed.), *Perspectives on disability* (pp. 3-13). Palo Alto, CA: Health Markets Research.

Banja, J. D. (1990). Rehabilitation and empowerment. *Archives of physical medicine and rehabilitation, 71*, 614-615.

Barnartt, S., N. (1996). Disability culture or disability consciousness. *Journal of Disabiity Policy Studies, 7*(2), 1-19.

Bickenbach, J. E. (1993). *Physical disability and social policy*. Toronto: University of Toronto.

Brannon, R. (1995). The use of the concept of disability culture: A historian's view. *Disability Studies Quarterly, 15*(4), 3-15.

Brown, S., E. (1995a). Disability culture: Here and now. *Disability Studies Quarterly, 15*(4), 2-3.

Brown, S. E. (1995b). *Pain, plain and fancy rappings: Poetry from the disability culture*. Las Cruces: NM: Institute on Disability Culture.

Brzuzy, S. (1997). Deconstructing disability: The impact of definition. *The journal of poverty, 1*(1), 81-91.

Buss, D. M. (1998). *Evolutionary Psychology*. Boston: Allyn & Bacon.

Callahan, J. (1989). *Don't worry, he won't get far on foot: The autobiography of a dangerous man*. New York: Vintage.

Callahan, J. (1990). *Do not disturb any further*. New York: William Morrow.

Chamberlin, J. (1990). The ex-patient's movement: Where we've been and where we're going. *Journal of Mind and Behavior, 11*(3&4), 323-336.

Chelberg, G., & Kroeger, S. (1995). Tenets of disability discovery. *Disability Studies Quarterly, 15*(4), 19-21.

Conyers, L. M., Koch, L. C., & Szymanski, E. M. (1998). Life-Span perspectives on disability and work: A qualitative study. *Rehabilitation Counseling Bulletin, 42*(1), 51-75.

Crewe, N. M. (1993). Aging and severe physical disability: Patterns of change and implications for change. In M. Nagler (Ed.), *Perspectives on disability* (2nd ed., pp. 355-361). Palo Alto, CA: Health Markets Research.

Davis, L. (Ed.). (1997). *The disability studies reader*. London: Routledge.

Dougan, M. J. (1993). *Able to laugh* [Video]. Boston: Fanlight productions.

Dunn, K. (1989). *Geek love*. New York: Warner.

Enright, M., Conyers, L., & Szymanski, E. M. (1996). Career and career-related educational concerns of college students with disabilities. *Journal of Counseling and Development, 74*, 103-114.

Equal Employment Opportunity Commission. (1992). *A technical assistance manual on the employment provisions of Title I of the Americans with Disabilities Act.* Washington: DC: Author.

Fine, M., & Asch, A. (1988). Disability beyond stigma: Social interaction, discrimination, and activism. *Journal of Social Issues, 44*(1), 3-21.

Finkelstein, V. (1994). The commonality of disability. In J. Swain, V. Finkelstein, S. French, & M. Oliver (Eds.), *Disabling barriers - Enabling environments* (pp. 9-17). London: Sage in association with the Open University Press.

Fowler, C. A., & Wadsworth, J. S. (1991). Individualism and equality: Critical values in North American culture and the impact on disability. *Journal of Applied Rehabilitation Counseling, 22*(4), 19-23.

French, S. (1994). Disability, impairment or something in between? In J. Swain, V. Finkelstein, S. French, & M. Oliver (Eds.), *Disabling barriers - Enabling environments* (pp. 17-25). London: Sage in association with the Open University Press.

Fries, K. (Ed.). (1997). *Staring back: The disability experience from the inside out.* New York: Penguin Putnam, Inc.

Gans, L. (1994). *To live with grace and dignity.* Horsham: PA: LRP Publications.

Garland Thompson, R. (1997). *Extraordinary bodies: Figuring physical disability in American culture and literature.* London: Routledge.

Gill, C. (1995). A psychological view of disability culture. *Disability Studies Quarterly, 15*(4), 16-19.

Gilson, S. F., & Depoy, E. (2000). Multiculturalism and disability: A critical perspective. *Disability and Society, 15*(2), 207-218.

Gliedman, J., & Roth, W. (1980). *The unexpected minority.* New York: Harcourt Brace Jovanovich.

Hahn, H. (1985). Toward a politics of disability: Definitions, disciplines, and policies. *The Social Science Journal, 22*(4), 87-105.

Hahn, H. (1986). Disability and the urban environment: A perspective on Los Angeles. *Society and Space, 4,* 273-288.

Hahn, H. (1993). The political implications of disability definitions and data. *Journal of Disability Policy Studies, 4*(2), 41-52.

Hahn, H. (1997). Advertising the acceptably employable image: Disability and capitalism. In L. J. Davis (Ed.), *The disability studies reader* (pp. 172-186). New York: Routeledge.

Hales, G. (Ed.). (1996). *Beyond disability: Toward an enabling society.* London: Sage in association with the Open University Press.

Herrnstein, R., & Murray, C. (1994). *The bell curve: Intlligence and class sturcture in American life.* New York: Free Press.

Hevey, D. (1992). *The creatures time forgot: Photography and disability imagery.* London: Routledge.

Higgins, P. C. (1992). *Making disability: Exploring the social transformation of human variation.* Springfield: IL: Charles C. Thomas.

Hunt. ().

Ingstad, B., & Whyte, S. R. (1995). *Disability and culture.* Los Angeles, CA: University of California Press.

Jenkins, W., M., Patterson, J. B., & Szymanski, E. M. (1992). Philosophical, historical, and legislative aspects of the rehabilitation counseling profession. In R. M. Parker & E. M.

Szymanski (Eds.), *Rehabilitation counseling: Basics and beyond* (second ed., pp. 1-40). Austin: Pro-ed.

Kincheloe, J. L., Steinberg, S. R., & Gresson, A. D. I. (1997). *Measured lies: The bell curve examined*. New York: St. Martin's.

Kirshbaum, M. (1996). Mothers with physical disabilities. In D. M. Krotoski, M. Nosek, A., & M. Turk, A. (Eds.), *Women with physical disabilities* . Baltimore: Brooks Publishing Company.

Lane, H., Hoffmeister, R., & Bahan, B. (1996). *Journey into the Deaf-World*. San Diego: Dawn Sign Press.

Longmore, P. K., & Umansky, L. (2001). Disability history: From the margins to the mainstream. In P. K. Longmore & L. Umansky (Eds.), *The new disability history: American perspectives* (pp. 1-32). New York: New York University Press.

Mackelprang, R., & Salsgiver, R. (1999). *Disability: A diversity model*. Pacific Grove, CA: Brooks/Cole Publishing Company.

Marks (1999a).                    London: Routledge.

Marks, D. (1999b). *Disability: Controversial debates and psychosocial perspectives*. London: Routledge.

McMahon, B. T. (2000). Frank Bowe. In B. McMahon & L. Shaw (Eds.), *Enabling lives: Biographies of six prominent Americans with disabilities* (pp. 107-132). New York: CRC Press.

Middleton, R. A., Rollins, C. W., & Harley, D. A. (1999). The historical and political context of the civil rights of persons with disabilities: A multicultural perspective for counselors. *Journal of Multicultural Counseling and Development, 27*, 105-120.

Miller, V. (1985). *Despite this flesh: The disabled in stories and poems*. Austin: University of Texas Press.

Mitchell, D. T., & Snyder, S. L. (2000). Disability studies and the double bind of representation. In D. T. Mitchell & S. L. Snyder (Eds.), *The Body and Physical Difference: Discourses of Disability* (pp. 1-31). Ann Arbor: The University of Michigan Press.

Myerson, L. (1990). The social psychology of physical disability: 1948 and 1988. In M. Nagler (Ed.), *Perspectives on Disability* (pp. 13-23). Palo Alto, CA: Health Markets Research.

Nagi, S. Z. (1976). An epidemilogy of disability among adults in the United States. *Milbank Memorial Fund Quarterly, 54*, 439-467.

Nagi, S. Z. (1977). The disabled and rehabilitation services: A national overview. *American Rehabilitation, 2*(5), 26-33.

Nosek, M., A. (1992). Independent Living. In R. M. Parker & E. M. Szymanski (Eds.), *Rehabilitation counseling: Basics and beyond* (pp. 103-134). Austin: Pro-Ed.

Oliver, M. (1996). Defining impairment and disability: Issues at stake. In G. Barnes and G. Mercer (Eds.) *Exploring the divide: Illness and disability*. Leeds: Disability Press.

Padden, C. (1989). The deaf community and the culture of deaf people. In S. Wilcox (Ed.), *American deaf culture: An anthology* (pp. 1-16). Burtonsville, MD: Linstock.

Pelka, F. (1997). *The ABC-CLIO companion to the disability rights movement*. Santa Barbara, CA: ABC-CLIO.

Peters, S. (2000). Is there a disability culture? A syncretisation of three possible world views. *Disability and Society, 15*(4), 583-601.

Pfeifer, D. (1994). Eugenics and disability discrimination. *Disability and Society, 9*(4), 481-499.

Pratt, C. W., Gill, K. J., Barrett, N. M., & Roberts, M. M. (1999). The experience of mental illness: An introduction to psychiatric rehabilitation. In C. W. Pratt, K. J. Gill, N. M. Barrett, & M. M. Roberts (Eds.), *Psychiatric Rehabilitation* (pp. 4-23). San Diego: Academic Press.

Reeve, D. (2000). Opression within the counseling room. *Disability and Society, 14*(4), 669-682.

Rehabilitation Services Administration. (1993). *Rehabilitation Act of 1973 as Ammended by the Rehabilitation Act of 1992 (PL 102-569)*. Washington, DC: U.S. Department of Education.

Reid, C. (2000). Justin Dart, Jr. In B. McMahon & L. Shaw (Eds.), *Enabling lives: Biographies of six prominent Americans with disabilities* (pp. 65-86). New York: CRC Press.

Rusk, H. (1972). *A world to care for*. New York: Random House.

Shakespeare, T. (1996). Disability, identity, and difference. In G. Barnes and G. Mercer (Eds.) *Exploring the divide: Illness and disability*. Leeds: Disability Press.

Shakespeare, T. (Ed.). (1998). *The disability studies reader: Social science perspective*. London: Cassell.

Shapiro, J. P. (1993). *No pity*. New York: Times Books.

Shaw, L., R. (2000). Judy Heumann. In B. McMahon & L. Shaw (Eds.), *Enabling lives: Biographies of six prominent Americans with disabilities* (pp. 87-106). New York: CRC Press.

Smart, J. (2001). *Disability, society, and the individual*. Gaithersburg, MD: Aspen Publishers, Inc.

Smart, J. F. (1997). The racial/ethnic demography of disability. *Journal of Rehabilitation*, 9-15.

Stein, H., F. (1979). Rehabilitation and chronic illness in American culture: The cultural psychodynamics of a medical and social problem. *Journal of Psychological Anthropology, 2* (2), (pp. 153-176).

Stone, M. H. (1997). *Healing the mind: A history of psychiatry from antiquity to the present*. New York: W.W. Norton & Company.

Swain, J., Finkelstein, V., French, S., & Oliver, M. (Eds.). (1994). *Disabling barriers - Enabling environments*. London: Sage in association with the Open University Press.

Vernon, A. (1999). The dialectics of multiple identities and the disabled people's movement. *Disability and Society, 14*, 385-398.

Walmsley, J. (1994). 'Talking to top people': some issues relating to the citizenship of people with learning disabilities. In J. Swain, V. Finkelstein, S. French, & M. Oliver (Eds.), *Disabling barriers - Enabling environments* (pp. 257-267). London: Sage in association with the Open University Press.

West, J. (1991). *The Americans with Disabilities Act: From policy to pratice*. New York: Milbank Memorial Fund.

Wilson, K. B., Jackson, R. L., & Doughty, J. D. (1999). Vocational rehabilitation acceptance: A tale of two races in a large midwestern state. *Journal of Applied Rehabilitation Counseling, 30*(2), 25-31.

World Health Organization. (1980). *International classification of impairments, disability, and handicaps: A manual of classification relating to the consequences of disease.* Geneva: World Health Organization.

Wright, B. A. (1983). *Physical disability: A psychosocial approach.* (Vol. Second edition). New York: Harper & Row.

Zemenchuk, J. K., Rogosch, F. A., & Mowbray, C. T. (1995). Women with serious mental illness in the role of parent: Characteristics, parentling sensitivity, and needs. *Psychosocial Rehabilitation Journal, 18*(3), 77-92.

Ziegler, D. (2001). *Personal communication*, November 8, 2001.

# Chapter 8

# COUNSELING WITH INDIVIDUALS FROM THE LESBIAN AND GAY CULTURE

*Mark Pope*[*]

University of Missouri - St. Louis

## INTRODUCTION

Providing counseling for individuals who have a cultural identity as gay or lesbian is a complicated process, and requires a counselor who has a high level of multicultural counseling competence (Pope, 1995; Pope & Barret, in press). In order to provide culturally effective treatment for any cultural group, Sue, Arredondo, and McDavis (1992) reported that a counselor must have appropriate attitudes, knowledge, and skills. Terndrup, Ritter, Barret, Logan, and Mate (1997) have developed special multicultural counseling competencies for working with gays and lesbians.

### Culture versus Diversity

There is a debate ongoing among multicultural counseling leaders and within the multicultural counseling community as to the scope of the definition of "multiculturalism" (Arredondo et al., 1992; Hughes & Brinks, 1992; Pedersen & Locke, 1999; Pope, 1995). On one side of the debate are those who favor an inclusive definition of multiculturalism (including racial, ethnic, and sexual minorities), and on the other side are those who support an exclusive definition (including only ethnic and racial minorities). The split centers on the inclusion of lesbians and gays as part of that definition.

Pope (1995) has argued persuasively for an inclusive definition of multiculturalism and that lesbians and gays must be a part of that definition. Locke (1990) has responded to that position by asserting that sexual orientation is an aspect of "diversity" but does not fit his definition of "culture."

[*] Correspondence may be addressed to Mark Pope, EdD, Division of Counseling, College of Education, University of Missouri - St Louis, 8001 Natural Bridge Road, St. Louis, Missouri 63121-4499, USA, pope@umsl.edu.

The aspects of gay and lesbian culture which are salient for counseling with this population include: (a) that the multicultural counseling skills which are required for dealing with racial and ethnic minorities are also important ones for dealing with sexual minorities as well; (b) that the identity formation tasks which racial and ethnic minorities must accomplish are the same for sexual minorities; (c) that there is indeed a lesbian and gay culture; (d) that *families* are functional and not biological for gays and lesbians; (e) that whether a cultural minority is *hidden* or *visible* is not the issue; (f) that gay and lesbian oppression as well as the results of oppression by the majority culture are very real, having real effects on real people's lives, development, and career; and (g) that there are specific gay and lesbian cultural counseling competencies.

## MULTICULTURAL COUNSELING SKILLS ARE SIMILAR BETWEEN CULTURAL GROUPS

Herr and Cramer (1988), Pedersen (1988), Sue, Arredondo, and McDavis (1992), and Pope (1995) discussed the role of the counselor in a multicultural society, especially when dealing with individuals who are members of a minority culture different from their own. Herr and Cramer stated that it is very important for counselors who provide counseling to special populations to reduce the "stereotypes, discrimination, environmental barriers, and other forms of bias that typically impede the development of such groups" (p. 154). Further, in order to counsel such individuals--that is, members of a cultural minority--counselors must have some familiarity with the culture of that minority. Counselors must be familiar with the gay and lesbian culture as well as well as the status of gays and lesbians within other multicultural communities if they hope to adequately serve their clients from the gay and lesbian community (Pope, 1991; Pope, Rodriguez, and Chang, 1992).

The American Counseling Association's multicultural counseling competencies and standards (Sue, Arredondo, & McDavis, 1992) along with the American Psychological Association guidelines on cultural sensitivity (Herr & Cramer, 1988) both recommended that counselors must be culturally aware of their own backgrounds and values and biases emanating from their experiences, be comfortable with the differences which may exist between counselor and client, and be sensitive to specific circumstances which would indicate the need to refer a client to someone better able to fulfill that client's needs.

Counselors who have lesbian and gay clients must become aware of that culture in order to be knowledgeable facilitators of developmental processes. Elliot (1990) stated that counselors should become aware of the sociopolitical issues, specific knowledge, necessary information, and institutional barriers that confront gay and lesbian clients who are seeking career counseling. Counselors must also be aware of the history, culture, ethics, jargon, and sense of community that define the gay and lesbian culture.

The special needs of this cultural minority arise from the historic discrimination which has helped to define the gay and lesbian community, including the lack of civil rights, secret or semi-secret lives, oppression, rejection or ostracism by their family of origin, societal censure, lowered self-esteem due to internalized homophobia, fear and reality of physical violence, and being the object of campaigns of hatred and vilification by right-wing political groups and fundamentalist religious groups (Cooper, 1989). One difference between most ethnic and racial minorities and the gay and lesbian minority is the fear of ostracism and rejection by their family of origin, and although this is an important difference, alone it is not sufficient to deny cultural status.

Croteau and Hedstrom (1993) described the process of counseling with members of socially oppressed cultural groups as "a process of flowing back and forth between recognizing and appreciating the similarities or common humanity of the individual and recognizing and appreciating the differences or uniqueness of the client's particular culture and social oppression." (p. 201). These authors were especially discussing career counseling with lesbian women and gay men.

It is obvious from the above authors' comments that multicultural counseling skills are also applicable to lesbian and gay clients. Additionally, knowledge of gay and lesbian culture is very important for counselors who work with that population.

## ON COMING OUT: THE IDENTITY DEVELOPMENT PROCESS FOR LESBIANS AND GAYS

*Coming out* has been defined by Altman (1971) as,

the whole process whereby a person comes to identify himself/herself as homosexual, and recognizes his/her position as part of a stigmatized and semi-hidden minority. . . . The development of a homosexual identity is a long process that usually begins during adolescence, though sometimes considerably later. Because of the fears and ignorance that surround our views of sex, children discover sexual feelings and behavior incompletely, and often accompanied by great pangs of guilt. . . . [Many of us] manage to hide into our twenties a full realization that [we are] not like [them] (pp. 15-16).

Further, McDonald (1982) has described coming out as a very difficult developmental process that may not be completed well into an individual's adult years.

Myers and colleagues (1991) have identified the phases that members of marginalized groups must accomplish on their path to a positive self-identity, which they call the OTAID model (Optimal Theory Applied to Identity Development). Briefly these phases include: 0) absence of conscious awareness, 1) individuation, 2) dissonance, 3) immersion, 4) internalization, 5) integration, and 6) transformation. In this very comprehensive model the authors "provide a unifying system for understanding and conceptualizing the identity development process and describe the effect of oppression on self-identity" (p. 58).

Cass (1979) identified the specific developmental stages that gays and lesbians must accomplish: 1) identify confusion, 2) identity comparison, 3) identity tolerance, 4) identity acceptance, 5) identity pride, and 6) identity synthesis. These stages are part of what is widely termed the *coming out* process. Myers et al. (1991) acknowledged the work of Cass (1979) in expanding the scope of identity formation in a multicultural context.

Further, Pope and Jelly (1991) described the coming out process as a self-identity process. They compared the developmental stages in self-identity formation for gays and lesbians to those of major developmental theorists, including Freud, Erickson, Piaget, Kohlberg, and Super.

Further, coming out is an important and necessary developmental task for anyone who is gay or lesbian. Coleman, Butcher, and Carson (1984) provided explanation and context of general developmental tasks:

> If developmental tasks are not mastered at the appropriate stage, the individual suffers from immaturities and incompetencies and is placed at a serious disadvantage in adjusting at later developmental levels--that is, the individual becomes increasingly vulnerable through accumulated failures to master psychosocial requirements. . . . Some developmental tasks are set by the individual's own needs, some by the physical and social environment. Members of different socioeconomic and sociocultural groups face somewhat different developmental tasks (p. 111).

Pope (1992) stated that this developmental task of discovery and acceptance of who we are and how we function sexually plays an important role especially in adolescence. This is, however, also the time for many gay males and lesbians when there exists the most denial of differences with the peer group. Unfortunately, if the developmental tasks of sexual orientation identification are not accomplished during this critical time and are denied and delayed, then other tasks are also delayed causing an identification *chain reaction* and thereby delaying other tasks such as relationship formation. It is very common to hear gay men who came out when they were substantially past adolescence have all the problems associated with those of teenagers who have just begun dating. It is important to note that once the critical period has passed in the developmental task, it may be very difficult or impossible to correct the psychological difficulties that have occurred as a result of this.

## CULTURAL MINORITY IN A MULTICULTURAL SOCIETY

Gay males and lesbians are surely a sexual minority according to any measure that has been used (Bell & Weinberg, 1978; Kinsey, Pomeroy, & Martin, 1948; Kinsey, Pomeroy, Martin, & Gebhard, 1953). They are also a psychological minority in the sense that lesbians and gay men were labeled as "diseased" by the psychological community until 1973 and the 7th printing of the *Diagnostic and Statistical Manual of Mental Disorders* (2nd ed.) (American Psychiatric Association, 1980, p. 380). This change in definition was a result of a protracted professional discussion that eventually led to a membership vote on whether homosexuality *per se* was a mental disease (Bayer, 1981). Gays and lesbians, therefore, are certainly a minority created by the psychological community out of the prejudices of the majority culture.

Are lesbians and gays then a cultural minority as well? Pope (1995) found that cultural minority status has been given to groups who are minorities within the majority culture and have their own geographic living areas, economic and social organizations, cultural traditions, and rituals. Further, a definition of what constitutes a cultural minority must transcend national boundaries, although which specific groups meet the requirements of this definition may vary from country to country. For example, Chinese are a minority culture within the United States even though they are numerically the majority in China, Singapore, Taiwan, Hong Kong, Macau, and substantial minorities within several other countries, including Malaysia, Vietnam, Thailand, Burma, and Cambodia.

Within many large cities in the United States and around the world, gay males and lesbians have developed geographic communities: for example, Greenwich Village/Christopher Street in New York, Castro Street in San Francisco, the West End in St. Louis, New Town in Chicago, West Hollywood in Los Angeles, Coconut Grove in Miami. Gay- and lesbian-owned businesses abound in these areas catering to the special needs of this minority. Here you find bookstores such as the Oscar Wilde Memorial Bookshop, Judith's Room, A Different Light, and Lambda Rising Bookstore; clothing stores such as Leather Forever, Great Western Wear, Rolo, and All-American Boy; restaurants such as the Patio, Hot and Hunky Hamburgers, and Welcome Home; bars such as Twin Peaks, Clementine's, Uncle Charlie's, Ninth Circle, the Box, Girl-Spot, Rawhide, Maud's, Eagle, and Detour; and newspapers and other periodicals such as San Francisco's *Bay Area Reporter*, Boston's *Gay Community News*, *Washington Blade*, *Christopher Street*, *St. Louis Vital Voice*, and *The Edge*. These resources for the gay and lesbian community are collected and distributed through international, national, and local directories such as *Spartacus Gay Guide*, the *Gayellow Pages,* and the *Gay Book*.

Each major religious denomination, political organization, and professional organization has a lesbian and gay caucus or group associated with it. The American Counseling Association has the Association for Gay, Lesbian, and Bisexual Issues in Counseling. The National Career Development Association has its Gay, Lesbian, Bisexual Career Development Special Interest Group. The American Psychological Association has Division 44: The Society for the Psychological Study of Lesbian and Gay Issues. The American Medical Association has the Physicians for Human Rights. The Episcopalians have Integrity. The Catholics have Dignity. The Methodists have Affirmation. There is even a specific Protestant church having its origins in the lesbian and gay community, the Metropolitan Community Church. The Democrats have the Harvey Milk Democratic Club and others. The Republicans have the Log Cabin Republican Clubs. There are Gay and Lesbian Sierrans in the Sierra Club, the Golden Gate Business Association for businesses, and High Tech Gays for individuals in high technology industries. The newest additions to this panoply of cultural organizations are the employee clubs encouraged by many large corporations, including Microsoft, Hewlett-Packard, IBM, Apple, United Airlines among others.

The rituals and traditions of lesbians and gays include those like most families--long-term relationships, marriages, raising children, the celebration of anniversaries--as well as the lesbian and gay marches and parades around the world to commemorate the Stonewall Riot in 1969, the event which marks the beginning of the modern gay and lesbian rights movement (Altman, 1971; Pope & Schulz, 1990a; Pope & Schulz, 1990b).

## FAMILY FOR GAYS AND LESBIANS

One of the differences between gay and lesbian culture and the racial and ethnic cultures is the concept of family. Elliott (1990) described coming out as a unique process that differentiates lesbians and gay men from other minority cultures in that they are probably the only group where the family of origin has to be informed about their membership status. This presents a powerful cohesive experience for gay males and lesbians--a right of passage. Conversely, it is the only group where the family of origin may also reject the person for their cultural minority status.

During the coming out process, individuals gather a family around them for support of their new identity. This new family is composed of gays and lesbians--most older chronologically and most who have been *out* for a much longer period of time. This family mentors the person through the coming out process and into the gay and lesbian culture. Sometimes these individuals take on the titles as well as roles of the family of origin members. In a gay Filipino family, one older gay man took on the role of mother, and was referred to by that title. The process is, however, one of mentoring the younger person into their new identity and new culture. There may or may not be a sexual attraction or sexual involvement in these relationships. Many do not have such a sexual component; some may have begun with a sexual attraction that has faded. These chosen families--as opposed to biological families--are powerful institutions within the gay and lesbian culture. They serve many of the same functions that biological families do for their own children: (a) nurturance; (b) transmitting social and cultural mores (in this situation, for those of the lesbian and gay culture); (c) setting behavioral boundaries; (d) self-esteem and identity issues. Yet they are different precisely for the procedure of determining membership. In the chosen family, the individuals who are members are both self- and group-selected; however, because the process of coming out and of acknowledging one's sexual orientation is such a difficult and traumatic process, the individuals who band together to assist this process develop an even more fundamental tie to each other and the group. This tie is often eternal, and is a tie that is difficult to break even in the most trying circumstances. Because this tie is chosen, it is often stronger than that of biological families.

## ON BEING A HIDDEN OR VISIBLE MINORITY AND DISCLOSING SEXUAL ORIENTATION

One of the arguments which proponents of an exclusive definition of multiculturalism have raised for the exclusion of gays and lesbians from their definition is that lesbians and gays can hide their sexual orientation, that their sexual orientation is generally not automatically visible, therefore, it is not of the same quality of oppression that racial and ethnic minorities must endure (Vontress, 1992). The same argument can be raised that any person who is a member of a racial or ethnic minority and does not conform to the visible features of their group is somehow not really a part of their group. They may be able to "pass" for a member of the majority culture, but at the most fundamental level of identity formation they are required to confront this. They remain a member of their own minority and possess special issues that deserve to be addressed within their own minority as well as the majority culture.

Vontress (1992) is right in one aspect of this: few gay males or lesbians can be identified merely by appearance (Goffman, 1983). This aspect of lesbian and gay oppression, however, has its own insidious consequences. The decision to come out, therefore, is a very important one for all lesbians and gays.

For those minorities, in general, who can "hide" their membership and for sexual minorities, specifically, there are profound reasons to not hide from their family, friends, co-workers, and employers. For lesbians and gays these include their own individual mental health as well as three categories of other reasons: (a) personal and moral reasons such as honesty, integration of their sexuality into every aspect of their life, recognition of who they are as a person, and support from those around them; (b) professional/political/societal reasons such as providing a role model for other gay males and lesbians, desensitizing their co-workers and themselves toward the issue, and eliminating any fear of blackmail; and (c) practical reasons such as so that their domestic partner can get benefits, come to events, and in order to prevent slips of the tongue and embarrassment when it inevitably slips out in everyday conversation with co-workers. The most important reason, however, is the full integration of every aspect of who the person is into one fully functioning human being.

Coming out is a continuous process that has no end; gay males and lesbians must make this decision to come out any time they meet a new person, in a new situation. Pope and Schecter (1992) have identified the different methods which briefly include simply using the correct gender-specific pronouns when speaking of dates or love relationships, matter of fact statements of reality, or defiant announcements based on pejorative homophobic, racist, or sexist comments made in the workplace.

Many gays and lesbians and some racial and ethnic minorities can "pass" as nonminority individuals, but this is not a very effective method of creating a positive self-identity. In fact "passing" behavior is antithetical to creating this positive self-identity. The consequences of passing include lower self-esteem (Berger, 1982), along with feelings of inferiority and the internalization of negative self-concepts (Weinberg & Williams, 1975). The cumulative effect of this devaluing of self and like-others is emotionally unhealthy (Fischer, 1972; Freedman, 1971; Weinberg, 1971).

## GAY AND LESBIAN CULTURAL COUNSELING COMPETENCIES

Sue, Arredondo, and McDavis (1992) outlined the knowledge, attitudes, and skills which are important for providing effective multicultural counseling. Terndrup and colleagues (1997) followed their article and provided specific multicultural counseling competencies for working with clients from the gay/lesbian/bisexual/transgenderd (GLBT) culture. Terndrup and colleagues modeled their competencies after the generic professional competencies of the Council on the Accreditation of Counseling and Related Educational Programs (CACREP) using the same eight CACREP categories to organize their contribution: Human Growth and Development, Social and Cultural Foundations, Helping Relationships, Group Work, Career and Lifestyle Development, Appraisal, Research, and Professional Orientation. Competencies include, for example, counselors' familiarizing themselves with the cultural traditions, rituals, and rites of passage specific to GLBT populations (Social and Cultural Foundations) and seeking consultation or supervision to ensure that their own biases or knowledge deficits about GLBT persons do not negatively influence the helping relationship (Helping Relationships). The competencies are presented in Table 1.

In the case example that follows, the numbers corresponding to the GLBT cultural counseling competencies are placed in the text to illustrate when such competencies are required and being displayed.

## Table 1: Competencies for Counseling Gay, Lesbian, Bisexual and Transgendered (GLBT) Clients, by A. I. Terndrup, K. Y. Ritter, R. Barret, C. Logan, and R. Mate[*]

As more and more sexual minorities seek counseling services for assistance with their life challenges, all counselors need to be well versed in understanding the unique needs of this diverse population. The Association for Gay, Lesbian, and Bisexual Issues in Counseling (AGLBIC) developed the competencies that follow in order to promote the development of sound and professional counseling practice.

When integrated into graduate counseling curricula, these competencies will assist counselors-in-training in the examination of their personal biases and values regarding GLBT clients, expand their awareness of the world views of sexual minorities, and lead to the development of appropriate intervention strategies that insure effective service delivery.

### 1.0 Human Growth and Development
Competent counselors will:

1.1) understand that biological, familial, and psychosocial factors influence the course of development of GLB orientations and transgendered identities;
1.2) identify the heterosexist assumptions inherent in current lifespan development theories and account for this bias in assessment procedures and counseling practices;
1.3) consider that, due to the coming out process, GLBT individuals often may experience a lag between their chronological ages and the developmental stages delineated by current theories;
1.4) recognize that identity formation and stigma management are ongoing developmental tasks that span the lives of GLBT persons;
1.5) know that the normative developmental tasks of GLBT adolescents frequently may be complicated or compromised by identity confusion; anxiety and depression; suicidal ideation and behavior; academic failure; substance abuse; physical, sexual, and verbal abuse; homelessness; prostitution; and STD/HIV infection;
1.6) understand that the typical developmental tasks of GLBT seniors often are complicated or compromised by social isolation and invisibility; and
1.7) affirm that sexual minority persons have the potential to integrate their GLB orientations and transgendered identities into fully functioning and emotionally healthy lives.

### 2.0 Social and Cultural Foundations
Competent counselors will:

2.1) acknowledge that heterosexism is a worldview and value-system that may undermine the healthy functioning of the sexual orientations, gender identities, and behaviors of GLBT persons;
2.2) understand that heterosexism pervades the social and cultural foundations of many institutions and traditions and may foster negative attitudes toward GLBT persons;

---

[*] Reprinted with permission of Association for Gay, Lesbian, and Bisexual Issues in Counseling (AGLBIC) and the authors.

2.3) recognize how internalized prejudice, including heterosexism, racism, and sexism, may influence the counselor's own attitudes as well as those of their GLBT clients;

2.4) know that the developmental tasks of GLBT women and people of color include the formation and integration of their gender, racial and sexual identities; and

2.5) familiarize themselves with the cultural traditions, rituals, and rites of passage specific to GLBT populations.

### 3.0 Helping Relationships
Competent counselors will:

3.1) acknowledge the societal prejudice and discrimination experienced by GLBT persons and assist them in overcoming internalized negative attitudes toward their sexual orientations and gender identities;

3.2) recognize that their own sexual orientations and gender identities are relevant to the helping relationship and influence the counseling process;

3.3) seek consultation or supervision to ensure that their own biases or knowledge deficits about GLBT persons do not negatively influence the helping relationship; and

3.4) understand that attempts to alter or change the sexual orientations or gender identities of GLBT clients may be detrimental or even life-threatening, and, further, are not supported by the research and therefore should not be undertaken.

### 4.0 Group Work
Competent counselors will:

4.1) be sensitive to the dynamics that occur when groups are formed that include only one representative of any minority culture and consider the necessity of including supportive allies for GLBT clients when screening and selecting group members;

4.2) establish group norms and provide interventions that facilitate the safety and inclusion of GLBT group members;

4.3) shape group norms and create a climate that allows for the voluntary self-identification and self-disclosure of GLBT participants; and

4.4) intervene actively when either overt or covert disapproval of GLBT members threatens member safety, group cohesion and integrity.

### 5.0 Career and Lifestyle Development
Competent counselors will:

5.1) counter the occupational stereotypes that restrict the career development and decision-making of GLBT clients;

5.2) explore with GLBT clients the degree to which government statutes and union contracts do not protect workers against employment discrimination based on sexual orientation and gender identity to help GLBT clients make career choices that facilitate both identity formation and job satisfaction.

5.3) acquaint GLBT clients with sexual minority role models that increase their awareness of viable career options.

*6.0 Appraisal*
Competent counselors will:

6.1) understand that homosexuality, bisexuality, and gender nonconformity are neither forms of psychopathology nor necessarily evidence of developmental arrest;

6.2) recognize the multiple ways that societal prejudice and discrimination create problems that GLBT clients may seek to address in counseling;

6.3) consider sexual orientation and gender identity among the core characteristics that influence clients' perceptions of themselves and their worlds;

6.4) assess GLBT clients without presuming that sexual orientation or gender identity is directly related to their presenting problems;

6.5) differentiate between the effects of stigma, reactions to stress, and symptoms of psychopathology when assessing and diagnosing the presenting concerns of GLBT clients; and

6.6) recognize the potential for the heterosexist bias in the interpretation of psychological tests and measurements.

*7.0 Research*
Competent counselors will:

7.1) formulate research questions that acknowledge the possible inclusion of GLBT participants yet are not based on stereotypic assumptions regarding these subjects;

7.2) consider the ethical and legal issues involved in research with GLBT participants;

7.3) acknowledge the methodological limitations in regard to research design, confidentiality, sampling, data collection, and measurement involved in research with GLBT participants; and

7.4) recognize the potential for heterosexist bias in the interpretation and reporting of research results.

*8.0 Professional Orientation*
Competent counselors will:

8.1) know the history of the helping professions including significant factors and events that have compromised service delivery to GLBT populations;

8.2) familiarize themselves with the needs and counseling issues of GLBT clients and use nonstigmatizing and affirming mental health, educational, and community resources;

8.3) recognize the importance of educating professionals, students, supervisees, and consumers about GLBT issues and challenge misinformation or bias about minority persons; and

8.4) use professional development opportunities to enhance their attitudes, knowledge, and skills specific to counseling GLBT persons and their families.

# THE CASE OF MARIO

Mario was a 24-year old man of Italian descent who was just beginning to come out to himself (1.3). He had five different sexual encounters with men over his life. In two of those encounters he was the active initiator and had made sexual advances to the men. In the other three he was the more passive receiver of the sexual advances. He was quite comfortable in either situation and reported that to his counselor (1.7).

He had come to the counselor initially for career counseling because he was undecided as to what occupation he should pursue. He had a breadth of interests and was overwhelmed by all that he liked to do, so he thought that by talking to a counselor at his college, he could gain some direction (5.1, 5.2, 5.3).

As he and his counselor talked, Mario became quite comfortable with the counselor.

Mario had already conducted a homophobia environmental assessment and had noticed that the counselor had several GLBT-oriented books on his shelf, had a "safe zone" sticker on his door, and used the terminology *sexual orientation* instead of *preference* when talking about GLBT issues (2.2).

Mario began to talk about his coming out process and how excited he was to find his true identity. Mario's counselor inquired if he would like to talk about that process (6.4) and Mario replied that he would like to. Mario's counselor identified that Mario was at the third stage in Cass' model, namely, identity tolerance (1.7). During this stage, individuals who are coming out begin to experience themselves as "probably" gay. There remains a small piece of doubt, and they are looking for answers to their identity questions (2.3).

The counselor and Mario determined that for Mario to more effectively answer those questions would require more experience than five sexual encounters and more social-political contact with the GLBT community in all its many manifestations (2.3, 2.5). Working together they devised a schedule of GLBT events for Mario to attend, providing for more exposure to the community. These events included: (a) attending the weekly GLBT and questioning youth group meeting; (b) volunteering to work on the organizing committee for the Gay and Lesbian Pride Festival held at the end of June each year; (c) volunteering to staff the Lesbian and Gay Crisis Line; and (d) joining the local Gay Sierra Club to go hiking.

They also decided that Mario could use two additional skills, dating skills and assertiveness training (1.3). Because Mario had rarely dated either women or men, training in dating skills would be imperative. This would include all the necessary skills required to secure and participate in a date. The assertiveness training was chosen because Mario had a difficult time saying no to people he did not really want to date or have sex with. Assertiveness training was necessary for him to say no and still feel good about himself. This became the contract for the counseling sessions and preceded the career counseling sessions.

# SUMMARY AND CONCLUSIONS

This chapter has presented the aspects of gay and lesbian culture that are salient for counseling with this population: (a) that the multicultural counseling skills which are required for dealing with racial and ethnic minorities are also important ones for dealing with sexual minorities as well; (b) that the identity formation tasks which racial and ethnic minorities must accomplish are the same for sexual minorities; (c) that there is indeed a lesbian and gay culture; (d) that families are functional not biological for gays and lesbians; (e) that whether a cultural minority is hidden or visible is not the issue, gay and lesbian oppression as well as the results of that oppression by the majority culture are very real, having real effects on real people's lives, development, and career, and finally (f) that there are specific gay and lesbian cultural counseling competencies.

As Pedersen (1991a)--another of the parents of multicultural counseling--stated so forthrightly in his introduction to the special issue of the *Journal of Counseling & Development* on multiculturalism as a fourth force in counseling:

> One advantage to the term multiculturalism is that it implies a wide range of multiple groups without grading, comparing, or making them as better or worse than one another and without denying the very distinct and complementary or even contradictory perspectives that each group brings with it. (Pedersen, 1991a, p. 4)

In another article in that same issue he expands on this concept when he stated, "the broad definition of culture is particularly important in preparing counselors to deal with the complex differences among clients from or between every cultural group" (Pedersen, 1991b, p. 7).

Finally, Savickas (1992) and Pope (1995) have discussed the difference between a *salad bowl* and a *melting pot* as analogies for American multiculturalism in the 1990s. In the melting pot, each distinct group loses its characteristics and melts together into one homogeneous amalgam. Savickas described the salad bowl as a place where every culture is mixed together into a heterogeneous cornucopia of interests, beliefs, traditions, rituals, and so forth, but where each still retains its own specific character. Pope said that the multicultural counseling salad bowl is large enough to include sexual minorities, ethnic and racial minorities, and all of the other contextual issues that make us human. Without this inclusive definition, there would indeed be something missing.

## SUGGESTED EXPERIENTIAL ACTIVITIES

1. "The Closeted Conversation" -- Pair up with another person and each of you conduct a conversation about a date you had last night with someone of the same sex as you are. For the first three minutes, speak about your dating partner without mentioning their gender. For the next three minutes, speak about your date using opposite sex gender pronouns. For the next three minutes, speak about your date using same sex gender pronouns. Process this by asking the question: How did it feel to lie about the gender of your date or to not tell the truth about your date?

2. "The GLBT Cultural Plunge" -- Go to a gay, lesbian, or drag bar by yourself. Pay attention to your feelings preceding, during, immediately after, and 24-hours after you go the bar. What were your expectations? What actually happened?

# REFERENCES

Altman, D. (1971). *Homosexual: Oppression and liberation.* New York: Avon Books.

American Psychiatric Association. (1980). *Diagnostic and statistical manual of mental disorders* (3rd ed.). In "Appendix C, Comparative listing of DSM-II and DSM-III", p. 380. Washington, DC: Author.

Arredondo, P., Lee, C., Leong, F., Ponterotto, J., Redleaf, V., & Vontress, C. (1992, September). Valuing pluralism: Community building for the 21st century. In C. Lee (Chair), *Valuing pluralism.* A panel presented at the meeting of the Association for Counselor Education and Supervision, San Antonio, TX.

Bayer, R. (1981). *Homosexuality and American psychiatry: The politics of diagnosis.* New York: Basic Books.

Bell, A. P, & Weinberg, M. S. (1978). *Homosexualities: A study of diversity among men and women.* London: Mitchell Beazley.

Berger, R. (1982). *Gay and gray: The older homosexual man.* Boston: Alyson Publications.

Cass, V. C. (1979). Homosexual identity formation: A theoretical model. *Journal of Homosexuality, 4,* 219-235.

Coleman, J. C., Butcher, J. N., and Carson, R. C. (1984). *Abnormal psychology and modern life* (7th ed.). Glenview, IL: Scott, Foresman and Company.

Cooper, C. (1989, April). Social oppressions experienced by gays and lesbians. In P. Griffin and J. Genasce (Eds.). *Strategies for addressing homophobia in physical education, sports, and dance.* Workshop presented at the annual convention of the American Alliance for Health, Physical Education, Recreation, and Dance. Boston, MA.

Croteau, J. M., & Hedstrom, S. M. (1993). Integrating commonality and difference: The key to career counseling with lesbian women and gay men. *Career Development Quarterly, 41,* 201-209.

Elliott, J. E. (1990, August). *Career development with lesbian and gay clients.* Paper presented at the meeting of the American Psychological Association, Boston, MA.

Elliott, J. E. (1993). Career development with lesbian and gay clients. *Career Development Quarterly, 41,* 210-226.

Fischer, P. (1972). *The gay mystique: The myth and reality of male homosexuality.* New York: Stein & Day.

Freedman, M. (1971). *Homosexuality and psychological functioning.* Belmont, CA: Brooks/Cole.

Goffman, E. (1983). *Stigma: Notes on the management of a spoiled identity.* Englewood Cliffs, NJ: Prentice-Hall.

Herr, E., & Cramer, S. (1988). *Career guidance and counseling through the lifespan* (3rd ed.). Glenview, IL: Scott, Foresman and Company.

Hughes, M., & Brinks, D. (1992, September). *Looking forward through diversity.* A professional development institute presented at the meeting of the Association for Counselor Education and Supervision, San Antonio, TX.

Kinsey, A. C., Pomeroy, W. B., & Martin, C. E. (1948). *Sexual behavior in the human male.* Philadelphia: W. B. Saunders Company.

Kinsey, A. C., Pomeroy, W. B., Martin, C. E., & Gebhard, P. H. (1953). *Sexual behavior in the human female.* Philadelphia: W. B. Saunders Company.

Locke, D. C. (1990). A not so provincial view of multicultural counseling. *Counselor Education and Supervision, 30*, 18-25.

McDonald, G. J. (1982). Individual differences in the coming out process for gay men: Implications for theoretical models. *Journal of Homosexuality, 8*, 47-60.

Myers, L. J., Speight, S. L., Highlen, P. S., Cox, C. I., Reynolds, A. L., Adams, E. M., & Hanley, C. P. (1991). Identity development and worldview: Toward an optimal conceptualization. *Journal of Counseling & Development, 70*, 54-63.

Pedersen, P. (1988). *A handbook for development of multicultural awareness*. Alexandria, VA: American Counseling Association.

Pedersen, P. (1991a). Introduction to the special issue on multiculturalism as a fourth force in counseling. *Journal of Counseling & Development, 70*, 4.

Pedersen, P. (1991b). Multiculturalism as a generic approach to counseling. *Journal of Counseling & Development, 70*, 6-12.

Pedersen, P., & Locke, D. (Eds.) (1999). *Cultural and diversity issues in counseling*. Greensboro, NC: ERIC/CAPS.

Pope, M. (1991, December). *Issues in career development for gay males and lesbians*. Paper presented at the Multicultural Counseling Conference, San Jose State University, Gilroy, California.

Pope, M. (1992). Bias in the interpretation of psychological tests. In F. Gutierrez and S. Dworkin (Eds.), *Counseling gay men & lesbians: Journey to the end of the rainbow*, (pp. 277-292). Alexandria, VA: American Counseling Association.

Pope, M. (1995). Career interventions for gay and lesbian clients: A synopsis of practice knowledge and research needs. *Career Development Quarterly, 44*, 191-203.

Pope, M., & Barret, B. (in press). Career counseling with gay, lesbian, bisexual, and transgender persons. In S. Niles (Ed.), *Adult career development: Concepts, issues, and practices for the 21st century* (3rd ed.). Columbus, OH: National Career Development Association.

Pope, M., & Jelly, J. (1991). MBTI, sexual orientation, and career development [Summary]. *Proceedings of the 9th International Biennial Conference of the Association for Psychological Type, 9*, 231-238.

Pope, M., Rodriguez, S., & Chang, A. P. C. (1992, September). *Special issues in career development and planning for gay men*. Presented at the meeting of International Pacific Friends Societies, International Friendship Weekend 1992, San Francisco, California, USA.

Pope, M., & Schecter, E. (1992, October). *Career strategies: Career suicide or career success*. Paper presented at the 2nd Annual Lesbian and Gay Workplace Issues Conference, Stanford, California.

Pope, M., & Schulz, R. (1990). Sexual attitudes and behavior in midlife and aging homosexual males. In J. A. Lee (Ed.), *Gay midlife and maturity*. New York: Haworth.

Pope, M., & Schulz, R. (1990). Sexual attitudes and behavior in midlife and aging homosexual males. *Journal of Homosexuality, 20* (3/4), 169-177.

Savickas, M. (1992, August). Innovations in counseling for career development. In L. J. Richmond (Chair), *New perspectives on counseling for the 21st century*. Symposium conducted at the annual convention of the American Psychological Association, Washington D.C.

Sue, D. W., Arredondo, P., & McDavis, R. J. (1992). Multicultural counseling competencies and standards: A call to the profession. *Journal of Counseling & Development, 70*, 477-486.

Terndrup, A. I., Ritter, K. Y., Barret, R., Logan, C., & Mate, R. (1997). *Competencies for counseling gay, lesbian, bisexual and transgendered (GLBT) clients* [On-line]. Available: http://www.aglbic.org/competencies.html

Vontress, C. E. (1971). Racial differences: Impediments to rapport. *Journal of Counseling Psychology, 18*, 7-13.

Vontress, C. (1992, September). Valuing pluralism: Community building for the 21st century. In C. Lee (Chair), *Valuing pluralism*. A panel presented at the meeting of the Association for Counselor Education and Supervision, San Antonio, TX.

Weinberg, G. H. (1971). *Society and the healthy homosexual*. New York: St. Martin's Press.

Weinberg, M. S., & Williams, C. J. (1974). *Male homosexuals*. New York: Oxford University Press.

*Chapter 9*

# MULTICULTURAL COUNSELING FOR CAREER DEVELOPMENT

## *Roger D. Herring*
University of Arkansas-Little Rock


The following quote from Herr and Cramer (1996) illustrates the dynamic status of career counseling in the United States and in much of the world:

> Maturing theoretical perspectives; transitions to transnational and global economies, dramatic shifts in occupational structures; high unemployment rates among some groups of youths and adults; demands for higher levels of literacy, numeracy, flexibility, and leachability in the labor forces of industrialized nations; concerns about the quality of work life and worker productivity; and changes in the composition of the labor force have combined to change the content, processes, and consumers of career interventions and services. (p. xi)

These factors illustrate the continual importance of the appropriate delivery of career guidance, career counseling, and career education. Multicultural sensitivity should be embedded in the delivery of career development (Herring, 1998).

The demographics of the United States are changing at such a rapid rate that educators, at all levels, are having difficulty meeting the needs of culturally diverse populations. No longer is the cultural portrait predominantly Western European; and nowhere are the demographic changes more evident than in the nation's public schools (Herring, 1998). Herring (1998) summarized the situation in this fashion:

> To attain the desired goal of eliminating the barriers to successful career development will require multifaceted, multicultural interventions. Such interventions will entail improving counseling techniques (individual and group) and improving the current, inequitable career opportunity structure and poor educational system that created the disparity in achievement and the low expectations levels of certain ethnic minority groups. . . . The reality that these populations do internalize the negative aspects of their historical and contemporary experiences deserves to become a primary concern of school counselors as well as other helping and service personnel in educational settings. (p. 22)

This chapter will review the four most salient variables inherent in the delivery of appropriate career development to multicultural populations. The first variable emphasizes the applicability of various career development theories to diverse populations. A second variable concerns the availability of career counseling models specific to the major ethnic groups in the United States. A third variable relates to available multicultural models of career assessment. A fourth variable addresses the interaction effects of gender, ethnicity, socioeconomic status (SES), and disability status in career development.

## APPLICABILITY OF THE MAJOR CAREER DEVELOPMENT THEORIES TO DIVERSE POPULATIONS

Numerous criticisms have arisen relative to the inadequacy of theory to explain the career development of ethnic minority and special needs students. For example, Fitzgerald and Betz (1994) suggested that gender and cultural factors have been ignored in theories of career development. Cultural factors are defined by these authors as those "beliefs and attitudes commonly found among group members-often these are socialized by society (i.e., occupational gender stereotypes, internalized homophobia)" (p. 107). Three themes are considered in this lack of attention to multicultural concerns: (a) the theories are based on erroneous assumptions; (b) particular theoretical concepts are not applicable; and (c) important career determinants are omitted from the theories (Brown, Brooks, & Associates, 1996).

### Erroneous Assumptions

One erroneous assumption is that individuals have multiple choices. That is, they are free to choose among alternatives that represent their interests, values, and abilities (Herring, 1998). Patton and McMahon (1999) concluded that "the assumption that options and choices are available to individuals without some form of social discrimination operating to distort individual characteristics is violated with respect to racial and ethnic group members" (p. 102).

### Lack of Applicability

The major career theoretical models were developed to explain the development of middle-class European American men, thus resulting in aspects that are inapplicable to ethnic minority and gender populations (Herring, 1998). A number of reviews (e.g., Brooks,1990; Fitzgerald & Betz, 1994; Hackett & Lent, 1992; Leong, 1995) have concluded that no model specifically explains the career development of ethnic populations. Several authors have noted the various effects of ethnicity in their models (Gottfredson, 1981; Holland, 1985a; Super, 1990); however, these claims have not been theoretically incorporated (Patton & McMahon, 1999). In addition, some have been critical of current theories due to their reliance on attempting to confirm internal validity at the expense of external or ecological validity

(Leong & Brown, 1995; Leong 1996). That is, theorists have not paid enough attention to how well their theories generalize to various groups.

## Lack of Sufficient Determinants

Career theories omit variables that are important career determinants for ethnic minority individuals. They most frequently focus on the constraining factors of mainstream society's sociopolitical system, especially ethnic discrimination and the effects of a differential opportunity system (Herring, 1998). In addition, their attention to the perceived barriers in career development has been greatly underemphasized. Albert and Luzzo (1999) suggested that "The use of the term *perceived* to refer to such barriers implies that the career-related barriers an individual believes currently exist or may be encountered in the future are not necessarily grounded in reality or based on factual information. Yet even those barriers with no basis in reality can, and often do, have a direct impact on the career decision-making process of the individual" (p. 431).

# CAREER COUNSELING MODELS SPECIFIC TO ETHNIC GROUPS IN THE U.S.

Patton and McMahon (1999) categorized currently popular career theories according to their relevance to ethnic groups (see Table 1). Each of these categories has some relevance to multicultural populations. They also represent a continuum from least relevance to more specific relevance. These groups deserve additional and more detailed attention (see Table 1).

### Table 1 Multicultural Relevance of Career Theories

| Category | Theorists | Relevance |
|---|---|---|
| traditional | Holland (1985)<br>Super (1990) | attempts to incorporate minority issues into their conceptualizations |
| broader theories | Hackett & Betz (1981)<br>Lent & Hackett (1994)<br>Mitchell & Krumboltz (1996)<br>L.S. Gottfredson (1981) | models that may be applicable across cultures |
| recent conceptual proposals | Osipow & Littlejohn (1995)<br>Arbona (1990)<br>Cheatham (1990) | attempt to incorporate cultural validity through culture specificity |

*Source:* Adapted from *Career development and systems theory: A new relationship*, by W. Patton & M. McMahon, 1999, pp. 102-107.Pacific Grove, CA: Brooks/Cole.

## Traditional Theories

Holland (1985a) agreed that characteristics such as age, race, class, disability, and gender may restrict career options. He also contended that such affected individuals would choose the next most dominant aspect of their personality in their career choice. Holland also contended that the structure of interests conforms to his hexagon model "even when the data, sexes and cultures vary" (p. 119). However, research efforts with Mexican engineers (Fouad & Dancer, 1992), African American college students (Swanson, 1992), Black South Africans (Watson, Stead, & Schonegevel, 1997), structural meta-analysis of 20 American ethnic matrices and 76 international matrices from 18 countries (Rounds & Tacey, 1996) have demonstrated that Holland's model does not address the "specific sample differences [that] reflect the individual differences of cultures" (Hansen, 1992a, p. 188).

Similarly, Super (1990) accepted issues of ethnicity; but he did not explain how they influence the career process. Additional research is needed to determine the interactions of ethnicity with Super's three major components--self concept, developmental stages, and career patterns. Also, other important variables may be needed to explain the career development of ethnic-group members.

## Broader Theories

Gottfredson (1981), through her circumscription and compromise model, explicitly noted the effect of social factors on career choice. She defined risk factors as "attributes of the person or of the person's relation to the environment that are associated with a higher than average probability of experiencing the types of problems under consideration" (Gottfredson, 1986, p. 204). Gottfredson (1981) also acknowledged gender and occupational prestige as important social influences on the choice of careers.

The learning principles within the social learning model (Mitchell & Krumboltz, 1996) are likely to have broad applicability to various groups. The process element also has potential efficacy for ethnic groups. For example, if a member of an ethnic group has had limited learning experiences in a particular area, the counselor works with the client to structure new learning experiences (Krumboltz, 1996). However, some elements of this model (e.g., self-observation generalizations) need to be further related to specific ethnic groups (Patton & McMahon, 1999).

# MULTICULTURAL MODELS OF CAREER
## ASSESSMENT AND COUNSELING

Assessment provides the data counselors and other career personnel require to determine whether their students or clients have retained the knowledge, skills, abilities, and other objectives of career education, counseling, and development. Assessment instruments are often criticized as being biased when they are used in the assessment of ethnic minority clients. They are criticized for being inattentive to clients' socioeconomic, linguistic, contextual, conditions-of-disability, and gender characteristics. The following discussion addresses some of these concerns and attempts to enlighten helping professionals to those concerns. Attention is given to the more popular assessment devices and how they reflect multicultural efficacy. The discussion also suggests how career counselors can avoid discriminatory assessments by selecting appropriate nonbiased, nonsexist materials and procedures.

## Standards for Multicultural Assessment

The Association for Assessment in Counseling (AAC; 1993) identified 34 standards with multicultural relevance from five of their major sets of standards. These standards included 10 concerning the selection of assessment instruments according to content, 9 related to the use of reliability, validity, and norming, 4 involving scoring and administration, and 11 addressing the use and interpretation of the results of assessment. The major theme permeating these standards is the selection process.

The *Code of Fair Testing Practices in Education* (APA, 1988) included two standards in the area of content. One emphasizes the need to define the purpose of assessment and the population to be assessed. The second standard addresses the need to evaluate the test instrument for any insensitive/inappropriate content and language.

The *Responsibilities of Users of Standardized Tests* (AACD, 1989) included four standards regarding content appropriateness. The test examiner has the responsibility to (a) determine the limitations to testing created by the test taker's age, ethnic, sexual, and cultural characteristics; (b) ascertain how the assessment instrument addresses variation of motivation, pace of work, linguistic issues, and test-taking experience of the test takers; (c) ascertain whether one common or several different assessments are necessary for accurate measurement of special populations; and (d) determine whether individuals of dissimilar language groups need assessment in either or both languages.

The *Standards for Educational and Psychological Measurement* (APA, 1985) included four multiculturally appropriate standards. A test's publisher should provide the data necessary for appropriate test use and interpretation when recommending a test for linguistically diverse test takers. School and career counselors must review the interpretive test materials to ensure stereotypical and traditional roles are not depicted in case studies or examples.

The *Code of Fair Testing Practices in Education* (APA, 1988) and the *Responsibilities of Users of Standardized Tests* (AACD, 1989) require test examiners to validate that test content and normative data are congruent with test takers from diverse backgrounds. The manual needs to be reviewed and previous performance by test takers of dissimilar ethnic and racial, cultural, and gender backgrounds needs to be noted, as well as reliability and validity indicators. Normative groups need to represent sufficient numbers of diverse test takers.

The *Standards for Educational and Psychological Testing* (APA, 1985) stresses the value of reviewing the criterion-related evidence of validity. The simple translation of a test from one language to another language does not necessarily transfer the validity and reliability. Any research that investigates the degree of predictive bias due to differential prediction for groups also needs reviewing.

*Responsibilities of Users of Standardized Tests* (AACD, 1989) emphasizes the need for test examiners to use verbal clarity, calmness, empathy, and impartiality toward all test takers. Test examiners need to consider potential effects of examiner-examinee dissimilarity in ethnic, cultural, and linguistic backgrounds, attitudes, and value systems. *Standards of Educational and Psychological Testing* (AERA, APA, & NCME, 1985) also suggest examiners ensure that linguistic modifications recommended by test publishers are described in the test manual.

*Multicultural Counseling Competencies and Standards* (Sue, Arredondo, & McDavis, 1992) included three standards related to multicultural assessment. In April 1995, the Executive Board of the Association for Multicultural Counseling and Development adopted these Competencies (Arredondo et al., 1996).

H.  Culturally skilled counselors must be aware of the potential bias of assessment instruments and when interpreting findings keep in mind the client's cultural and linguistic characteristics.
I.  They also need an awareness and understanding of how culture and ethnicity may affect personality formation, vocational choices, manifestations of psychological disorders, help-seeking behavior, and the appropriateness of counseling approaches.
J.  Counselors not only must understand the technical aspects of the instruments, they must also be aware of the cultural limitations.

The American Counseling Association (ACA) revised its ethical standards (American Counseling Association, 1995) to ensure that counselors are providing specific orientation to test takers prior to and following test administration. The standards state that assessment results should be considered in proper perspective with other factors (e.g., effects of SES, ethnic, and cultural factors).

## Biases in Testing

Reynolds and Brown (1984) suggested six areas of test bias: inappropriate content, inappropriate standardization samples, examiner and language bias, inequitable social consequences, measurement of different constructs, and differential predictive validity. Bilingual and English as Second Language (ESL) students also have difficulty with oral and written instructions as well as vocabulary and syntax of test items (Drummond, 1996).

*Test taker bias factors*. Test takers require adaptations in the assessment process to avoid bias. Overgeneralizations and stereotypical statements must be avoided. The ethnic, SES, and gender differences discussed in this chapter are meant to sensitize helping professionals to differences, not to encourage them to judge students by their ethnic background, name, skin color, social class, conditions of disability, gender, or lifestyle preference. The most common test taker bias factors are test wiseness and text anxiety.

*Familiarity with the assessment process*. The test administrator cannot assume that test takers are test wise. Not all individuals are accustomed to being assessed, especially in a one-to-one situation (Grossman, 1995) such as individually administered intelligence tests. Test takers who are unfamiliar with the assessment process often become anxious (Dao, 1991). Research indicates that even a small amount of anxiety can interfere with performance (Hill, 1980).

For example, immigrant and refugee students who have never been assessed are likely to be anxious during the process (Dao, 1991). Evidence also indicates that African American and poor students are more anxious in assessment procedures than European American and middle-class students (Hill, 1980). For example, some Hispanic Americans come from countries where students are seldom appraised individually (Grossman, 1984). Many Native American Indians also fail to exhibit successful test-taking behaviors due to cultural beliefs that prevent competitive behaviors in schools.

*Motivation.* Many students and clients are not equally motivated to do their best when they are assessed. Some may not realize that the assessment is designed to evaluate them. This situation is especially true of Hispanic Americans, Native American Indians, and Southeast Asian Americans, who come from cultures where they are not evaluated in ways common in mainstream U. S. culture (Grossman, 1995). The test administrator must consider the attitudinal characteristics and encourage test takers to do their best.

*Test administrator and examiner bias.* Test administrators may themselves introduce bias to the test setting. They must recognize personal bias and how it may influence the interpretation of test results (Drummond, 1996). In testing culturally and ethnically different students, Drummond (1996) advised test administrators and examiners to:

A.  become familiar with the characteristics and learning styles of different groups,
B.  avoid stereotypes,
C.  treat all students equally and with respect and dignity, and
D.  be sure that the tests used are culturally valid and appropriate. (p. 350)

*Assessment materials and procedures.* Test administrators and examiners must have basic knowledge of the trends/issues related to the treatment of ethnically and culturally different individuals, appropriate tests and assessment procedures, and sources of referral and support (Drummond, 1996). Test administrators, examiners, and counselors need to be alert to important behavioral signals that may affect the reliability and validity of the instrument.

## Selection of Appropriate Test Instruments

In adapting instruments for career counseling and development in general, Osipow (1991) concluded that: (a) cross-cultural adaptation is extremely difficult; (b) reliance on judges' ratings has inherent difficulties; and (c) theoretical notions on which to build instruments must be very clear and made operational. The following discussion will address several of the most viable considerations in the selection of ethnically and culturally appropriate assessment materials and procedures.

The top three inventories currently in use are the *Strong Interest Inventory* (SII; Hansen, 1992b), the *Myers-Briggs Type Indicator* (MBTI; Myers & McCaulley,1985), and the *Wechsler Adult Intelligence Scale* (Wechsler, 1981). What are the multicultural implications of these and other assessment instruments? For example, Haviland and Hansen (1987) found that the *SII* has adequate criterion validity for Native American Indian college students. This section will discuss selected assessment instruments and their applicability for multicultural student populations.

*Emic and etic perspectives.* Another way of viewing the assessment of dissimilar ethnic and cultural individuals exists in the differentiation of the examiner's perspective. The terms *emic* and *etic* are used to describe the phenomena that have culture-specific (emic, culturally localized) or universal (etic, culturally generalized) application (Atkinson, Morten, & Sue, 1997; Johnson, 1990). More specifically, an etic perspective stresses the universal qualities among ethnic groups by examining and comparing many cultures from a position external to those cultures. Conversely, an emic perspective is culture-specific and examines behavior from within a culture, using criteria relative to the internal characteristics of that culture (Dana, 1993). From the etic perspective, assessment involves comparing students' scores to a normative population and comparing different students from different cultures on a construct that is assumed to be universal across all cultures.

Dana (1993) contended that examples of etic personality instruments are the *California Psychological Inventory* and the *Eysenck Personality Questionnaire*. Examples of etic intelligence/cognitive functioning instruments are the *Wechsler Intelligence Scales, System of Multicultural Pluralistic Assessment, Kaufman Assessment, Battery for Children, McCarthy Scales of Children's Abilities*, and *Stanford-Binet Intelligence Scale*. Other single construct tests for identification of psychopathology are the *State-Trait Anxiety Scale, Beck Depression Inventory, Michigan Alcoholism Screening Test*, and *Minnesota Multilphasic Personality Inventory*. All of these tests have been translated into other languages.

Emic assessment instruments include observations, case studies, studies of life events, picture story techniques, inkblot techniques, word association, sentence completion, and drawings (Drummond, 1996). Most of these methods are classified as projective, and can generate a personality description of the individual that reflects the data and mirrors the culture and ethnic group (Dana, 1993). An excellent example of the use of holistic and indigenous assessment techniques for Native American Indian and Alaska Native students, especially in gifted and talented assessment, can be reviewed in Herring (1997). Thematic apperception test versions are also available. Examples of such tests are (Drummond, 1996):

> *Thompson Modification of the* rAT-10-card version for African Americans *Themes Concerning Blacks Test-20* charcoal drawings depict aspects of African American culture and lifestyle.
> *Tell Me a Story Test* (TENIAS)-designed for Spanish speaking populations. *Michigan Picture Story Test-designed* for use with Hispanic American and African American children and adolescents.

Sentence completion methods have been used with many different cultures. The items can be designed to appraise the social norms, roles, and values of students and clients from different cultures. One caution is that formal scoring systems for emic tests are not always available or consistently reliable.

*Degree of culturation.* Culturation (whether enculturation or acculturation) is a major and complex construct (Domino & Acosta, 1987). The construct describes "the changes in behaviors and values made by members of one culture as a result of contact with another culture" (Burnam, Telles, Hough, & Escobar, 1987, p. 106). The degree of culturation to mainstream society and the extent to which the original culture has been kept provide valuable information in interpreting assessment results (Drummond, 1996).

Two examples of instruments that can provide data on the variables that affect assessment interpretation are the *Developmental Inventory of Black Consciousness* (DIBC) and the *Racial Identity Attitude Scale* (RIAS). Another useful scale is the *African Self-Consciousness Scale* (ASC), which has four dimensions: (a) awareness of Black identity; (b) recognition of survival priorities and affirmative practices, customs, and values; (c) active participation in defense of survival, liberation, and the like; and (d) recognition of racial and ethnic oppression (Baldwin & Bell, 1985).

*Interpretation of data.* Counselors may desire to review new and innovative graphic approaches to demonstrating to students what their multivariate profiles mean (Strahan & Kelly, 1994). Students frequently do not grasp data depicted in forms such as bars, stanines, percentiles, and plots. More creative visual displays coupled with raw data from a variety of interest inventories might simplify interpretations of the often-complex information in test results.

*Students with disabilities.* While vocational training and career counseling for students with disabilities is mandated, assessment of vocational potential has continued to be incongruent with placement outcomes (Vandergoot, 1987). Federal support for research projects emphasizing transition of youth with disabilities from school to work has promoted community-referenced assessment procedures, relegating psychometric tests and traditional vocational evaluations to a "nonfunctional assessment tools" category (Rusch, 1986, p. 9). Assessment strategies that can survive such charges of invalidity must meet these criteria: the assessment must consist of multiple components and be included in multiple settings by multiple assessors over a period of time (Guidubaldi, Perry, & Walker, 1989). A continuum of assessment components is beginning to emerge, as domains are defined, that relate to the environments in which students with disabilities are expected to live and work (Daniels, 1987).

McConnell (1999) addressed the effectiveness of a strategy that examined the exploration stage of career development with visually impaired high school students. The strategy employed manualized structured career planning exercises designed to be completed by students at home in collaboration with their parents. "Results indicated that students confirmed their career choices, became more aware of their career values, and were encouraged to explore future career alternatives" (p. 120).

Numerous assessment instruments are available for students with disabilities. The *Standards for Educational and Psychological Tests* (APA, 1985) also have explicit standards for the appropriate use and interpretation of standardized tests that school counselors and other appraising professionals need to know. Table 1 lists a number of tests for these populations.

## Assessment and Treatment of Abnormal Behavior

A brief discussion of abnormal behavior is important to career counseling and development. Frequently, ethnic minority students are misdiagnosed as manifesting symptoms of pathology. Such assessment errors result in these students being labeled and assigned to educational programs that potentially limit their career choices in life. Thus, the rationale exists for this section. (see Table 2)

Assessment of abnormal behavior involves identifying and describing an individual's symptoms "within the context of his or her overall level of functioning and environment" (Carson, Butcher, & Coleman, 1988, p. 531). The methods of assessment should be sensitive to ethnic, cultural, and other environmental influences on behavior and functioning. The literature involving standard assessment techniques, however, indicates that problems of bias and insensitivity exist when psychological tests and other methods developed in one cultural-ethnic context are used to assess behavior in other cultures (Nystul, 1993).

### Table 2 Examples of Assessment Instruments With Special Populations

*USES Non Reading Aptitude Test Battery (NATB)*--United States Employment Service
This test is designed for use with disadvantaged and semiliterate students, grades 9 to 12. It measures intelligence, verbal, numerical, spatial, form perception, clerical perception, motor coordination, finger dexterity, and manual dexterity.

*Wide Range Achievement Test (WRAT)*--Jastak Assessment Systems
This test can be administered to individuals 5 years to adult. It measures spelling, arithmetic, and reading. It is best used in a clinical setting as a screening device to determine approximate educational achievement levels.

*Reading-Free Vocational Interest* Inventory--Elbem Publications
This test is designed to provide information about the vocational preferences for persons with mental retardation and learning disabilities through the use of pictorial illustrations of individuals engaged in various occupational tasks.

Source: Adapted from Herring, 1998, p. 256.

For example, standard diagnostic instruments to measure depressive disorder may miss important cultural expressions of the disorder in African Americans (Adebimpe, 1997) and Native American Indians (Manson, Shore, & Bloom, 1985). In a major study of depression among Native American Indians (Manson & Shore, 1981; Manson et al., 1985), the *American Indian Depression Schedule (AIDS)* was developed to assess and diagnose depressive illness. The investigators found that depression among the Hopi Indians includes symptoms not measured by standard measures of depression such as the *Diagnostic Interview Schedule* (DIS) and the *Schedule for Affective Disorders and Schizophrenia* (SADS*)*. These measures failed to capture the short, but acute dysphoric moods sometimes reported by the Hopi (Manson et al., 1985).

In reviewing the limitations of standard assessment techniques, several authors (Higginbotham, 1979; Lonner & Ibrahim, 1989; Marsella, DeVos, & Hsu, 1979) suggested that sensitive assessment methods examine both sociocultural norms of healthy adjustment and culturally based definitions of abnormality. There is evidence that people whose problems match cultural categories of abnormality are more likely to seek folk healers (Left, 1986). Assessment of culturally sanctioned systems of cure will enhance the planning of treatment strategies (Carson et al., 1988).

Fischler and Booth (1999) presented many of the mental disorders (American Psychiatric Association, 1994) that vocational rehabilitation counselors may encounter. Each chapter offers case studies to illustrate specific psychological and psychiatric symptoms and their vocational impact. Yip (1999) described a vignette to illustrate a vocational counseling model for clients with schizophrenia. An evaluation of a vocational program designed to help young adults with severe psychiatric disabilities develop the skills necessary to choose and implement a career plan indicated that the program had positive effects on the participants' vocational and educational status, self-esteem, and hospitalization rates (see Ellison, Danley, Bromberg, & Palmer, 1999).

## The Inter-Domain Model

Unless an occupation requires exclusively intellectual abilities, career assessments should include multiple patterns of ability, not just for variable patterns of intellectual aptitude. Appraising only cognitive factors, in the ability domain, is generally limiting (Lowman, 1993). In addition, unless a counselor is dealing with a well defined problem clearly specific to a particular domain, a single test or domain driven approach to career assessment represents poor practice.

Extensive literature exists on the career implications of abilities (Lowman, 1991) and interests (e.g., Holland, 1985a), and an emerging literature on occupationally relevant personality characteristics is available as well (e.g., Hough, Eaton, Dunnette, Kamp, & McCloy, 1990; Lowman, 1991). The potential sources of bias in the inter-domain model are troublesome. Although this model might work for middle-class European American males, ability-interest-personality maps might be very different for African Americans, other European Americans, Hispanic Americans, and, especially for females (Fitzgerald & Betz, 1994).

## The Career-Development Assessment and Counseling Model

The *Career-Development Assessment and Counseling Model* (C-DAC; Hartung et al., 1998; McDaniels, 1989) recognizes that in an age of increasingly rapid cultural and economic change, no simple process of matching people and jobs can adequately meet the needs of individuals and society. Developmental career counseling initially involves sharing with clients an understanding of the normal sequence and nature of life stages and of life space (Super, Osborne, Walsh, Brown, & Niles, 1992). The Life Career Rainbow is, for this purpose, a good teaching device (Super, 1990).

The *Life Career Rainbow* (Super, 1990,1992) portrays the development of the life career of an individual from birth until death. The two outside arcs of the Rainbow show the name of the life stages and the approximate ages of transition from one stage to another. The Rainbows depict the person's career in terms of a life span and life space, formed by nine roles played first only as a child with other roles of pupil-student, leisurite, citizen, worker, spouse, homemaker, parent, and pensioner.

The C-DAC model offers the best of differential methods and an implementation of the developmental theories of career choice (Super et al., 1992). This model is founded on the three models of career development, career maturity and adaptability importance, and career determinants. The career development model is presented graphically with the Life Career Rainbow (Super, 1990). Maturity and adaptability indicate the viability of various roles in an individual's life and is a relatively recent area of investigation. Determinants incorporates many of the variables central to the *trait and factor* approach.

## The Personal Styles Inventory

The *Personal Styles Inventory* (PSI; Kunce, Cope, & Newton, 1986a, 1986b, 1989) is an empirically derived, self-report instrument designed to measure enduring and common personality characteristics. The inventory is based on the personal styles model of personality (Kunce & Cope, 1987), which uses a circumplex format to integrate data on personality characteristics in relation to two bipolar dimensions: (a) *extroversion* versus *introversion* and (b) the need for *stability* versus *change*. The 24 PSI scales relate to either one or both of these two dimensions. Style scores indicate strength of a characteristic and are unrelated to either mental health or psychopathology. The adaptive and maladaptive implications of an individual's personal styles are determined by environmental circumstances and the psychological state of the individual.

In regards to career counseling, the PSI is used to evaluate the *fit* of an individual's personal styles with career roles and expectations (Kunce, Cope, & Newton, 1991)). The use of the PSI differs from interest inventories in that the results of the *PSI* can be used to *fine tune* an individual's selection of a specific position within an occupation (Kunce et al., 1991). A major advantage is that the results do not imply either adjustment or maladjustment (Kunce at al., 1991). Schauer (1991) concluded that additional assets of the PSI are its reliability and validity, the use of precise language, and a variety of available interpretive tools. Limitations include the lack of reliability and validity data on the PSI-120 or short form and computerized narratives (Kunce et al., 1991). Schauer (1991) points out the lack of linkage to a theoretical model, the test's interpretive complexity, and assuming normality, the omission of a clear check on the validity of a person's responses.

## Holland's Typology Assessments

Holland's (1985b, 1994) *Self-Directed Search* (SDS) is considered the most widely used career interest inventory in the world. The SDS family of career assessment tools provides accurate career guidance for individuals. These easy-to-use instruments are self-administered and self-scored. The SDS system assists individuals to explore their interests and competencies, and to discover careers and occupations that best match their own personalities. These instruments are offered in English, Spanish, English Canadian, and French Canadian languages. A companion software system is also available.

The SDS is based on Holland's RIASEC theory and extensive research which asserts that most individuals can be categorized as one of six personality types: Realistic, Investigative, Artistic, Social, Enterprising, or Conventional. The normative sample for the *Assessment Booklet* (4th Ed.; Holland, 1994) was composed of 2,602 students and working adults. The sample included 1,600 females and 1,002 males ranging in age from 17-65 years (M=23.5), with 75% Caucasians, 8% African Americans, 7% Hispanics, 4% Asian Americans, 1% Native American Indians/Alaskan Natives, and 5% from other ethnic backgrounds.

Gade, Fuqua, and Hurlburt (1988) examined a sample of 596 Native American Indian high school students (321 females, 275 males) enrolled in eight schools in Manitoba, Canada. The *Self-Directed Search* (Holland, 1985b) was used to determine personality types and the Teacher Approval and Education Acceptance scales of the *Survey of Study Habits and Attitudes-Form H* (SSHA; Brown & Holtzman, 1967) was used to measure educational satisfaction. Results of an analysis of variance indicated that students with an Investigative or Social personality type had significantly higher scores on educational satisfaction than students with a Realistic type code. These results are in the direction hypothesized by Holland and provide support for the generalizability of this hypothesis to a Native American Indian population.

## Qualitative Evaluation

Researchers and scientist-practitioners often do not use qualitative measures in their evaluations of career awareness and career maturity. This omission only serves to infer that only quantitative procedures are useful. Objective researchers contend that both modes are needed to obtain a total picture of career education and guidance.

In one study, 166 high school juniors (including both honors and nonhonors students) attending a Midwestern public high school participated in a joint guidance and language arts (writing skills) unit (Lapan, Gysbers, Hughey, & Arni, 1993). This sample included European American (86% males, 90% females), African American (11.7% males, 6.6% females), and Asian American (2.1% males, 2.6% females) students. Results indicated that for many students, participation in the program led to the achievement of specific guidance competencies such as vocational identity and attainment of higher English grades for females.

A key element of this cooperative guidance-language arts career unit was that students learned the career process even though they may not have made a definite decision. Cooperative activities can be effective in addressing needs of students and involving others in the guidance delivery service (Herring, 1995; Herring & White, 1995). Cooperative activities also appeal to ethnic minority youth, especially Native American Indians and Hispanic Americans (Herring, 1997).

## Multiple Interventions

The need for a variety of modes and tests is evident, ranging from nonverbal culture-free tests in the language of linguistic minorities to tests in standard English. The individual's level of culturation into the mainstream culture is vitally important. Understanding the individual's educational level and background, language facility, and receptive and expressive vocabulary can also help test selection (Drummond, 1996).

## Self-Efficacy Measurement

One of the major limitations of research on career self-efficacy has been the absence of a general measure useful under a variety of circumstances (Hackett, 1991). Osipow and Rooney's (1989) *Task-Specific Scale of Occupational Self-Efficacy* represents one example of a sound intervention for this emphasis. Osipow's (1991) work also represented an advance in the development of instruments to be used in counseling. The self-efficacy model does have potential to be applicable to ethnic minority groups (Lent & Hackett, 1987). Studies have demonstrated the relevance of self-efficacy to academic and career behavior of different cultural and ethnic groups (e.g., Arbona, 1995). Self-efficacy is also relevant to other career-related variables (e.g., self-concept; Osipow & Littlejohn, 1995).

Individuals need to be able to cope with and accept the influences of perceived barriers in career development. Increasing individuals' self-efficacy for overcoming perceived barriers and helping individuals to adopt more of an optimistic attributional style toward career-related barriers are appropriate strategies. However, not all barriers can be overcome. Albert and Luzzo (1999) suggested that "Individuals need to distinguish between barriers for which personal control and responsibility are appropriate and barriers that the individual may not have the capacity to overcome" (p. 434). Social cognitive career theory (Lent, Brown, & Hackett, 1996; Lent & Hackett, 1987) and attribution theory (Weiner, 1986) are useful approaches to increase understanding of the role that perceived barriers play in career development.

## INTERACTION EFFECTS OF GENDER, ETHNIC, SOCIOECONOMIC, LIFESTYLE, AND DISABILITY STATUS IN CAREER DEVELOPMENT

Time and space constraints prohibit extensive discussions of the variables of gender, ethnicity, SES, lifestyle, and disability. However, two excellent resources that discuss these interactions and others are recommended. Peterson and Gonzalez's (2000a) *Career Counseling Models for Diverse Populations* helps fill the void for adapting vocational counseling skills to various populations. Various emphases within theories and approaches exist, but very little actual application of these theories is found in which a particular individual's background, needs, and options are basic to the success of career intervention. This resource describes a variety of career and vocational counseling models that can be used for many types of individuals and groups across the life span, from age four to age eighty-four.

These authors also have provided a companion text that has additional applicability. *The Role of Work in People's Lives: Applied Career Counseling and Vocational Psychology* (Peterson & Gonzalez, 2000b) emphasizes an integrated coverage of theory, the impact of technology and differences in multicultural, gender, and sexual orientation. Work values, job satisfaction, postmodernism, and future trends are discussed throughout. Separate chapters present school counseling, postsecondary counseling, and career transitions for adults.

Another group of very relevant research efforts involves the studies of Trusty and his colleagues. (Trusty & Ng, 2000; Trusty, Ng, & Plata, 2000; Trusty, Robinson, Plata, & Ng, 2000). Trusty, Ng, and Plata (2000) examined the independent effects of gender and SES and the Gender x SES interaction among U.S. late adolescents (National Education Longitudinal Study—NELS:88, 1996) who had attended a postsecondary institution within 2 years of high school graduation and had selected a field of study. Their findings were very similar to the findings of Trusty, Robinson, Plata, and Ng (2000), who used a different subsample from NELS:88 (1996). Clear interactions existed among gender, SES, and race-ethnicity in the form of the three-way and multiple two way interactions. "That is, the strength of the effects of race-ethnicity was concomitantly conditional on gender and SES in predicting Holland type of major" (p. 54). The researchers reported, "within racial-ethnic groups, gender, and SES differences seemed to contribute to heterogeneity in educational choices. Among or across various racial-ethnic groups, increases in SES seemed to contribute to homogeneity in educational choices." (pp. 54-55) That is, gender and SES were a major source of variability within racial-ethnic groups. Also, at higher levels of SES, between-group differences in choices in types of majors disappeared. Attention will be given to each of these variables in the following discussions.

*Gender status*. Historically, gender status has determined the choice of available career areas. Career options were decided in traditional ways--education or medical fields for females, the physical sciences and math fields for males. Career interventions must begin in the lower grades to dispel the notion of traditional gender stereotyped career areas. Unfortunately, the identities of adolescent females are often based on their physical attributes, not their talents, abilities, or interests (Herr & Cramer, 1996). "These young women are valued more for their appearance, manners, and respect for rules than for their academic achievements" (Craig, Contreras, & Peterson, 2000, p. 22). To develop a healthy life, adolescent females need love from family and friends, meaningful work, respect, challenges, and physical and psychological safety (Pipher, 1994).

Craig et al. (2000) conducted an excellent intervention for the career development of adolescent females. The Teen Exploratory Career System (TECS) was designed to process adolescent female students through the growth and explorative developmental career level. The various areas selected were (a) societal roles, (b) sexual identity, (c) interpersonal skills, (d) aptitude tests, (e) family influences, (f) personal traits and strengths, (g) goal setting, and (h) decision making. "The TECS model is general in nature so that every racial or ethnic group can be processed through the system without losing any of its integrity" (p. 28). The results indicated that "both boys and girls worked at the model differently, and most differences were addressed by gender variables" (p. 34).

Trusty and Ng's (2000) longitudinal study of the effects of achievement perceptions on choice of postsecondary major has import for this discussion. Their result that English achievement perceptions were a stronger predictor, overall, for women and mathematics achievement perceptions were a stronger predictor for men coincides with earlier research. Trusty, Robinson, and colleagues (2000), in an earlier study using NELS:88 (1996) data, found that for women, reading scores were a stronger predictor of choice of major; whereas for men, mathematics scores were a stronger predictor.

The research of Trusty, Ng, and Plata (2000) found gender to be a strong predictor of Holland type of major. Largest differences between men and women were in S, R, and C types. Within genders and across Holland types, men were most likely to be in I, E, and S majors, respectfully. Women were most likely to be in S, I, and E majors, respectfully.

*Race-Ethnicity and socioeconomic status* (SES). Recent research has examined the potential effects of ethnicity on children's educational and occupational aspirations (Wahl & Blackhurst, 2000). Most of these research studies have compared students of various ethnic backgrounds in an effort to determine how variables associated with high educational aspirations and actual college attendance may operate differently across ethnic groups. Several consistent themes emerge from these research efforts.

First, among students from all ethnic backgrounds, SES plays a major role in determining educational and occupational aspirations and educational choices (e.g., Solorzano, 1992; Trusty, Robinson, et al., 2000). Valadez (1998) investigated the role of individual, peer, parental, and educational variables in the decision to attend college for 24,599 students in their 8th-, 10th- and 12th-grade years. Valadez concluded that students from low SES backgrounds (a) do not have access to valuable resources, and (b) are not as skilled at using available resources as students from higher SES backgrounds.

Trusty, Ng, and Plata's (2000) study revealed that the strongest relationship between SES and Holland type of major for men was in the R category, and this relationship was negative. That is, an increase in SES resulted in a sharp decrease in participants' selecting R majors. For women, the strongest relationships were in C, A, and R types, with C and R types being negative. That is, increases in SES resulted in decreases in the choices of those majors by women. The relationship for A majors was positive which indicates that as increases in SES resulted in an increase in participants choosing A majors.

Second, Native American Indian and Hispanic students have among the lowest and least stable educational aspirations (e.g., Kao & Tienda, 1998; Mau, 1995). For example, in a national survey of 8th-, 10th-, and 12th-grade students, Kao and Tienda (1998) found that Hispanic students had the lowest aspirations at each of the three grade levels. These results supported the findings of Mau (1995), who found that among 8th-grade students in a national survey, Hispanic girls and Native American Indian boys and girls had the lowest educational aspirations.

Third, the effects of SES, gender, and race-ethnicity are conditional upon one another. Trusty, Ng, and Plata's (2000) research indicated that "the effects of SES were stronger for women than for men; race-ethnicity was a stronger predictor for men and women with lower SES; and the effects of race-ethnicity were stronger for men than for women" (p. 55). To provide examples of how SES, gender, and ethnicity interacted, for Asian and Pacific Islanders, the choice of E and S majors was conditional on gender and SES; and choice of R majors was conditional on gender. At low SES, Asian Pacific Island men chose E majors more frequently than expected; and at high SES, they chose E majors less frequently than expected. For Asian Pacific Island women, only those at middle SES chose E majors more frequently than expected. For Hispanics, selecting an E-type major was conditional on gender and SES. Hispanic women chose E majors at approximately expected levels. Hispanic men with low and middle SES chose E majors more frequently than expected; but Hispanic men with high SES chose E majors less frequently than expected. For African American men, choice of S-type majors was conditional on gender and SES. African American men with low and middle SES chose S majors more often than expected, but those with high SES chose S majors less often than expected. The number of Native American Indian participants was relatively small. However, generally, Native American Indian women with low and middle SES may be likely to choose S majors and may not be likely to choose E majors.

The above results reveal the dynamic interactions of gender, SES, and race-ethnicity. That is, these variables work separately and together to influence the career development of young people. These results, among others, underscore the need for counselors and researchers to consider multiple contexts regarding career-related choices.

Third, parental expectations and support appear to be key variables influencing the college aspirations of ethnic students (Hossler & Maple, 1993; Ramos & Sanchez, 1995). For example, Mau (1995) found that middle school students' educational aspirations paralleled their perceived parental expectations within each ethnic minority group. Such expectations have also been shown to influence students as early as junior high school (Wahl & Blackhurst, 2000).

Finally, a lack of realistic information about college is often discovered among ethnic students, as well as a mismatch between aspirations and academic preparation (Wahl &

Blackhurst, 2000). Dai (1996) found that whereas intellectual ability predicted the educational aspirations of European American high school seniors, there was no parallel relationship between ability and aspirations among African American students. In addition, several studies have suggested that among ethnic minority students with high educational aspirations, there is frequently a lack of realistic information about college (Kao & Tienda, 1998; Valadez, 1998). These factors my combine to result in a greater mismatch between aspirations and attainment for ethnic minority students than for European American students (Solorzano, 1992).

*Lifestyle status.* Many issues for lesbian women and gay men are similar to those identified for women and ethnic minority groups (Patton & McMahon, 1999). One issue is not to assume heterogeneity of gay men and lesbians. Several issues relevant to identity development for lesbians and gay men tend to exacerbate the complexities within this population. For example, Fassinger (1995) suggested that the demands of lesbian identity issues may result in the neglect of career development. Because lesbian identity is not usually solidified until late adolescence or adulthood, the inclusion of an individual identity into career planning may not occur until after important early periods of career development (Morgan & Brown, 1991).

Second, the identification of oneself as gay may eliminate potential career options for men, particularly those in which being gay has marked negative consequences (e.g., teaching, military; Patton & McMahon, 1999). Third, many lesbians may experience estrangement from families, a major influence on women's career development. Finally, the coming-out process frequently results in "a temporary (but dramatic) decrease in self-esteem and new complexities in self-concept" (Fassinger, 1995, p. 155).

In addition, a few researchers have identified environmental issues relevant to the career development of lesbians and gay men (e.g., Fassinger, 1995). These include occupational stereotyping (assumptions that certain occupations are lesbian and gay specific) and occupational discrimination (rejecting or discouraging lesbians and gays in particular career areas).

# IMPLICATIONS FOR PRACTICE AND RESEARCH

The available theory and research suggest students' occupational aspirations may be formed in early elementary school and that these earliest aspirations are relatively stable and realistic (e.g., Trice & McClellan, 1993). These aspirations are often limited, however, by interactive effects of prevailing gender and ethnic stereotypes (e.g., Kao & Tienda, 1998; Mau, 1995), SES and class differences (e.g., Solozano, 1992), lack of adult role models (e.g., Trusty, 1999), and lack of parental support for occupational and educational attainment (e.g., Hossler & Maple, 1993; Ramos & Sanchez, 1995; Trusty, 1999). However, increasing students' and parents' occupational and educational aspirations can only be achieved by providing realistic information about postsecondary options and discussing students' chances of success (e.g., Dai, 1996; Valadez, 1998).

Research results previously presented suggest that "effective career guidance programs should (a) be developmentally appropriate, (b) actively dispel limiting occupational stereotypes and broaden students' awareness of potential occupations, (c) be responsive to cultural values, and (d) furnish practical and realistic information about a wide range of postsecondary options" (Wahl & Blackhurst, 2000, p. 371). (see Table 3). The following discussions will focus on appropriate multicultural examples (noninclusive) of the implications set forth in previous sections.

### Table 3 Student Career Development

Successful implementation and maintenance of effective career guidance and counseling programs will facilitate students' development of several key Competencies (Wahl & Blackhurst, 2000, p. 371):

- Identifying and rejecting gender-, race-, culture-, and class-based occupational stereotypes
- Investigating potential careers
- Identifying postsecondary training requirements for careers of interest
- Acquiring practical information about postsecondary education or training

## The Career Path Tournament

The Career Path Tournament (Scholl, 1999) uses a round-by-round elimination format to illustrate the constraining effects of sociological forces on career advancement. This intervention has four goals: (a) to stimulate awareness of sociological barriers to career advancement; (b) to increase participants' awareness of feelings (e.g., anger, anxiety, and confusion); (c) to gain a better understanding of the career advancement process as it is reflected in education practices, professional training, and hiring interviews; and (d) to increase awareness of the need to intentionally cope with discriminatory practices.

This game is intended for junior high, high school, and college students in a classroom setting. Undergraduate participants' (N = 74) quantitative and qualitative evaluation of the game indicated that the game raised awareness of sociological barriers and provided participants with helpful suggestions for adoptively coping with these barriers (Scholl, 1999). Additional gains cited included awareness of the following: the importance of detern-dnation, the importance of positive self-presentations, the need to acquire "symbols of completion," concerns of employers, and the nature of of the career advancement process.

## A Narrative Approach

Traditionally, the practice of career counseling and education has emphasized an objective perspective. In recent years, increasing attention has focused on the use of "a subjective narrative approach to career counseling that emphasizes meaning and meaning-making while retaining the merits of the traditional, objective approach" (Cochran, 1997, p. ix). As Howard (1989) noted:

> People tell themselves stories that infuse certain parts of their lives and actions with great meaning and de-emphasize other aspects. But had any of them chosen to tell himself or herself a somewhat different story, the resulting pattern of more-meaningful and less-meaningful aspects of his or her life would have been quite different" (p. 168).

A narrative is the most pervasive and suitable activity for actualizing meaningful experiences (Cochran, 1997). Cochran has presented three ways of creating meaning through the use of narratives that can be used to enhance career representations:

> First, a narrative provides a temporal organization, integrating a beginning, middle, and end into a whole.... Second, a story is a synthetic structure that configures an indefinite expansion of elements and spheres of elements into a whole.... Third, the plot of a narrative is a point. (pp. 5-7)

## Planned Happenstance

Chance plays an important role in an individual's career, but career counseling is still perceived as a process designed to eliminate chance from career decision making. Traditional career counseling interventions are no longer sufficient to prepare students and adults to respond to career uncertainties and need to adopt a counseling intervention that views unplanned events as both inevitable and desirable (Mitchell, Levin, & Krumboltz, 1999).

The planned happenstance theory offers some radically different advice for career counselors (Mitchell et al., 1999):

1. Acknowledge that it is normal, inevitable, and desirable for unplanned events to influence careers.
2. Think of indecision not as a problem to be remedied, but as a state of planful open-mindedness that will enable clients to capitalize on unforeseen future events.
3. Teach clients to take advantage of unplanned events as opportunities to try new activities, develop new interests, challenge old beliefs, and continue lifelong learning;
4. Teach clients to initiate actions to increase the likelihood of beneficial unplanned events in the future.
5. Follow through with clients to provide continuing support for their learning throughout their careers. (p. 123)

Some of the client questions about planned happenstance, as summarized from Mitchell et al. (1999) are:

1. Isn't it amazing how chance events have affected my life?
2. If chance events play such a big role in everyone's life, do we have any power to control our own destiny?
3. Would you agree that there are constraints on my power to decide?
4. What kinds of constraints are there?
5. What should I do with the rest of my life?
6. What if I make a plan and something happens to interrupt it?

Henderson (2000), in her qualitative study of "Follow Your Bliss," indicated that participants (a) demonstrated a dogged commitment to follow their interests, what they succeeded in, and enjoyed; (b) exhibited a breadth of personal competencies and strengths;

and (c) functioned in work environments characterized by freedom, challenge, meaning, and positive social atmosphere. Using individual experiences as inspiration, individuals can be encouraged to respect career indecision as an opportunity to explore and to create their own luck by getting out into the world of opportunity. Active career exploration (e.g., networking, attending lectures and conferences, making site visits, or shadowing) can maximize the chances of encounters that have the potential to propel their careers in new and enjoyable directions (Henderson, 2000; Mitchell et al., 1999).

## SUMMARY

Most of the major theories of career development were first articulated in the 1950s and 1960s when the labor force was predominantly male and European American. The last 20 years have witnessed a tremendous influx of both women and ethnic groups. Leong and Brown (1995) stressed the narrow population that most career theory has addressed, the limited nature of the theoretical assumptions, the lack of recognizing broader "sociopolitical, socioeconomic, social-psychological, and sociocultural realities of cross-cultural individuals" (p. 146), and the inappropriateness and limitations of much use of the terms *race*, *ethnicity*, and *minority*. Rather, they suggested the use of the terms *ethnic group* and *cultural group* to avoid such a narrow target population.

Many factors can bias the assessment of diverse groups and individuals, leading to possible sources of misinterpretation. Ethical and legal standards hopefully ensure that these groups and individuals are appraised appropriately. To increase their multicultural understanding, career counselors can utilize research on the multicultural counseling process, case studies in the literature, experiences of other helping professionals, their own personal experiences with culturally dissimilar individuals, and other first-hand experiences with various ethnic and cultural groups (Draguns, 1989; Nutall, Romero, & Kalesnik, 1992).

Arbona's (2000) review of research efforts emphasizing practice and theory in career counseling and development during 1999 offers some positive feedback. This recent research indicates an increasing attention to the application of the career theoretical and practical knowledge base to diverse populations, including women, racial and ethnic minorities, and persons with disabilities. Findings from the research published in 1999 indicate that many factors regarding career counseling and development with non-postsecondary students also apply to ethnic minority college students with or without disabilities. These research efforts have increasingly examined particularly relevant factors in understanding the career development of diverse populations, including acculturation, ethnic identity, discrimination, and the experience of being an ethnic minority in the context of educational and work settings.

The most important task for career counselors is to be fully aware of the uniqueness of every individual (Isaacson & Brown, 1993). Herring (1998) stated: "The counselor can then address the psychological and sociological factors that are central to each of the career development and choice theories. This approach ensures that personal characteristics such as gender, culture, class, ethnic group membership, alternative lifestyle, and conditions of disability are considered" (p. 52).

# EXPERIENTIAL ACTIVITIES

## Case Study 8. 1: Gender and Ethnic Influences

One of a teacher's best students, an eighth-grade Hispanic American girl, informs the school counselor that she is not going to continue in her program because she is not planning to go to college. When the counselor asks why, she replies that in her family and culture, college is for boys. She says her plans are to finish high school, find a temporary job, get married, have four or five children, and stay home. The counselor believes that girls should be encouraged to go on to college so they can have the career and other opportunities a college degree provides. (adapted from Grossman, 1995. p. 214, and Herring, 1998, p. 125)

## Case Study 8. 2: Playground Bias?

Johnny attended a private school where the playgrounds were segregated by gender. In one playground, the girls skipped and jumped rope, in the other, the boys played football. Johnny often stood on the sidelines and chatted with several other nonathletic boys. Johnny's teacher was concerned and arranged privately with several of the male athletes to include Johnny and his friends in the daily football games. The teacher warned that if they failed to do this, all of the boys in the class would be punished (adapted from Herring, 1998, p. 126)

## Case Study-8. 3: Harold

Harold is a middle class African American 16-year-old boy who ran away after experiencing years of abuse from his father because of a gay relationship. He worked in a grocery store in the evenings and attended high school during the day, resolving to complete high school. Instead of a supportive environment at his school, Harold found his peers hostile and harassing. Openly gay to his classmates and teachers, Harold was teased during class by other students and received no support from teachers. After he was physically assaulted at the bus stop after school, Harold felt pushed to the point of either quitting school or demanding action. (adapted from Herring, 1998, p. 166).

1. Refer to Case Study 8. 1. Disregard the description of the teacher's perspective. Instead, imagine what your viewpoint would be and how would you deal with the problem. If you prefer a number of options, try to determine the factors that led you to select the particular approaches you would use. How are these approaches congruent with a traditional Hispanic gender role description?
2. Refer to Case Study 8. 2.How do you feel about the gender separation that existed on the playground? What is your opinion about the way the teacher responded to Johnny and his friends' behavior. What might have been the teacher's reason for responding in that manner? How would you have responded?
3. Participate in a dyadic encounter with an individual from a different ethnic or cultural group, or an individual with disabilities. Describe your experiences.
4. How would your school respond to Case Study 8. 03?

5.  Have students name characters from their favorite TV shows who either fit or contradict a common stereotype. How might their perceptions of other people be influenced by what they see on TV? (adapted from Aronson, 1994).

# REFERENCES

Adebimpe, V. R. (1997). Mental illness among African Americans. In I. Al-Issa & M. Tousignant (Eds.) *Ethnicity, immigration and psychopathology* (pp. 95-120). New York: Plenum.

Albert, K. A., & Luzzo, D. A, (1999). The role of perceived barriers in career development: A social cognitive perspective. *Journal of Counseling & Development, 77(4)*, 431-436.

American Association for Counseling and Development & Association for Measurement and Evaluation in Counseling and Development (AACD). (1989, May). The responsibilities of users of tests. AACD *Guideposts*, 12-28.

American Counseling Association (ACA). (1995). *Code of ethics and standards of practice.* Alexandria, VA: Author.

American Educational Research Association (AERA), American Psychological Association (APA), & National Council on Measurement in Education (NCME) (1985). *Standards for educational and psychological testing.* Washington, DC: American Psychological Association.

American Psychiatric Association. (1995). *Diagnostic and statistical manual of mental disorders* (4th ed.). Washington, DC: Author.

American Psychological Association. (APA) (1985). *Standards for Educational and Psychological Testing.* Washington, DC: Author.

American Psychological Association. (APA) (1988). *Code of fair testing practices.* Washington, DC: Joint Committee on Testing Practices, Author.

Arbona, C. (1995). Theory and research on racial and ethnic minorities: Hispanic Americans. In F.T.L. Leong (Ed.), *Career development and vocational behavior of racial and ethnic minorities* (pp. 37-66). Hillsdale, NJ: Erlbaum.

Arbona, C. (2000). Practice and research in career counseling and developmental. *The Career Development Quarterly, 49,* 98-134.

Aronson, D. (1994). Changing channels. *Teaching Tolerance, 3*(2), 28-31.

Arredondo, P., Toporek, R., Brown, S. P., Jones, J., Locke, D., Sanchez, J., & Stadler, H. (1996). Operationalization of the multicultural counseling competencies. *Journal of Multicultural Counseling and Development, 24*, 42-78.

Association for Assessment in Counseling (AAC). (1993). *Standards for assessment in counseling.* Washington, DC: Author.

Atkinson, D. R., Morten, G, & Sue, D. W, (1997). *Counseling American minorities: A cross-cultural perspective* (5th ed.). Dubuque, IA: Brown & Benchmark.

Baldwin, J. A., & Bell, Y. R. (1985). The African Self-Consciousness Scale: An Africentric personality questionnaire. *Western Journal of Black Studies, 9*(2), 65-68.

Brooks, D. (1990). Summary, comparison, and critique of the major theories. In D. Brown & L. Brooks (Eds.), *Career choice and development: Applying contemporary theories in practice* (2nd ed., pp. 338-363). San Francisco: Jossey-Bass.

Brown, D., Brooks, L., & Associates. (1996). *Career choice and development: Applying contemporary theories to practice* (3rd ed.). San Francisco: Jossey-Bass.

Brown, W., & Holtzman, W. (1967). *Manual, Survey of Study Habits and Attitudes*. New York: The Psychological Corporation.

Burnam, M. A., Telles, C. A., Hough, R. L., & Escobar, J. 1. (1987). Measurement of acculturation in a community population of Mexican Americans. *Hispanic Journal of Behavioral Science, 9*, 105-130.

Carson, R. C., Butcher, J. N., & Coleman, J. C. (1988). *Abnormal psychology and modern life* (8th ed.). Glenview, IL: Scott, Foreman.

Cochran, L. (1997). *Career counseling: A narrative approach*. Thousand Oaks, CA: Sage.

Craig, M.P., Contreras, M., & Peterson, N. (2000). Multicultural career exploration with adolescent females. In N. Peterson & R.C. Gonzalez (Eds.), *Career counseling models for diverse populations* (pp. 22-35). Belmont, CA: Wadsworth/Brooks Cole.

Dai, Y. (1996). Educational plans after high school: A national survey of high school seniors. *Journal of Research and Development in Education, 30*, 22-30.

Dana, R. H. (1993). *Multicultural assessment perspectives from professional psychology*. Boston: Allyn & Bacon.

Daniels, J. (1987). Transition from school to work. In R. Parker (Ed.), *Rehabilitation counseling: Basics and beyond* (pp. 283 317). Austin, TX: Pro-Ed.

Dao, M. (1991). Designing assessment procedures for educationally at-risk Southeast Asian-American students. *Journal of Learning Disabilities, 24*, 594-601.

Domino, G., & Acosta, A. (1987). The relation of acculturation and values in Mexican Americans. *Hispanic Journal of Behavior Sciences, 9*, 191-250.

Draguns, J. G. (1989). Dilemmas and choices in cross-cultural counseling: The universal versus the culturally distinctive. In P.B. Pedersen, J.G. Draguns, J. Lonner, & J.E. Trimble (Eds.), *Counseling across cultures* (3rd ed.; 3-21). Honolulu: University of Hawaii Press.

Drummond, R. J. (1996). *Assessment procedures for counselors and helping professionals* (3rd ed.). Columbus, OH: Merrill.

Ellison, M. L., Danley, K.S., Bromberg, C., & Palmer, E.V. (1999). Longitudinal outcome of young adults who participated in a psychiatric rehabilitation program. *Psychiatric Rehabilitation Journal, 22*, 337-341.

Fassinger, R. E. (1995). From invisibility to integration: Lesbian identity in the workplace. *The Career Development Quarterly, 44*, 146-167.

Fischler, G.L., & Booth, N. (1999). *Vocational impact of psychiatric disorders: A guide for rehabilitation professionals*. Gaithersburg, MD: Aspen.

Fitzgerald, L. F., & Betz, N. E. (1994). Career development in a cultural context: The role of gender, race, class, and sexual orientation. In M. L. Savickas & R. W. Lent (Eds.), *Convergence in career development theories: Implications for science and practice* (pp. 103-117). Palo Alto, CA: Consulting Psychologists Press.

Fouad, N.A., & Dancer, L.S. (1992). Cross-cultural structure of interests: Mexico and the United States. *Journal of Vocational Behavior, 40*, 129-143.

Gade, E., Fuqua, D., & Hurlburt, G. (1988). The relationship of Holland's personality types to educational satisfaction with a Native American high school population. *Journal of Counseling Psychology, 35*, 183-186.

Gottfredson, L. S. (1981). Circumscription and compromise: A developmental theory of occupational aspirations. *Journal of Counseling Psychology,21*, 545-579.

Gottfredson, L.S. (1986). Special groups and the beneficial use of vocational interest inventories. In W.B. Walsh & S.H. Osipow (Eds.), *Advances in vocational psychology: Assessment of interests* (pp. 127-198). Hillsdale, NJ: Erlbaum.

Grossman, H. (1984). *Educating Hisipanic students: Cultural implications for instruction, classroom management, counseling, and assessment.* Springfield, IL: Charles C, Thomas.

Grossman, H. (1995). *Teaching in a diverse society.* Boston: Allyn and Bacon.

Guidubaldi, J., Perry, J. D., & Walker, M. (1989). Assessment strategies for students with disabilities. *Journal of Counseling & Development, 68*, 160-165.

Hackett, G. (1991). Career-efficacy measurement: Reactions to Osipow. *Journal of Counseling & Development, 70*, 330-331.

Hackett, C., & Lent, R. W. (1992). Theoretical advances and current inquiry in career psychology. In S. D. Brown & R. W. Lent (Eds.), *Handbook of counseling psychology* (pp. 419-451). New York: Wiley.

Hansen, J. C. (1992a). Does enough evidence exist to modify Holland's theory to accommodate the individual differences of diverse populations? *Journal of Vocational Behavior, 40*, 188-193.

Hansen, J. C. (1992b). *User's guide: Strong interest inventory.* Palo Alto, CA: Consulting Psychologists Press.

Hartung, P. J., Vandiver, B. J., Leong, F. T. L., Pope, M., Niles, S. G, & Farrow, B. (1998). Appraising cultural identity in career-development assessment and counseling. *Career Development Quarterly, 46*, 276-293.

Haviland, M. G., & Hansen, J. C. (1987). Criterion validity of the Strong Campbell Interest Inventory for American Indian college students. *Measurement and Evaluation in Counseling and Development, 19*, 196-201.

Henderson, S. J. (2000). "Follow your bliss": A process for career happiness. *Journal of Counseling & Development, 78*, 305-315.

Herr, E. L., & Cramer, S. H. (1996). *Career guidance and counseling through the life span: A systemic approach* (5th ed.). New York: Harper Collins.

Herring, R. D. (1995). Creating culturally compatible classrooms: Roles of the school counselor. The *North Dakota Journal of Counseling & Development*, l(l), 28-33.

Herring, R. D. (1997). *Counseling diverse ethnic youth: Synergetic strategies and interventions for school counselors.* Fort Worth, TX: Harcourt Brace.

Herring, R. D. (1998). *Career counseling in schools: Multicultural and developmental perspectives.* Alexandria, VA: American Counseling Association.

Herring, R. D., & White, L. (1995). School counselors, teachers, and the culturally compatible classroom: Partnerships in multicultural education. *The Journal for the Professional Counselor, 34*, 52-64.

Higginbotham, H. N. (1979). Culture and mental health services. In A.J. Marsella, G. DeVos, & F.L.K. Hsu (Eds.), *Perspectives on cross-cultural psychology* (pp. 307-332). New York: Academic Press.

Hill, K. T. (1980). *Eliminating motivational causes of test bias. Final report, October 1, 1976, through March 31, 1980.* Ann Arbor, MI: University of Michigan. (ERIC Reproduction Document Series No. ED 196-936).

Holland, J. L. (1985a). *Making vocational choices: A theory of vocational personalities and work environments*. Englewood Cliffs, NJ: Prentice-Hall.

Holland, J. L. (1985b). *The Self-Directed Search Professional Manual*. Palo Alto, CA: Consulting Psychologists Press.

Holland, J. L. (1994). *Self-Directed Search (SDS) Form* R (4th ed.). Odessa, FL: Psychological Assessment Resources (PAR).

Hossler, D., & Maple, S. (1993). Being undecided about postsecondary education. *The Review of Higher Education, 16,* 285-307.

Hough, L. M., Eaton, N. K., Dunnette, M. D., Kamp, J. D., & McCloy, R. A. (1990). Criterion-related validity of personality constructs and the effect of response distortion on those validities. *Journal of Applied Psychology Monograph, 75,* 581-595.

Howard, G. (1989). *A tale of two stories*. Notre Dame, IN: Academic Publications.

Isaacson, L. E., & Brown, D. (1993). *Career information, career counseling, and career development* (5th ed.). Boston: Allyn & Bacon.

Johnson, S. D. (1990). Toward clarifying culture, race, and ethnicity in the context of multicultural counseling. *Journal of Multicultural Counseling and Develolpment, 18,* 41-50.

Kao, G., & Tienda, M. (1998). Educational aspirations of minority youth. *American Journal of Education, 106,* 349-384.

Krumboltz, J. D. (1996). A learning theory of career counseling. In M. L. Savickas & W. B. Walsh (Eds.), *Handbook of career counseling theory and practice* (pp. 55-80). Palo Alto, CA: Davies-Black.

Kunce, J. T., & Cope. C. S. (1987). Personal styles analysis. In N.C. Gysbers & E.J. Moore (Eds.), *Career counseling: Skills and techniques for practitioners* (pp. 100-130). Englewood Cliffs, NJ: Prentice-Hall.

Kunce, J. T., Cope, C. S., & Newton, R. M. (1986a). *The Personal Styles Inventory*. Columbia, MO: Educational & Psychological Consultants.

Kunce, J. T., Cope, C. S., & Newton, R. M. (1986b). *Personal Styles Inventory: Manual for counselors and clinicians*. Columbia, MO: Educational & Psychological Consultants.

Kunce, J. T., Cope, C. S., & Newton, R. M. (1989). *Personal Styles Inventory: Interpretation guide and scoring directions-* Columbia, MO: Educational & Psychological Consultants.

Kunce, J. T., Cope, C. S., & Newton, R. M. (1991). Personal Styles Inventory. *Journal of Counseling & Development, 70,* 334-341.

Lapan, R. T., Gysbers, N., Hughey, K., & Arni, T. J. (1993). Evaluating a guidance and language arts unit for high school juniors. *Journal of Counseling & Development, 71,* 444-451.

Left, J. (1986). The epidemiology of mental illness. In J.L. Cox (E d.), *Transcultural psychiatry* (pp. 23-36). London: Croom Helm.

Lent, R. W., Brown, S. D., & Hackett, G. (1996). Career development from a social cognitive perspective. In D. Brown, L. Brooks, & Associates (Eds.), *Career choice and development* (3rd ed., pp. 373-421). San Francisco: Jossey-Bass.

Lent, R.W., & Hackett, G. (1987). Sociocognitive mechanisms of personal agency in career development: Pantheoretical aspects. In M. L. Savickas & R. W. Lent (Eds.), *Convergence in career development theories* (pp. 77-101). Palo Alto, CA: CPP.

Leong, F. T. L. (Ed.). (1995). *Career development and vocational behavior of racial and ethnic minorities*. Hillsdale, NJ: Erlbaum.

Leong, F. T. L. (1996). Challenges to career counseling: Boundaries, cultures, and complexity. In M. L. Savickas & W. B. Walsh (Eds.), *Handbook of career counseling theory and practice* (pp. 333-346). Palo Alto, CA: Davies-Black.

Leong, F. T. L., & Brown, M. T. (1995). Theoretical issues in cross-cultural career development: Cultural validity and cultural specificity. In W. B. Walsh & S. H. Osipow (Eds.), *Handbook of vocational psychology* (2nd ed., pp. 143-180). Mahwah, NJ: Erlbaum.

Lonner, W. J., & Ibrahim, F. A. (1989). Assessment in cross-cultural counseling. In P.B. Pedersen, J. Draguns, W.J. Lonner, & J.E. Trimble (Eds.), *Counseling across cultures* (3rd ed.; pp. 299-334). Honolulu: University of Hawaii Press.

Lowman, R. L. (1991). *The clinical practice of career assessment: Interests, abilities, and personaliiy*. Washington, DC: American Psychologists Association.

Lowman, R. L. (1993). The Inter-Domain Model of career assessment and counseling. *Journal of Counseling & Development, 71*, 549-554.

Manson, S. M., & Shore, J. H. (1981). Psychiatric epidemiological research among American Indian and Alaska Natives: Some methodological issues. *White Cloud Journal, 2*, 48-56.

Manson, S. M., Shore, J. H., & Bloom, J. D. (1985). The depressive experience in American Indian communities: A challenge for psychiatric theory and diagnosis. In A. Kleinman & B. Goods (Eds.), *Culture and depression: Studies in the anthropology and cross-cultural psychiatry of affect and disorder* (pp. 331-368). Berkeley, CA: University of California Press.

Marsella, A. J., DeVos, G., & Hsu, F. L. K. (Eds.) (1979). *Perspectives on cross-cultural psychology*. New York: Academic Press.

Mau, W. (1995). Educational planning and academic achievement of middle school students: A racial and cultural comparison. *Journal of Counseling & Development, 73*, 518 -526.

McConnell, J. (1999). Parents, adolescents, and career plans of visually impaired students. *Journal of Visual Impairment and Blindness, 93*, 498-515.

McDaniels, C. (1989). *The changing workplace*. San Francisco: Jossey-Bass.

Mitchell, K. E., Levin, A. S., & Krumboltz, J. D. (1999). Planned happenstance: Constructing unexpected career opportunities. *Journal of Counseling & Development, 77*,115-124.

Mitchell, L.K., & Krumboltz, J.D. (1996). Krumboltz's learning theory of career choice and counseling. In D. Brown & L. Brooks (Eds.), *Career choice and development* (3rd ed., pp. 233-280). San Francisco: Jossey-Bass.

Morgan, K., & Brown, L. (1991). Lesbian career development, work behavior, and vocational counseling. *Counseling Psychologist, 19, 273*-291.

Myers, I. B., & McCaulley, M. H. (1985). *Manual: A guide to the development and use of the Myers-Briggs Type Indicator*. Palo Alto, CA: Consulting Psychologists Press.

*National Education Longitudinal Study: 1988-1994: Data files and electronic codebook system* [CD-ROM data files and documentation] (NELS). (1996). Washington, DC: National Center for Education Statistics [Producer and Distributor].

Nutall, E. V., Romero, J., & Kalesnik, J. (1992). *Assessing and screening preschoolers: Psychological and educational dimensions*. Boston: Allyn & Bacon.

Nystul, M.S. (1993). *The art and science of counseling and psychotherapy*. New York: Merrill.

Osipow, S. H. (1991). Developing instruments for use in counseling. *Journal of Counseling & Development, 70*, 322-326.

Osipow, S, H, & Littlejohn, E. M. (1995). Toward a multicultural theory of career development: Prospects and dilemmas. In F.T.L. Leong (Ed.), *Career development and vocational behavior of racial and ethnic minorities* (pp. 251-261). Hillsdale, NJ: Erlbaum.

Osipow, S. H., & Rooney, R. (1989). *The task-specific scale of occupational self-efficacy.* Columbus, OH: Author.

Patton, W., & McMahon, M. (1999). *Career development and systems theory: A new relationship.* Pacific Grove, CA: Brooks/Cole.

Peterson, N., & Gonzalez, R. C. (Eds.). (2000a). *Career counseling models for diverse populations: Hands-on applications by practitioners.* Belmont, CA: Wadsworth/Brooks Cole.

Peterson, N., & Gonzalez, R. C. (Eds.). (2000b). *The role of work in people's lives: Applied career counseling and vocational psychology.* Belmont, CA: Wadsworth/Brooks Cole.

Pipher, M. (1994). *Reviving Ophelia: Saving the selves of adolescent girls.* New York: Ballantine Books.

Ramos, L., & Sanchez, A. R. (1995). Mexican-American high school students: Educational aspirations. *Journal of Multicultural Counseling and Development, 23,* 212-221.

Reynolds, C. R., & Brown, R. T. (1984). Bias in mental testing. In C. R. Reynolds & R.T. Brown (Eds.), *Perspectives on bias in mental testing.* New York: Plenum.

Rounds, J.B., & Tracey, T.J. (1996). Cross-cultural structural equivalence of RIASEC models and measures. *Journal of Counseling Psychology, 4,* 310-329.

Rusch, F. (1986). *Competitive employment issues and strategies.* Baltimore, MD: Brookes.

Schauer, A. H. (1991). Ruuotion: Personal Styles Inventory. *Journal of Counseling & Development, 70,* 342-343.

Scholl, M. B. (1999). The Career Path Tournament: Developing awareness of sociological barriers to career advancement. *The Career Development Quarterly, 47,* 230-242.

Solorzano, D. G. (1992). An exploratory analysis of the effects of race, class, and gender on student and parent mobility aspirations. *Journal of Negro Education, 61(l),* 30-43.

Strahan, R. F., & Kelly, A. E. (1994). Showing clients what their profiles mean. *Journal of Counseling & Development, 72,* 329-331.

Sue, D. W., Arredondo, P., & McDavis, R. J. (1992). Multicultural counseling competencies and standards: A call to the profession. *Journal of Counseling & Development, 70,* 64-88.

Super, D. E. (1990). A life-span, life space, approach to career development. In D. Brown & L. Brooks (Eds.), *Career choice and development* (2nd ed.; pp. 197-261). San Francisco: Jossey-Bass.

Super, D. E. (1992). Toward a comprehensive theory of career development. In D. J. Montross & C. J. Shinkman (Eds.), *Career development: Theory and practice* (2nd ed.; pp. 35-64). Springfield, IL: Charles C, Thomas.

Super, D. E., Osborne, W. L., Walsh, D. J., Brown, S. D., & Niles, S. G. (1992). Developmental assessment and counseling: The C-DAC model. *Journal of Counseling & Development, 71,* 74-80.

Swanson, J.L. (1992). The structure of vocational interests for African American college students. *Journal of Vocational Behavior, 40,* 129-143.

Trice, A. D., & McClellan, N. (1993). Do children's career aspirations predict adult occupations? An answer from a secondary analysis of a longitudinal study. *Psychological Reports, 72* 368 -370.

Trusty, J. (1999). Effects of eighth-grade parental involvement on late adolescents' educational expectations. *Journal of Research and Development in Education, 32,* 224-233.

Trusty, J., & Ng, K-M. (2000). Longitudinal effects of achievement perceptions on choice of postsecondary major. *Journal of Vocational Behavior, 57,* 123-135

Trusty, J., Ng, K-M., & Plata, M. (2000). Interaction effects of gender, SES, and race-ethnicity on postsecondary choices of U.S. students. *The Career Development Quarterly, 49,* 45-59.

Trusty, J., Robinson, C. R., Plata, M., & Ng, K-M. (2000). Effects of gender, socioeconomic status, and early academic performance on postsecondary educational choice. *Journal of Counseling & Development, 78,* 463-472.

Valadez, J. R. (1998). Applying to college: Race, class, and gender differences. *Professional School Counseling, 1*(5), 14-20.

Vandergoot, D. (1987). Review of placement research literature: Applications for practice. *Rehabilitation Counseling Bulletin, 30,* 243-272.

Wahl, K. H., & Blackhurst, A. (2000). Factors affecting the occupational and educational aspirations of children and adolescents. *Professional School Counseling, 3*(5), 367-374.

Watson, M.B., Stead, G.B., & Schonegevel, C. (1997, July). *Does Holland's career hexagon shape up for disadvantaged students?* Paper presented at the 20th International School Psychology Colloquium, Melbourne, Australia.

Wechsler, D. (1981). *WAIS-R manual-Wechsler Adult Intelligence Scale revised.* San Antonio, TX: The Psychological Corporation.

Weiner, B. (1986). *An attributional theory of motivation and emotion.* New York: Springer-Verlag.

Yip, K. S. (1999). Normalized vocational counseling for clients with schizophrenia. *International Journal of Mental Health, 28,* 86-100.

# Chapter 10

# MULTICULTURAL GROUP COUNSELING

*Michael Mann*
Truman State University
*Changming Duan*
University of Missouri—Kansas City

Due to their therapeutic efficacy and cost effectiveness, group counseling and group therapy as treatment modalities have increased; and their use is expected to increase (Corey, 1995). As the population of the United States continues to diversify ethnically (see U.S. Census Bureau, 1992) and as the needs of individuals belonging to various minority and oppressed groups are gradually recognized, it is foreseeable that group counseling will be increasingly multicultural in nature. It is imperative that counselors in the 21st century be multiculturally competent in serving the varied needs of our increasingly diverse clientele. In fact, failing to do so has been deemed as unethical by the governing organizations in the professions of counseling and psychology (see American Counseling Association, 1995; American Psychological Association, 1981, 1996; and Council for Accreditation of Counseling and Related Education Programs, 2001).

Although the importance of offering group counseling that is culturally sensitive and fits all group members' needs has been widely recognized, the research and theory-building effort in multicultural group counseling is strikingly lacking in the literature. The need for professional and scholarly attention to theory development in how to do effective multicultural group counseling is loud and obvious. In an attempt to provide group counselors with some direction in their exploration of how to work effectively with multicultural groups, we discuss the following topics in this chapter: how multicultural group is defined, different types of multicultural groups, and factors that may affect multicultural group dynamics. In addition, we provide counselors with a list of practical guidelines for facilitating multicultural groups. This list is not meant to be comprehensive or conclusive, but to serve heuristic roles in helping counselors to start their own journey of theory development in multicultural group counseling.

## THE DEFINITION OF MULTICULTURAL GROUP COUNSELING

The designation *multicultural group counseling* has been traditionally used to refer to group counseling where more than one race or ethnicity are represented (Locke, 1990). In many professional writings, the discussion of multicultural group counseling is really about the four major U.S. ethnic minority groups, African Americans, Asian Americans, Hispanic Americans, and Native American Indians (see Merta, 1995). When being defined in this way, multicultural groups in counseling consist of individuals with exclusive racial-ethnic group memberships.

However, multicultural group counseling can also be broadly defined. It can be seen as a situation where two or more people with different ways of perceiving their social environment are brought together in a helping relationship (Pedersen, 1994). Consistent with this definition, Sue et al. (1982) viewed multicultural group counseling as any group counseling relationship "in which two or more of the participants differ with respect to cultural background, values, and lifestyle" (p. 47). Although all groups may potentially qualify to be considered as multicultural groups under such a broad definition, the term multicultural group counseling, inclusively defined, is mainly used to refer to group counseling offered to groups with certain diverse compositions. These groups would consist of members being different from each other in some distinct cultural characteristics that are recognized by the society as associated with social oppression. These cultural characteristics include: sex, religion, affectional orientation, disability status, and so forth, as well as race and ethnicity. It is clear that some cultural differences are visible (e.g., race and sex) and some are not (e.g., affectional orientation and religion), and individual invisible differences cut across their visible differences.

The advantage of having a broad and inclusive definition of multicultural group counseling is apparent. It may help prevent the group members who experience social oppression due to their invisible cultural characteristics (e.g., being gay, lesbian or bisexual) from feeling misunderstood or marginalized in counseling. It may also help counselors understand that it is their professional and ethical responsibility to understand and accept all the cultural aspects that have contributed to shaping their clients.

Although we strongly endorse the broad definition of multicultural group counseling, we will mainly focus on discussing the implication of race and ethnicity in group counseling to fulfill the objectives of this chapter. This decision is also a reflection of our lack of expertise in many areas related to the issue. Readers are strongly encouraged to go to the literature for more information on how to run groups with multiple layers of individual and cultural differences.

## TYPES OF GROUPS

Multicultural group counseling takes place in the specialized therapeutic setting of a group. The group composition can be determined by considering the needs or demands for the service and the therapeutic goals of the group. Groups can be homogeneous or heterogeneous along one or more criteria (e.g., needs, demographic characteristics, diagnoses, etc). Members of a homogeneous group share similarity along the chosen criteria (Johnson & Johnson, 1994; Unger, 1989), and heterogeneous group members differ on the criteria (Merta, 1995). From a cultural perspective, there can be culturally homogeneous or heterogeneous groups. For instance, when race-ethnicity is considered, an African American therapy group will be a homogeneous group and a therapy group consisting of both White and non-White members will be a heterogeneous group. If gender is considered, an Asian American women's support group will qualify as a homogeneous group and an Asian American student support group with both men and women will be a heterogeneous group.

Both culturally homogeneous groups--also called culture-specific groups (Fukuyama & Coleman, 1992)--and heterogeneous groups can have advantages and disadvantages, and they may pose different challenges for the group facilitator. In this section, we first present a brief description of the cultural characteristics of racial-ethnic homogeneous groups from the four largest ethnic minorities in the United States. We then discuss the general issues related to working with ethnically/racially heterogeneous groups.

To avoid inaccurate assumptions and stereotypical ideas in understanding racial-ethnic minorities, we also discuss a few concepts that we think have critical roles in our understanding of racial-ethnic minority group members. These concepts include: racial/ethnic/cultural identity, acculturation, and cultural values. We feel strongly that group counselors need to attend to these phenomena in offering multicultural group counseling to racially heterogeneous groups, and to a lesser degree, racially homogeneous groups. The understanding of these phenomena may help the counselor see within group differences as well as between group differences. Not all ethnic minority members feel the same about their ethnic and cultural heritage. The group counselor needs to understand each individual in cultural context.

## Racially/Ethnically Homogeneous Groups

Homogeneous groups have been assumed to have the advantage of "having less conflict, being more cohesive, affording more support, being better attended, and providing more rapid relief than heterogeneous groups" (Merta, 1995, p.572). It is apparent that the ethnic similarities between and among the group members may help them appreciate each other's experiences and may constitute a source of support for all members. It is believed that a homogeneous counseling group may offer its members the opportunity of immersing themselves in their own racial-ethnic culture, and such immersion experience at times can result in the affirming of their own racial-ethnic identity (Fukuyama & Coleman, 1992).

However, being involved in a racially homogeneous counseling group is not without limitations. Some researchers believe that such groups may be at risk for being superficial and less creative and productive than heterogeneous group (Johnson & Johnson, 1994; Unger, 1989). As pointed out by Sue (1990), sometimes racially homogeneous groups may raise the possibility of reinforcing cultural stereotypes (e.g., reticence among Asian Americans). Fukuyama and Coleman (1992) advised that this situation may be prevented by considering a potential group member's stage of racial identity development (discussed in a later section) before placing individuals in a culturally specific group. In running such groups, needless to say, the group counselor would need to be knowledgeable about the specific cultures that the group members share.

Within the context of homogeneous groups, the following four types of groups represent the four largest racial-ethnic minorities in the United States (African Americans, Native

American Indians, Asian Americans, Hispanic Americans). The group processes and dynamics of these groups will be largely influenced and shaped by their distinct cultures.

### African Americans

Numerous scholars (Baruth & Manning, 1991; Gladding, 1991; Rollack, Westman, & Johnson, 1992) have advocated the use of a group treatment approach for African American clients throughout the life span because of its compatibility with many African American values (i.e., interdependence, group identity). Rollack et al. (1992) contended disclosure might be easier in a group setting where there is "safety in numbers" and where one's experiences can be validated by others. Because many African American clients expect a quick solution to their identified concerns (as do other multicultural clients), a problem-solving orientation may be warranted (Paniagua, 1998). Finally, African American group participants--because of experiences with racism--may be initially suspicious and distrustful, especially when there is evaluative component of the group (Sue & Sue, 1999).

### Native American Indians

Native American Indians tend to emphasize nonverbal forms of communication (e.g., body language, tone of voice, avoiding eye contact) that may impede traditional group approaches (Paniagua, 1998). In fact, listening is often considered more important than talking (Matheson, 1986; Richardson, 1981). Also, a preference for group harmony and cooperation might render group confrontation unacceptable for many Native Americans (Newlon & Arciniega, 1992). Paniagua (1998) emphasized the importance of preparation for the group, structuring the group, and controlling the intensity of group conflict when doing group work with Native American Indians. Some writers (Manson, Walker, & Kivlahan, 1987; Thompson, Walker, & Silk-Walker, 1993), despite these considerations, have recommended a group format with Native American clients as long as it is combined with traditional American Indian activities.

### Asian Americans

Asian Americans are often perceived as lacking receptivity and responsiveness to group work (Baruth & Manning, 1991; Gladding, 1991; Leong, 1992). Because of loyalty to parents and to the family name, Asian Americans might be hesitant to disclose personal information in groups (Ho, 1984; Vander Kolk, 1985). Because of the indirect communication style of many Asian Americans (i.e., politeness, avoiding offending others, lack of eye contact), the traditional group interactional process may be undermined (Paniagua, 1998). Also, Asian Americans may expect the therapist to be an expert and authority, and to offer concrete advice on how to solve their problems (Paniagua, 1998). A structured, problem-oriented focus seems to foster more positive outcomes than a free-floating interactional approach (Kitano, 1989; Leong, 1992). Despite these reservations, Leong (1992) has noted that careful screening, selection, and preparation can lead to beneficial outcomes for Asian Americans in groups.

### Hispanic Americans

Hispanic Americans may be hesitant to disclose in groups because of commitment to one's family, and disclosure may threaten traditional males' perception of machismo or masculinity (Baruth & Manning, 1991; Gladding, 1991). Between-group differences (e.g., Mexican Americans, Puerto Ricans; Newlon & Arciniega, 1992) and within-group differences (e.g., acculturation level, identity development; Baron, 1991) should be recognized by the group leader because of wide diversity within the Hispanic American community. More acculturated Hispanics will likely respond to traditional group counseling approaches, whereas immigrants and first generation individuals will be reluctant to engage in these practices such as interpersonal processing (Newlon & Arciniega, 1992). A problem-solving focus to the group work is recommended (Paniagua, 1998). Despite these considerations, a group counseling modality is advocated with Hispanic American clients because of their natural inclination toward groups (Avila & Avila, 1988).

## Racially/Ethnically Heterogeneous Groups

Although the designation *heterogeneous group* may imply differences and conflicts within the group, many theorists view such groups as being advantageous in that they provide opportunities for "greater in-depth work, individuation, character change, productivity, and creativity" (Merta, 1995, p. 570). Avila and Avila (1988) contended that in racially heterogeneous groups there is greater potential for interaction and understanding between individuals of diverse racial-ethnic backgrounds. It is believed that the rich feedback from a heterogeneous group will challenge members' biases and promote positive changes (Corey, 1995; Walsh, 1989). The challenge for successfully maximizing these benefits in heterogeneous groups lies in the practice that truly adopts a multicultural perspective or non-Euro-American perspective in facilitating the group in its culture and norm building (Corey, 1995). An authentic multicultural outlook would enable the group counselor to understand and consider the cultural characteristics of all group members (within-group differences) in addition to their racial-ethnic-cultural memberships (between-group differences) in group dynamics and processes.

The benefits listed above are not automatically realized in all racially heterogeneous groups. Johnson and Johnson (1994) pointed out that heterogeneous groups can be, if not effectively managed, at risk for excessive conflict and alienation of members. As observed by Gladding (1991), some groups do not overcome their biases and become mired in conflict whereas others simply deny any racial-ethnic differences. Thus, the challenge for the group counselor lies in the intention and effort to face the differences and utilize the potential conflict resolutions for group members' learning and growth. In fact, Burke's (1984) research supports this engaging approach, showing that groups that are intentionally led in exploring racial or cultural differences serve to modify racial attitudes better than groups in which exploration is haphazard.

## Hypothetical Case Example:

A Mexican American man in a racially and ethnically heterogeneous therapy group expressed depressive moods and negative thoughts about himself due to the fact that he was criticized and yelled at by his boss at work. He was afraid that he might lose his job as the result. One of two Caucasian men in the group perceived that the Mexican American man probably suffered from low self-esteem because he could not bring himself to reason with his unfair boss. He saw that it was the Mexican man's responsibility to protect his interest. The second Caucasian man was very sympathetic and expressed helplessness, saying "What can you do? He is your boss!" The only African American member immediately expressed anger and pointed out that racial discrimination was involved, and it was the boss's problem, not the problem of the

Mexican American man. Then, the first Caucasian man and the African American man heatedly argued about "who has and should have control over us." All three women members of the group, one Asian American, one Caucasian, and one African American, and one biracial man (half Native American and half Caucasian) remained silent even after the group leader encouraged them to share how they felt.

To understand the group dynamics at this moment, the group leader needs to, *at least*, be sensitive to:

1.  The extent to which group members' perceptions were related to their own racial-ethnic backgrounds and experiences, as well as their related personal concerns and issues. For instance, the views expressed by the first Caucasian man and the African American man probably reflected their life experience and their social sensitivity to racial discrimination.
2.  Differences in how much the group members identified themselves with their own racial-ethnic group or adopted the values held by their group. The two Caucasian men had different reactions. Perhaps they felt differently about being a member of the dominant group and about the value that one should stand up for his or her own interests.
3.  The gender differences in social perception and emotional reactions. Among the various possible explanations of why all women members were silent, at least one might be gender socialization differences.
4.  Differences among ethnic minority members' acculturation level. The Mexican American man's reaction to what happened at work might reflect his values, and his willingness to change would be limited by his acculturation level. The silence of some group members might also reflect their comfort level in expressing themselves in an openly manner.

From a multicultural perspective, to facilitate growth of this group, the group leader needs to accept and respect the cultural differences at all levels so that members' behaviors and expressions would not be misunderstood. Perhaps the Mexican American man's perceived lack of assertiveness should not be interpreted as reflecting a weak ego, it could be interpreted as a manifestation of the value *respeto* (respect for persons in positions of authority). The African American man's anger might be understood in relation to the social oppression and discrimination he and his group have experienced. The silence of other group members should not be viewed as only exhibiting resistance or lack of involvement. Perhaps, the Asian American member will feel less comfortable about the conflicts than the African American and the Caucasian members.

However, focusing attention on between-group differences only is not sufficient, and in fact, could be harmful. These ethnic minority members may or may not identity themselves closely with their racial-ethnic groups. It is not uncommon that two members of the same cultural group perceive things in totally different ways. There are undoubtedly numerous influences on the perceptions and behavior of members in counseling groups, many are likely cultural, and many are likely situational or personal.

Considering the composition of the group in the example, the group leader will need to be vigilant in challenging or otherwise blocking any discriminatory or destructive behavior. To protect group members' cultural identity and cultural pride, it seems advisable that the group leader lead the group to an open expression of observations from a racial-ethnic-cultural perspective. Having group members engage in thoughtful reflection on such an interchange could lead to learning of new multicultural coping skills. Group members could then put new skills into action, first within the safety of the group, then in their lives.

## CULTURAL FACTORS THAT MAY AFFECT GROUP PROCESSES

Significant factors that play an important role in shaping the cultural characteristics and interpersonal interactions of group leaders and group members include racial-ethnic-cultural identity, acculturation level, and cultural values. The understanding of these cultural phenomena may be the key for the group counselor understanding within-group, individual differences. Individual group members differ from each other not only in their racial-ethnic cultural background but also in their felt identification with their cultural heritage, their ability to function in a multicultural environment, and their adherence to learned cultural values. These individual differences will no doubt influence how they interact with other group members, whether or not with similar or dissimilar racial-ethnic backgrounds. These differences will also influence individual and group responses to the group counselor's interventions.

### Racial-Ethnic-Cultural Identity

In a multicultural environment, individuals are confronted with the psychological task of defining themselves in racial-ethnic-cultural terms. They have to define themselves not only as individuals but also as members of their heritage group in relation to other groups. According to Phinney (1990), ethnic or racial identity refers to an individual's fundamental aspect of the self that involves a sense of membership in an ethnic group and the attitude, behavior, and feelings that are associated with the group. Obviously, not all individuals from the same ethnic group feel and think the same about their group membership. An Asian American living in America, for instance, may feel very Asian or very American, or somewhere in between, in defining himself or herself; and the Asian American may or may not have positive attitudes and feelings toward other Asian Americans. This sense and feeling of belonging to one's ethnic group provides one dimension where differences between individuals with the same ethnic background are exhibited.

Different ethnic-racial-cultural identity development models have been presented in the literature. Some of the examples are: Black racial identity development models (Cross, 1971; Jackson, 1975; Thomas, 1971), the White Racial Consciousness Development Model (Helms, 1984), the Hispanic Identity Model (Ruiz, 1990), and the Racial/Cultural Identity Model (Atkinson, Morten, & Sue, 1998), which is more general and applicable to Asian Americans. All of these models are stage models and share the common understanding that racial-ethnic-cultural identity development progresses through initial confusion and a poor, diffuse sense of identity to later ethnic acceptance and identity integration.

The difference between and among the various stages will reflect itself in the individual's behaviors and interpersonal interactions. In group interactions, both the members' and group leaders' racial and ethnic group membership may interact with their racial-ethnic identity stages in influencing the group communication process (e.g., for a detailed description of a Black and White model of communication patterns see Helms, 1984). It should be noted that not all ethnic minorities feel the same about their heritage or about the dominant culture, nor do all White people feel the same toward their own or other ethnic groups. A true multicultural group counseling perspective would be sensitive to how group members feel about their own race-ethnicity-culture and about those of other members. To achieve this goal, the group counselor must understand his or her racial-ethnic-cultural identity and be aware of her or his own racial and cultural biases (Greeley, Garcia, Kessler, & Gilchrest, 1992). This self-awareness and self-understanding forms the foundation for an accurate understanding of group members' racial and cultural attitudes and behaviors.

## Acculturation

Living in a cultural environment in which one's own ethnic culture is not the dominant one, ethnic minority individuals face the need to adapt their behaviors and attitudes so that they can navigate in the dominate culture. This adaptation is called acculturation. According to Berry (1980), acculturation refers to the changes within an individual in cultural attitudes, values, and behaviors as a result of contact with another culture. Theorists believe that, as a result of acculturation, ethnic minority members vary in their attitudes and behavioral adaptation toward their own ethnic culture as well as the dominant culture (LaFromboise, Coleman, & Gerton, 1993).

Research has shown that acculturation varies with age, length of residency in the U.S., educational attainment, and generational status (e.g., Yasuda & Duan, 2000). Individuals who have lived in the U.S. longer, have achieved a higher level of education, and have been higher in generational status tend to be more acculturated into the American mainstream culture than those being lower on these variables (Sodowsky & Carey, 1988). In terms of the consequences of acculturation, it has been found that the level of acculturation may be related to ethnic minority members' psychological adjustments (see Nagata, 1994), positive attitudes toward counseling, and participation in group counseling activities. Individuals with a higher level of acculturation tend to be more effective in communicating with members of the dominant cultural group, more likely to seek counseling, and more active in participating in group counseling activities.

However, it should be noted that although acculturation may help ethnic minority members' adjustment in living in the mainstream culture, its role in their psychological well-being is not as important as it has been assumed. Research has failed to show meaningful correlations between the level of acculturation and psychological well-being indicators such as self-esteem (e.g., Houston, 1984), and emotional state (e.g., Yasuda & Duan, 2000). Both empirical and theoretical research has suggested that ethnic identity (knowing who you are)--but not acculturation (knowing what to do)--is an important predictor of psychological well being for ethnic minority members (e.g., Yasuda & Duan, 2000)

In order to facilitate every group member's learning and growth, the group counselor needs to be sensitive to group members' acculturation experience and understand how their acculturation may affect their involvement in the group. Stereotypical expectations for individuals with ethnic minority status need to be avoided. For instance, not all Asian

American members are "quiet" or "non-assertive." The degree to which they have acculturated into the mainstream culture needs to be considered.

## Cultural Values

Theorists and researchers have suggested that individuals from racial and ethnic minority groups have value systems and worldviews that differ significantly from individuals from the dominant culture (e.g., Carter, 1995; Sue & Sue, 1999). It is imperative that the group counselor's perception of the group dynamics be built on an understanding of value differences among the group members. Behaviors should be understood in the context of these cultural values. For instance, some important White Euro-American values such as independence, autonomy, assertiveness, and competition may not be regarded as important or as positive by people from cultures that are more collectivistic in nature. On the other hand, many values that are endorsed by some ethnic groups, such as modesty, conforming, and self-criticizing, are not commonly respected by the dominant culture. As the result, different behaviors may stem from different values, and these behaviors may carry different meanings when being viewed in different cultural contexts.

The group counselor should take the professional and ethical responsibility to understand that these differences in values will affect how group members present themselves, interact with others, and participate in group activities. It should be recognized that values that are not consistent with the dominant culture do not necessarily indicate psychological problems, pathology, or resistance. For instance, not every individual who does not possess a "strong ego" has low self-worth, and not every individual who relies on others for making personal decisions is incompetent. Further, being passive or non-responsive is not always a sign of resistance.

Cultural value differences not only exist in these general human tendencies, but also are present in all areas of human perception and functioning. Individuals with different cultural backgrounds may differ in their view of the environment and self, in their processing of events around them, and in their expectations of themselves and others. For example, individuals in a group setting who value relatedness more than individualism in interpersonal relationships may be less assertive or confrontational than those who value individualism. Those who value authority may expect control and dominance from the group leaders, and those who value autonomy may expect assistance and support from those leaders. Thus, group counselors must understand value differences among group members to fully understand group dynamics.

## PRACTICAL GUIDELINES FOR FACILITATING MULTICULTURAL GROUPS

Based on a review of the literature, the following guidelines are recommended when facilitating multicultural groups:

1.  Multicultural group leaders should resist cultural encapsulation. Wrenn (1985) defined cultural encapsulation as accepting untested stereotypes of racial/ethnic

minorities as fact, not recognizing cultural differences within multicultural groups, and not being aware of the cultural-specific nature of one's own personal values. As stated above, this is foundational when facilitating multicultural groups. If not, one is likely to impose one's values and expectations on the group experience.

2.  Properly preparing members for the group experience is essential in the success of any multicultural group. Appropriately screening, selecting, and orienting participants is vital to the positive outcome of any group, but may be even more so with multicultural groups (Corey, 1995). Baruth and Manning (1991) advocated the use of a pre-group interview to select and prepare individuals for multicultural group counseling.

3.  Structuring the group sessions to lessen and reduce ambiguity and anxiety should be an ongoing concern of group leaders who facilitate multicultural groups (Merta, 1995). Baron (1991) and Leong (1992) have suggested a structured, problem-focused approach for members of racial-ethnic minorities who are unfamiliar with group work.

4.  Conflict and confrontation are necessary and helpful elements of the group process. However, excessive conflict may negatively affect the participation of multicultural group members. Merta (1995) recommended that group leaders be aware of "cultural differences in communication style and tolerance for confrontation" (p. 579).

5.  Because of various factors such as differing cultural values, varying communication styles, and language difficulties, trust and group cohesion might take longer to develop in multicultural groups than other groups. Thus, pressing for disclosure or confronting resistance too early may in fact be counterproductive (Corey, 1995).

## CLASSROOM ACTIVITIES UTILIZING CONCEPTS FROM THIS CHAPTER

The following classroom activities are suggested for utilizing concepts and ideas from the chapter to enhance student learning:

*   Students define for themselves the term "multicultural group counseling," and then discuss the rationale for their definition.
*   Students form teams and debate the pros and cons of the *inclusive* or *exclusive* perspectives (definitions) of multicultural counseling.
*   Students interview each other, afterwards discussing similarities and differences, especially in terms of racial-ethnic-cultural identity, acculturation, and cultural values.
*   Students discuss the benefits and disadvantages of homogeneous and heterogeneous groups.
*   Students describe any personal experiences in multicultural groups and discuss what was beneficial and problematic about these group experiences.
*   Students in groups develop a pregroup interview to appropriately screen, select, and orient potential group participants for a future multicultural counseling group experience.

- Students role play possible problematic situations in a multicultural counseling group and then develop appropriate responses to these situations.
- Students form into groups and develop their own guidelines for leading multicultural counseling groups.

These represent some ideas for incorporating concepts and ideas into classroom activities from this chapter. An instructor is limited only by her or his creativity.

## REFERENCES

American Counseling Association (1995). *Code of ethics and standards of practice.* Alexandria, VA: Author.

American Psychological Association. (1981). Ethical principles of psychologists. *American Psychologist, 36,* 633-681.

American Psychological Association. (1996). *Guidelines and principles for accreditation of programs in professional psychology.* Washington, DC: Author.

Atkinson, D. R. , Morten, G, & Sue, D. W. (1998). *Counseling American minorities* (5th ed.) Boston: McGraw-Hill.

Avila, D. L., & Avila, A. L. (1988). Mexican-Americans. In N. A. Vacc, J. Wittmer, & S. DeVaney (Eds.), *Experiencing and counseling multicultural and diverse populations* (2nd ed., pp. 289-316). Muncie, IN: Accelerated Development.

Baron, A. (1991). Counseling Chicano college students. In C. C. Lee & B. L. Richardson (Eds.), *Multicultural issues in counseling: Approaches to diversity* (pp. 171-184). Alexandria, VA: American Association for Counseling and Development.

Baruth, L. G., & Manning, M. L. (1991). *Multicultural counseling and psychotherapy: A lifetime perspective.* New York: Merrill.

Berry, J. W. (1980). Acculturation as varieties of adaptation. In A. M. Padilla (Ed.). *Acculturation: Theory, models and some new findings* (pp. 9-25). Boulder, CO: Westview Press

Burke, A. W. (1984). The outcome of the multi-racial small group experience. *International Journal of Social Psychiatry, 30,* 96-101.

Carter, R. T. (1995). *The influence of race and racial identity in psychotherapy.* New York: John Wiley.

Corey, G. (1995). *Theory and practice of group counseling* (4th ed.). Pacific Grove, CA: Brooks/Cole.

Council for Accreditation of Counseling and Related Educational Programs (2001). *CACREP accreditation manual.* Alexandria, VA: Author.

Cross, W. E. (1971). The Negro-to-Black conversion experience: Towards a psychology of Black liberation. *Black World, 20,* 13-27.

Fukuyama, M. A., & Coleman, N. C. (1992). A model for bicultural assertion training with Asian-Pacific college students: A pilot study. *Journal for Specialists in Group Work, 17,* 210-217.

Helms, J. E. (1984). Toward a theoretical explanation of the effects of race on counseling: A Black and White model. *The Counseling Psychologist, 12,* 153-165.

Jackson, B. (1975). Black identity development. *Journal of Educational Diversity, 2,* 19-27.

Johnson, D. W., & Johnson, F. P. (1994). *Joining together: Group theory and group skills.* Boston: Allyn & Bacon.

Gladding, S. T. (1991). *Group work: A counseling specialty.* New York: Merrill.

Greeley, A. T., Garcia, V. L., Kessler, B. L. & Gilchrest, G. (1992). Training effective multicultural group counselors: Issues for a group training course. *Journal for Specialists in Group Work, 17,* 196-209.

Helms, J. E. (1984). Toward a theoretical model of the effects of race on counseling: A Black and White model. *Counseling Psychologist, 12* (4), 153-165.

Ho, M. K, (1984). Social group work with Asian/Pacific Americans. *Social Work with Groups, 7,* 49-61.

Houston, L. N. (1984). Black consciousness and self-esteem. *Journal of Black Psychology, 11,* 1-7.

Kitano, H. H. L. (1989). A model for counseling Asian-Americans. In P. Pedersen, J. G. Draguns, J. Lonner, & J. E. Trimble (Eds.), *Counseling across cultures* (3rd ed., pp. 139-151). Honolulu: University of Hawaii Press.

LaFromboise, T., Coleman, H. L. K., & Gerton, J. (1993). Psychological impact of biculturalism: Evidence and theory. *Psychological Bulletin, 144,* 395-412.

Leong, F. T. (1992). Guidelines for minimizing premature termination among Asian American clients in group counseling. *Journal for Specialists in Group Work, 17,* 218-228.

Locke, D. C. (1990). A not so provincial view of multicultural counseling. *Counselor Education and Supervision, 30,* 18-25.

Manson, S. M., Walker, R. D., & Kivlahan, D. R. (1987). Psychiatric assessment and treatment of American Indians and Alaska Natives. *Hospital Community Psychiatry, 38,* 165-173.

Matheson, L. (1986). If you are not an Indian, how do you treat an Indian? In H. P. Lefley & P. B. Pedersen (Eds.), *Cross-cultural training for mental health professionals* (pp. 115-130). Springfield, IL: Charles C. Thomas.

Merta, R. J. (1995). Group work: Multicultural perspectives. In J. G. Ponterotto, J. M. Casas, L. A. Suzuki, & C. M. Alexander (Eds.), *Handbook of multicultural counseling* (pp. 567-585). Thousand Oaks, CA: Sage.

Nagata, D. K. (1994). Asian American and Pacific Islanders' mental health issues: A historical perspective. *Asian American and Pacific Islander Journal of Health, 2,* 108-124.

Newlon, B. J., & Arciniega, M. (1992). Group counseling: Cross-cultural considerations. In D. Capuzzi & D. R. Gross (Eds.), *Introduction to group counseling* (pp. 285-306). Denver, CO: Love.

Paniagua, F. A. (1998). *Assessing and treating culturally diverse clients: A practical guide.* Thousand Oaks, CA: Sage.

Pedersen, P. B. (1994). *A handbook for developing multicultural awareness* (2nd ed.). Alexandria, VA: American Counseling Association.

Phinney, J. S. (1990). Ethnic identity in adolescents and adults: Review of research. *Psychological Bulletin, 108,* 499-514.

Richardson, E. H. (1981). Cultural and historical perspectives in counseling American Indians. In D. W. Sue (Ed.), *Counseling the culturally different: Theory and practice* (pp. 216-255). New York: John Wiley.

Rollack, D. A., Westman, J. S., & Johnson, C. (1992). A Black student support group on a White university campus: Issues for counselors and therapists. *Journal for Specialists in Group Work, 17*(4), 243-252.

Ruiz, A.S.(1990). Ethnic identity: Crisis and resolution. *Journal of Multicultural Counseling and Development, 18,* 29-40.

Sodowsky, G.R. & Carey, J.C. (1988). Relationships between acculturation-related demographics and cultural attitudes of an Asian-Indian immigrant group. *Journal of Multicultural Counseling and Development, 16,* 117-136.

Sue, D. W. (1990). Culture specific techniques in counseling: A conceptual framework. *Professional Psychology: Research and Practice, 21,* 424-433.

Sue, D.W., Bernier, J. E., Durran, A., Feinberg, L., Pedersen, P., Smith, E. J., & Vasquez-Nuttal, E. (1982). Position paper: Cross-cultural counseling competencies. *The Counseling Psychologist, 10*(2), 45-52.

Sue, D.W., & Sue, D. (1999). *Counseling the culturally different: Theory and practice* (3rd ed.). New York: John Wiley.

Thomas, C. W. (1971). *Boys no more.* Beverly Hills, CA: Glencoe Press.

Thompson, J., Walker, R. D., & Silk-Walker, P. (1993). Psychiatric care of American Indians and Alaska Natives. In A. C. Gaw (Ed.), *Culture, ethnicity, and mental illness* (pp. 189-243). Washington, DC: American Psychiatric Press.

U.S. Census Bureau. (1992). *Statistical abstract of the United States: The national data book* (112th ed.). Washington, DC: Bureau of the Census.

Unger, R. (1989). Selection and composition criteria in group psychotherapy. *Journal for Specialists in Group Work, 14*(3), 151-157.

Vander Kolk, C. J. (1985). *Introduction to group counseling and psychotherapy.* Columbus, OH: Merrill.

Walsh, R. (1989). Asian psychotherapies. In R. J. Corsini & D. Weddings (Eds.), *Current psychotherapies* (4th ed., pp. 546-559). Itasca, IL: Peacock.

Wrenn, C. G. (1985). Afterward: The culturally encapsulated counselor revisited. In P. Pedersen (Ed.), *Handbook of cross-cultural counseling and therapy* (pp. 323-329). Westport, CT. Greenwood Press.

Yasuda, T., & Duan, C. (2000). Ethnic identity, acculturation and emotional well-being among Asian American and Asian international students. *Paper presented at the American Psychological Association Annual Convention*, Washington DC.

*Chapter 11*

# INTERPERSONAL COMMUNICATION SKILLS AS A BASIS FOR MULTICULTURAL COUNSELING

**M. Sylvia Fernandez**
Florida Atlantic University
**Jerry Trusty**
Pennsylvania State University
**Reba J. Criswell**
Texas A&M University-Commerce

## INTRODUCTION

Communication between individuals from the same culture is often difficult. When communicating with individuals from a culture or background different from our own, the difficulty is compounded. Communication skills, interpersonal skills, empathy, and counseling relationship-building skills are the cornerstones of effective multicultural counseling. This chapter will stress the importance of basic counseling skills in becoming a competent multicultural counselor. This chapter will also serve as a basis for applying the models presented in other chapters.

Cultural knowledge should go beyond customs, food, language, and religion to other human dynamics. As counselors, it is critical that we develop an awareness of how cultural issues such as gender, ethnicity and race, spirituality, affectional orientation, age, physical or emotional issues, and socioeconomic status affect the way we and our clients construct meaning in the world. As a result, our understanding of clients' sources of stress is enhanced (Brislin, 1981; Parker, 1987; Pedersen, 1988). Only then can we work with our clients with *cultural intentionality*. Ivey, Ivey, and Simek-Morgan (1997) defined cultural intentionality as the ability to generate thoughts, words, and behaviors to communicate with self and others within a given culture and with a variety of diverse groups; to understand other cultures; and to formulate plans. It is important that counselors act on as many possibilities existing within a culture and reflect on these actions. Communication skills then are essential if one is to counsel with cultural intentionality.

# COMMUNICATION SKILLS

One of the more important counseling skills that a counselor should possess is the ability to effectively communicate both verbally and nonverbally. In counseling, communication moves first from the client to counselor then counselor to client (Sue & Sue, 1999). Communication skills become even more critical when communicating and counseling across cultures.

It would be inaccurate to assume that behaviors or rules of speaking are universal, conveying a consistent meaning across various contexts. In multicultural communication, verbal and nonverbal communications differ according to cultural contexts. That is, one's personal culture influences the dynamics of one's communication. We can arrive at the same conclusions about communication only if we share the same cultural and social upbringing (Locke, 1995). Therefore, the culture of the counselor is as equally important as the culture of the client.

# COMMUNICATION DYNAMICS

The effectiveness of interpersonal communication is influenced by communication dynamics such as verbal communication, nonverbal communication, and patterns of communication. Verbal communication includes translation, word choice, and paralanguage. Nonverbal communication is comprised of proxemics and kinesics. Patterns of communication involve the level of formality, level of directness and explicitness, and show of emotion (Baruth & Manning, 1999; Hogan-Garcia, 1999; Ismail, 2001a; Sue & Sue, 1999). Okun, Fried, and Okun (1999) noted that verbal and nonverbal communications as well as patterns of communication make up conversational style.

## Verbal Communication

When we communicate with clients whose primary language is not the same as our own, it is helpful to be able to speak a few words or phrases in their language to establish affinity. Beyond that, becoming aware of the pitfalls of translation, word choice and meaning, and paralanguage is essential if we are to continue working with these clients.

### Translation
When we translate messages from our primary language to that of the client's, or vice versa, there is the potential for miscommunication and misunderstandings. Translation could lead to distortion and misinterpretation of counselor or client verbalizations. Paniagua (1998) noted that the core essence of the verbalization might be lost because cultural concepts expressed are not easily translated by literal translation of the words. Also, the use of a translator adds a third person to the counseling relationship that may facilitate or hinder the therapeutic process.

### Word Choice and Meaning
Rules as well as exceptions to the rules contribute to the complexity of the English language. Additionally, definition and meaning attribution further compound potential

problems. That is, the same word may have different interpretations in different cultures. For example, the word *family* in Asian countries refers to spouses, parents, siblings, grandparents, uncles, aunts, cousins, and other relatives; whereas, in the United States and some European countries family refers to spouses, parents, and siblings.

In order to avoid miscommunication, there are simple measures individuals could take to achieve greater clarity and meaning. To begin, choose words carefully by making sure they are not ambiguous in meaning, are quite commonly used, and are easily understood. Next, provide qualifications and definitions to terms that are likely to cause misunderstandings. Finally, ask for feedback to ensure that the message has been clearly understood.

### *Paralanguage*

Paralanguage refers to vocal cues such as loudness, pauses, silences, hesitations, rate, and inflections. Volume and intensity of speech are influenced by cultural values (Sue & Sue, 1999). For example, loudness of speech may be viewed as boisterous or aggressive. However, speaking loudly may not indicate anger or hostility, and speaking softly may not be a sign of shyness or weakness. Rules of conversation such as how we greet and address each other, and how we use silence may be influenced by age, gender, or ethnicity. Euro-Americans tend to feel uncomfortable with long silences in conversations, and feel obligated to end silences with more verbal communication. Among Arabs, silence is a form of privacy, whereas the Spanish see it as a sign of agreement. Asians view silence as a sign of politeness and respect (Hall, 1976; Ismail, 2001b). To facilitate effective communication, counselors need to adapt their tone of voice, style, and behavior to what is culturally acceptable to their clients.

## Nonverbal Communication

The majority of any message is communicated nonverbally and occurs outside our level of awareness (Locke, 1995; Ramsey & Birk, 1983; Singelis, 1994). Therefore, what is said may be enhanced or negated by nonverbal behavior. For example, if a woman tears up and becomes choked when she states, "I'm not upset," she is clearly contradicting the content of the communication. In all communications, nonverbal messages influence verbal messages and vice versa (Locke, 1995). Additionally, the same nonverbal behaviors may mean something different from one culture to another. There is a wide spectrum of nonverbal cues that one can attend to in multicultural counseling. Two common nonverbal cues presented below are proxemics and kinesics.

### *Proxemics*

Proxemics involves the study of perception and the use of interpersonal space in interpersonal relationships, as well as work and professional relationships. Clear norms exist concerning the use of physical distance in social interaction (Goldman, 1980; Pearson, 1985). For example, the *little dance* individuals do when trying to decide and establish what's the appropriate standing distance within a certain context. Or, the choice of standing distance based on the relationship with another person of status and power. The use of physical space in the workplace has implications for how office furniture is arranged to accommodate seating for both counselors and their clients. For example, Latin Americans are not comfortable with a desk between them and the other person (Hall, 1982; LaBarre, 1985; Sue & Sue, 1999).

### Kinesics

Kinesics is the study of bodily movement such as facial expression, posture, gestures, and eye contact as ways of communication or ancillaries to speech. For example, using the right hand versus the left to shake hands, or to give and receive things, has significance in many cultures. Sue and Sue (1999) noted that in some Asian countries, touching someone with the left hand is considered rude because the left hand is used as an aide to the process of elimination (unclean), whereas the right hand is used for eating (clean). Gestures and bodily movements also have different meanings. For example, the up-and-down head movement to Euro-Americans indicates consent or agreement, but to Sri Lankans the side-to-side head movement means agreement (Eakins & Eakins, 1985; Jensen, 1985). Another example involves placing one's feet on the table. In the American culture, this is a sign of informality and relaxation. In some Asian cultures, it is considered rude to place one's feet (the lowest part of the body) at the same level as someone's face, or to show the bottom of feet.

In counseling, we assume that facial expressions provide cues to responsiveness, emotions, and involvement in the therapeutic process (Sue & Sue, 1999). The use of smiling, eye contact, or lack thereof, may be interpreted as shy, reserved, or sneaky. Smiling is an ambiguous behavior that may or may not imply trust and friendliness. According to Pederson (1988), outside of its learned context the smile has no fixed meaning. Eye contact has a great deal of power and varies in meaning from one culture to the next. In Western cultures, direct eye contact may be an invitation to conversation, whereas a stare may be a statement of defiance. In many cultures, eye contact may be forbidden with those who have more power, or of a different gender. Okun et al. (1999) found that "the amount of eye contact between two people is determined by their cultures, their personal relationship, and the topic of conversation" (p. 87).

## Patterns of Communication

According to Okun et al. (1999), patterns of communication or conversational traits may include, but are not limited to, level of formality, level of directness and explicitness, and show of emotion. These rules of conversation are governed by age, gender, status, and power.

### Level of Formality

Level of formality can be viewed as a continuum. On the high-end, individuals are referred to by their title and on the low-end by their first name. High-end formality is used when the person being addressed is perceived to be of power and status, based on education, social position, or economic wealth. For many Asian cultures, high-end formality is used as a way of showing respect. On the other hand, in the American culture as a means of equalizing the relationship, a person perceived to be of the same power and status may be addressed on the low-end level of formality.

### Level of Directness and Explicitness

The amount of verbal expressiveness such as freely entering into conversations, asking questions, stating thoughts and opinions, and showing proper respect varies from culture to culture. Because many cultures value indirectness, quickly getting to the point may be considered rude. Valuing indirectness has the potential to alienate, or to negatively label an individual as being evasive or afraid to confront the problem. Counselors may run the risk of misinterpreting or inaccurately ascribing meaning and motives to behaviors (Banks & Banks, 1993; Irvine & York, 1995).

Most people from Asian and Middle Eastern cultures place a high reliance on shared experience, nonverbal cues, and the context in which the communication takes place. Consequently, they appear indirect and vague in their verbal communications. In countries like the United States, Switzerland, and Germany people are very direct, precise, and explicit in their communication because they rely heavily on the spoken word for meaning. Reliance on context and nonverbal cues is low. Consequently, they may appear too direct and overly talkative.

According to Sue and Sue (1999), in some cultures indirectness is a strategy to avoid causing another person to lose face and is a consideration for another person's sense of dignity. However, in cultures that are direct and explicit in their communication, indirectness may be seen as dishonesty, suggesting that the speaker may have something to hide. Therefore, when communicating with individuals who do not value directness and explicitness we need to be careful of what and how we say things so as not to unintentionally offend them by being too direct. To obtain an accurate meaning of the message, it is also important to pay close attention to nonverbal cues, shared experiences, and the circumstances within which the communication takes place.

On the other hand, if you are communicating with someone who values directness and explicitness, say exactly what you mean. Do not be easily offended when your ideas or opinions are attacked with a degree of directness you are not accustomed to, keeping in mind that this directness is a technique used to achieve clarity and meaning. It is important to be objective in hearing what they have to say. Also, remember that attacks on ideas are not personal and are not voiced to deliberately embarrass you. In addition, keep in mind that in such cultures reliance on context is low; so be especially attentive to the spoken word as this will usually serve as your main source of information in your communication (Ismail, 2001a; Sue & Sue, 1999).

### Show of Emotion

Finally, cultures also differ in their expression of emotion. Members of some cultures tend to be more expressive with their emotions, whereas in other cultures, members tend to be more reticent and do not show their feelings openly. Rather, they keep them carefully controlled and subdued. Consequently, people from a more expressive culture may view those from a reticent culture as cold or unfeeling. On the other hand, people from a reticent culture may view those from a more expressive culture as immature and eccentric. Yamamoto and Kubota (1983) found that among some Chinese and Japanese, restraint of strong feelings (both positive and negative) is seen as a sign of maturity and wisdom.

When discussing the subject of communication across cultures, language is something that cannot be ignored. Language is the primary mode of message transmission and very much a part of culture. However, because of its central importance, factors pertaining to language can also be the source of many misunderstandings in multicultural communication.

# COUNSELING AS A COMMUNICATION STYLE

In multicultural counseling, the practice of counseling is in and of itself a communication style. The process of counseling, the theoretical orientation of the counselor, and the individual counselor as a cultural being are influential pieces in the counseling relationship.

Sue and Sue (1999) defined counseling as "a process of interpersonal interaction, communication, and social influence" (p. 76). They also determined that for effective counseling to occur, both the counselor and the client must be able to send and receive verbal and nonverbal messages accurately and appropriately. Counseling style goes beyond the content of what is said to include all aspects of nonverbal communications and patterns of communication that were discussed in an earlier section of this chapter.

Counseling has been conceptualized as a social influence process. It can be described as a process designed to influence clients toward constructive change. According to Kottler and Brown (1985), the personal skills and level of functioning of a counselor can determine the direction of the counseling process and the impact of the counselor on the client. The unique personalities of the client and the counselor influence each other and the counseling process and outcome. Social influence theorists stress counselor expertise as the important factor in the client's acceptance of communication from the counselor. Client behavior change is viewed as a function of the strength of counselor social power, which impels compliance and changes resisting forces within the client. Pietrofesa, Hoffman, and Splete (1984) identified the client's perception of the counselor as one of the potential social power bases of counselors.

Developing multicultural awareness is a professional obligation of every trained counselor. Six divisions of the American Counseling Association have adopted a set of multicultural competencies that serves as a guide to developing multicultural awareness, knowledge, and skills (Fuertes, Bartolomeo, & Nichols, 2001). Awareness, in this case, is the ability to accurately assess a cultural situation from both the counselor and the client's cultural viewpoint (Ivey, 1987a; Pedersen, 1988). The operative word here is "both." According to Wittmer (1992), counselors need to recognize that they are a cultural entity with a cultural viewpoint or bias that comes into play in the counseling situation. Developing a sense of cultural awareness is to be aware of what it means to be from one's own culture. Parker (1987) noted that counselors' awareness of their own biases is a prerequisite to effective facilitation of a counseling relationship. When counseling across cultures, counselors refrain from any sentiments of ethnocentrism. That is, the tendency to judge all other groups according to one's own group standards, behaviors, and customs and to view other groups as inferior by comparison.

"If one accepts the premise that counselor effectiveness is a function of accuracy of the counselor's understanding of the client, then the invisible filters ascribed to the counselor culture assume major importance" (Holiman & Lauver, 1987, p. 188). Because clients of different cultures do things differently, counselors must be tolerant of deviations from the norm. What may be the norm for the counselor may not be the norm for the client coming from a different culture. Developing multicultural awareness is a means toward increasing a person's power, energy, and freedom of choice in a multicultural world (Pandey & Kakkar, 1982; Wittmer, 1992). Therefore, multiculturally aware counselors increase their power to facilitate change in their clients, as well as empower their clients to understand themselves within their own cultures.

A multicultural counselor is one who is accepting of a multiplicity of realities. Riddle (1982) identified such individuals as being able to see both the specific and the universal, and to understand attitudes and behaviors as appropriate and relevant within a specific context. Matsumoto (1996) noted that the ability to recognize cultural filters is a key to showing respect for other cultural ways and to learning about those ways. Who counselors are as individuals and professionals is a reflection of themselves as cultural beings. "The way you frame the world and what it means to you is also a story you tell about what you experience and observe throughout your life" (Ivey et al., 1997, p. 2). Counselors need to be able to see themselves as verbal and nonverbal communicators, with an understanding of their verbal conversational style. This, in turn, has an impact on the counselor's theoretical orientation. Skillfully integrating theories will allow counselors to meet the differing developmental and cultural needs of their clients (Herring, 1997; Ivey et al., 1997). Counselors who recognize their preferred counseling and cultural styles are able to be flexible in order to best meet the unique styles of their clients (Ramirez, 1999).

Different theories of counseling represent different communication styles. That is, the basic assumptions and principles of each theory influence the focus of counseling and the skills used. Theories of counseling are highly culture-bound. Techniques that may be counterproductive and definitions of what constitutes desirable outcomes vary widely. Different theories may contradict clients' personal beliefs and values. For example, counseling modes that rely on introspection, reflection, and extreme client verbalization to open and eventually reorganize one's thinking style and feelings do not meet with the disposition of most Asians. Asians value modesty and reservation in self-disclosure. Openness may be construed as an invasion of privacy or an affront to their dignity (Church, 1982; Fernandez, 1988; Tanaka-Matsumi & Higginbotham, 1996). Each theory tells a distinct story, and different cultural groups are receptive to different counseling and communication styles.

## INTERPERSONAL SKILLS

The cultural context of the counseling relationship is influenced by age, gender, ethnicity, education, as well as other factors. The cultural context of communication, discussed in a preceding section, is a salient aspect of multicultural counseling. Two aspects of interpersonal communication that tend to receive little attention are the individual's perception of time and the perception of the individual versus that of the group.

### Perception of Time

According to Okun et al. (1999), time is based on cycles. That is, cycles of the sun and moon, which can be measured mechanically (e.g., minutes, hours, days, etc.). Every culture has its own concept of time. Hall (1976) described time in terms of being monochronic or polychronic. Monochronic-time cultures view time as fixed and linear. Members place a high emphasis on schedules, a precise reckoning of time, and promptness. In such cultures, schedules take precedence over interpersonal relations. Because of this urgency to remain on schedule, members attempt to get to the point quickly when communicating. As a result, they may appear rather rude or brash. In polychronic-time cultures, time is viewed as fluid and cyclical. Members do not observe strict schedules. In such cultures, preset schedules are subordinate to interpersonal relations. Most Western and European countries are monochronic-time cultures, whereas most Asian, Latin American, and Middle Eastern countries are polychronic-time cultures.

When communicating from a monochronic-time culture, counselors must exhibit patience with clients from a polychronic-time culture. If clients fail to show for an appointment at a scheduled time, counselors should not immediately interpret this as rudeness, callousness, or resistance. Conversely, if counselors from a polychronic-time culture are communicating with clients from a monochronic-time culture, adhering to schedules as much as possible is important. Adherence to an allocated time for counseling sessions may be easier for a client and counselor from a monochronic- rather than a polychronic-time culture (Hall, 1976; Ismail, 2001a; Okun et al., 1999).

## Perception of the Individual versus that of the Group

Cultures can be characterized as being either individual-centered (individualist) or group-centered (collectivist) in orientation. In individual-centered cultures, ties between individuals are loose. Everyone is expected to look after himself or herself and his or her immediate family; the individual takes center stage; independence is highly valued; and a single person can earn credit or blame for success or failure. In group-centered cultures, individuals are integrated into strong, cohesive groups. Throughout their lifetime, they continue to protect one another in exchange for unquestioning loyalty. Individuals are regarded as part of the group. There is a high degree of interdependence among individuals in the same group, and credit or blame goes to the group (Fernandez, 1988; Ismail, 2001a; Sue & Sue, 1999). Therefore, counselors may need to focus at the individual as well as the systems level. Ivey et al. (1997) identified the importance of counselors recognizing that individual counseling exists within a social context.

## EMPATHY AND MULTICULTURAL COUNSELING

Perhaps no counseling skill has received as much attention as the skill of empathy. Since Roger's (1957) description of empathy as a basic condition in the counseling process, numerous authors have studied and theorized upon the empathy construct. From almost all counseling theoretical perspectives, empathy is seen as an integral part of counseling (Carlozzi, Bull, Eells, & Hurlburt, 1995; Hartley, 1995; Ivey, Ivey, & Simek-Morgan, 1993).

Empathy has been described and defined as a state (e.g., Baston, Fultz, & Schoenrade, 1987; Rogers, 1957), a personality trait (e.g., Davis, 1983; Mehrabian & Epstein, 1972), and as a process (e.g., Gladstein, 1983; Rogers, 1975). Empathy has also been characterized in terms of cognition and affect. Duan and Hill (1996) described these dimensions. Cognitive empathy is intellectual understanding of the experience of the client, or intellectual role-taking. Affective empathy, or emotional empathy, is experiencing the emotions of the client.

Duan and Hill (1996) noted that some researchers have found evidence that intellectual and emotional empathy are largely independent of one another, whereas other researchers have found connections between the two. Researchers (Baston et al., 1987; Carlozzi et al., 1995; Grace, Kivlighan, & Knuce, 1995; Krebs, 1975; Mehrabian & Epstein, 1972; Ridgway & Sharpley, 1990; Toi & Baston, 1982) have reported that various components and dimensions of empathy are related to many helping behaviors, positive counseling outcomes, and counseling skills, including multicultural counseling skills (Constantine, 2000).

Even though empathy holds such theoretical and practical prominence, Duan and Hill (1996) noted that the amount of research on empathy has declined over the last several years. In particular, they called for more research regarding the influences of culture on the communication and experience of empathy. This knowledge could increase counselors' potential to understand and help clients with diverse cultural backgrounds. Authors (Lago & Thompson, 1996; McClure & Teyber, 1996; Scott & Borodovsky, 1990; Vontress, 1969) agree that cultural differences compound the difficulties in empathizing with clients. According to Lago and Thompson (1996), responding to clients' emotions and communicating intellectual understanding to clients are naturally more difficult when the counselor and client are culturally different. These same authors and others (e.g., Ford, Harris, & Schuerger, 1993; Hanna, Bemak, & Chung, 1999; Ivey, 1987b; Pedersen, Draguns, Lonner, & Trimble, 1996) also believe that empathy is essential to effective multicultural counseling.

## Ivey's Expanded Conceptualization of Empathy

Duan and Hill (1996), in tracing the history and development of the empathy construct, described the phenomenological qualities of empathy. Ivey (1987b) also noted that empathy, as traditionally defined and practiced, focuses on the unique perspective of the individual client. Historical, social, and environmental dimensions of the individual are either secondary or ignored. These cultural dimensions definitely influence the counseling process; and they influence formal and informal assessments made by the counselor, as well as decisions regarding counseling interventions. If, however, cultural influences are outside the awareness of the counselor and client, counselors and clients are likely to make erroneous assessments and decisions.

A framework from research and statistics is useful to demonstrate, in concrete terms, how such errors are made. In statistics, failing to account for all variables that are related to some criterion or outcome is called *specification error*. That is, the researcher failed to specify (include) all variables that were meaningful to the criterion or outcome (see Asher, 1983). For example, a researcher finds that the number of stop signs in towns and cities in Illinois is strongly related to the number of accidental deaths in those towns and cities. The more stop signs, the more deaths. The researcher therefore concludes that eliminating stop signs will decrease the number of accidental deaths. People who are aware know that population is the unspecified variable that dominates the relationship between number of stop signs and number of accidental deaths. The true causal relationship is between population and accidental deaths, and stop signs serve only as proxy for population.

The conclusion to eliminate stop signs reached by the researcher in the above example is ridiculous. Conclusions reached by counselors and clients are likely to be equally ridiculous if cultural influences are not specified in the equation. All theories that we use in counseling, psychology, and human development specify variables and causal linkages among variables; and according to the literature (Atkinson & Lowe, 1995; Ivey, 1987b, 1995, 2000; Pedersen et al., 1996; Ridley & Lingle, 1996), failing to specify or account for cultural variables is common in many conventional counseling approaches. However, several of these traditional approaches can be modified to account for cultural influences (e.g., see Atkinson & Lowe, 1995; Leong, 1995).

Ivey (1987b), in conceptualizing empathy multiculturally, stated "Empathy requires not only awareness and understanding of the unique individual before one, but also the broad array of cultural/historical factors that may underlie individual experiencing" (p. 199). In addition, counselors need to be aware of the influences of their own cultural and historical background; and counselors can facilitate clients in understanding counselors' individuality and culture. Ivey termed this *dialectical empathy*. In this framework, counseling is a co-construction in which the counselor and client focus upon interpersonal and intercultural awareness. The counselor's goal is understanding clients' individuality and cultural being. Other authors (e.g., Coleman, 1997; McClure & Teyber, 1996; Ridley & Lingle, 1996) suggest a similar integrated and balanced approach to multicultural counseling.

## Cultural Empathy

Ridley and Lingle (1996) described *cultural empathy* as a learned, interpersonal, and multidimensional process. They defined cultural empathy as the counselor's ability to attain an accurate understanding of the experiences of clients from other cultural backgrounds, "an understanding informed by counselors' interpretation of cultural data" (p. 32). The ability of counselors to communicate their interpretation of this understanding with an attitude of concern enhances cultural empathy. Similarly, authors (e.g., Constantine, 2000; Mullavey-O'Byrne, 1997; Sodowsky, Kuo-Jackson, Richardson, & Corey, 1998) noted the importance of active involvement in the collection of cultural data from both affective and cognitive dimensions for purposes of better understanding clients' experiences. In addition, Ivey et al. (1993) identified respect of the worldviews of others as a major component of cultural empathy.

For a more thorough understanding of cultural empathy, Ridley and Lingle (1996) defined the following relevant characteristics:

1. *Cultural empathy is multidimensional.* Counselors must genuinely empathize with clients from multiple capacities--"a perceptual-affective-cognitive-communicative process" (p. 32).
2. *Cultural empathy is an interpersonal process.* This process involves separate acts of (a) understanding and (b) communicating that understanding across cultures as a way of relating interpersonally.
3. *Cultural similarity between counselors and clients may be helpful but is not necessary for achieving empathy.* Counseling culturally similar clients does not guarantee adequate understanding. The development of insensitivity to within-cultural differences may occur. By learning how to interpret cultural data, skilled

counselors will have the advantage of communicating their understanding effectively.

4. *Cultural empathy does not depend upon cultural neutrality.* Failing to examine one's own cultural values increases counselors' risks of inappropriate value judgments of clients from other cultural backgrounds. Owning their own cultural values contributes to the likelihood that counselors will be successful at differentiating their values from those of their clients.

5. *Cultural empathy can be learned.* The first step in the development of cultural empathy is to possess generic empathy skills. More refined process skills are then learned, allowing the counselor to communicate cultural understanding in a meaningful way.

In this section, a model of cultural empathy developed by Ridley and Lingle (1996) will be summarized. This model interrelates three processes: (a) superordinate processes--cultural empathic understanding and cultural responsiveness; (b) cultural sensitivity; and (c) subordinate processes—"cognitive, affective, and communicative" (p. 33).

### Superordinate Processes

Ridley and Lingle (1996) identified superordinate processes, cultural empathic understanding, and cultural empathic responsiveness, as central and supported by all other processes. Cultural empathic understanding includes the notion that clients' self-experiences must be understood from within their cultural framework. As noted by Deen (1985), counselors must determine how cultural norms, values, and assumptions underlie clients' self-experiences. Clients' "feelings, attitudes, thoughts, values, motivations, coping patterns, and behaviors" (Ridley & Lingle, 1996, p. 35) constitute unique experiences of the self. To be effective, counselors must develop an understanding that recognizes their clients as cultural beings.

Cultural empathic responsiveness involves counselors' ability to empathically communicate their understanding to clients. Some of the behaviors related to cultural empathic responsiveness, as noted by Ridley and Lingle (1996), include the counselor: (a) verbally describing understanding of clients' self-experiences; (b) expressing interest in learning about clients' cultural values; (c) assisting clients in increasing their knowledge regarding themselves; and (d) expressing a desire to help clients with personal conflicts and struggles.

### Cultural Sensitivity

To differentiate their model of cultural empathy from traditional empathy as well as other models of cultural empathy, Ridley and Lingle (1996) identified *cultural sensitivity* as "the most distinguishing feature" (p. 33). Specifically, Ridley, Mendoza, Kanitz, Angermeier, and Zenk (1994) regarded cultural sensitivity as a "prerequisite for culturally responsive counseling interventions" (p. 129) and "for effective cultural empathic processing" (Ridley & Lingle, 1996, p. 33). Wade and Bernstein (1991) also reported cultural sensitivity to be a significant component leading to increased empathic responding when counseling culturally different clients.

Ridley et al. (1994) found five nomological subprocesses that contribute to counselors' ability to be culturally sensitive. These include: "counselor cultural self-processing, counselor ability to act purposively in information gathering and processing, counselor ability to apply active-selective attention, counselor ability to maintain plasticity in applying schemata, and counselor motivation" (p. 131).

### Subordinate Processes

Subordinate processes include cognitive, affective, and communicative processes. Cognitive processes involve counselors taking the perspective of their clients and differentiating between their own values and those of their clients. Ridley and Lingle (1996) determined the following regarding assessing client values: "What clients are least willing to change shows their strongest cultural preferences" (p. 38).

The two components of affective processes include vicarious affect and expressive concern. According to Ridley and Lingle (1996), vicarious affect relates to the counselor's ability to "identify vicariously with the client's self-experience" (p. 39). In other words, to experience *as* clients experience themselves rather than *how*. Expressive concern entails the capability of counselors to communicate with an attitude of concern and a genuine interest in the struggles of their clients.

Lastly, Ridley and Lingle (1996) identified two communicative processes: *probing for insight* and *conveying accurate understanding*. Probing for insight involves counselors listening attentively, gathering information regarding clients' self-experience, and gaining feedback from clients through probing and asking questions. In order to decrease client vulnerability often felt in multicultural counseling, counselors must convey accurate understanding of clients in words and language easily understood by their clients.

## A Caveat

Although empathy is a basic and necessary condition for effective multicultural counseling to occur, and although we have presented many positive aspects of empathy, empathy is not a panacea. All empathy may not be helpful. Gladstein (1983) discussed the appropriateness and usefulness of empathy based on (a) the various stages in the counseling process and (b) clients' needs and preferences. Empathy seems most useful in the initial stages of counseling when the relationship is forming. Empathy is also useful in facilitating clients' self-awareness. Empathy may not be as useful when the focus of counseling is on problem solving or action. Duan and Hill (1996) noted evidence that the usefulness of empathy seems to change as the counseling process progresses. Regarding clients' needs and preferences, some clients desire a close emotional relationship with the counselor; whereas others do not. Some clients also expect counselors to present themselves, and some clients expect counselors to be directive. These desires and expectations are often culturally linked (e.g., Atkinson & Lowe, 1995; Duan & Hill, 1996; Ford et al., 1993; Hanna et al., 1999; Lindermuth, 1998; Wehrly, 1988).

## COUNSELING RELATIONSHIP-BUILDING SKILLS

The foundation for successful counseling is the counseling relationship. Paniagua (1998) identified three levels involved in the development of this relationship, namely, the conceptual, behavioral, and cultural levels. The conceptual level includes the counselor's and client's perception of constructs such as openness, honesty, motivation, empathy, sensitivity, and credibility. The behavioral level involves the client's perception of the counselor's competence in specified areas relating to the identified problem, as well as the counselor's perception of the client's motivation and ability to successfully implement a treatment plan. The cultural level entails compatibility (minimizing cultural barriers between the counselor and the client); cultural universals, that is, common elements that cut across diverse groups (counselor credibility and counselor contribution to the therapeutic relationship); and cultural competence (awareness of variables that may affect the counseling relationship and outcome).

## Clients' Perspectives

The counseling relationship is a contrived professional relationship. For this relationship to result in positive outcomes, a strong level of trust must be established. In multicultural counseling, the task of developing and establishing a trusting relationship is compounded by the many barriers that inherently exist among and between cultures. A lack of trust could lead to guardedness, inability to establish rapport, and lack of self-disclosure. Counselors' effectiveness depends on their perceived expertness, trustworthiness, and attractiveness to clients. Clients will test counselors' expertness and trustworthiness through challenges aimed at getting counselors to self-disclose. According to Sue and Sue (1999), clients attempt to determine counselors' awareness of their own racism. They also attempt to identify how this racism may interfere with the counseling relationship. Common verbal tests include:

How can you possibly understand the minority experience?
Have you ever laughed at racist jokes?
How do you feel about interracial relationships?

How these questions are answered will either enhance or diminish the counselor's credibility.

## Conceptualization of Clients and Client Outcomes

To be effective multicultural counselors, individuals need to be able to tolerate ambiguity, be adaptable to new social and professional roles, and be flexible. It is necessary to use alternate counseling approaches and techniques to meet the needs of culturally different groups (Ivey, 1987a; Locke & Velasco, 1987; Parker, 1987).
Ramirez (1999) identified seven tasks of multicultural counselors:

1. *Matching clients in an atmosphere of acceptance.* Counselors provide a nonjudgmental, accepting atmosphere, being careful to avoid any pressure or expectations for clients to conform. Clients feel free to express their preferred cognitive and cultural styles. Counselors work at gaining client trust and matching communication styles in order to remove any barriers to the process.
2. *Making a formal assessment of preferred styles.* Counselors assess clients' preferred cognitive and cultural styles through observations and possibly formal inventories.

3. *Conducting a life history interview.* This provides information about times when clients have felt pressured to conform and to suppress a preferred style. It also assists in identifying people and institutions where clients felt most matched or mismatched, as well as identifying personal and environmental strengths/assets.

4. *Making a self-assessment.* Counselors evaluate their own preferred personal and professional style, identify biases and prejudices, and determine match or mismatch with clients.

5. *Introducing cognitive and cultural flex and the multicultural model.* Given that client involvement is essential, counselors introduce clients to the major concepts of their theoretical approach to counseling and multicultural coping and functioning. This further facilitates client involvement in the therapeutic process and outcome.

6. *Assessing progress in flex development.* This is a time for assessing progress toward clients' goals and making changes in the treatment plan as needed.

7. *Encouraging clients to become change agents.* Clients learn how to foster change in their environment and to regain control.

When the counselor's communication style does not match with the communication style of the client, difficulties may arise. Fernandez (1990) identified such difficulties as the inability to establish rapport and premature termination of counseling. During the counseling process, counselors must be able to recognize when clients feel discriminated against and respond by acknowledging and validating their feelings, then processing those feelings with the client. Authors (Brislin, 1993; Sue & Sue, 1999) noted that for effective communication and counseling to occur, the counselor and client must be able to send and receive both verbal and nonverbal messages accurately and appropriately. Ivey et al. (1997) emphasized the importance of both clients and counselors communicating within their own culture and possessing the ability to understand other cultures as well.

Social constructivism is a frame of reference that encourages counselors to think about the social contexts in which clients' concerns developed. What clients experience in their families of origin, their communities, and their cultures deeply affect the way they think about the world" (Ivey et al., 1997, p. 51).

By entering their clients' world, counselors develop new respect and understanding for their clients' world. In addition, counselors are better able to recognize differences that exist. When counselors achieve this level of understanding and are able to communicate this understanding to clients, counseling becomes a true coconstruction, and counseling therefore has enhanced potential for helping clients reach their goals.

## CONCLUSION

Multiculturalism implies integration across cultures, which facilitates development of a flexible and adaptable approach to interpersonal relating (Riddle, 1982). Ivey (1987a) used the term cultural intentionality to describe the ability to look at oneself and others as unique human beings in a cultural context. Cultural intentionality requires the integration of individual and multicultural awareness, which is, individual uniqueness and cultural norms in interaction with one another. Counselors must be able to synthesize relevant information and make appropriate generalizations (Hood & Arceneaux, 1987; Sue & Morishima, 1982). The use of empathy in multicultural counseling enhances counselors' understanding of clients' individuality and cultural being. It is important that counselors take to heart Ivey's (1981, 1986) belief that different theories as well as different cultures generate different constructs. Interpersonal communication skills of counselors are the bases for effective multicultural counseling.

## ACTIVITIES

### Individual

1.  Respond to the following questions:

    a.  When you hear the term *culturally different*, what group comes to mind first? Describe the members of this culture in regard to their physical features, language, behaviors, attitudes, and lifestyles.
    b.  Think of the significant people in your life when you were a child (e.g., relatives, friends, or teachers). What do you remember about their attitudes toward other ethnic minority groups (e.g., African, European, Hispanic, Native and/or Asian Americans)? What do you remember them saying to you? What did you overhear that was intended for someone else? What did you learn about these groups from: (1) your parents, (2) significant others (e.g., relatives, friends, or teachers), and (3) movies? What messages do *you* give others today about these groups?
    c.  Think of the cultural group to which you belong. When did you first become aware, and how did you learn that you were a member of a group that was different from other groups?

Adapted from Wittmer, J. (1992). *Valuing diversity and similarity: Bridging the gap through interpersonal skills*. Minneapolis, MN: Educational Media Corporation.

2.  Videotape yourself in a counseling session. Analyze the session using the "Communication Dynamics" section of the chapter. Then answer the following questions:

    a.  What have you discovered about your communication style?
    b.  What have you discovered about your interpretation of your client's verbal and nonverbal behaviors?
    c.  Can you identify your personal communication style?
    d.  From what theoretical orientation did you operate?
    e.  What techniques did you use?
    f.  How culturally empathic were you?
    g.  Can you identify your professional communication style?

3.  Venture into your client's environment. Spend one day or at least eight hours participating in an experience that is totally *alien* to you. For example, attend a

different worship experience (i.e., synagogue, mosque, or temple if you are Christian); participate in an activity in your client's neighborhood.

4. Read a book that portrays a distinctive culture.

5. How were you socialized to interact with others? What influence did your age, gender, and so forth, and that of the person with whom you were communicating, have on your interaction?

## Small Group

1. Use the individual activity #1 above to facilitate a group discussion. After the individual activity is complete, in small groups, share responses to the activity. In addition, respond to the following questions:

   a. What have you learned, or relearned, about yourself by responding to questions regarding different groups?

   b. What are you aware of now about yourself or the groups?

   c. What struck you most about this activity?

   d. What did you learn about yourself that surprised you?

   e. What did you learn about yourself that has the strongest implication for multicultural communications?

   f. What experiences or events did you recall that have had the greatest impact on your present attitudes and feelings toward culturally distinct persons?

   g. Now that you have brought many of these feelings to your awareness, what, if anything, would you like to change and/or do?

2. Play Barnga (see Thiagarajan & Steinwachs, 1994). A brief description of the Barnga activity and questions for group processing are included in the following paragraphs.

   Thiagarajan and Steinwachs (1994) noted that in spite of similarities, there are differences that must be discovered, understood, and reconciled within individuals' beliefs and values in order to function effectively with others. Barnga is an activity, which sensitizes participants to the affective component of cross-cultural encounters. It simulates misperceptions and consequent communication difficulties, focusing on understanding and bridging conflict.

   Barnga is played in small groups consisting of four to six players using a modified deck of cards and rule sheets. After each group becomes familiar with the rules by playing several hands, the rule sheets are removed leading to the beginning of a tournament. The tournament consists of two rules: (1) there is absolutely no verbal or written communication; and (2) players may only use gestures or draw pictures to communicate. The silent tournament begins. After several hands are played, a winner is declared at each table. The winners then move to the next table. The pattern is repeated several times. After the game is played, the following questions may be used to debrief:

   a. Describe your experience with the game.

   b. What are you thoughts and feelings right now?

    c.   What do you think was going on?

    d.   How did it feel to go to a different table?

    e.   How did it feel to have someone new at your table?

    f.   How did your thoughts and feelings change toward the end of the tournament?

    g.   What were your greatest successes?

    h.   What were your greatest frustrations?

    i.   What do you now know, or are aware of, regarding encounters with those different from yourself?

# REFERENCES

Asher, H. B. (1983). *Causal modeling*. Newbury Park, CA: Sage.

Atkinson, D. R., & Lowe, S. M. (1995). The role of ethnicity, cultural knowledge, and conventional techniques in counseling and psychotherapy. In J. G. Ponterotto, J. M. Casas, L. A. Suzuki, & C. M. Alexander (Eds.), *Handbook of multicultural counseling* (pp. 387-414). Thousand Oaks, CA: Sage.

Banks, J. A., & Banks, C. A. (1993). *Multicultural education*. Boston: Allyn and Bacon.

Baruth, L. G., & Manning, M. L. (1999). *Multicultural counseling and psychotherapy: A lifespan perspective*. Upper Saddle River, NJ: Prentice Hall.

Baston, C. D., Fultz, J., & Schoenrade, P. A. (1987). Distress and empathy: Two qualitatively distinct vicarious emotions with different motivational consequences, *Journal of Personality, JJ,* 19 39.

Brislin, R. W. (1981). *Cross-cultural encounters*. New York: Pergamon.

Brislin, R. W. (1993). *Understanding culture's influence on behavior*. Honolulu, HI: East West Center.

Carlozzi, A. F., Bull, K. S., Eells, G. T., & Hurlburt, J. D. (1995). Empathy as related to creativity, dogmatism, and expressiveness. *Journal of Psychology, 29,* 365-373.

Church, A. T. (1982). Sojourner adjustment. *Psychological Bulletin, 91,* 540-572.

Coleman, H. L. K. (1997). Conflict in multicultural counseling relationships: Source and resolution. *Journal of Multicultural Counseling and Development, 25,* 195-200.

Constantine, M. G. (2000). Social desirability attitudes, sex, and affective and cognitive empathy as predictors of self-reported multicultural counseling competence. *The Counseling Psychologist, 28,* 857-872.

Davis, M. H. (1983). Measuring individual differences in empathy: Evidence for a multidimensional approach. *Journal of Personality and Social Psychology, 44,* 113-126.

Deen, N. (1985). Cross-cultural counseling from a Western-European perspective. In P. Pedersen (Ed.), *Handbook of cross-cultural counseling and therapy* (pp. 45-53). Westport, CT: Greenwood Press.

Duan, C., & Hill, C. E. (1996). The current state of empathy research. *Journal of Counseling Psychology, 43,* 261-274.

Eakins, B. W., & Eakins, R. G. (1985). Sex differences in nonverbal communication. In L. A. Samovar & R. E. Porter (Eds.), *Intercultural communication: A reader* (pp. 290-307). Belmont, CA: Wadsworth.

Fernandez, M. S. (1988). Issues in counseling Southeast-Asian students. *Journal of Multicultural Counseling and Development, 16,* 157-166.

Fernandez, M. S. (1990). *Asian students expectations about counseling: Implications for counselors on American university campuses.* Unpublished doctoral dissertation, Southern Illinois University at Carbondale, Carbondale, Illinois.

Ford, D. Y., Harris, J., III, & Schuerger, J. M. (1993). Racial identity development among gifted Black students: Counseling issues and concerns. *Journal of Counseling & Development, 71,* 409-417.

Fuertes, J. N., Bartolomeo, M., & Nichols, C. M. (2001). Future research directions in the study of counselor multicultural competency. *Journal of Multicultural Counseling and Development, 29,* 3-12.

Gladstein, G. A. (1983). Understanding empathy: Integrating counseling, development, and social psychology perspectives. *Journal of Counseling Psychology, 30,* 467-482.

Goldman, M. (1980). Effect of eye contact and distance on the verbal reinforcement of attitude. *The Journal of Social Psychology, 111,* 73-78.

Grace, M., Kivlighan, D. M., Jr., & Knuce, J. (1995). The effect of nonverbal skills training on counselor trainee nonverbal sensitivity and responsiveness and on session impact and working alliance ratings. *Journal of Counseling & Development, 73,* 547-552.

Hall, E. T. (1976). *Beyond culture.* New York: Anchor Press.

Hall, E. T. (1982). *The hidden dimension.* New York: Anchor/Doubleday.

Hanna, F. J., Bemak, F., & Chung, R. C. (1999). Toward a new paradigm for multicultural counseling. *Journal of Counseling & Development, 77,* 125-134.

Hartley, G. D. (1995). Empathy in the counseling process: The role of counselor understanding in client change. *Journal of Humanistic Education and Development, 34,* 13-23.

Herring, R. D. (1997). *Counseling diverse ethnic youth.* Fort Worth, TX: Harcourt Brace.

Hogan-Garcia, M. (1999). *The four skills of cultural diversity: A process for understanding and practice.* Toronto, Ontario: Wadsworth.

Holiman, M., & Lauver, P. J. (1987). The counselor culture and client-centered practice. *Counselor Education and Supervision, 26,* 184-191.

Hood, A. B., & Arceneaux, C. (1987). Multicultural counseling: Will what you don't know help you? *Counselor Education and Supervision, 26,* 173-175.

Irvine, J. J., & York, D. E. (1995). Learning styles and culturally diverse students: A literature review. In J. A. Banks & C. A. McGee Banks (Eds.), *Handbook of research on multicultural education* (pp. 484-497). New York: McMillan.

Ismail, N. (2001a). *Communicating across cultures (Part 1).* [On-line]. http://www.pertinent.com/pertinfo/business/yaticom.html [2001, April 5].

Ismail, N. (2001b). *Communicating across cultures (Part 2).* [On-line]. http://www.pertinent.com/pertinfo/business/yaticom1.html [2001, April 5].

Ivey, A. E. (1981). Counseling and psychotherapy: Toward a new perspective. In A. J. Marsella & P. B. Pedersen (Eds.), *Cross-cultural counseling and psychotherapy.* New York: Pergamon.

Ivey, A. E. (1986). *Developmental therapy.* San Francisco: Jossey-Bass.

Ivey, A. E. (1987a). Cultural intentionality: The core of effective helping. *Counselor Education and Supervision, 26,* 168-172.

Ivey, A. E. (1987b). The multicultural practice of therapy: Ethics, empathy, and dialectics. *Journal of Social and Clinical Psychology, 5,* 195-204.

Ivey, A. E. (1995). Psychology as liberation: Toward specific skills and strategies in multicultural counseling and therapy. In J. G. Ponterotto, J. M. Casas, L. A. Suzuki, & C. M. Alexander (Eds.), *Handbook of multicultural counseling* (pp. 53-72). Thousand Oaks, CA: Sage.

Ivey, A. E. (2000). *Developmental therapy: Theory into practice.* North Amherst, MA: Microtraining Associates.

Ivey, A. E., Ivey, M. B., & Simek-Morgan, L. (1993). *Counseling and psychotherapy: A multicultural perspective* (3rd ed.). Boston: Allyn and Bacon.

Ivey, A. E., Ivey, M. B., & Simek-Morgan, L. (1997). *Counseling and psychotherapy: A multicultural perspective* (4th ed.). Boston: Allyn and Bacon.

Jensen, J. V. (1985). Perspective on nonverbal intercultural communication. In L. A. Samovar & R. E. Porter (Eds.), *Intercultural communication: A reader* (pp. 256-272). Belmont, CA: Wadsworth.

Kottler, J. A., & Brown, R. W. (1985). *Introduction to therapeutic counseling.* Monterey, CA: Brooks/Cole.

Krebs, D. (1975). Empathy and altruism. *Journal of Personality and Social Psychology, 32,* 1134-1146.

LaBarre, W. (1985). Paralinguistics, kinesics, and cultural anthropology. In L. A. Samovar & R. E. Porter (Eds.), *Intercultural communication: A reader* (pp. 272-279). Belmont, CA: Wadsworth.

Lago, C., & Thompson, J. (1996). *Race, culture and counseling.* Philadelphia: Open University Press.

Leong, F. T. L. (Ed.). (1995). *Career development and vocational behavior of racial and ethnic minorities.* Mahwah, NJ: Lawrence Erlbaum Associates.

Lindermuth, D. C. (1998). Counseling African American families: Implications for White counselors. *Family Therapy, 25,* 41-49.

Locke, D. C. (1995). Counseling interventions with African American youth. In C. C. Lee (Ed.), *Counseling for diversity* (pp. 21-40). Boston: Allyn and Bacon.

Locke, D. L., & Velasco, J. (1987). Hospitality begins with the invitation: Counseling foreign students. *Journal of Multicultural Counseling and Development, 15,* 115-117.

Matsumoto, D. (1996). *A world of diversity: Facilitator's guide.* Pacific Grove, CA: Brooks/Cole.

McClure, F. H., & Teyber, E. (1996). The multicultural-relational approach. In F. H. McClure & E. Teyber (Eds.), *Child and adolescent therapy: A multicultural-relational approach.* Fort Worth, TX: Harcourt Brace.

Mehrabian, A., & Epstein, N. (1972). A measure of emotional empathy. *Journal of Personality, 40,* 525-543.

Mullavey-O'Byrne, C. (1997). Empathy in cross-cultural communication. In K. Cushner & R. W. Brislin (Eds.), *Improving intercultural interactions: Vol. 2. Modules for cross-cultural training programs* (pp. 205-220). Thousand Oaks, CA: Sage.

Okun, B. F., Fried, J., & Okun, M. L. (1999). *Understanding diversity: A learning-as-practice primer.* Pacific Grove, CA: Brooks/Cole.

Pandey, J., & Kakkar, S. (1982). Cross-cultural differences and similarities in ingratiation tactics as social influence and control mechanisms. In R. Rath, H. S. Asthana, D. S. Sinha, & J. B. P. Sinha (Eds.), *Diversity and unity in cross-cultural psychology* (pp. 295-301). Lisse, Netherlands: Swets and Zeitlinger.

Paniagua, F. A. (1998). *Assessing and treating culturally diverse clients: A practical guide.* Thousand Oaks, CA: Sage.

Parker, W. M. (1987). Flexibility: A primer for multicultural counseling. *Counselor Education and Supervision, 26,* 176-183.

Pearson, J. C. (1985). *Gender and communication.* Dubuque, IA: W. C. Brown.

Pedersen, P. (1988). *A handbook for developing multicultural awareness.* Alexandria, VA: American Association for Counseling and Development.

Pedersen, P. B., Draguns, J. G., Lonner, W. J., & Trimble, J. E. (Eds.). (1996). *Counseling across cultures* (4th ed.). Thousand Oaks, CA: Sage.

Pietrofesa, J. J., Hoffman, A., & Splete, H. H. (1984). *Counseling: An introduction.* Boston: Houghton Mifflin.

Ramirez, M., III. (1999). *Multicultural psychotherapy: An approach to individual and cultural differences.* Needham Heights, MA: Allyn and Bacon.

Ramsey, S., & Birk, J. (1983). Preparation of North Americans for interaction with Japanese: Considerations of language and communication style. In D. Landis & R. Brislin (Eds.), *Handbook of intercultural training: Volume III* (pp. 227-259). New York: Pergamon.

Riddle, D. T. (1982). Multiculturalism: Moving beyond cultural definition. In R. Rath, H. S. Asthana, D. S. Sinha, & J. B. P. Sinha (Eds.), *Diversity and unity in cross-cultural psychology* (pp. 285-294). Lisse, Netherlands: Swets and Zeitlinger.

Ridgway, I. R., & Sharpley, C. F. (1990). Multiple measures for the prediction of counselor trainee effectiveness. *Canadian Journal of Counselling, 24,* 165-177.

Ridley, C. R., & Lingle, D. W. (1996). Cultural empathy in multicultural counseling. In P. B. Pedersen, J. G. Draguns, W. J. Lonner, & J. E. Trimble (Eds.), *Counseling across cultures* (4th ed., pp. 21-46). Thousand Oaks, CA: Sage.

Ridley, C. R., Mendoza, D. W., Kanitz, B. E., Angermeier, L., & Zenk, R. (1994). Cultural sensitivity in multicultural counseling: A perceptual schema model. *Journal of Counseling Psychology, 41*(2), 125-136.

Rogers, C. R. (1957). The necessary and sufficient conditions of therapeutic personality change. *Journal of Consulting Psychology, 21,* 95-103.

Rogers, C. R. (1975). Empathic: An unappreciated way of being. *The Counseling Psychologist, 5*(2), 2-10.

Scott, N. E., & Borodovsky, L. G. (1990). Effective use of cultural role taking. *Professional Psychology: Research and Practice, 21,* 167-170.

Singelis, T. (1994). Nonverbal communication in intercultural interactions. In R. W. Brislin, T. Yoshida, & K. Cushner (Eds.), *Improving intercultural interactions: Modules for cross-cultural training programs* (pp. 268-294). Thousand Oaks, CA: Sage.

Sodowsky, G. R., Kuo-Jackson, P. Y., Richardson, M. F., & Corey, A. T. (1998). Correlates of self-reported multicultural competencies: Counselor multicultural social desirability, race, social inadequacy, locus of control racial ideology, and multicultural training. *Journal of Counseling Psychology, 45,* 256-264.

Sue, D. W., & Sue, D. (1999). *Counseling the culturally different: Theory and practice.* New York: John Wiley & Sons, Inc.

Sue, S., & Morishima, J. K. (1982). *The mental health of Asian Americans.* San Francisco: Jossey-Bass.

Tanaka-Matsumi, J., & Higginbotham, H. N. (1996). Behavioral approaches to counseling across cultures. In P. B. Pedersen, J. G. Draguns, W. J. Lonner, & J. E. Trimble (Eds.), *Counseling across cultures*. (4th ed., pp. 266-292). Thousand Oaks, CA: Sage.

Thiagarajan, S., & Steinwachs, B. (1994). *Barnga: A simulation game on cultural clashes*. Yarmouth, ME: Intercultural Press.

Toi, M., & Baston, C. D. (1982). More evidence that empathy is a source of altruistic motivation. *Journal of Personality and Social Psychology, 43,* 281-292.

Vontress, C. E. (1969). Cultural barriers in the counseling relationship. *Personnel and Guidance Journal, 48*(1), 11-17.

Wade, P., & Bernstein, B. L. (1991). Cultural sensitivity training and counselor's race: Effects on Black female clients' perceptions and attrition. *Journal of Counseling Psychology, 38*(1), 9-15.

Wehrly, B. (1988). Cultural diversity from an international perspective. *Journal of Multicultural Counseling and Development, 16,* 3-15.

Wittmer, J. (1992). *Valuing diversity and similarity: Bridging the gap through interpersonal skills*. Minneapolis, MN: Educational Media Corporation.

Yamamoto, J., & Kubota, M. (1983). The Japanese American family. In J. Yamamoto, A. Romero, & A. Morales (Eds.), *The psychosocial development of minority group children* (pp. 237-247). New York: Brunner/Mazel.

# Chapter 12

# NON-WESTERN HELPING MODALITIES

### *Roger D. Herring*
University of Arkansas-Little Rock
### *Carmen Salazar*
Texas A&M-Commerce

Indigenous culture and value systems directly influence the development of the constructs inherent to helping processes with diverse ethnic populations. "It is essential for the reader to discern that values do not emanate from a vacuum, but rather are influenced by worldview, cultural ideology, and personal philosophy" (Robinson & Howard-Hamilton, 2000, p. 49). This axiom applies to both clients and counselors. Specific Western helping approaches do not directly link mental growth and development to Indigenous cultural and ethnical perspectives. It is therefore necessary for counselors to bridge the gaps between and among themselves, their clients, and counseling itself.

Demographic projections reveal that by 2040 the U.S. population will be comprised of approximately 56% White, 21% Hispanic American, 14% African American, 8% Asian American, and 1% Native American Indian/Alaska Native (U.S. Census Bureau, 1998). The increasing diversity in this nation presents multiple obstacles for diverse groups and multiple challenges for counselors, and these obstacles and challenges span the developmental spectrum. For example, in the area of parenting, Diller (1999) described the situation in this manner:

> Ethnic parents face a most difficult and thankless task of preparing their children for entry into a society that does not value them. Their children, in turn, may encounter difficulties navigating some of the normal developmental tasks of childhood because of the preponderance of negative messages they receive about themselves from the White world (p. 66).

The available literature on specific and appropriate helping endeavors for ethnic minority individuals is limited and not generally well-grounded, although resources are expanding. In this chapter, we synthesize available literature in presenting an appropriate perspective for the helping of people from non-mainstream groups. The chapter is intended as a general introduction to various non-Western helping models. Barriers to educational, career, and personal development often preclude the possibility of ethnic minority individuals' full participation in mainstream culture (see Arbona, 1996; Leung, 1995); therefore, the particular focus of this chapter is on young people from ethnic minority groups. We first present a brief overview of critical influences on the development of ethnic minority individuals.

## CRITICAL INFLUENCES ON WORLDVIEWS

The authors' intent is not to deliberately exclude other minority persons, such as gay-lesbian individuals and persons with disabilities. Rather, the introductory nature of this chapter precludes discussions of all who are ethnically or otherwise culturally different from mainstream, dominant society. Some comparisons are made across groups in these discussions; however, within group differences require recognition.

### Sociocultural and Psychosocial Factors

People from ethnic minority groups present unique issues because of their developmental status and membership in their cultures. Some of the issues are related to sociocultural conditions (e.g., poverty, prejudice, racism), whereas others are developmental issues faced by all people. Developmental tasks, however, are also influenced by cultural factors. Most children are reared within the context of a family, whose members bear primary responsibility for the socialization of the children. Understanding the culture's concept of family is vital to effective interventions. The effective helping professional must address sociocultural issues and intrapsychic concerns.

#### Poverty, Low Socioeconomic Status (SES), and Class

Socioeconomic concerns are frequently the least discussed, and therefore the least addressed multicultural issue. Apparently unnoticed are 40 million poor people—the populations of Maine, Vermont, New Hampshire, Connecticut, Rhode Island, and New York combined—with a growth-rate increasing twice as fast as the general population in the United States (Mantsios, 2001). Economic deprivation and workplace discrimination are only two of the multiple issues faced by less economically advantaged people. The effect of unemployed and underemployed parents on ethnic youth is tremendous. For example, a central issue has been a tendency for male counselors to dominate ethnic minority students and "guide" them into stereotypical career choices (Herring, 1998).

The high rates of poverty in ethnic minority families is well documented in census data. For example, in 1998, 26% of African American, 26% of Hispanic American, and 13% of Asian American families are poor, as compared to 9% of non-Hispanic Whites (U.S. Census Bureau, 1999). Perhaps, the most direct effect of poverty is restricted access to environmental resources with which to combat substandard housing, lack of comprehensive health care, and inadequate nutrition (Rivers & Morrow, 1995). The relationship of low SES, its concomitant stressors, high rates of psychological maladjustment, and limited resources present viable concerns to ethnic minority individuals. For example, studies (e.g., Hanson, 1994; Reinolds, 1996; Trusty & Harris, 1999) indicate that the lower the parents' income and education, the less likely a child is to enter college or acquire a bachelor's degree. And this holds true even for low SES young people who demonstrate academic talent (see Hanson, 1995; Trusty & Harris, 1999).

### Language Issues

Younger youth generally learn second languages more easily and more quickly than older youth and adults. As a result, the language skills of bilingual children may threaten the traditionally strict hierarchical role of monolingual parents and children (Huang, 1994). Language issues may also interfere with academic achievement. For example, traditional learning styles for Native American Indian and Alaska Native children rely heavily on nonverbal communication, observation, and enactment, as well as linguistic structures that are entirely different from those of English (Herring, 1997a). As a result, the English skills of these youth are among the poorest of any group in the United States, which partially explains their historical academic underachievement (Herring, 1997a, 1997b).

### Stereotypes

Stereotypes are transmitted through overtly negative images and attitudes as well as in covert omissions of the positive aspects of ethnic minority cultures. These pervasive messages can become internalized if not countered by evidence to the contrary (Rivers & Morrow, 1995). When they are internalized, identity exploration may be restricted and a dichotomous mode of thinking can result (e.g., White is "good," color is "bad"). Ethnic minority individuals often find themselves having to choose between identifying with dominant values in order to achieve, thereby fulfilling the prophecy and acting out the negative stereotype. Such dichotomies are represented in derogatory slurs that ethnic minority individuals sometimes use to refer to one who has "sold out" to the dominant culture. For example, "apple" refers to a Native American Indian person who is considered "Red on the outside but White on the inside" (Herring, 1997a, 1999).

### Academic Underachievement and School Dropout

A primary concern of school personnel is lowering the dropout rates of students. The frequency of school dropout for the general population ranges from 5% to 30%, whereas ethnic minority students have a much higher rate, especially in inner cities (U.S. Census Bureau, 2001). Their value orientations, low SES, and familial conditions are often not conducive to completing secondary education. An ethnic appropriate example is reflected in the cooperation value clash between some ethnic youth and the mainstream Western value of competition. Some Native American Indian students may feel uncomfortable when praised for their work as *individuals*, yet feel quite proud when they receive praise for *group* success; or may resist competing if they believe that their own success will contribute to their classmates' failures (Grant & Gomez, 1996). In addition, some Native American Indian/Alaska Native communities may value nonlinguistic forms of expression (e.g., art and drawing) more than reading and writing (Garrett, 1995; Trawick-Smith, 1997).

## Major Psychosocial Factors

Multiple psychosocial factors also influence the developmental processes of many ethnic individuals. Such factors as substance abuse, increasing populations, teen pregnancy, and delinquency serve to exacerbate other ethnic and cultural factors in contemporary U.S. society. These factors warrant brief attention for the reader's edification.

### Substance Abuse

The problem of alcohol and other drug abuse in the United States continues to be of great concern. Three factors need to be recognized in this problem: physiological, sociological, and psychological (Lawson & Lawson, 1989). Physiological studies have indicated a genetic factor for some forms of substance abuse; sociological research has demonstrated the influence of family and peers; and psychological factors have been found to play a role. Although substance experimentation is relatively common among all youth, additional characteristics are present among ethnic minority youth. Within groups differences limit generalizing from a particular subgroup to the larger group (e.g., differences exist between reservation/nonreservation Native American Indians, as well as among and within tribes).

### Demographics

Ethnic minority youth are the fastest growing segment of the U.S. population. By the year 2000, ethnic minority youth will comprise nearly 30% of the population, with the Native American Indian and Alaska Native populations having the largest percentage of children and adolescents--over 37% under 18 years of age (U.S. Census Bureau, 1992). Ethnic minority youth deserve an appropriate and ethnic-specific perspective from helping professionals.

### Teenage Pregnancy

Given the lack of role models, skills, and self-confidence necessary to pursue alternative paths, many ethnic minority girls, especially those from low SES families, may actively seek the traditional role of mother as the only rite of passage by which to enter into adult womanhood (Rivers & Morrow, 1995). Teenage pregnancy is associated with educational setbacks, unemployment, family problems, and welfare dependency (Herring, 1997a, 1997b).

### Delinquency

Youth under the age of 21 account for about 30% of police arrests in the United States (U.S. Department of Justice, 1991). Factors related to chronic delinquency include low verbal intelligence, poor school performance, peer rejection in childhood, and membership in antisocial groups. A consistent factor is a family environment low in warmth, high in conflict, and characterized by inconsistent discipline. Non-peer and non-familial factors also influence adolescents' choice of gang membership and delinquency.

## Impact of Sociocultural and Psychosocial Factors

Helping professionals, especially those working with youth, must understand how sociocultural and ethnic-group contexts influence the development of mental health problems in ethnic minority individuals. Concurrently, the negative influences of these problems on ethnic minority students' social, mental/emotional, and career development must be understood. Some researchers (e.g., Phinney, Lochner, & Murphy, 1990) contend that the common element among ethnic minority youth at risk for future psychological maladjustment is the maintenance of a foreclosed or diffused identity status. In addition, cultural marginality and the stress associated with acculturation results in heightened anxiety, lowered self-esteem, and aggressive acting-out or withdrawal behavior, which can contribute to such problems as substance abuse, academic underachievement or dropout, teenage pregnancy, delinquency, and suicide and homicide among ethnic minority youth (Rivers & Morrow, 1995).

This brief discussion of sociocultural and psychosocial influences on ethnic individuals' personal development illustrates the numerous obstacles inherent in their attempts to participate in contemporary society. The obvious results can be shattering. The impact of these factors continues to be counterproductive to successful social, emotional/mental, and career development. Attention will now be directed to more appropriate and indigenously sensitive helping approaches with the major ethnic minority populations. For the purposes of continuity and clarity, the term *helping professional* will be the primary referent term within these discussions.

## HISPANIC AMERICANS

The term *Hispanic* is frequently used by governmental institutions and the media to designate those individuals who reside in the United States and who were born in, or can trace their ancestry to, one of the Spanish-speaking nations of the world. However, this label is not an inclusive self-identifier used by individuals within this population. Many prefer to use their country of origin to identify their nationality. Members of this group recognize the terms *Latino* (masculine) and *Latina* (feminine) as more accurate descriptions of their origin (Lopez-Baez, 1997). Nevertheless, this author will use the more familiar term *Hispanic Americans*.

### Overview of Hispanic Helping Systems

Three popular *ethnomedical systems* exist in the United States among Hispanics: *Espiritismo* (Spiritism), *Santeria,* and *Curanderismo*. These traditional, folk systems of healing contrast with biomedical systems (Koss-Chioino, 2000). Each system synthesizes beliefs and practices derived from the separate colonial histories of the three ethnic communities with which they are associated (See Myers, 1999, for a detailed discussion of the historical roots of *Espritismo* and *Santeria*).

*Espiritismo* (Spiritism), primarily associated with Puerto Ricans, is also practiced in the Oriente region of Cuba (Bernal & Gutierrez, 1988), as a synthesis of European (French) and Afro-Caribbean traditions (Koss-Chioino, 2000). Ramos-McKay, Comas-Diaz, and Rivera (1988) stated that "a significant number of Puerto Ricans believe in *espiritismo*" (p. 210), which the authors describe as "a form of mental health care" (p. 211).

*Santeria* is associated with Cubans (Koss-Chioino, 2000) and Puerto Ricans (Evanchuk, 1999; Zea, Quezada, & Belgrave, 1997). It blends folk Catholicism and West African traditions (Koss-Chioino, 2000). Zea et al. noted that "The influence of African culture on the beliefs and behaviors of some Latino groups has been overlooked by psychologists and has been more often examined by anthropologists and sociologists" (1997, p. 256). Puerto Ricans and Cubans have kept and transmitted African-based spiritual beliefs and practices. The African influence (Nigerian Yoruba traditions) is strong in *Santeria*, which is practiced in both groups, and which is "very much alive in urban enclaves such as the Bronx, Harlem, and Miami" (Zea et al., 1997, p. 259), and other urban locations, including Chicago, Detroit, and Gary, Indiana (Lefever, 1996).

*Santeria* and *Espiritismo* are not limited to Caribbean, African, Latin American people, working class, or poor people. These practices are also becoming more popular among individuals of other ethnic groups and among middle-class professionals (Evanchuk, 1999; Lefever, 1996; Myers, 1999).

*Curanderismo*, which synthesizes folk Catholicism and Mexican Indian traditions (Koss-Chioino, 2000), is "a set of folk/medical beliefs, rituals, and practices that address the psychological, social, and spiritual needs of Mexican and Mexican American populations" (Cervantes & Ramirez, 1992, p. 114). Martinez (1988) noted that beliefs in folk healing and associated folk illnesses occur with enough frequency among the Mexican American population to warrant the attention of medical/health care providers.

Echeverry (1997) described a help-seeking pattern among Hispanics who tend to rely on alternative approaches to wellness. First, they will try to resolve physical and mental problems within the extended family, consult a trusted friend (*compadre*), priest/minister, or a folk healer (i.e., a *santero*, *curandera*, or *espiritista*). If these strategies do not work, they may go to a mental health practitioner or emergency room. For other Hispanics, healing rituals may represent an important adjunct to conventional medical care (e.g., Evanchuk, 1999).

Some recognition exists among traditional folk healers that combinations of spiritual, medical, and mental health treatment may be needed. An informal practice common among Hispanic healers is referring somatic complains to medical doctors, and simultaneously referring spiritual aspects of the problem to traditional treatments (Koss-Chioino, 2000). An increasing recognition also exists among Western-focused practitioners that utilization of traditional healing practices may be an important aspect of wellness for Hispanic clients. As Bernal and Gutierrez (1988) observed: "With some individuals, mobilizing the folk-healing system of support can be an important leverage in therapeutic change" (pp. 243-244).

## Illness Etiologies

*Espiritismo* involves belief in an invisible world, inhabited by spirits, that surrounds the visible world. Spirits communicate with those in the material world through mediums, and can penetrate the visible world and attach themselves to human beings (Ramos-McKay et al., 1988). Benevolent spirits and misguided spirits of those who died an untimely death are also available (Myers, 1999). Misguided spirits are the cause of suffering (Koss-Chioino, 2000; Myers, 1999) and are attracted to people who behave immorally (Koss-Chioino, 2000).

In the *Espiritismo* belief system, the person is composed of spirit and matter, so illness can have physical or spiritual causes (Myers, 1999). Physical and psychological well-being are not separated, and health involves both emotional and physical states. For example, "Anxiety can be expressed as headaches or 'pain in the brain'" (Ramos-McKay et al., 1988 , p. 211). Puerto Rican cultural beliefs consistent with *Espiritismo* include communication between living and dead through dreams (Ramos-McKay et al., 1988).

Most information on *Santeria* has been transmitted through oral tradition, and only recently have written materials been available (Perez y Mena, 1998; Zea et al., 1997). Basic beliefs of the Yoruba tradition include respect for ancestors, and interconnection between the living and dead. Natural and supernatural forces are considered causes of physical and emotional problems (Bernal & Gutierrez, 1988; Zea et al. 1997). The term *Santeria* means "worshiping of saints." The Yoruban deities (*Orishas*) worshipped in this system are identified with Catholic saints (Myers, 1999; Perez y Mena, 1998). Each *Orisha* represents or controls a force of nature (Zea et al., 1997) and is identified with a human interest or endeavor (Myers, 1999). The underlying assumption in *Santeria* is that deities are the direct cause of suffering. "Like people [they] can do both good and evil, and the only way to cope is to ally with and manipulate these powerful beings for your own ends" (Koss-Chioino, 2000, p. 152).

*Curanderismo* embraces a holistic view of life, with no artificial boundaries between mind and body. Cervantes and Ramirez (1992) described four views of illness and health associated with this system:

A. Life is ordained by divine will; a person must focus his or her thoughts, intentions, and behaviors on good deeds. Physical or emotional illness stems from loss of purpose and direction in life; the person is no longer in harmony.
B. Supernatural causes figure strongly in illness and health.
C. Health is viewed as a "naturalistic process."
D. Physical or emotional illness is a direct reflection of interpersonal relationships within the family and community.

These authors drew attention to similarities between the *Curanderismo* belief system and family therapy: "Similar to the idea of family homeostasis in family therapy, a healthy body is maintained through the balancing of biological needs and social-interpersonal expectations, physical and spiritual harmony, and individual and cultural-familial attachments." Physical, mental and spiritual dysfunctions are attributed to spirit loss, possession, punishment from God, *and* an imbalanced family system. (Cervantes & Ramirez, 1992, p. 115).

Koss-Chioino (2000) described the view of imbalance as a moral issue in the *Curanderismo* (and *Espiritismo*) belief system: "Those who 'break the rules' (including 'uncleanliness' in the moral sense) often become ill because they threaten the integrity of social fabric. Transgressions are sinful both because they unbalance the 'good' within an individual and because they generate conflict among persons" (p. 152).

Myers' (1999) observations about etiology (and treatment) in *Espiritismo* have implications for beliefs, in all three systems, about locus of responsibility. The client is suffering from external *causas*, so is not accountable for symptoms or behavior. Moreover, the client is required to passively follow the *espiritista's* treatment. This process differs from traditional therapy models in which the focus is on the client's personal responsibility and on internal (psychodynamic) causes. The counselor must find a way to bridge these two systems.

Koss-Chioino (2000) described the "causal paradigm" of Hispanic ethnomedical systems: "Malicious or unaware other-than-human beings or forces are the final causes of physical suffering, emotional distress, or personal problems" (pp. 151-152). Illnesses are "culturally constructed as syntheses of somatic and psychological factors," which contrasts with the biomedical model in which mind and body are separated (p. 156). The unifying theme for all three systems is harmony and balance of individuals, within and between them, and within the cosmos. Imbalance is perceived as a moral issue (Koss-Chioino, 2000).

## Diagnosis

In these three systems, little distinction is made among physical illness, emotional disorder, and social problems. In contrast to diagnoses of biomedicine or psychotherapy, the traditional Hispanic healer "knows" what the client's complaint is without verbal input from the client. Diagnosis is obtained by a variety of means (Koss-Chioino, 2000).

In *Espiritismo*, diagnostic divination takes place through spirit communication. The healer-medium's personal spirit-guides help him or her identify the spirit causing the client's problems. The healer then describes the client's complaints and the client confirms or denies them (Koss-Chioino, 2000). Diagnosis in *Santeria* is through a different form of divination as the *santero* reads shells (*los caracoles*) or palm nuts that are thrown onto a straw mat. The pattern of thrown shells is interpreted according to the position of the shells (Koss-Chioino, 2000; Lefever, 1996; Zea et al., 1997). In *Curanderismo*, diagnosis is accomplished through reading cards (tarot or a Spanish deck), or an egg is broken after the client is cleansed or "swept" with it (Koss-Chioino, 2000). Cervantes and Ramirez (1992) observed that "as in mainstream psychological and medical practice, [diagnosis in *Curanderismo*] includes the naming of the disease, the description of its etiology, and the prescribed treatment--all of which strengthen the relationship to the healer and enhance his or her credibility" (p. 115).

## Healing Process

Some aspect of balance (i.e., harmony) is central to healing in all three systems. In *Espiritismo*, the medium-healer (*espiritisto/espiritista*) is the vehicle for healing, not the agent of intervention (Koss-Chioino, 2000). The healer's task is to exorcise illness-causing spirits through working the cause (*causa*). The healer is possessed by the spirit causing the illness, then educates the spirit regarding what it is doing wrong, resulting in the spirit's request for forgiveness. Simultaneously, the client is treated with cleansing remedies that involve candles, herbs, special baths, and protective fetishes (Myers, 1999). Culturally appropriate treatment includes use of the client's words to describe the symptoms, treatment of cultural manifestations of illness, and the use of the extended family system in the healing process (Myers, 1999; Ramos-McKay et al., 1988).

The use of image and metaphor are central to the group healing rituals of *Espritismo*: "The feelings of clients are literally 'shaped' or 'formed' inside the healer through the action of the particular spirit causing the distressing feelings in the suffering client" (Koss-Chioino, 2000, p. 154). The healer models these feelings and emotions, and a "cycle of resonating feelings is set up" that includes the healers and other mediums in attendance, and the audience of participants (Koss-Chioino, 2000, p. 154). This group form of healing has been compared with psychodrama (Koss-Chioino, 2000; Ramos-McKay et al., 1988). Ramos-McKay et al. highlighted the relevance of group therapy for Puerto Rican culture and noted that "The Puerto Ricans' acceptance of the dramatic aspects of *espritismo* can be utilized in therapy by incorporating drama into the therapeutic sessions" (1988, p. 224).

In *Santeria*, healers and priests deal with problems and emotional distress (Koss-Chioino, 2000). Through divination, the *Orishas* reveal themselves, diagnose problems, and provide solutions (Lefever, 1996). Healers also prescribe herbal remedies and amulets "to protect against future harm or to bring about a desired event. These latter services, actual manipulations of the future, appear to be most sought after" (Koss-Chioino, 2000, p. 153). As expressions of gratitude and praise, food offerings and animal sacrifices are given to the *Orishas*. Santeria practice may also involve drum and dance festivals in which specific *Orishas* are honored. Participants may attain an altered state of consciousness that opens the channels of communication with the spirits (Lefever, 1996).

In *Curanderismo*, the healer is viewed as an instrument for a higher power that is the origin of the healing process (Cervantes & Ramirez, 1992; Koss-Chioino, 2000). The healer's role includes consultant to the spirit world, intercessor of positive energy, and restorer of family and community balance and harmony. Treatment involves sacred words, chants, specific cures, and creative imagery that is "culturally appropriate and therapeutically relevant to the presenting problem." This imagery takes shape through "prayer, ritual, or a directed sequence of thoughts" (Cervantes and Ramirez, 1992, p. 116). These authors compare characteristics of the *curandero/curandera* and the family therapist, and conclude that they "are remarkably similar and further suggest the dynamic role of spirituality in these functions. The philosophy of curanderismo serves as the connecting bridge between the penitent (client), the confessor/healer, the presenting problem, and the impaired interpersonal functioning in the social and familial system" (pp. 116-117).

Zea et al. (1997) described a case illustrating that utilization of folk healing systems is not limited to clients of a particular social class or educational level. It also highlights the interplay between indigenous healing practice and Western helping approaches:

> Sandra, a Latina woman of Caribbean descent, was encouraged by some friends to consult an *italero* (shell reader) about some job-related concerns. Much to her surprise, the *italero* mentioned patterns in her reading associated with back pain, a problem Sandra had been struggling with since a car accident several years before. According to the reading, she needed to help herself before the Orishas would do anything for her. Although she had never been a believer in Santeria, in her own words "this made me diet and exercise regularly in order to help my back pain." She received an *eleque* (necklace) for her health protection and job instability. In Sandra's case, although she was not brought up within the Santeria tradition, this intervention motivated her to change health-related behaviors. A well-educated woman, she already knew that diet and exercise would help, but she had never complied with physicians' recommendations (p. 261).

## ASIAN AMERICANS

The term *Asian American* refers to individuals living in the United States whose ancestors were native inhabitants of Asia and who are categorized by the U.S. Census Bureau as Asian Americans. According to the U.S Census Bureau (2001), the largest four Asian American groups in the United States are Chines Americans (1,645,427), Filipino Americans (1, 406, 770), Japanese Americans (847, 562), and Asian Indians (815, 447). Asian Americans, however, consist of over 29 distinct subgroups, representing three geographical regions: South Asia (India, Pakistan, Bangladesh), Southeast Asia (Burma, Cambodia, Laos, Vietnam, Thailand, Malaysia, Indonesia, the Philippines, and thousands of islands south and east of China), East Asia (China, Hong Kong, Japan, North and South Korea, and Taiwan), and Pacific Islands (Samoa, Tonga, Guam, Tahiti, Fuji, and other smaller islands). Many of these groups came to the Hawaiian Islands as well as to the U.S. mainland. The focus of this chapter, however, is on the mainland U.S.

Profound differences exist between the mental health concepts of Asian Americans and Western helping approaches. Acknowledging within-group differences, Asian Americans, however, do share some cultural and ethnic helping patterns. The authors' intent is not to deny the existence of differences among the various Asian American subgroups, but rather to describe their common indigenous helping systems and compare them with that of European American (i.e., Western) concepts. Our approach is general because of the diversity between and within Asian ethnic groups, and also because of the limited scope of this chapter.

The term *Asian culture* refers to the cultures of these countries from which Asians in the United States originated; cultures that were basically influenced by Hinduism, Islam, Confucianism, and Buddhism. Researchers (e.g., Sue & Sue, 1999) have identified numerous common values among Asian Americans as a group.

## Overview

A substantial variation is evident between ethnomedical systems among Asian groups (Koss-Chioino, 2000). Chinese medicine, a major influence, has a history of more than 5,000 years (see Koss-Chioino, 2000 for a more detailed discussion of this history). Traditional Chinese Americans are highly influenced by religious and spiritual beliefs, and by concepts of health and illness in Chinese medicine (Lee, 1997). They may utilize many types of traditional healing methods for physical and emotional problems. According to Lee (1997), many traditional healing methods are available in larger Asian communities in the U.S. The most popular are herbal medicine, acupuncture, therapeutic massage, and religious faith healing. Ritual treatments are usually conducted by Buddhist monks. Geomancy and fortune telling are also used "to prevent or remove `bad spirit'" (Lee, 1997, p. 61).

Ethnomedicine among Japanese Americans is based on Chinese traditional medicine and religious healing within Buddhist and Shinto traditions. Japanese Americans may also turn to healing cults such as the Salvation Cult (*Gedatsukai*), and more Western-like therapies such as Naikan and Morita, which focus on Japanese values (Koss-Chioino, 2000). Gee and Ishii (1997) noted that in Japan, people consult folk healers; however, Japanese Americans usually do not. Chinese medicine has influenced the belief systems of most people in Southeast Asia, and Chinese folk remedies are "widely practiced among the Vietnamese, Khmer, Hmong, and Mien (but not significantly among the Lao)" (Muecke, 1983). Members of Southeast Asian groups living in the U.S. may consult shamans and tend to utilize traditional herbal remedies (Koss-Chioino, 2000; Muecke, 1983; Sue & Sue, 1999).

Descriptions of the utilization patterns of Asian Americans suggest that families will turn to Western mental health services as well as traditional ethnomedical systems (e.g., Lin & Cheung, 1999; Moore & Boehnlein, 1991), although level of acculturation to Western values can modify help seeking patterns (Gee & Ishii, 1997). For some Asian Americans, mental health help is seen as a last resort. For example, Lee (1997) observed that traditional Chinese American families will turn to family members first for help with psychological problems, and then to trusted outsiders. Helpers within the ethnic community include elders, indigenous healers, spiritual leaders, and physicians. If the illness persists, families will turn to Western mental health professionals when all other resources have been exhausted (Lee, 1997).

Korean American clients who visit a mental health practitioner will often have already attempted various folk healing methods. For example, Kim (1997) noted that Korean clients sought mental health services only when problems were severe, and only when other means of help were exhausted. Most had sought other treatments, including herbal medicine, acupuncture, Christian counseling, and medical services. Conversely, clients may turn to mental health treatment first. Lo and Lau (1997) described the help seeking of Chinese in Canada when a condition does not respond quickly to conventional treatment. "Many Chinese do not hesitate to consult traditional practitioners, some of whom even advertise to specialize in treating different anxiety symptoms" (p. 313). Others may simultaneously seek traditional help and Western treatment. Chao (1992) described Southeast Asian families as being often "caught between the conflicting pulls" of traditional practices and modern U.S. psychological practices (p. 171). Mollica and Lavelle (1988) stated, "In general, a Western physician can assume that Indochinese patients are concurrently utilizing" a traditional cure for their symptoms along with Western medical treatment (pp. 273-274). While there is variation between Southeast Asian communities in the degree of reliance on community resources such as indigenous healers and those providing cures (Mollica & Lavelle, 1988), Chao (1992) noted that it is important for helping professionals to realize that traditional healers are a common resource in Southeast Asian communities.

A split between mind and body does not exist in Asian culture (Chao, 1992; Lin & Cheung, 1999). Chao (1992) noted that the person suffering from emotional distress will most likely experience fatigue, aches in joints and limbs, and headaches, and suggested the need for mental health practitioners to honor these symptoms: "This does not mean that the psychologist is practicing beyond his or her realm of expertise; it means that he or she is being aware of the whole person" (Chao, 1992, p. 161).

## Illness Etiologies

Harmony and balance, unity of body and mind, and the existence of the spirit realm are all key elements in Asian ethnomedical systems. Balance is the central tenet of the Chinese conception of health. This includes booth inner (within the person), and outer balance (with nature and the world). Balance between *yin* (dark, heavy, inner, female) and *yang* (bright, light, outer, male) is especially important (Koss-Chioino, 2000). Life energies are kept in balance by dualities. When imbalance occurs, the body's immunity is disturbed and the body becomes susceptible to illness.

The universe and human beings are subject to laws of five elements: fire, earth, metal, water, and wood. These elements correspond to five visceral organs and five emotions (Lee, 1997). Koss-Chioino (2000) described the importance of the heart, which "presides over all the organ systems and governs all mental activities. If the heart malfunctions (i.e., symbolic imbalance), palpitations, memory loss, insomnia, or mental disorders can occur" (p. 158). This unity of body and mind is exemplified in the Chinese written character for "joyless," the literal meaning of which is "the heart locked inside the door;" and the character for "happiness," the meaning of which is "the heart opened inside the door" (Lee, 1997, p. 60). The literal translation of the term *psychologist* in several Asian languages illustrates the concept that "heart issues encompass both the mind and the body." The Chinese characters for psychologist translate as "'expert of the inner heart,'" and in Vietnamese a psychologist is an "'expert of the heart, or soul,' or the 'expert who helps one understand the heart'" (Chao, 1992, p. 160).

Emotional problems and mental illness result from an imbalance of *yin/yang*; from excessive accumulation or decrease of *qi* (Gee & Ishii, 1997; Koss-Chioino, 2000; Lee, 1997), and imbalance in the five elements (Gee & Ishii, 1997). Mental illness is also explained as a form of spiritual unrest caused by a ghost or vengeful spirit; or *karma*; that is, causes arise from deeds from past lives, or punishment from God. Mental illness may also be caused by genetic vulnerability/hereditary defects, physical and emotional strain resulting from external stresses, character weakness, or may be a manifestation of physical disease (Lee, 1997).

Similarly, traditional Korean American clients may view mental illness as resulting from an imbalance of *yin* and *yang* within the body, from hereditary weakness, character weakness, or physical or emotional strain. Mental illness may be also perceived as a supernatural intervention, caused by evil or vengeful spirits (Kim, 1997).

Balance is also central to indigenous healing traditions of India, including Ayurvedic medicine. Individuals exist simultaneously in the three realms of the physical body, a reincarnated soul, and a social being invested with a particular dharma (i.e., clearly defined rules of conduct). Emotional distress is viewed as a disturbance in any of these realms; and disturbance in one realm affects functioning in other realms (Prathikanti, 1997).

The supernatural realm figures strongly in the Southeast Asian belief system, which includes the existence of good and evil spirits who are intelligent, and able to affect the life circumstances of the living. The spirits may be unhappy, and may be punishing. Hmong beliefs include the existence of good spirits who can protect against the workings of evil spirits (Sue & Sue, 1999). Human beings may communicate with spirits. Chao (1992) noted that "most Southeast Asian clients and friends will relate either a personal experience or that of a close friend or relative with a spirit" (p. 172). Gee and Ishii (1997) pointed out that Southeast Asians and Filipinos commonly believe spirit possession to be the cause of schizophrenia. Filipinos believe psychosis is caused by possession by agents of God, souls of the dead, spirits of life, or curses placed by shamans. Koss-Chioino (2000) observed that along with the belief in spirits as omnipresent, causal forces, a central concept of traditional Southeast Asian medical systems is the belief that "continued health depends on the continued residence of many souls; absence of one or more causes illness or death" ( p. 159).

## Diagnosis

Similarities exist between indigenous healers in the Asian American ethnomedical system and Western health practitioners. Both have diagnostic tools to help identify the nature of the problem, both provide interpretations to the patient, and both have treatment methods. However there are also differences. Traditional healers are likely to make a diagnosis and prescribe treatment based on assessment of the basic cause of illness, which may be natural or supernatural. Indigenous systems of healing tend to treat illness, which is recognized as a psychosocial process that must be treated in the context of the individual's family, social network, and community. In contrast, Western health practitioners are more biopsychologically oriented, focus on treatment of disease, and usually treat the individual without attention to context (Lee, 1997).

## Healing Process

In Chinese medicine, focus is on the somatic in diagnosis and treatment, but the psychological approach is an integral aspect, due to the essential relationship between the mind and the state of a person's health (Koss-Chioino, 2000). Illness may result from strong emotional states and imbalance in the types of foods eaten (Sue & Sue, 1999). Consequently, nutrition is important for restoring health. Foods are categorized into five groups: hot, cold, allergic, moderate, and nutrient (Lee, 1997). Treatment may include herbal prescriptions (Lo & Lau, 1997), or dietary changes which include eating specific types or combinations of foods (Sue & Sue, 1999); therapeutic foods that give *good qi* (energy) are a popular treatment for physical and emotional problems (Lee, 1997). Massage treatments, acupuncture, (Sue & Sue, 1999), and exercise type treatments such as *tai chi chuan, qi-gong*, and others, bring harmony to body and mind (Lee, 1997; Lo & Lau, 1997). Treatment for emotional problems may also include consultation with *feng-shui* masters or other practitioners of fortune telling (Lo & Lau, 1997).

The underlying assumption of Naikan and Morita therapies is that harmony with others is a desirable state; and treatment involves reestablishing harmony. The Japanese concept of *sunao* forms the basis of these therapies, which "refers to a pristine state of mind, like that of a baby, an unconditional state of trust in others" (Koss-Chioino, 2000, p. 159). The goals of therapy involve helping "to move clients toward being more in tune with others and society, to move away from individualism, and to move toward interdependence and connectedness" (Sue & Sue, 1999, p. 200).

For East Indian Americans, treatment also involves restoration of balance and harmony. Because body, soul, and social being are interrelated, treatment in any one realm can positively affect the other realms, regardless of the realm in which the distress originated. In Ayurvedic tradition, there is no treatment to address mental illness as distinct from the underlying aspects of being. Remedies to restore balance in the three realms involve "prayers, purification, rituals, soothing ointments, dietary instructions, and behavioral changes" (Prathikanti, 1997, p. 91).

Southeast Asian families may utilize a variety of remedies to restore balance within the body and balance of the body with its environment. These include modifications of Chinese treatments, such as acupuncture, massage, and herbal remedies (Muecke, 1983); as well as dermabrasive practices such as cupping, and moxibustion (Chao, 1992, Muecke, 1983). Massage and dermal treatments produce changes in the skin, which may be misread by teachers, health care practitioners, and others, as signs of physical abuse (Muecke, 1983; Sue & Sue, 1999). However, as Muecke observed: "The practices rarely, if ever, present a threat to the physical integrity of the person, and almost always nurture the person's sense of being cared for and his or her sense of security in being able to do something actively about disturbing symptoms" (1983, p. 437).

Shamanic healing may also be used to restore balance and harmony. Chao (1992) described the work of an American school psychologist with a Hmong family. A seven year old Hmong boy who was born in the United States to refugee parents from Laos was referred to the psychologist for school phobia following a car accident with his mother. The psychologist called a meeting with the parents and the boy. When they arrived, along with two older siblings and the boy's paternal grandmother who spoke minimal English, the psychologist decided on an "intuitive hunch" to meet with everybody. After speaking with first the father, then the mother, as a gesture of politeness the psychologist asked the grandmother for her opinion of the situation. With the father acting as translator, the grandmother explained that the car accident has caused the souls of the mother and son to be frightened out of their bodies; their souls were wandering lost, and now were vulnerable to attack by harmful spirits. The psychologist learned that some extended family members had advised visiting a highly respected shaman in another city for treatment. The psychologist validated the family's discussion about seeing the shaman, and intervened on their behalf with the school, assuring the family there would be no reports of truancy or child abuse or neglect. On the Monday morning following the visit to the shaman,

> the boy was back in school. His teacher reported that he had even come a bit early and that there had been no signs of the earlier reluctance. He had a twine necklace and two strings tied around his wrist. The boy tried to describe the ceremony. The shaman shook a lot, there was a gong and a bowl of water, the shaman tied on the strings. The boy no longer felt worried about coming to school. He said the shaman did some things for his mother and she felt stronger (Chao, 1992, p. 174).

During a follow-up visit with the family in their home, the psychologist learned that the family was suffering from grief and guilt due to the death of an infant during their escape from Laos, as well as post-traumatic stress. The school psychologist wondered if a future ceremony with a shaman might help heal the family; and desired consultion with a Hmong psychologist to learn how best to heal these matters of the heart (Chao, 1992).

# NATIVE AMERICAN INDIAN/ALASKA NATIVES

Helping professionals are confronted with major tasks in promoting the career, academic, and social development of Native American Indian/Alaska Natives. For the purposes of this discussion, the term "Native" will be used as the identifying label for this population. Before examining helping practice for these individuals, however, an overview of important issues is necessary.

## Overview

Many Natives exist as both Natives and as non-Natives—attempting to retain their traditional values but seeking as well to live in the dominant culture. This dualistic life increases the developmental stress on Natives. Also, to further complicate helping efforts, within-group differences negate the treating of these people homogeneously. Effective helping with Natives requires helping professionals to recognize a minimum of three within-group variances: cultural commitment, use of humor, and view of seeking help.

### Cultural Commitment

The historical idea of cultural assimilation as a solution to the so-called "Indian problem" remains untenable (Herring, 1999). Traditional Native people do not wish to be assimilated into the dominant culture and this recognition is important. A Chippewa described it in this way:

We view this place [North America] as being given to us by the Creator to take care of and to pass onto our future generations. We believe all other people are visitors, and when they leave, we'll still be here to pick up the pieces, no matter what shape it's in (Mulhern, 1988, p. 1).

Fifty percent of Native populations live off reservations (Herring, 1999). This physical separation from reservation culture has resulted in a varied degree of commitment to tribal customs and values. Natives are a people of many peoples whose diversity is reflected in a variety of customs, languages, and family types (Garrett & Herring, 2001). This diversity exists not only between members of different tribes and nations but also among members within a single tribe. Helping professionals need to be cautious of making assumptions about the cultural orientation of Natives. The continuum of acculturation found in Native families can be described as comprising the following types (Herring, 1989, 1999; Garrett & Garrett, 1996; Garrett & Garrett, 1993):

- *Traditional*. This family pattern attempts to adhere to culturally defined styles of living. Family members generally speak and think in their Native language and practice only traditional beliefs and values. This family desires to return to an ancestral culture of nomadism (depending on the tribe or nation) and isolation from non-Native peoples.
- *Transitional*. The transitional family retains only rudimentary elements of historical family life, preferring to live within the majority culture. The members generally speak both the Native language and English. This family does not fully accept the cultural heritage of their tribal group nor identify with mainstream culture and values.
- *Bicultural*. This family is generally accepted by dominant society. Family members are simultaneously able to know, accept, and practice both mainstream values and the traditional values and beliefs of their cultural heritage.
- *Assimilated*. The assimilated family generally is accepted by the dominant society. The family members embrace only mainstream culture and values.

In addition to these diverse family types, other influences (e.g., negative socioeconomic, cultural, and political influences) experienced by many Native youth may produce a high degree of alienation by the time they have reached adolescence. These youth not only experience the identity crisis of adolescence (i.e., as defined by tribal socialization mores and not necessarily Eriksonian) but also the additional burden of the identity crisis of their ethnicity. Psychological helplessness and hopelessness may serve to further alienate the youth from helping professionals (Herring, 1999).

## Use of Humor

Contrary to the stereotype of Native peoples as solemn, stoic figures poised against a backdrop of tepees, horses, tomahawks, and headdresses, they love to laugh. Humor is important in bringing people together and reaffirming bonds of kinship. Laughter relieves stress and creates an atmosphere of sharing and connectedness. Native humor is unique in its pragmatism, especially in its observation of the obvious and the use of exaggeration. From the use of the clown motive in ceremonies and rituals to the use of practical jokes, humor is a prominent feature of Native culture (Herring, 1994). People who cannot accept teasing or cannot handle laughing at themselves probably cannot handle being part of the group. Native humor serves the purpose of reaffirming and enhancing the sense of connectedness experienced in being part of the group (Garrett & Garrett, 1996; Garrett & Garrett, 1993). Nevertheless, helping professionals are cautioned to use humor very discreetly and to ensure tribal specificity.

### Use of Folklore

Native folklore communicates the appreciation and relationship to the Earth and its animals. The Earth is a family member and should be respected, cherished, and not controlled. Caduto and Bruchac (1991) wrote, "to the native people of North America, what was done to a frog or a deer, to a tree, a rock or a river, was done to a brother or sister" (p. xviii). Beliefs are passed inter-generationally through storytelling. Native folk tales are meant to teach as well as to entertain. Bruchac (1991) wrote that if a child misbehaves, he or she will be told a story rather than punished because "striking a child breaks that child's spirit, serves as a bad example and seldom teaches the right lesson, But a story goes into a person and remains there" (p. i). Chiricahua and Mescalero Apache use folklore as a group-supported means of expressing and transiently resolving unresolved, repressed infantile conflicts. Apache also use their folklore as a complement to the defensive and adoptive functions of individual dreams, fantasies, and daydreams.

### View of Seeking Counseling

Effective helping with Natives also involves a varied orientation to helping professionals and helping in general. Research indicates that traditional Native Americans seldom look to Western helping processes as a means of improving their chosen way of life (LaFromboise, 1998), and recognize the need for professional help only when community-based networks are unavailable or undesirable (Herring, 1999). Such reluctance may also be attributable to Natives' memory of the historical negative interactions they have had with non-Native people. Moreover, many Natives believe that mental illness is a justifiable outcome of human weakness or the result of avoiding the discipline necessary to keep cultural values and community respect. Native individuals who do enter counseling often express concern about how conventional Western psychology superimposes biases onto their problems and molds their behavior in a direction that conflicts with Native cultural lifestyle orientations (LaFromboise, 1998). This incompatibility between conventional counseling approaches and indigenous approaches constitutes a cultural variance that may hinder effective counseling by the unknowing counselor.

## Illness Etiology

If Natives want assistance from federal Native American Indian programs, they must prove their status of being a Native in terms of the definition established by the federal government. This definition states that individuals must have at least one-quarter "Indian blood" and a proof of tribal status (Harjo, 1993). However, the federal government does not have the final word in that definition. The federal government must also recognize the sovereign status of each tribal definition of "Indian." Without this verification, Natives cannot avail themselves of mental health services funded by the federal government.

## Cultural-bound Syndromes

Culture-specific disorders are known as cultural-bound syndromes in the literature. Simons and Hughes (1993) proposed the term *cultural-related syndromes* because many of these syndromes have been observed across different cultures. Examples of cultural-related syndromes that helping professionals are most likely to find in their practices with Native youth include the following (Simons & Hughes, 1993):

- Ghost sickness (weakness, dizziness resulting from the action of witches/evil).
- Wacinko (feeling of anger, withdrawal, mutism, suicide ideation).

Native individuals of the Southwest may also display cultural-related syndromes that are associated with their long history of interactions with Mexicans and Mexican Americans—who have had considerable influence on Native cultures in that region. These syndromes include the following:

- Ataque de nervios (out-of-consciousness state resulting from evil spirits)
- Mal puesto hex, root-work, voodoo death (unnatural diseases and death resulting from the power of people who use evil spirits)
- Wind/cold illness (a fear of the cold and the wind; feeling weakness and susceptibility to illness resulting from the belief that natural and supernatural elements are not balanced)

The impact of cultural-related syndromes upon the assessment of Natives, however, are not generally considered by helping professionals in their practices. Two reasons account for this omission (Paniagua, 1999). First, current standard clinical ratings and diagnostic instruments do not include criteria for the assessment of such syndromes. Second, reimbursement for clinical services regarding cultural-related syndromes is not a practice among major private insurance, Medicaid, and Medicare.

Helping professionals should have some familiarity with cultural-related syndromes shared by Natives. For example, a Native youth reporting manifestations (e.g., weakness, loss of appetite, and fainting) as the result of the action of evil supernatural forces would be an example of a schizophrenic to a helping professional unfamiliar with the effect of ghost sickness among Native peoples. If the individuals' belief is not shared by family members, this belief is probably not a culturally supported belief (Westermeyer, 1993; Paniagua. 1999).

## Diagnosis

Helping professionals have to be careful not to generalize Natives' performance on assessment instruments due to the multitude of distinct tribes within this population. Traditions and values differ tribally, and performance on aspects of assessment tools also tends to vary. For example. a general finding in intelligence testing is that Native youth seem to score lower on the verbal scales as compared to the performance scales (Neisser et al., 1996). In addition, McShane and Plas (1984) suggested that Native youth are plagued by chronic middle-ear infections that can negatively effect their development in the verbal area. Native youth may also be misperceived by test examiners as they tend to be deferential to a non-Native test examiner, and they may be seen as lacking motivation.

The Minnesota Multiphasic Personality Inventory (MMPI) has been cited as the most "useful psychological test available in clinical and counseling settings for assessing the degree and nature of emotional upset" (Walsh & Betz, 1990, p. 117); and it is one of the most well-researched instruments currently in use (Suzuki & Kugler, 1995). The MMPI-2 was developed with a representative sample of Native individuals; and examination of scores and profiles indicates no substantial mean differences between Natives and the general normative sample on the MMPI-2 validity scales and standard scales (Butcher & Williams, 1992). Suzuki and Kugler (1995), however, cautioned professionals "not to rely upon a computer report, which cannot possibly integrate all of the relevant cultural information" (p. 503).

The California Personality Inventory (CPI; Gough, 1987) is an inventory that measures folk concepts—"concepts that arise from and are linked to the ineluctable processes of interpersonal life, and that are found everywhere that humans congregate into groups and establish societal functions" (p. 1). Some of these concepts include responsibility, tolerance, sociability, empathy, and sense of well-being. The CPI was developed to assess overall well-adjusted individuals in relation to social, educational, vocational, and family issues (Walsh & Betz, 1990). Dana (1993b), however, reported the presence of item differences between ethnic groups. Davis, Hoffman, and Nelson (1990) also found that differences exist in CPI response patterns between Native samples and European American samples equated on age, occupation, and education. They noted scaled score differences due to an interaction between gender and ethnic group and concluded that ethnic background should be considered in usage of the CPI.

To be effective with Natives, helping professionals must broaden their base of cultural knowledge and be willing to develop new structures, policies, and strategies that are more responsive to the uniqueness of Native individuals. Synergetic assessment is the integrating of multiple approaches into an organized paradigm of delivering appraisal services successfully to Natives (Herring, 1997a, 1997b). Integrative theorizing is currently becoming more common and influential. Theoretical approaches involving cognitive behavioral theory and developmental counseling have brought diverse theories together in a coherent fashion. For example, Attneave's (1969, 1982) network therapy involves multiple interventions and assessments with Native individuals, families, and the community to produce and maintain change.

The initial assessment session requires that the helping professional be alert to specific qualities inherent to effective diagnosis. The following procedures are offered as guidelines to initiate the assessment and helping process (adapted from Herring, 1999).

1. Recognize the limited understanding of Native culture and the positive feeling of being a Native. Non-Native helping professionals should begin with a clear statement regarding their limited knowledge of values, religions, and traditions.
2. Avoid pseudo-secrecy statements, and do not ask questions unrelated to the core problem.
3. Do not discuss medicinal resources. Synthetic medicine is not preferred by traditional Native individuals. They have their natural herbal and spiritual medicines.
4. Accept relatives, friends, Medicine Men/Women, and tribal leaders. The elders in the tribe and traditional medicine men/women have a special place in the family; they are seen as an integral part of the extended family (Dana, 1993a) and would be included in the extended family tree of Native Americans.

5.  Avoid taking many notes. Doing anything other than listening is considered a sign of disrespect.
6.  Listen rather than talk.
7.  Confidentiality versus resistance. Traditional Natives may not answer personal questions, and the helping professional may interpret this as resistance. The appropriate approach is not to label the behavior as resistance but to consider it as a sign indicating that issues of confidentiality have not been resolved (Paniagua, 1999).

In most educational settings, the school counselor coordinates the assessment of students' characteristics and behaviors with a variety of assessments. School counselors may administer standardized achievement tests, interest inventories, behavior rating scales, and nonstandardized procedures (Herring, 1997b). A culturally responsive school counselor needs to consider the dynamics of culture and ethnicity when interpreting data from assessment tools (Lee, 1995). The school counselor also needs to recognize potential influences of cultural bias in assessment instruments.

Dana (1993a, 1993b) provided an assessment model that helping professionals and clinicians could use in an overall approach to minimizing biases during the assessment of Native clients. Dana recommended assessing acculturation, selecting measures consistent with clients' preferences, and being culture-specific in communication regarding assessment. All assessment strategies have some degree of bias (Dana, 1993a). The important guideline to remember is to emphasize assessment techniques in which interpretations and speculations are minimized (Paniagua, 1999). The helping professional should also make an effort to select measures with evidence of cross-cultural validity,

In summary, our central purpose is to alert helping professionals who engage in intellectual and personality assessments to the uniqueness of the Native populations, especially those who remain pantraditional or traditional. This alertness is mandatory if appropriate and ethnic-specific diagnoses are to be rendered. If these ethnic specific parameters are overlooked, misdiagnosis and mislabeling will continue (Herring, 1999).

# Healing Process

Effective helping with Natives is predicated on adopting a proactive developmental perspective, including a thorough knowledge of past and current Native cultures (Herring, 1997a, 1997b). Helping professionals need to develop strategies to modify the effects of political, psychosocial, and socioeconomic forces on Natives. They also may need to become systemic change agents, intervening in environments that impede the development of Natives (Eberhard, 1989). The most appropriate and effective helping approach for integrating the multiple influences on Native Americans may rest in synergetic helping strategies.

### Directions for Synergetic Counseling

Successful helping often hinges on understanding traditional cultural attitudes, beliefs, and values, and being able to incorporate them into counseling strategies. Helping professionals need to become familiar with both content and process concerns when working with Natives as well (Herring, 1990b). Content concerns include worldview differences between helper and helpee, or the special needs and unique problems of Natives; whereas process concerns include varied levels of acculturation or differences in socioeconomic status. Inherent with process and content concerns, helping professionals might heed the following cautions and recommendations relative to the counseling environment and atmosphere.

## Creating a Culturally Affirmative Environment

Despite pressure from the dominant culture to conform to the "majority," and thereby subjugate their heritage, most Natives survive by becoming bicultural in a functional sense. This cultural fluency has implications for helping in light of recommendations that helpers do not "go Native" (Eldredge, 1993). If a non-Native professional attempts to use Native practices (e.g., burning herbs, conducting rituals, wearing Native jewelry and clothing), traditional Natives may be offended or alienated. They may view these pseudo-Native practices with distrust or disdain, which would be injurious to the helping relationship (Eldredge, 1993). Their ability to exist in two cultures makes Natives aware of the dominant culture's values of professional dress and demeanor (Trimble & Fleming, 1989).

Some practical, synergetic recommendations that may help create a culturally affirmative environment for helping Natives, but which do not require the professional to deny his/her own culture include the following (Garrett & Herring, 2001; Herring, 1999):

1.  Address openly the issue of dissimilar ethnic relationships rather than pretending that no differences exist.
2.  Evaluate the degree of acculturation of the Native.
3.  Schedule appointments to allow for flexibility in ending the session.
4.  Be open to allowing other family members to participate in the helping session.
5.  Be open to integrating indigenous interventions with Western traditions.

## Integration of Indigenous Strategies

Manson (1986) reported that "many traditional Indian and Native healing practices are gradually being incorporated into contemporary approaches to mental health treatment" (p. 64). He described three such practices as (1) *four circles*—concentric circles of relationship between client and Creator, spouse, nuclear family, and extended family as a culturally based structural concept of self-understanding; (2) *talking circle*—a forum for expressing thoughts and feelings in an environment of total acceptance without time constraints, using sacred objects (e.g., feathers or stones), the pipe, and prayer; and (3) *sweat lodge*—a physical and spiritual self-purification ritual emphasizing the relationship of the human being to all of creation. If the helping process is concerned with finding one's way and with the recovery of purpose and meaning, then the vision quest is an important, culturally relevant metaphor for school counselors (Heinrich, Corbine, & Thomas, 1990).

Broken Nose (1992) described the sweat lodge ceremony in these words:

The sweat lodge is a dome-like structure, usually constructed from willow branches and covered with heavy cloth and canvas. (The construction materials may vary as long as steam is contained and light is kept out). It serves as a sacred place of prayer. When the boys gathered there, the leader poured water over a pile of rocks in the middle of the circle, filling the lodge with steam. Each boy prayed aloud. Sometimes the boy received a sign from the spirits—lights around his head or the touch of an eagle feather. The spirits spoke to the leader about the prayers of each boy. The leader, in turn, passed along the spirits' suggestions and advice (p. 383).

The work of healing is effectively done with metaphors: "Traditional healing systems draw on metaphors resonant within the culture to construct the illness reality and then symbolically manipulate it to effect healing" (Good & Good, 1986, p. 18). The helping professional must be able to identify what these metaphors are within the Native's reality. "Now, if a patient believes in rituals and sacraments, I put down cedar. I use feathers and herbs. It isn't that I have any magic; it's the rituals and their sacramental quality—they *are* healing" (Hammerschlag, 1988, p. 87). Familiarity with traditional healing practices can provide access to those metaphors.

Using helping strategies that elicit practical solutions to problems is frequently effective. A nondirective approach may allow self-exploration and self-generated goals. A blend of techniques to fit with each individual is beneficial. Helpers should avoid direct and provocative confrontation. Even if the Native avoids eye contact (a culturally-appropriate behavior), the helping professional may maintain eye contact (without staring) sufficient for appropriate conversation, especially with a Native who is hearing challenged or deaf.

Respect the uses of silence. Silence may be the beginning of an important disclosure or may signify deep thought. Demonstrate honor and respect for the client's culture(s). Traditional Natives are socialized not to ventilate feelings, especially feelings relative to death or dying (Broken Nose, 1992). To grieve for someone who is in the process of dying is viewed as hurrying the person on his or her way. And to talk about someone who has died is viewed as holding his or her spirit back from the spirit world. One can talk to the person during the four days and nights wake period. Maintain the highest level of confidentiality. Native American Indian communities are extremely close. A wrong word or questionable ethical practice can rapidly destroy credibility and trust. Honesty and genuineness are vital.

### Conducting the Initial Session

The initial session or contact is vital to developing a helping relationship with Natives. From the beginning, Natives may be evaluating the total presentation of the professional (e.g., manner of greeting, physical appearance, ethnicity, nonverbal behavior and communication, and other subtle characteristics). The first few minutes of the session are very important to its success or failure. Content knowledge of the culture needs to be demonstrated to gain respect from Native clients. For example, awareness of tribal identity and familial pattern may need to be acknowledged immediately. Such an acknowledgment will convey to the client the attitude and concern of the professional relative to his or her understanding of Native culture.

### Within-Group Variances

As discussed earlier, three important characteristics must be acknowledged: cultural commitment (i.e., familial pattern); place of residence (reservation, rural, or urban setting), and tribal affiliation (Garrett & Garrett, 1996). Given the variance in family patterns, residences, and tribes, several ideas can be suggested to enhance effective helping with Natives.

Most Native history and culture are characterized by an oral tradition of communication (Herring, 1990a). The professional must pay attention to and subtly match the client's tone of voice, pace of speech, and degree of eye contact (LaFromboise, 1990; Thomason, 1991). This oral tradition can easily be integrated with the Native respect for elders. Tribal leaders can be effective resources in sharing customs and the *old way* through oral histories. Assessments of cultural commitment and tribal structure, customs, and beliefs will provide useful information on how to proceed (Garrett & Garrett, 1996). But remember, every Native client should be approached as an individual.

Helping professionals might consider using various authentic and nonstereotypical media resources. Videos and films are available depicting Native art, crafts, and music. Media materials can be obtained by contacting tribal organizations, Bureau of Indian Affairs offices, federal and state offices of Native education, and other such agencies. Such media examples can supplement non-Native perspectives, as well as expand Native views about tribal and clan characteristics. In addition, both Natives and non-Natives can benefit through these vicarious experiences *the Indian way*.

Another way of demonstrating respect for the traditional way is to encourage extended family members to participate. Working in the presence of a group, giving people a choice about the best way to proceed with the process, and allowing participation of family members and friends are all natural components of the traditional healing-way (Garrett & Garrett, 1996).

A traditional Native person who seeks assistance from an indigenous healer looks to the healer to identify the cause of the problem and work the cures (Peregoy, 1999). A professional must demonstrate patience exemplified by not offering advice or interpretation without being invited to do so. At the same time, possibilities must be described and solutions suggested with the realization that no one knows as well as the client what is best to be done (Garrett, 1991, 1994; Garrett & Garrett, 1996).

Another culturally appropriate technique is the use of guided imagery (Peregoy, 1999). For example, a Native female student comes to the school counselor's office with presenting concerns related to her self-concept. The school counselor may want to use guided imagery techniques to have the student visualize herself as she perceives herself to be, and then, have her visualize how she would ideally like to be. Once this is done the student then develops steps, with the assistance of the counselor, to work toward the goal of how she would like to perceive herself in the future. An excellent resource to use with this student is the discussion of the Pocahontas Perplex as discussed by Portman and Herring (2001).

## Summary

This discussion attempted to convey to future and current helping professionals appropriate information relative to helping Native Americans. A primary emphasis was placed on within-group differences and how professionals can ascertain these differences within the counseling context. A few basic recommendations for counseling with Natives include the following (Garrett & Herring, 2001; Herring, 1999):

- Ask permission whenever possible and always give thanks.
- Never interrupt—allow sufficient time for responding.
- Be patient.
- Use silence whenever appropriate (or even when it isn't).
- Use descriptive statements rather than questioning.
- Model self-disclosure through anecdotes or short stories.
- Make use of metaphors and imagery when appropriate.

- Try not to separate the person from the spirituality or from affiliation. with the tribal group. Honor those sacred relationships.
- Recognize the relative nature of value judgments such as "right or wrong" and "good or bad."

If helping professionals will heed the content and process information within the preceding discussions, the gap existing between cultural worlds, and between harmony and disharmony, can be bridged. If Natives are expected to learn and practice mainstream culture, then professionals also should enter the helping situation with a willingness to learn. Garrett and Garrett (1996) concluded that if professional helpers come first as students, and second, as professionals, they might be surprised at how much growth would take place by members of both worlds.

## AFRICAN AMERICANS

African Americans represent the largest ethnic minority group in the United States, currently about 13% of the total population, with nearly 32% being youth (U.S. Census Bureau, 1999). Although African Americans reflect a highly diverse group in terms of physical appearance, geographic preference, and SES, they remain a culturally distinct group united by ideology and a functional system of values and beliefs (Butler, 1992). Helping professionals must be cognizant of within-group variations.

## Overview

This discussion of African Americans' educational, social, emotional, and mental development will begin, as the other discussions have, with a brief overview of the potential and realistic obstacles in their quests for success. The degree of success or failure for these individuals is largely dependent on the various helping professionals with which they interact. As with all ethnic groups, helping professionals must possess content knowledge and process skills to ensure effective interventions; and subsequently, success in achieving goals.

### Social Class Distinctions

Gordon (1978) defined *social class* as social hierarchical arrangements of persons on the bases of differences in power, political power, or social status. He coined the term *ethclass* to refer to the social participation and identity of individuals who are confined to their own social class and ethnic group. It is a subculture that falls under the social structure of a society, within which members interrelate with each other and with society as a whole. African American families' ethclass distinctions have been described as being affluent, working class, or poor (Lum,1992):

*Affluent Families*: Affluent African American families are termed *conformists*; families are middle class, with husband and wife employed outside the home. Both spouses also cooperate at home, encourage education, and are involved in community affairs. They are achievement- and work-oriented, upwardly mobile, and are personal property owners.

*Working Class Families*: Working-class African American families are termed *innovators*, struggling to survive and depend on the cooperative efforts of the entire family. Parents are usually literate, their income bordering on the poverty line, and they tend to have five or more children. Racial discrimination and insufficient education limit their employment chances. Yet, the families usually own their own homes, rear their children with a strong sense of morality, and are self-reliant.

*Poor Families*: Poor African American families are considered *rebels*. They cope with low incomes through their extended households. Frequent relocation and unemployment are the norm. Marriage and child rearing occur during the teenage years, and parents are usually school dropouts. These families tend to reject society and experience failure and disappointment. With no hope, violent rebellion may become a means of resistance. The reader will heed that within-group differences among African Americans are more complex than the preceding descriptions, as these descriptions can be subdivided.

### Family Structure and Life Patterns

Contemporary studies on African American family structure indicate viable systems (e.g., Gary & Glasglow, 1983). However, this observation does not infer a denial that the African American family is presently experiencing a great deal of internal (family conflicts) and external (victim systems) stress (Ho, 1992). Rather, these stresses have spurred the development of diversified, changing African American family systems and structures.

As a result of responding adaptively to daily stressors, three types of African American families have emerged (Billingsley,1987): nuclear, external, and augmented families. The *nuclear family* consists of spouses and children and no other person living with them. Such a nuclear household can be *incipient* when there are no children, *simple* if composed of husband and wife their children, or *attenuated* if there is a single parent with no other parent figure present.

In *extended families*, other relatives or in-laws of the husband and wife share the same household with the nuclear family. Extended families may be incipient, simple, or attenuated, depending upon whether children are present or whether there is only one parent. *Augmented families* include the presence of nonrelatives in the household.

### Religious Influences

Religious institutions have traditionally played an important role in the lives of African Americans. Their religious denominations were organized as a means of coping with the social isolation that African Americans encountered during a history of slavery and oppression. Many West African cultural traditions were preserved in the lives of slaves in the United States. Jules-Rosette (1980, p. 275) identified six distinctive features of West African spirituality incorporated into the religious practices of African Americans:

1.  The direct link between the natural and supernatural
2.  The importance of human intervention in the supernatural world through possession and spiritual control
3.  The significance of music to invoke the supernatural
4.  The strong tie between the world of the living and the world of the dead
5.  The importance of participatory verbal performance, including call-response
6.  The primacy of both sacred and secular verbal performance

The central focus of African American religion has been on interpreting the African American experience in a meaningful way. The chief function of the African American preacher has been, and continues, to make the Christian Bible relevant to current events. Henry (1990) illuminated this function as follows:

> Black preaching is based on the Bible but not tied to pat legalistic or literalistic answers. Black worshipers are seeking the strength and assurance to survive another day rather than solutions to abstract theological problems. (p. 65)

African American ministers have also become busy participants and leaders in civil rights movements. Henry (1990) explained the religious base of civil rights movements: "Black theology condemns capitalism, does not condemn violence, contends that God is actively working for black liberation, and demands reparations for past injustices" (p 66). African American churches have always been more than religious institutions, according to Locke (1992),

> During slavery, churches were centers for the development of leadership, educational institutions, and agents for the transmission of traditions and values of the African-American community. After emancipation, the functions of the churches increased as they became agents for strengthened family ties, employment agencies providing assistance to newcomers in locating housing and jobs, and cultural centers providing opportunities for African Americans to learn about and appreciate their own heritage. (p 24)

Even if African American families do not actively become involved in a particular church, their religious heritage will shape their beliefs and values, their views on marital relationships and divorce, abortion, adoption, and child-rearing practices. Helping professionals' awareness of religious backgrounds will enhance their understanding of attitudes and values that may affect intervention decisions (Gibbs, 1990).

In becoming familiar with the various religious traditions, helping professionals need to be knowledgeable about local church and denominational laws and attitudes toward the role of women in the church and society, divorce and remarriage, drugs and alcohol, homosexuality, and healing (Richardson, 1991). In addition, helping professionals need to identify local African American ministers as resource and referral contacts. *The Black Church in the African American Experience* (Lincoln & Mamiya, 1990) is an excellent resource that can provide helping professionals with essential background information on the history and status of the African American church and its varied roles in African American society.

## Indigenous Healing Practices

Traditional healing as practiced in various parts of Africa has several implications for helping professionals who work with first-generation African Americans or international students from Africa. Vontress (1991) summarized these implications under five headings: (1) the cross-cultural counseling relationship, (2) the setting, (3) diagnostic procedures, (4) intervention strategies, and (5) the training of cross-cultural counselors (pp. 248-249). A brief discussion of these intervention areas will be presented--according to Vontress's research except when otherwise noted.

### Cross-Cultural Counseling Relationship

People socialized in Africa's small, rural, and collectivistic communities within consanguineous extended families headed by an elder will present unique cultural qualities to helping professionals. They are inclined, as a courtesy, to inquire about the helping professional's health and family before stating the reason for counseling. Helping professionals need to reciprocate the personal focus and thus minimize concerns about their ability to relate to their culturally and ethnically different clients (Herring, 1999). However, immediate acceptance should not be expected. Youth will need to consult with the family elder first, as the family serves a role in which members pool information and then advise the indecisive member on what to do.

All African Americans are not alike or Westernized simply because they dress and talk as other citizens of the United States. Many contrasts, contradictions, and differences are produced by the nearly 6,000 tribes and multitude of languages found in Africa. Nearly 95% of Africans live in areas of less than 20,000; but others may reside in much larger urban areas, or even in European cities prior to their arrival in the United States (Cowan,1987).

### The Setting

African Americans, and youth in particular, may feel comfortable bringing a family member or a friend when they meet with the helping professional. If they do, these individuals should be invited to participate in the discussions. For some clients, the display of African artifacts and the presence of African music in the background alleviate initial anxieties.

### Diagnosis Procedures

Helping professionals who focus exclusively on the psychological component of human existence are apt to misdiagnose the problems of African Americans. They must explore many of the traditional African beliefs held by the person. For example, the belief in *animism* acts as a powerful force on the traditional African's understanding of life's difficulties.

### Intervention Strategies

Traditional African healers utilize many different methods to help their patients, such as dream interpretation (e.g., Mpolo, 1974), possession dances (e.g., Stoller & Olkes,1987), sacrifices (e.g., Gonzalez-Wippler,1988), pharmacotherapy (e.g., Torrey, 1986), shock therapy (e.g., Vontress, 1991), exorcism (e.g., Spence,1988), and music as therapeutic accompaniment (e.g., Stoller,1989). If the helping professional does not feel adequate to attempt an integrated approach, the best advice is to refer the client to a more qualified person or obtain the assistance of a recognized and knowledgeable African.

### Cross-Cultural Counselor Training

Counselor training programs need to require courses in anthropology and sociology to help counselors to understand the belief systems of various African societies and to recognize how these systems influence the well-being of people holding these beliefs. Pre-service helping professionals, as well as in-service professionals, also need training in sensitization to cultural differences and how these differences influence the counseling process.

# Healing Process

The ethnic-aware helping professional becomes familiar with the cultural possibilities of African Americans. Continuing with a central theme of this chapter, a synergetic approach is recommended. Using this approach, the helping professional selects the most appropriate intervention or strategy, considering cultural and environmental influences.

## *Cultural Antecedents*

White and Parham (1990) suggested that "the experiences of slavery, Jim Crow legislation, de facto and de jure segregation, institutional racism, and the on-going economic oppression" in the United States teach African Americans "to distrust White folks" (p. 76). In addition, the deliberate dissolution of family units during slavery continues to affect current African American families and economies.

For example, African American males were perceived as economic threats and competition for White males. Consequently, a primary motivation for the enactment of Jim Crow laws was to control African American men's access to the workplace. Because African American females were not perceived similarly, women were allowed to enter certain areas of the workplace, forcing women to become the breadwinners (Grier & Cobbs, 1968). Such historical acts of discrimination and racism have negative impacts on contemporary African Americans in ways that may cause them to voluntarily seek counseling (White & Parham, 1990). The negative effects of history and its influences on African Americans must be acknowledged in order to provide effective counseling.

## *Cultural Commitment*

The cultural commitment of African American youth will generally reflect familial perspectives. The extent to which the family is integrated into mainstream culture and has accepted its values and norms are also relevant to helping African American youth. Adolescents with varying levels of exposure to integrated schools and neighborhoods may present different patterns of symptoms, problem behaviors, and adaptation to the community (Gibbs, 1990).

## *View of Seeking Help*

One forgotten or overlooked variable, however, is African American youth's cultural view of seeking counseling. African American families generally do not voluntarily seek treatment for the emotional or behavioral problems of their children. Many African American youth and their families still view counseling as a process for "strange" or crazy" people only (Ho, 1992). Contact with mental health services is usually precipitated by a crisis and happens when other sources of help have been depleted. Most African American youth are referred by the school, the juvenile court, or the social welfare system (e.g., Herring, 1999). Although this tendency varies by SES and acculturation levels, African American families are more likely to seek counseling initially from family doctors, ministers, and friends or relatives than from counseling professionals (Neighbors,1985).

Counseling is frequently perceived by African Americans as a process that requires them to relinquish their independence by first having to tell their personal business to a stranger and then having to listen and follow this same stranger's advice. This attitude is especially pervasive among low-income male students (e.g., Kirk,1986). In addition, the distrust of authority by some African Americans, notably the very poor, extends to those in the community that have reached middle-class status. An African American professional may have an initial advantage with ethnic-similar person; however, even he or she must overcome this mistrust.

African Americans rely heavily upon extended family ties and church organizations during times of crisis. They seek help from mutual aid and informal helping networks, such as the extended family and kin network (Martin & Martin, 1985). In African American communities, when an individual believes that she or he is experiencing difficulties in living, the primary source of mental and emotional sustenance remains prayer, spirituality, and the minister (e.g., Nobles, 1986). A subsequent decision to see a helping professional should be considered and addressed. Another consideration involves the extent to which clients are willing to be open with their helping professionals. African Americans frequently operate under the cultural more that one does not disclose personal or family business to strangers, especially when that person is not of similar ethnicity or is considered a member of an oppressor ethnic group (Priest, 1991).

School counselors need to be cognizant that by the time African American youth are referred to them for counseling and or guidance, their symptoms may be severe and the intervention required may be intensive (Gibbs, 1990). In addition, school counselors may be challenged by African American youth who identify their difficulties as societal as opposed to internal (personal shortcomings) (Priest, 1991).

In contrast to the challenges helping professionals face regarding African Americans' view of seeking help for mental health concerns, views are more positive regarding career development. Trusty, Watts, & Crawford (1996), using a nationally representative sample, studied parents' perceptions of various career-development resources for their children. Trusty et al. found that of the five major U.S. racial-ethnic groups, African American parents perceived schools and school counselors most positively. Lower SES parents also perceived school counselors more positively than middle- or high-SES parents; and this likely reflects limited resources for low SES families. Therefore, African American and low SES parents want and need the help of schools and school counselors for the career development of their children. In addition, career development can be a means by which African American youth can come to know and trust counselors, thereby enhancing youth's help-seeking for mental health concerns.

Economic reality among African American youth deserves specific consideration by helping professionals. A primary need for helping professionals is to actively solicit African American youth (especially low SES groups) in terms of college admission and selection process. Helping professionals need to stress the importance of equal opportunity programs, as well as the role of traditionally Black colleges. African American youth need these services, and frequently school helping professionals are the only ones to open the door to them.

## Summary

The success or failure of African Americans depends upon many factors. Slavery and subsequent discrimination experiences have pervasive and enduring effects. Churches and family-community networks are salient resources for social, psychological, and economic support. The ability to overcome obstacles depends on the nature of African Americans' relationship with the schools (Ho, 1992). An African American youth's performance and academic achievement also are related to attitudes of teachers and staff. If helping professionals, especially school counselors, are to make significant contributions to the educational, emotional, and mental development of African American youth, they must develop awareness of both African and African American cultures. Content knowledge, however, is not enough; they must develop and implement specific programs to make contributions to the success of African Americans (Locke, 1995).

## SELF-ASSESSMENT ACTIVITIES

A. Diller (1999) presented several excellent activities to stimulate increased self-awareness. As Diller proposed, such exercises "are useful to the extent that the reader takes them seriously, gives sufficient time to adequately process and complete them, and approaches them with candor" (p. 42). One altered example of these exercises is the following (p. 43).

This exercise gives you (the student) an opportunity to verbalize and identify your experiences with, attitudes toward, and beliefs about members of different racial-ethnic groups. Answer the following questions in relation to each of the following groups: (a) African Americans, (b) Hispanic Americans, (c) Asian Americans, (d) Native American Indians, and (e) Biethnic/Biracial Americans.

1. Describe in detail experiences you have had with members of this group.
2. What are your feelings about members of this group and how has that changed?
3. What are any characteristics, traits, or other things about members of this group that make it difficult for you to approach them?
4. Without censoring yourself, generate a list of characteristics that describes your beliefs and perceptions about members of this group.
5. What reactions come to mind when you think about working professionally with members of this group?
6. What kinds of answers, information, learning experiences, contact, and so forth do you need to become more comfortable with members of this group?

B. Malcolm McFee (1968) believed that those who are comfortably half in the Indian world and half in the non-Indian world possess a third dimension stemming from biculturality that renders them "150% men." How do you interpret this statement? Do you agree or disagree? State your rationale.

C. As a helping professional, how can you incorporate the cultural values presented in this chapter in strategies and interventions in your professional setting (i.e., schools, private practice, agency, and so forth)?

# REFERENCES

Arbona, C. (1996). Career theory and practice in a multicultural context. In M. L. Savickas, & W. B. Walsh (Eds.), *Handbook of career counseling theory and practice* (pp. 45-54). Palo Alto, CA: Davies-Black.

Attneave, C. L. (1969). *Therapy in tribal settings and urban network interventions. Family Process, 8,* 192-210.

Attneave, C. L. (1982). American Indian and Alaska native families: Emigrants in their own homeland. In M. McGoldrick, J. K. Pearce, & J. Giordana (Eds.), *Ethnicity and family therapy* (pp. 55-83). New York: Guilford.

Bernal, G., & Gutierrez, M. (1988). Cubans. In L. Comas-Diaz & E. E. H. Griffith (Eds), *Clinical guidelines in cross-cultural mental health* (pp. 233-261). New York: John Wiley & Sons.

Billingsley, A. (1987). Black families in a changing society. In J. Dewart (Ed.), *The state of Black America* (pp. 101-154). New York: National Urban League.

Broken Nose, M. A. (1992). *Working with the Oglala Lakota: An outsider's perspective. Families in Society, 73*(6), 380-384.

Bruchac, J. (1991). *Native American stories.* Golden, CO: Fulcrum.

Butcher, J. N., & Williams, C. L. (1992). *Essentials of MMPI-2 and MMPI-A interpretation.* Minneapolis: University of Minnesota Press.

Butler, J. (1992). Of kindred minds. In M. Orlandi (Ed.), *Cultural competence for evaluators: A guide for al school and other drug abuse prevention practitioners working with ethnic/racial communities* (pp. 1-35). Rockville, MD: U.S. Department of Health and Human Services.

Caduto, M. J., & Bruchac, J. (1991). *Keepers of the animals: Native American stories and wildlife activities for children.* Golden, CO: Fulcrum.

Cervantes, J. M., & Ramirez, O. (1992). Spirituality and family dynamics in psychotherapy with Latino children. In L. A. Vargas & J. D. Koss-Chioino (Eds), *Working with culture: Psychotherapeutic interventions with ethnic minority children and adolescents* (pp. 103-128). San Francisco: Jossey-Bass.

Chao, C. M. (1992). The inner heart: Therapy with Southeast Asian families. In L. A. Vargas & J. D. Koss-Chioino (Eds), *Working with culture: Psychotherapeutic interventions with ethnic minority children and adolescents* (pp. 157-181). San Francisco: Jossey-Bass.

Cowan, L. G. (1987). Africa. In *The encyclopedia Americana* (International ed., Vol. 1, pp. 256-260). Danbury, CT: Grolier.

Dana, R. H. (1993a, November 5). *Can "corrections" for culture using moderator variables contribute to cultural competence in assessment?* Paper presented at the annual convention of the Texas Psychological Association, Austin, TX.

Dana, R. H. (1993b). *Multicultural assessment perspectives for professional psychology.* Boston: Allyn & Bacon.

Davis, G. L., Hoffman, R. G., & Nelson, K. S. (1990). Differences between Native Americans and Whites on the California Psychological Inventory. *Psychological Assessment, 2*(3), 238-242.

Diller, J. V. (1999). *Cultural diversity: A primer for the human services.* Belmont, CA: Wadsworth/Brooks Cole.

Echeverry, J. J. (1997). Treatment barriers: Accessing and accepting professional help. In J.G. Garcia & M.C. Zea (Eds), *Psychological interventions and research with Latino populations* (pp. 94-107). Boston: Allyn and Bacon.

Eberhard, D. R. (1989). American Indian education: A study of dropouts, 1980-1987. *Journal of American Indian Education, 29,* 32-40.

Eldredge, N. M. (1993). Culturally affirmative counseling with American Indians who are deaf. *Journal of Rehabilitative Counseling, 26*(4), 1-18.

Evanchuk, R. (1999). "Bring me a pumpkin": A healing ceremony in Orisha worship for women of all ages. *Southern Folklore, 56*(3), 209-221.

Garrett, J. T. (1991). Where the medicine wheel meets medical science. In S. McFadden (Ed.), *Profiles in wisdom: Native elders speak about the earth* (pp. 167-179). Santa Fe, NM: Bear & Company.

Garrett, J. T. (1994). Understanding Indian children, learning from Indian elders. *Children Today, 22,* 18-21, 40.

Garrett, J. T., & Garrett, M. (1996). *Medicine of the Cherokee: The way of right relationship.* Santa Fe, NM: Bear & Company.

Garrett, M. T. (1996). "Two people": An American Indian narrative of bicultural identity. *Journal of American Indian Education, 36*(1), 1-21.

Garrett, M. T., & Herring, R. D. (2001). Honoring the power of relation: Counseling Native adults. *Journal of Humanistic Counseling, Education and development, 40*(2), 139-160.

Garrett, M. W. (1995). Between two worlds: Cultural discontinuity in the dropout of Native American youth. *The School Counselor, 42,* 186-195.

Garrett, M. W., & Garrett, J. T. (1993). *Full circle: A path to healing and wellness.* Unpublished manuscript. Greensboro: University of North Carolina-Greensboro.

Gary, L., & Glasglow, D. (1983). *Stable Black families.* Washington, DC: Howard University Press.

Gee, K. K., & Ishii, M. M. (1997). Assessment and treatment of schizophrenia among Asian Americans. . In E. Lee (Ed.), *Working with Asian Americans: A guide for clinicians* (pp. 227-251). New York: Guilford.

Gibbs, J. T. (1990). Black American adolescents. In J.T. Gibbs & L.N. Huang (Eds.), *Children of color: Psychological interventions with minority youth.* San Francisco: Jossey-Bass.

Gonzalez-Wippler, M. (1988). *The complete book of spells, ceremonies and magic.* St. Paul. MN: Llewellyn Publications.

Good, B. J., & Good, M. J. D. V. (1986). The cultural context of diagnosis and treatment: A view from medical anthropology. In M. R. Miranda & H. H. L. Kitano (Eds.), *Mental health research and practice in minority communities: Development of culturally sensitive training programs* (pp. 1-27). Rockville, MD: National Institute of Mental Health. (ERIC Document Reproduction Service No. ED 278 754)

Gordon, M. M. (1978). *Human nature, class, and ethnicity.* New York: Oxford University Press.

Gough, H. G. (1987). *Manual for the California Psychological Inventory.* Palo Alto, CA: Consulting Psychologists Press.

Grant, C. A., & Gomez, M. L. (Eds.). (1996). *Making schooling multicultural: Campus and classroom.* Upper Saddle River, NJ: Merrill/Prentice-Hall.

Grier, W.H., & Cobbs, P. M. (1968). *Black rage.* New York: Bantam.

Hammerschlag, C. A. (1988). *The dancing healers: A doctor's journey of healing with Native Americans*. New York: HarperCollins.

Hanson, S. L. (1994). Lost talent: Unrealized educational aspirations and expectations among U.S. youths. *Sociology of Education, 67,* 159-183.

Harjo, S. S. (1993). The American Indian experience. In H. P. McAdoo (Ed.), *Family ethnicity: Strength in diversity* (pp. 199-216). Newbury Park, CA: Sage.

Heinrich, R. K., Corbine, J. L., & Thomas, K. R. (1990). Counseling Native Americans. *Journal of Counseling & Development, 69*(2), 128-133.

Henry, C. P. (1990). *Culture and African American politics*. Blomington, IN: University Press.

Herring, R. D. (1990a). Attacking career myths among Native Americans: Implications for counseling. *The School Counselor, 38,* 13-18.

Herring, R. D. (1990b). Counseling Native American children: Implications for elementary guidance. *Elementary School Guidance & Counseling: Special Issue on Cross-Cultural Counseling, 23,* 272-281.

Herring, R. D. (1994). The clown or contrary figure as a counseling intervention strategy with Native American Indian clients. *Journal of Multicultural Counseling and Development, 22,* 153-164.

Herring, R. D. (1997a). *Counseling diverse ethnic youth: Synergetic strategies and interventions for school counselors*. Fort Worth, TX: Harcourt Brace.

Herring, R. D. (1997b). *Multicultural counseling in schools: A synergetic approach*. Alexandria, VA: American Counseling Association.

Herring, R. D. (1998). *Career counseling in schools: Multicultural and developmental perspectives*. Alexandria, VA: American Counseling Association.

Herring, R.D. (1999). *Counseling with Native American Indians and Alaska Natives: Strategies for helping professionals*. Thousand Oaks, CA: Sage.

Ho, M. K. (1992). *Minority children & adolescents in therapy*. Newbury Park, CA: Sage.

Huang, L. N. (1994). An integrative view of identity formation: A model for Asian Americans. In E. P. Salett & D. R. Koslow (Eds.), *Race, ethnicity, and self-identity in multicultural perspective* (pp. 42-61). Washington, DC: National MultiCultural Institute.

Jules-Rosette, B. (1980). Creative spirituality from Africa to America: Cross-cultural influences in contemporary religious forms. *Western Journal of Black Studies, 4,* 273-285.

Kim, S. C. (1997). Korean American families. . In E. Lee (Ed.), *Working with Asian Americans: A guide for clinicians* (pp. 125-135). New York: Guilford.

Kirk, A. R. (1986). Destructive behaviors among members of the Black community with a special emphasis on males: Causes and methods of intervention. *Journal of Multicultural Counseling and Development, 14,* 3-9.

Koss-Chioino, J. D. (2000). Traditional and folk approaches among ethnic minorities. In J.E. Aponte & J. Wohl (Eds), *Psychological intervention and cultural diversity* (2nd ed; pp. 149-166). Boston: Allyn and Bacon.

LaFromboise, T. D. (1990). *Circles of women: Professionalization training for American Indian women*. Newton, MA: Women's Educational Equity Act Press.

LaFromboise, T. D. (1998). American Indian mental health policy. In D. R. Atkinson, G. Morten, & D. W. Sue (Eds.), *Counseling American minorities* (5th ed.; pp. 137-158). Boston: McGraw-Hill.

Lawson, G. W., & Lawson, A. W. (1989). *Alcoholism and substance abuse in special populations*. Rockville, MD: Aspen.

Lee, C. C. (1995). Multicultural literacy: Imperatives for culturally responsive school counseling. In C. C. Lee (Ed.), *Counseling for diversity: A guide for school counselors and related professionals* (pp. 191-198). Boston: Allyn & Bacon.

Lee, E. (1997). Chinese American families. In E. Lee (Ed.), *Working with Asian Americans: A guide for clinicians* (pp. 46-78). New York: Guilford.

Lefever, H. G. (1996). When the saints go riding in: Santeria in Cuba and the United States. *Journal for the Scientific Study of Religion, 35*, 318-330.

Leung, S. A. (1995). Career development and counseling: A multicultural perspective. In J. G. Ponterotto, J. M. Casas, L. A. Suzuki, & C. M. Alexander (Eds.), *Handbook of multicultural counseling* (pp. 549-566). Thousand Oaks, CA: Sage.

Lin, K. M., & Cheung, F. (1999). Mental health issues for Asian Americans. *Psychiatric Services, 50*(6), 774-780.

Lincoln, C. E., & Mamiya, L. H. (1990). *The Black church in the African American experience*. Durham, NC: Duke University Press.

Lo, H. T., & Lau, G. (1997). Anxiety disorders of Chinese patients. In E. Lee (Ed.), *Working with Asian Americans: A guide for clinicians* (pp. 309-319). New York: Guilford.

Locke, D. C. (1992). *Increasing multicultural understanding: A comprehensive model*. Newbury Park, CA: Sage.

Locke, D. C. (1995). Counseling interventions with African American youth. In C.C. Lee, (Ed.), *Counseling for diversity: A guide for school counselors and related professionals* (pp. 21-40). Boston: Allyn and Bacon.

Lopez-Baez, S. I. (1997). Counseling interventions with Latinas. In C.C. Lee (Ed.), *Multicultural issues in counseling: New approaches to diversity* (2nd ed.; pp. 257-268). Alexandria, VA: American Counseling Association.

Lum, D. (1992). *Social work practice and people of color: A process-stage approach* (2nd ed.). Montery, CA: Brooks/Cole.

Manson, S. M. (1986). Recent advances in American Indian mental health research: Implications for clinical research and training. In M.R. Miranda & H. L. Kitano (Eds.), *Mental health research and practice in minority communities: Development of culturally sensitive training programs* (pp. 51-89). Rockville, MD: National Institute of Mental Health. (ERIC Document Reproduction No. ED 278 754)

Mantsios, G. (2001). Media magic: Making class invisible. In M. L. Anderson & P. H. Collins (Eds.), *Race, class, and gender: An anthology* (4th ed., pp. 333-342). Belmont, CA: Wadsworth.

Martin, J., & Martin, E. (1985). *The helping tradition in the Black family and community*. Silver Springs, MD: National Association of Social Workers.

Martinez, C. (1988). Mexican-Americans. In L. Comas-Diaz & E. E. H. Griffith (Eds). *Clinical guidelines in cross-cultural mental health* (pp. 182-203). New York: John Wiley & Sons.

McFee, M. (1968). The 150% man: A product of Blackfeet acculturation. *American Anthropologist, 70*, 1096-1103.

McShane, D. A., & Plas, J. M. (1984). The cognitive functioning of American Indian children: Moving from the WISC to the WISC-R. *School Psychology Review, 13*, 61-73.

Mollica, R.F., & Lavelle, J.P. (1988). Southeast Asian refugees. In L. Comas-Diaz & E. E. H. Griffith (Eds), *Clinical guidelines in cross-cultural mental health* (pp. 262-304). New York: John Wiley & Sons.

Moore, L.J., & Boehnlein, J.K. (1991). Treating psychiatric disorders among Mien refugees from highland Laos. *Social Science and Medicine. 32*(9), 1029-1036.

Mpolo, M. (1974). *Une approche pastorale du probleme du la sorcellerie* (a pastoral approach to the problem of sorcery). Kinshasa, Republic of Zaire: Editions Cedi.

Muecke, M. A. (1983). Caring for Southeast Asian refugee patients in the USA. *American Journal of Public Health, 73*(4), 431-438.

Mulhern, B. (1988, September 26-October 1). Wisconsin's Indians: Their progress, their plight. *The Capital Times*, p. 1.

Myers, C. M. (1999). "Spirit will tell you to see a doctor": The viability of espiritismo in biomedicine. *Southern Folklore, 56*(3), 245-280.

Neighbors, H. W. (1985). Seeking professional help for personal problems: Black Americans' use of health and mental health services. *Community Mental health Journal, 21*, 156-166.

Neisser, U., Boodoo, G., Bouchard, T. J., Boykin, A. W., Brody, A. W., Brody, N., Ceci, S. J., Halpern, D. F., Loehlin, J. C., Perloff, R., Sternberg, R. J., & Ubina, S. (1996). Intelligence: Knowns and unknowns. *American Psychologist, 51*, 77-98.

Nobles, W. W. (1986). *African psychology: Toward its reclamation, reascension, & revitalization*. Oakland, CA: Black Family Institute Publication.

Paniagua, F. A. (1999). *Assessing and treating culturally diverse clients: A practical guide* (2nd ed.). Thousand Oaks, CA: Sage.

Perez y Mena, A. I. (1998). Cuban Santeria, Haitian Vodun, Puerto Rican spiritualism: A multiculturalist inquiry into syncretism. *Journal for the Scientific Study of Religion, 37*, 15-27.

Peregoy, J. J. (1999). Revisiting transcultural counseling with American Indians and Alaskan Natives: Issues for consideration. In J. McFadden (Ed.), *Transcultural counseling* (2nd ed.; pp. 137-170). Alexandria, VA: American Counseling Association.

Phinney, J. S., Lochner, B.T., & Murphy, R. (1990). Ethnic identity development and psychological adjustment in adolescence. In A. R. Stiffman & L. E. Davis (Eds.), *Ethnic issues in adolescent mental health* (pp. 53-72). Newbury Park, CA: Sage.

Portman, T. A., & Herring, R. D. (2001). Debunking the Pocahontas paradox: The need for a humanistic perspective. *Journal of Humanistic Counseling, Education and Development, 40*(2), 185-199.

Prathikanti, S. (1997). East Indian American families. In E. Lee (Ed.), *Working with Asian Americans: A guide for clinicians* (pp. 79-100). New York: Guilford.

Priest, R. (1991). Racism and prejudice as negative impacts on African American clients in therapy. *Journal of Counseling & Development, 70*, 213-215.

Ramos-McKay, J. M., Comas-Diaz, L., & Rivera, L. (1988). Puerto Ricans. In L. Comas-Diaz & E.E.H. Griffith (Eds), *Clinical guidelines in cross-cultural mental health* (pp. 204-232). New York: John Wiley & Sons.

Reinolds, C. (1996, June 20). Study: Income, not race, fuels education gap. *Arkansas Democrat Gazette,* pp. 1A, 11A.

Richardson, B. L. (1991). Utilizing the resources of the African-American church: Strategies for for counseling professionals. In C.C. Lee & B.L. Richardson (Eds.), *Multicultural issues in counseling: New approaches to diversity* (pp. 65-75). Alexandria, VA: American Association for Counseling and Development.

Rivers, R. Y., & Morrow, C. A. (1995). Understanding and treating ethnic minority youth. In J. F. Aponte, R. Y. Rivers, & J. Wohl (Eds.), *Psychological interventions and cultural diversity* (pp. 164-180). Boston: Allyn & Bacon.

Robinson, T. L., & Howard-Hamilton, M. F. (2000). *The convergence of race, ethnicity, and gender: Multiple identities in counseling.* Columbus, OH: Merrill/Prentice-Hall.

Simons, R. C., & Hughes, C. C. (1993). Cultural-bound syndromes. In A. C. Gaw (Ed.), *Culture, ethnicity, and mental illness* (pp. 75-93). Washington, DC: American Psychiatric Press.

Spence, L. (1988). *The encyclopedia of the occult.* London, England: Bracken Books.

Stoller, P. (1989). *Fusion of the worlds: An ethnography of possession among the Songhay of Niger.* Chicago: University of Chicago Press.

Stoller, P., & Olkes, C. (1987). *In sorcery's shadow: A memoir of apprenticeship among the Songhay of Niger.* Chicago: University of Chicago Press.

Suzuki, L. A., & Kugler, J. F. (1995). Intelligence and personality assessment: Multicultural perspectives. In J. G. Ponterotto, J. M. Casas, L. A. Suzuki, & C. M. Alexander (Eds.), *Handbook of multicultural counseling* (pp. 493-515). Thousand Oaks, CA: Sage.

Sue, D. W., & Sue, D. (1999). *Counseling the culturally different: Theory and practice.* (3$^{rd}$ ed.). NY: John Wiley & Sons.

Thomason, T. C. (1991). Counseling Native Americans: An introduction for non-Native American counselors. *Journal of Counseling and Development, 69,* 321-327.

Torrey, E. E. (1986). *Witchdoctors & psychiatrists: The common roots of psychotherapy and its future.* New York: Harper & Row.

Trawick-Smith, J. (1997). *Early childhood development: A multicultural perspective.* Upper Saddle River, NJ: Merrill/Prentice-Hall.

Trimble, J. E., & Fleming, C. M. (1989). Providing counseling services for native American Indians: Client, counselor, and community characteristics. In P. B. Pedersen, J. G. Draguns, W. J. Lonner, & J. E. Trimble (Eds.), *Counseling across cultures* (3rd ed., pp. 177-204). Honolulu: University of Hawaii Press.

Trusty, J., & Harris, M. B. C. (1999). Lost talent: Predictors of the stability of educational expectations across adolescence. *Journal of Adolescent Research, 14,* 359-382.

Trusty, J., Watts, R. E., & Crawford, R. (1996). Career information resources for parents of public school seniors: Findings from a national study. *Journal of Career Development, 22,* 227-238.

U. S. Census Bureau (1992). *Current population reports, P 25-1092, Population projections of the United States by age, sex, race, and Hispanic origin 1992-2050.* Washington, DC: U. S. Government Printing Office.

U.S. Census Bureau (1998). *Statistical abstracts of the U.S.: 1998.* Washington, DC: U.S. Department of Commerce.

U.S. Census Bureau (1999). *Poverty in the U.S.:1998.* Washington, DC: U.S. Department of Commerce.

U.S. Census Bureau (2001). *Statistical abstracts of the U.S.: 2000.* Washington, DC: U.S. Department of Commerce.

U. S. Department of Justice (1991). *Crime in the United States.* Washington, DC: U. S. Government Printing Office.

Vontress, C. E. (1991). Traditional healing in Africa: Implications for cross-cultural counseling. *Journal of Counseling & Development, 16*, 73-83.

Walsh, W. B., & Betz, N. E. (1990). *Tests and assessment* (3rd ed.). Englewood Cliffs, NJ: Prentice Hall.

Westermeyer, J. J. (1993). Cross-cultural psychiatric assessment. In A. C. Gaw (Ed.), *Culture, ethnicity, & mental illness* (pp. 125-144). Washington, DC: American Psychiatric Press.

White, C. B., & Parham, T. A. (1990). *Black psychology: An African American perspective* (2nd ed.). Englewood Cliffs, NJ: Prentice-Hall.

Zea, M. C., Quezada, T., & Belgrave, F. Z. (1997). Limitations of an acultural health psychology for Latinos: Reconstructing the African influence on Latino culture and health-related behaviors. In J. G. Garcia & M. C. Zea (Eds), *Psychological interventions and research with Latino populations* (pp. 255-266). Boston: Allyn and Bacon.

# Chapter 13

# Supervision from a Multicultural Perspective

***Karin Jordan***
George Fox University
***Jesse Brinson***
University of Nevada-Las Vegas
***Colleen Peterson***
University of Nevada-Las Vegas

"The more in touch I am with my beliefs, and acknowledge them, the more I give myself freedom to choose how to use those beliefs."

*-Virginia Satir*

Supervision involves a deep ethical commitment to self-knowledge, personal and professional growth, self-exploration, acquisition of counseling skills and theory, and mutual respect by both the supervisor and trainee. Another fundamental supervision component is cultural relativism, the idea that people (supervisors, trainees, and clients) of each culture or subculture are judged on their own terms--on their own perceptions, beliefs, and feelings (Thio, 1986). Unfortunately, supervisors have not always embraced cultural relativism and lived up to the commitment to understand and adjust to the trainee's need to become a multiculturally competent counselor, acknowledging the trainee's own cultural experience in the process.

## Key Issues in Multicultural Supervision

Multicultural supervision of trainees needs to center on (a) multicultural identity, (b) multicultural awareness, and (c) multicultural knowledge and skills. The supervisor is essential in this process of developing a multicultural (cultural-racial-ethnic diversification) professional identity and becoming a culturally competent counselor. The trainee should be familiar with the key issues and the developmental process in order to assess future supervisors' multicultural knowledge and skill for guiding them in this complex process.

## Identity

Developing a professional identity that reflects cultural relativism is a process with which trainees need help. The supervisor needs to help the trainee promote cultural-racial-ethnic *awareness* (cognitive process) and *sensitivity* (affective process). Didactic classes on multiculturalism generally

> over-emphasize characteristics of various cultural groups and often ignore the importance of the trainees' perception of and feelings toward their respective cultural background. As a result, trainees are rarely challenged to examine how their respective cultural identities influence understanding and acceptance of those who are both culturally similar and dissimilar (Hardy & Laszloffy, 1995, p. 227).

Therefore, supervisors must facilitate greater understanding and acceptance between the similar and dissimilar. This can be accomplished through techniques such as the cultural genogram, originally described by Hardy and Laszloffy (1995), which helps the trainees gain greater insight and appreciation of their own and their clients' cultures, and the impact cultures have on the counseling process. The primary goals of the cultural genogram are:

> (a) illustrating and clarifying the influence that culture has on the family system; (b) assisting trainees in identifying the groups which contribute to the formation of their cultural identity; (c) encouraging candid discussions that reveal and challenge culturally based assumptions and stereotypes; (d) assisting trainees in discovering their culturally based emotional triggers (i.e., unresolved culturally based conflicts); and (e) assisting trainees in exploring how their unique cultural identities may impact their therapeutic style and effectiveness. (p. 228)

The cultural genogram involves using the template of the basic genogram, which is a graphic depiction (where figures represent people and lines delineate relationships) of a family's structure and the relationships of family members who are biologically and legally related (McGoldrick & Gerson, 1985). After the basic (at least three generation) genogram has been constructed, the trainee is to "add the following elements: the (~) symbol to identify intercultural marriages, colors to illustrate the cultural composition of each person's cultural identity, and the symbols denoting pride/shame issues" (Hardy & Laszloffy, 1995, p. 231). Additionally, questions relating to trainees' and other family member's culture of origin, identity, relationship, intergenerational interactions, values, beliefs, pride/shame issues, and so forth, should be addressed.

Because cultural identity is a broad multidimensional process, the supervisor needs to help the trainee in this developmental process. Consequently, the supervisor must have gone through this process him/herself, as well as some personal soul searching, and have adequate knowledge for guiding the trainee in cultural-racial-ethnic diversification. Only then can the supervisor take on this necessary and essential task of helping the trainee develop a clear multicultural professional identity. In interviewing the potential supervisor, the trainee might ask the following questions.

1. Tell me what cultural-racial-ethnic diversification means to you. Do you perceive yourself to have a clear multicultural professional identity? Please explain.
2. How do you help trainees develop a cultural identity? How do you assist trainees in exploring their own pride and shame issues related to their culture? How do you guide the trainees in their work with clients to address issues of cultural identity, pride and shame?
3. Describe to me how you prepare trainees to be culturally competent.

## Awareness

In addition to cultural identity, cultural awareness needs to be taught during the supervision process, so that the trainee can put the client's behavior into a context consistent with the client's culture. Whereas miscommunication and misinterpretation of communication and behavior occur in all relationships, it is particularly important that intercultural communication occurs with as much knowledge and insight as possible. It is the supervisor's responsibility to help the trainee recognize that cultural awareness and sensitivity imply learning to recognize when old information no longer holds true (Pattersen, 1988). Additionally, there is a need to not create cultural stereotypes, which can be more problematic than cultural insensitivity.

The Person-in-Culture Interview (PICI; Berg-Cross & Chinen, 1995) is a 24-item, open-ended interview-training device that helps trainees reach cross-cultural understanding without stereotyping clients. It is rooted in psychodynamic, humanistic, family systems, and existential theory. This technique helps trainees become more cognizant of their cultural experiences and personal values that have shaped their sense of self. Trainees use the PICI while working with peers (preferably someone who is quite different from them), interviewing each other and following a protocol of questions. Some examples of these questions are: "Each little community has certain images of a successful person. In what ways would your community judge you to be successful or unsuccessful?" "If you 'fit in' at home and in your community, tell what a normal day would be like. What type of normal day are you striving for?" (Berg-Cross & Chinen, 1995, p.340). Answers to these questions should be discussed with the supervisor, serving as a springboard for further discussion and exploration. This kind of exercise can help trainees learn about a specific culture while encouraging broader communication with people from different cultural-racial-ethnic backgrounds.

When interviewing a supervisor for cultural awareness, trainees might ask the following questions:

1. Can you explain to me what cultural awareness means to you? What about cultural stereotyping?
2. How do you assist a trainee to become culturally aware, and to avoid cultural stereotyping?

## Knowledge and Skills

Assisting trainees in becoming multiculturally competent includes developing knowledge and skills for working with culturally diverse clients. Multiculturally competent trainees are knowledgeable about the different experiences of members of various cultural groups. Additionally, they understand that there are often barriers to communication across cultures as a result of these differences. More specifically, a multiculturally knowledgeable trainee is comfortable with the differences that exist between them and their clients' ethnicity and beliefs.

It is important that trainees develop multicultural counseling competencies in addition to basic counseling competencies such as counseling theories, techniques, and strategies. Basic counseling skills, although necessary when doing multicultural counseling, are often not sufficient. It is important that trainees also have developed cultural awareness and racial identity. Research by Sabnani, Ponterotto, and Borodovsky (1991) and Ottavi, Pope-Davis, and Dings, (1994) support the importance of racial identity. Multicultural competencies also include knowledge of certain cultural groups (their verbal and nonverbal communication, behaviors, beliefs, values, and experiences) that are most likely different from the trainee's own. It also includes the trainee being knowledgeable about the effects of multicultural barriers. Finally, multicultural competence means that trainees choose techniques and strategies on the client's behalf.

There are several self-report measures of multicultural counseling competencies: The Cross-Cultural Counseling Inventory-Revised (CCCI-R; LaFromboise, Coleman & Hernandez, 1991), the Multicultural Counseling Awareness Scale-Form B: Revised Self Assessment (MCAS:B; Ponterotto, Sanchez, & Magida, 1991), the Multicultural Counseling Inventory (MCI; Sodowsky, Taffe, Gutkin, & Wise, 1994) and the Multicultural Awareness-Knowledge-and-Skills Survey (MAKSS; D'Andrea, Daniels, & Heck, 1991). These measures are designed for evaluation of trainees' knowledge and skills by supervisors. In this chapter, the MAKSS will be examined at some length.

When choosing a supervisor who is multiculturally knowledgeable, trainees should ask questions such as:

1. How does knowledge in multicultural counseling differ from knowledge in basic counseling?
2. How do you assist trainees in becoming multiculturally knowledgeable?
3. What measures do you use to assess trainees' multicultural competencies?

The answers to these questions can help uncover supervisors' own cultural identity development. These questions are also designed to assist the trainee in assessing the supervisor's knowledge of the multicultural development process that trainees go through. Additionally, it is hoped that these questions stimulate additional conversation about this topic, as well as guide and infiltrate the supervision process from a multicultural stance.

# THE COMPLEX DYNAMICS OF THE SUPERVISORY RELATIONSHIPS: A CONCEPTUAL MODEL

Supervision, unlike a classroom experience, is a complex dynamic of the relationship between a supervisor, a trainee, and (generally) the trainee's client(s). The eleven components of this complex relationship are: (1) Choosing a Multicultural Supervisor, (2) Assessing for Certification and Training, (3) Assessing for Cultural Encapsulation, (4) Assessing for Theory and Practice, (5) Assessing Research Interests, (6) Multicultural Supervision and Power/Authority, (7) Multicultural Supervision and Shared Meaning, (8) Cultural Conditioning, (9) Discussing Cultural Differences, (10) Valuing the Trainee as a Person, and (11) Multicultural Supervision and Trust.

## Choosing a Multicultural Supervisor

As we have mentioned, supervision is an important component of counselor training. Supervision affords trainees an opportunity to work with individuals who help them integrate their formal academic training into the real world of professional counseling. To this end, the clinical supervisor makes sure that each trainee can implement traditional and contemporary models of therapy into working with people, and emphasizes the importance of the trainee's ability to follow the ethical standards and best practices. The application of theoretical concepts and effective ethical practices may be considered the heart of the supervisory process. More recently, however, as a consequence of professional accreditation standards and guidelines such as those developed by the Council for the Accreditation of Counseling and Related Education Programs (CACREP; Council for Accreditation, 2001), clinical supervisors are prompted to take a serious look at the multicultural development of counselors-in-training. Several scholars have been discussing the importance of providing trainees with a broader perspective for working with culturally diverse individuals and families (Leong & Wagner, 1993; Mio & Morris, 1990; Priest, 1994). Within the counseling field, multicultural supervision is receiving its place as a major training initiative for counselors-in-training.

Multicultural supervision is becoming ever more a reality given the fact that issues such as race, racism, oppression, stereotyping, racial and ethnic identity, and acculturation have become the focus of many cross-cultural counseling sessions (Petersen, 1991; Ponterotto, Alexander, & Grieger, 1995). In essence, the challenge for clinical supervisors is to prepare their trainees with sufficient awareness, knowledge, and skills to perform as professional helpers when working with American racial and ethic minorities, gay and lesbian clients, the aged, white males, physically challenged individuals, not to mention counseling with other underrepresented groups. For the trainee, this implies that he or she must take seriously his or her obligation to choose a supervisor with a deep understanding of and an appreciation for working with culturally diverse populations.

Finding a clinical supervisor with multicultural supervision experience and knowledge can be problematic, no matter how much therapeutic experience the supervisor might have. The literature reveals that supervisors are rarely trained in supervision (Hess & Hess, 1983). Most supervisors in agencies and schools are approved based on having a master's degree in counseling, and having a minimum of two years of work experience in the field. Hess and

Hess (1983) point out that even experienced counselor educators may not be trained in supervision. Thus, unless supervisors are taking it upon themselves to pursue post-degree training in supervision, and cross-cultural supervision in particular, one can reasonably assume that the average supervisor is not well-trained and may not feel qualified to supervise students in multicultural work. Second, the trainee should keep in mind that most organizations view supervision as a luxury, which typically means that there are few resources to provide for staff development in the area of supervision. In this climate of watching the bottom line, so to speak, many organizations do not provide in-service training in supervision strategies; if you are stuck or confused, you usually consult informally with a colleague. Therefore, finding a colleague with cross-cultural supervision experience is extremely difficult. Third, as we alluded to earlier in the chapter, some supervisors tend to be culturally encapsulated, as such, supervisors may not sensitively understand their culturally different clients' experiences, and they may relate to clients in a stereotypic manner. Clearly, most supervisors are from White, middle-class backgrounds; and they enter the professional world of counseling with limited prior contact with culturally different individuals and groups (Kiselica, 1998). Our ability to relate effectively to any event or person we experience is influenced by the quantity as well as the quality of experiences we have with similar events or persons (McGrath & Axelson, 1993). Fourth, academic training in counseling theory and practice continues to focus on preparation with the White, Anglo-Saxon, middle-class population. Current theories of counseling and psychotherapy inadequately describe, explain, predict, and deal with the richness and complexity of a culturally diverse population (Ivey, Ivey, & Simek-Morgan, 1993). This fact alone could mean that many supervisors focus their therapeutic energies on preparing trainees to work primarily with members of the dominant society. Fifth, the doctoral-level supervisor is typically required to do academic research as a means of securing professional recognition and merit increases. One would think that the clinical supervisor would have diversity issues integrated into his or her research agenda. However, we have found this is frequently not the case. Because the trainee may have the option of selecting a supervisor for counseling practicum and internship, we will provide some pragmatic ways for assessing the individual's potential as a multicultural supervisor. Of course, the more affirmative responses the trainee receives in each of these areas, the greater the likelihood of the supervisor having considerable interests in cross-cultural supervision issues.

## Assessing for Certification and Training

The current movement in the counseling field is to train master's level practitioners in clinical supervision either pre- or post-degree. The National Board for Certified Counselors (NBCC) offers a supervision credential, and a counselor that graduates from a CACREP approved program can sit for the certification. Trainees could inquire whether the supervisor holds a NBCC certificate, and whether he or she holds the credential in supervision. Given that the supervision credential is a recent add-on, the supervisor may not be aware of this credential. Securing the credential provides the supervisor with additional knowledge and skill in supervision. The student could also inquire whether multicultural coursework was required in the supervisor's training program. Typically, most programs offer one course in multicultural counseling. The trainee might inquire whether the supervisor has considered additional training in multicultural counseling and therapy. Whereas one course is insufficient for adequate training, we would add that one course is better than no course at all. Ask your supervisor whether he or she has attended training at the Multicultural Training Institute (MCT) in Washington, D.C. The MCT offers excellent training seminars on cultural diversity issues for mental health professionals.

## Assessing for Cultural Encapsulation

One of the most effective ways of assessing an individual's cultural encapsulation is to inquire about the regular, meaningful contact that he or she maintains with people outside of his or her cultural or racial group. More specifically, these are people outside his or her work environment. For example, the supervisor may have three good friends that are gay or lesbian. To ascertain this information, the student might ask the supervisor--within the proper context of course--what lessons the supervisor has learned from his or her relationship with culturally different individuals that impact his or her work in supervision. If the objective information the supervisor presents suggests limited contact with a variety of individuals and groups, perhaps this is a significant indicator that the person may hold rather traditional values and beliefs about cultural diversity issues. Having conservative views are neither right nor wrong, good nor bad. Conservative views become problematic, however, when people assume universality to the human experience (Sue & Sue, 1999).

## Assessing for Theory and Practice

More and more non-mainstream groups are seeking the services of counseling professionals. Given this fact, the supervisor must have theories of counseling which are not bound by one culture. For the supervisor, he or she should have knowledge of frameworks such as Sue, Ivey, and Pedersen's (1996) systematic theory on multicultural counseling and therapy (MCT). The MCT conceptual framework (or meta-theory) would apply to Euro-American culture, Asian, African, Latin American and other world cultures. MCT is one of the most important new theoretical perspectives to shape the field of counseling. Supervisors should be familiar with this trend toward multicultural counseling frameworks. By asking your supervisor about his or her familiarity with such perspectives or structures, the trainee can determine whether the supervisor has a blueprint for gender-and culture-sensitive therapeutic practice on a variety of levels (individual, family, group, community, and institutional).

## Assessing Research Interests

The clinical supervisor in a counselor-training program is typically a doctoral level counselor educator. That is, the individual teaches courses as well as supervises students in both practicum and internship. If the individual is tenured or in a tenure track position, he or she is required to maintain the pursuit of scholarship as means of gaining professional recognition in the field. The individual typically seeks to publish his or her work in notable journals such as those published by the American Counseling Association, American

Psychological Association and The American Association for Marriage and Family Therapy. The following journals represent the top journals in the field of counseling:

The Journal of Counseling & Development
Counselor Education and Supervision
Journal of Multicultural Counseling and Development
Journal of Mental Health Counseling
Journal of Humanistic Counseling and Development
Journal for Specialists in Group Work
Professional School Counseling
The Journal of Marriage and Family Therapy
The Clinical Supervisor
The Counseling Psychologist
The Journal of Counseling Psychology

Evaluating a supervisor's research interests can be a helpful tool in determining the extent of the supervisor's interest in cross-cultural supervision issues. If the research appears limited with respect to cross-cultural emphasis, the supervisor may have some difficulty responding to such issues in a supervisory forum. In the final analysis, we believe choosing a multicultural supervisor is an important consideration for every trainee. We also believe that finding a supervisor to work effectively with a variety of clients can be a significant challenge. We further believe that supervisors will meet the challenge of becoming knowledgeable in cross-cultural supervision training programs, agencies, and schools as these organizations begin to place more emphasis in this most important training perspective. Ultimately, however, supervisors take responsibility for educating themselves on supervision.

## Multicultural Supervision and Power/Authority

In a supervisory relationship there is the supervisor with power and authority and the trainee who is less influential. This power and authority is derived from the fact that the supervisor is perceived as more experienced and typically is older than the trainee. By contrast, because trainees are considered novices in their field, and are generally younger, they often show deferential respect for the more experienced supervisor. Trainees are likely to postpone expressing their feelings and concerns if issues exist between the supervisor and the trainee. Also, because there is general fear of negative evaluation from the supervisor, trainees may take few risks, and avoid being candid in their statements. When power and authority are paired with cultural or racial differences between supervisor and trainee, particularly when the supervisor is a person of color and the trainee is white, or vice versa, it becomes even more difficult for the trainee to be assertive in the relationship. Power differences between people of color and whites suggests that perceptual differences often contribute to a egocentric self-image of one's cultural group, negative stereotyping against other groups, and a more insidious belief of "we" against "them" mentality (Brinson & Morris, in press). From a supervisory perspective, this is frequently transmitted into the unconscious belief that in fact, the supervisor and trainee are biased against one another. Thus the supervisory relationship takes on an artificial quality during the entire time the trainee and supervisor are working together.

The key to addressing the power and cultural differences between supervisor and trainee is for both to reveal any of their professional limitations or personal obstacles with regard to different cultures. What happens in this instance is the trainee increases his or her status and power because he or she takes the risk to address an area where most tend to remain silent. Vicariously, the trainee empowers the supervisor because the supervisor must reveal his or her viewpoint of the discussion. One must keep in mind that discussing racial issues, for example, often puts people on the defensive and can create a significant amount of psychological stress within the person. Nonetheless, discussing these issues is an empowering experience for both involved. If a reasonable understanding is reached during the discussion, relationships are generally transformed for the better. The next section will continue to build on this idea of shared differences.

## Multicultural Supervision and Shared Meaning

In cross-cultural supervision, that is, when the supervisor and the trainee come from ethnically and culturally diverse backgrounds, the odds are greater that needless misunderstandings will occur. For example, the supervisor may be Black, the trainee may be White, and the client may be a person of color. As a consequence of these cultural differences and social statuses, different information processing and differential power elements could impact upon the supervisory relationship (Wehrly, 1995). How this is acknowledged and dealt with is to a large extent dependent on the experience, knowledge, skills, and ultimately the sensitivity of the supervisor. There are basically three things that the supervisor could do to minimize the potential for conflict between the supervisor and the trainee. First, the supervisor could discuss with the trainee the impact of cultural conditioning on individual development. Second, the supervisor could have a dialogue with the trainee about the advantages and disadvantages of racism awareness training. Third, the supervisor could express to the trainee that he or she truly valued as a person.

## Cultural Conditioning

What we have learned about our self in relation to others is that we often evaluate others based on how we have been taught to see our self. This may be referred to as our *cultural conditioning*. This cultural conditioning comes through the usual developmental influences of family, school, media and society-at-large. Most of us can remember our parents telling stories or making comments about different cultural groups. These messages continue to play out in our relationships with one another today. This accounts for why many of us raise our children in the manner in which we were raised. Cultural conditioning (consciously or unconsciously) accounts for our expectations or lack of expectations of culturally distinct individuals and groups. Both the supervisor and the trainee bring culturally conditioned attitudes towards each other's cultural group. Cultural conditioning is not necessarily a bad thing. The problem comes when our cultural conditioning causes us to interpret neutral or innocent behaviors negatively. Too often, our cultural conditioning leads us imagine that the other person has attitudes that he or she really does not have. As a result, we may explain the person's confusing behavior in terms of the person's race, nationality, or religion. When communication breaks down along cultural lines, unfortunately, the outcome is often negative. Perhaps a brief case illustration will help illuminate what we are attempting to communicate. Again, keep in mind that we are describing how cultural conditioning often distorts how we interpret information, in turn, leading to conflict.

> During a master's level practicum course, a Black male supervising a White female student assigns her a forty-year-old Black male client. During the first session, when asking about the client's presenting concerns, the client reports that he is dealing with a very racist boss. When the trainee proceeds to ask the client what makes him think his boss is racist, the client responds by saying "most Whites have difficulty dealing with a very dark skinned Black male." The student finds this to be a very troubling statement, and in fact, proceeds to offer suggestions as to why the statement is not true. During her supervision meeting, the trainee discusses this incident with the supervisor. The supervisor confirms the position of the client. The trainee is appalled at the supervisor's position. She states that she has lost respect for the supervisor. She then storms out of the session in tears.

Needless to say, what just happen were responses based upon cultural conditioning. The fact of the matter is many Black males have abundant stories of how their color negatively influences their interactions with many Whites in the United States. Very dark skinned men and women believe that society treats them differently based on their skin color. Most would add that this differential treatment is an overt sign of racism. On the other hand, the cultural conditioning of many Whites suggests that many perceive racism from a narrow viewpoint that is manifested in overt acts of behavior on the part of individuals and institutions. This raises an important question with respect to how both can address the issue of cultural conditioning. We believe it is important that the supervisor be aware of generalizing the culture of racism within mainstream society to the individual encounter. It is important to recognize and understand how much of the interpretation is distorted by a self-fulfilling prophecy in which the White person conforms to the cultural expectation of the Black person. For the trainee, it is important to recognize and accept the perceived racism that often characterizes the psychological domain of racial minorities in American society. Such a perspective could have implications for forming relations, assessment and diagnosis of clients, presenting issues, and the selection of appropriate treatment interventions.

## Discussing Cultural Differences

To work effectively in cross-cultural supervision, the supervisor and trainee must discuss distinct cultural differences such as communication style. That is, in some cultures social relationships tend to be hierarchical; whereas in others relationships are more egalitarian. When social relationships are hierarchical, which is more often the case for minority groups, the supervisor will likely be very formal in his or her interaction with the trainee. This would mean that the trainee is not expected to use the first name when referring to the supervisor. The supervisor expects to be addressed by Mr., Miss, or Dr. Jones. Within a more egalitarian social structure, which is generally a norm in the dominant culture, individuals could be expected to address the supervisor by his or her first name. Supervisors in the egalitarian format may view trainees as their equals. They may even, on occasion, have lunches together during or after work. A person from a hierarchical social structure may take a more rigid view of this behavior and may likely view it as unprofessional. In hierarchical relationships, the supervisor could expect that any formal or informal discussion of client cases only occur with the supervisor, unless the supervisor grants permission to the contrary. On the other hand, egalitarian supervisors may not take offense at the idea of informally discussing a case with a colleague. As long as the client's confidentiality is protected, the egalitarian supervisor may not take offense. The primary purpose of discussing cultural differences is to ensure that the supervisor and trainee know each other's expectations. Needless misunderstandings are less likely to occur if both understand the commonalties and differences of certain cultural patterns.

## Valuing the Trainee as a Person

Despite the cultural differences that may exist between the supervisor and the trainee, the trainee must know that he or she is valued as a person. Boyd-Franklin (1989) postulates that the key task of the supervisor is the empowerment of trainees through the "mobilization of their feelings of confidence and competence in themselves and their work" (p.244). Kiselica (1998) reinforces this idea as he describes his experiences with cross-cultural supervision:

> When I felt the need to talk about my family roots and the commonalties between my ancestors' experiences and those of my clients, my supervisors served as a caring sounding board, helping me to clarify what I was learning about my own identity. When I unknowingly behaved in an ethnocentric manner, they gently confronted in a supportive way that challenged my culturally encapsulated perspective while communicating to me that I was valued as a person. (p. 9)

Supervisors need to convey a real concern for their trainees. They should be interested in their trainees, care for them, and want to help them.

## Multicultural Supervision and Trust

Trust in multicultural supervision is complex, but crucial to the well-being of the supervisory relationship and essential for promoting personal and professional growth. For most trainees, respect, safety, and truism in their supervisory relationship are the keys to the feeling of trust. Adding the multicultural dimension helps address the importance of trust in the supervisor-trainee relationship.

*Respect* is usually defined as the supervisor's esteem for the trainee. The supervisor should express respect for the trainee's culture and the values and relevance of their life (professional and personal) experience. This includes expressing belief in the trainee's abilities. For example,

> I told my supervisor that I thought some self-disclosure with one of my clients was an appropriate way to establish some trust with this client, since she was unsure about being in counseling. I told the client that I understood how hard it was being a refugee and living in this country, since I myself was a refugee. I shared some of my experiences when I was in a refugee camp and I could see that she relaxed somewhat. She told me she would be back next week, since she thought I understood. My supervisor was not only supportive of my decision to self-disclose, but also of what I disclosed.

Trainees might expect that the legitimacy of the intervention will be questioned by their supervisor and met with a myriad of responses. However, the example demonstrates that in a respectful supervisory relationship, trainees can use interventions without feeling the need to legitimize them, but instead trusting their abilities.

*Safety* can be defined as the trainee feeling the freedom to take risks to push him or herself and the client past personal comfort, to promote growth and change, as well as being willing to make mistakes. Trainees will feel comfortable when they are allowed to tell the truth about themselves, their cultural values and beliefs, and their work--without feeling judged or shamed by their supervisor. Safety is generally experienced by trainees when they see their supervisor as accepting of them, despite being challenged. For example,

> I told my supervisor that I saw an African-American client for the first time. I wanted to be culturally sensitive, being Caucasian and all, and said to the client that I was not very knowledgeable about African-American culture, but would welcome her educating me in our sessions. I told my supervisor that I was surprised that the client got angry and said that she was not here to educate me, but to get help from me. When my supervisor challenged my approach with this client, being respectful and nurturing in the process, I knew that this was a safe situation to tell the truth and learn how to become culturally knowledgeable.

Because cross-cultural interactions are often uncomfortable for trainees, avoidance is often the result. However, in a safe supervisory relationship, trainees can comfortably explore unknown territories.

*Truism* can be described as the commitment to be honest about oneself and one's ability. It is essential in the process of accountability. The supervisor bears the primary responsibility in setting the stage for truism, however both the supervisor and trainee need to make the commitment to be honest, not only with themselves but also with each other. At that point, trainees can engage in discussions about their feelings about race without being stonewalled. For example,

> A trainee discussed a new client that she had worked with for two sessions. She identified having worked with a male client for one session and was frustrated that the client avoided any and all eye contact with her. In the following session this same client wore mirrored sunglasses, making any attempts for eye contact impossible. Halfway through the session she stopped the process of the session and asked the client if he would not mind taking his glasses off. The client explained that in his culture it was quite inappropriate for a female to have eye contact with a male and that he noticed her attempt to have eye contact with him. The supervisor explored with the trainee how knowledgeable she should be about her client's cultural and ethnic background, as a way to understand, analyze, promote, manage and affirm the client's culture.

In this example, the trainee who tells the truth about her counseling sessions does so based on past experiences of being treated fairly and non-diminishing in the supervision relationship, setting the foundation for a relationship of trustworthiness that promotes growth and accountability. Doherty (1995) suggested that people are obligated to be truthful in relationships with one another, to avoid disintegration.

*Multiculturalism*, in the context of supervision,

directly relates to understanding, analyzing, managing, promoting and affirming diversity. The promotion of diversity moves beyond tolerance, patronization, generosity, and 'good deeds', and even beyond common decency, to confronting differences and developing the flexibility that allows appreciation and respect for both differences and similarities" (Kavanagh & Kennedy, 1992, p.5).

It is important to remember that both the supervisor and the trainee bring their own experiences, values, and beliefs about what multiculturalism is to the relationship, which will influence how they relate to each other as well as to the trainee's client. Supervisors and trainees with dramatically different experiences, values, and beliefs about multiculturalism might experience difficulties in understanding, agreeing, and working together than those who are more similar. In a trusting supervision relationship these difficulties can be overcome.

# ASSESSMENT INSTRUMENTS AND CORRESPONDING DEVELOPMENTAL STAGES

As trainees embark on the process of developing a multicultural professional identity and becoming culturally competent counselors, not only should they be aware of the multicultural counseling competencies adopted by the Association for Multicultural Counseling and Development (AMCD) (Sue, Arrendondo, & McDavis, 1992), but they should also engage in the practice of monitoring their own attitudes, knowledge, and skills in this area. This assessment process includes informal methods such as self-evaluation, as well as more formal methods that involve the use of established instruments. Both the informal and formal methods have their purposes and limitations, and we will explore some of them in an effort to help trainees understand how they can be used to enhance their development as multiculturally competent counselors.

One of the first things trainees should do is explore their own multicultural identity. This involves becoming aware of one's own cultural attitudes, values, and beliefs. How does one do this? It is accomplished through the informal assessment process of asking oneself what his/her attitudes, values, and beliefs are and where they came from. For example:

- What is my belief about freedom of choice?
- Do all people have it or should all people have it?
- Where does my belief come from? (family of origin, religion, peers?)

The next developmental milestone in becoming multiculturally competent is increasing multicultural awareness. Once again this is accomplished through self-examination. In this area trainees might ask themselves questions such as:

- From what ethnic/cultural background are my friends, co-workers, neighbors, and so forth?
- What experience do I have with people who are African-American, Latino/Latina, Native-American Indian?

- What kind of emotional reactions do I have toward people from other racial and ethnic groups?
- What stereotypes or pre-conceived notions do I have of other racial and ethnic groups?

By asking these and similar questions, trainees challenge themselves to increase their multicultural awareness and heighten their sensitivity to differences.

Once trainees have examined their cultural attitudes, values, and beliefs, as well as their multicultural awareness, the next step is to examine what multicultural knowledge and skills they already have. Some questions one could ask might include:

- What do I know about different racial and cultural heritages, including my own?
- What do I know about oppression, racism, discrimination, and privilege?
- What do I know about different communication styles (verbal and non-verbal) for different ethnic groups?
- What educational and/or training experiences will help me acquire the necessary multicultural knowledge and skills?

Trainees should engage in self-evaluation and be conscientious in their ethical duty to be multiculturally sensitive and competent.

The aforementioned areas of multicultural attitudes and beliefs, awareness, knowledge and skills correspond with the dimensions of cultural competency identified in the literature (Sue, Arredondo, & McDavis, 1992). Whereas the self-evaluation and suggested questions are important and helpful, they are nonetheless informal and self-driven, and therefore subjective and potentially biased. Even the most well-intentioned trainee, or professional for that matter, can have blinders or can neglect questioning him or herself regarding areas of weakness. This calls for the use of more objective, psychometrically sound, research-based assessment instruments.

In the area of multicultural competence evaluation, there are essentially four different instruments that have been developed and have undergone some testing of psychometric properties (Ponterotto, Rieger, Barrett, & Sparks, 1994). The four were mentioned earlier in this chapter and include the CCCI-R (LaFromboise et al., 1991), the MCAS-B (Ponterotto et al., 1991), the MCI (Sodowsky et al., 1994), and the MAKSS (D'Andrea et al., 1991).

The CCCI-R has received the most empirical scrutiny and has acceptable levels of internal consistency and moderate evidence of content, criterion-related, and construct validity (Ponterotto et. al, 1994). The MCAS-B has been shown to have satisfactory internal consistency and criterion-related validity (Ponterotto, et al., 1994). The MCI has shown satisfactory internal consistency, promising criterion-related validity and moderate construct validity (Ponterotto et. al, 1994). The MAKSS has demonstrated satisfactory internal consistency and needs additional testing of psychometric properties (Ponterotto et al., 1994). All of these instruments were designed to measure various aspects of multicultural competencies.

A more detailed description of the MAKSS is provided, to illustrate how multicultural instruments are designed. The MAKSS (D'Andrea et al., 1991) is self-administered and is comprised of 60 items which are divided into three subscales (Awareness, Knowledge and

Skills). Subscale reliabilities were judged to be acceptable with internal consistency coefficients of .75, .90, and .96 for the subscales. After prompting for standard demographic information (e.g., gender, age, race, ethnic/cultural background), the instrument contains questions that ask the respondent to assess their multicultural values, awareness, knowledge, beliefs, and skills. Items assess perceptions, attitudes, and attributions regarding areas such as communication, sensitivity to groups, and professionalism. Items also require self-judgements by test-takers (see D'Andrea et al., 1991).

Trainees can benefit from completing a multicultural instrument as a way of exploring their present understanding of multicultural issues. This can also serve as a springboard for further discussions with the supervisor, raising multicultural sensitivity, and gaining insight into the dynamics in a client-counselor dyad (Korchin, 1976).

## STRUCTURE AND ASSESSMENT IN MULTICULTURALLY SENSITIVE PRACTICUM/INTERNSHIP COURSES

Throughout trainees' practicum and internship experiences, both informal and formal methods of assessment should be used. This assessment should be on-going and both supervisee and supervisor directed, with supervisee and supervisor alike asking questions regarding multicultural sensitivity regarding the trainee's interaction with clients. Multiculturally sensitive supervisors use formal assessments such as the MAKSS, to assess the trainee's current level of understanding and then facilitate appropriate learning opportunities for the trainee to increase or improve in those areas through written material, instruction, and practical application. Additionally, these assessments can be used as pre and post-tests to evaluate trainees' progress over the course of a practicum or internship experience. By using the formal assessments, trainees have a more objective measure of their multicultural competence and have an idea of specific areas for growth.

In addition to the formal assessments, the discussion of multicultural awareness and sensitivity should be a part of all case consultation. Trainees and supervisors alike should incorporate the contextual aspects of the client's world (racial, ethnic, cultural background and influences) into the discussion of the presenting problem, treatment plan development, and treatment techniques.

Examples of questions to be asked in such discussions are:

- What would the client's family say about the problem and how to solve it?
- What are the expectations within this client's cultural or ethnic background regarding his or her situation?
- Is my view of the client's presenting problem biased or skewed because of my own cultural or ethnic background?
- Are the changes I am helping my client make contrary to her or his cultural or ethnic background? And if so, what implications will they have in my client's life? And further, have I explored with my client if that is what he or she wants?

This type of question should be routine and expected. It is important to remember that only by broadening the lens for trainees to accurately see their clients experience within their multicultural context, and by possessing the appropriate multicultural knowledge and skills, can the trainee competently work with and help clients.

## MULTICULTURAL SUPERVISION AND ETHICAL AND LEGAL ISSUES

The Code of Ethics and Standards of Practice, American Counseling Association (ACA, 1995) presents principles that define ethical behavior for its members. The Code addresses the issue of diversity, which is identified as, but not limited to, age, gender, race, ethnicity, religion, sexual orientation, marital status, and so forth. Several sections of the ACA Code apply to the topic of supervision from a multicultural perspective (Corey, Corey & Callanan, 1998). Sections A.1. and 2., The Counseling Relationship, focus on the importance of being non-discriminatory and respecting the differences of both the client and counselor. Section C.5., Public Responsibility, focuses on the importance of nondiscrimination; and Section E.8., Diversity in Testing, underscores the importance of choosing measurement instruments that have been standardized on a sample that is representative of the client. For example, a test that is administered to a middle-aged African-American client should have normative data on that population. Finally, Section F.2., Counselor Evaluation and Training Program, emphasizes the importance of hiring, as well as maintaining diversity in the student body, faculty, and staff.

Whereas the ACA Code of Ethics addresses multicultural and diversity issues, including training; the Association for Multicultural Counseling and Development (AMCD, a division of the American Counseling Association, ACA) has developed a document that addresses these issues more thoroughly. This document is labeled the *Operationalization of Multicultural Counseling Competencies*. This document is based on four basic beliefs: (a) that we are all multicultural individuals; (b) that we all possess a personal, political and historical culture; (c) that we are affected by sociocultural, political, environmental and historical events; and (d) multiculturalism also intersects with multiple factors of individual diversity (Arredondo, Toporek, Brown, Jones, Locks, Sanchez, & Standler, 1996, p.3). In the document, multicultural competencies are divided into three areas: 1) counselor awareness of one's own cultural values and biases, 2) counselor awareness of client's worldview, and 3) culturally appropriate intervention strategies. Each of these sections is subdivided into *attitudes and beliefs*, *knowledge*, and *skills*.

There are three sections. Section I is titled Counselor's Awareness of Own Cultural Values and Biases. Subsection A focuses on the importance of counselors having insight into their own multicultural and diversity attitudes, beliefs, and values. Subsection B focuses on counselors' multicultural and diversity understanding and insight regarding counselors' impact on others. Subsection C stresses the importance of continuously developing multicultural and diverse attitudes, beliefs and values, and the importance of continuous training.

Section II is called Counselor Awareness of Client's Worldview. Subsection A encourages counselors to be aware of and assure that they do not let their own stereotypes enter the counseling session. Subsection B stresses the importance of exercising multicultural counseling competence when working with diverse clients, and subsection C's emphasis is on stereotypes and the importance of seeking out educational opportunities.

Section III is titled Culturally Appropriate Intervention Strategies. Subsection A stresses the importance of accepting the client's beliefs, values, and practices such as their religious observations and language. Subsection B focuses on the importance of counselor's awareness of possible client biases that might impact seeking mental health services, as well as institutional and assessment tool biases. It also points out that counselors should be aware of possible reverse discrimination. Subsection C addresses counselors' need for flexibility in treatment strategies and service delivery in accommodating clients' needs. Additionally, counselors should be aware and deal with potential issues of oppression and discrimination.

It is important to remember that both the ACA code of ethics and the Operationalization of Multicultural Counseling Competencies document are not intended to be a blueprint that precludes supervisors and trainees from ethical reasoning and decision making. Supervisors have the responsibility to guide the trainee in the process of becoming a culturally competent and ethical counselor. This process needs to be trainee-specific. When working with multicultural clients, trainees have the responsibility, to be client-specific, making ethical and competent decisions; and then assuming personal responsibility for the consequences (Lanning, 1997).

## SUMMARY

All of these suggestions could prove helpful in choosing a supervisor that could help the trainee with cross-cultural supervision issues. Between the supervisor and the trainee, both must remember the various factors that could define and determine a successful working relationship. We believe beginning level trainees, as well as more advanced trainees, could benefit from this information. We especially believe that it is essential for supervisors to be aware of these important ideas. At least, now, trainees should feel themselves empowered to have a more effective relationship in cross-cultural supervision.

## EXERCISES TO PROMOTE CRITICAL THINKING

1) Prepare your own cultural genogram as a way to gain understanding of your cultural identity. First, design your own basic genogram. If necessary, refer back to McGoldrick and Gerson's (1985) *Genograms in Family Assessment* or DeMaria, Weeks, and Hof's (1999) *Intergenerational Assessment of Individual, Couples, and Families: Focused Genograms*. Then, define your culture of origin (e.g., father is African American, mother is Asian, your culture of origin exists in two cultures). Next, identify organizational principles, such as perceptions, behaviors, and beliefs (acceptable/pride and unacceptable/shame) and develop symbols that depict these pride and shame issues graphically. Then, designate colors for each culture (e.g., you might chose red for African American and green for Asian). Now, identify intercultural marriages in your family. Lastly consider some of the following questions:

- Did anybody in your family immigrate? If yes, who? When? Under what circumstances?

- Are there intercultural marriages in your family? If yes, who? How do different members of the family feel about them?

2)      Identify past relationships that you perceived as safe. How was respect, safety, and truism shown in those relationships? Identify who was primarily responsible for truism in this relationship (you, the other person, or both of you)? Using this information and what you read, develop some questions that will help you determine what to ask your supervisor about her or his values about having a trusting supervisor-trainee relationship.

3)      Develop a list of peers, friends, colleagues, and relatives who live in your area and are of various ethnicities or cultures. Describe how these people have impacted your multicultural awareness.

# REFERENCES

American Counseling Association (1995). *Code of ethics and standards of practice.* Alexandria, VA: Author.

Andrea, M., & Danies, J. (1991). Exploring the different levels of multicultural counseling training in counselor education. *Journal of Counseling & Development, 70,* 78-85.

Arredondo, P., Toporek, R., Brown, S., Jones, J., Locke, D. C., Sanchez, J., & Stadler, H. (1996). *Operationalization of the multicultural counseling competencies.* Alexandria, VA: American Counseling Association.

Berg-Cross, L., & Chinen, R. T. (1995). Multicultural training models and the Person-in-Culture Interview. In J. G. Ponterotto, J. M. Casas, L. A. Suzuki, & C. M. Alexander (Eds.), *Handbook of multicultural counseling* (pp. 333-356). Thousand Oaks: Sage Publications.

Bernard, J. M., & Goodyear, R. K. (1992). *Fundamentals of clinical supervision.* Boston: Allyn & Bacon.

Bradshaw, W. H. (1982). Supervision in black and white: Race as a factor in supervision. In M. Blumenfield (Ed.), *Applied supervision in psychotherapy* (pp. 199-220). New York: Grune & Stratton.

Brinson, J. A., & Morris, J. R. (in press). Blacks' and whites' perceptions of real-life scenarios. *Journal of Humanistic Counseling and Development.*

Cook, D. A., & Helms, J. E. (1988). Visible racial/ethnic group supervisees? satisfaction with cross-cultural supervision as predicted by relationship characteristics. *Journal of Counseling Psychology, 35,* 268-274.

Corey, G., Corey, M. S., & Callanan, P. (1998). *Issues and ethics in the helping profession.* Pacific Grove, CA: Brooks/Cole.

Council for Accreditation of Counseling and Related Educational Programs (2001). *CACREP accreditation manual.* Alexandria, VA: Author.

D'Andrea, M., Daniels, J. & Heck, R. (1991). Evaluating the impact of multicultural counseling training. *Journal of Counseling & Development, 70,* 143-150.

DeMaria, R., Weeks, G. & Hof, L. (1999). *Intergenerational assessment of individuals, couples, and families: Focused genograms.* Philadelphia: Taylor & Francis.

Doherty, W. (1995). *Soul searching: Why psychotherapy must promote moral responsibility.* New York, NY: Basic Books.

Hardy, K. V. & Laszloffy, T. A. (1995). The cultural genogram: Key to training culturally competent family therapists. *Journal of Marital and Family Therapy, 21*(3), 227-237.

Hess, A. K., & Hess, K. A. (1983). Psychotherapy supervision: A survey of internship training practices. *Professional Psychology: Research and Practice, 14,* 504-513.

Hunt, P. (1987). Black clients: Implications for supervision of trainees. *Psychotherapy, 24,* 114-119.

Ivey, A. E., Ivey, M. B., & Simek-Morgan, L. (1993*). Counseling and psychotherapy: A multicultural perspective* (3rd ed.). Boston: Allyn & Bacon.

Kavanagh, K.H. & Kennedy P.H. (1992). *Promoting cultural diversity: Strategies for health care professionals.* Newbury Park, CA: Sage.

Kiselica, M. (1998). Preparing anglos for the challenges and joys of multiculturalism. *The Counseling Psychologist, 26,* 5-13.

Korchin, S. (1976). *Modern clinical psychology.* New York: Basic Books, Inc.

LaFromboise, T. D., Coleman, H. L.K., & Hernandez, A. (1991). Development and factor structure of the Cross-Cultural Counseling Inventory-Revised. *Professional Psychology: Research and Practice, 22,* 380-388.

Lanning, W. (1997). Ethical codes and responsible decision-making. In J. A. Kottler (Ed.). *Finding your way as a counselor* (pp. 111-113). Alexandria, VA: American Counseling Association.

McGoldrick, M. & Gerson, R. (1985). *Genograms in family assessment.* New York: W. W. Norton & Company.

McGrath, P. & Axelson, J. A. (1993). *Accessing awareness & developing knowledge: Foundations for skill in a multicultural society.* Pacific Grove, CA: Brooks/Cole.

Mio, J. S, & Morris, D. R. (1990). Cross-cultural issues in psychology training programs: An invitation for discussion. *Professional Psychology: Research and Practice, 21,* 434-441.

Ottavi, T. M., Pope-Davis, D. B., & Dings, J. G. (1994). Relationships between White racial identity and self-reported multicultural counseling competencies. *Journal of Counseling Psychology, 41,* 149-154.

Pedersen, P. (1988). The three stages of multicultural development: Awareness, knowledge, and skill. In P. Pedersen (Ed.), *A handbook for developing multicultural awareness* (pp. 3-18). Alexandria, VA: American Association for Counseling and Development.

Petersen, F. K. (1991). *Race and ethnicity.* New York: Haworth.

Ponterotto, J. G., Alexander, C. M., & Grieger, I. (1995). A multicultural competency checklest for counseling training programs. *Journal of Multicultural Counseling and Development, 23,* 11-20.

Ponterotto, J. G., Rieger, B. P., Barrett, A. & Sparks, R. (1994). Assessing multicultural counseling competence: A review of instrumentation. *Journal of Counseling & Development, 72,* 316-322.

Ponterotto, J. G., Sanchez, C. M., Magids, D. M. (1991, August). *Initial development and validation of the Multicultural Counseling Awareness Scale (MCAS).* Paper presented at the annual meeting of the American Psychological Association, San Francisco, CA.

Priest, R. (1994). Minority supervisor and majority supervisee: Another perspective of clinical reality. *Counselor Education and Supervision, 34,* 152-158.

Remington, G., & Da Costa, G. (1989). Ethnocultural factors in resident supervision: Black supervisor and White supervisees. *American Journal of Psychotherapy, 43*, 398-404.

Sabnani, H. B., Ponterotto, J. G., & Borodovsky, L. G. (1991). White racial identity development and cross-cultural counselor training: A stage model. *The Counseling Psychologist, 19*, 72-102.

Satir, V. (1987). The therapist's story. *Journal of Psychotherapy and the Family, 3*(1). In M. Baldwin and V. Satir (Eds.), *The use of self in therapy*. New York: Haworth.

Sodowsky, G. R., Taffe, R. C., Gutkin, T., & Wise, S. L. (1994). Development and applications of the Multicultural Counseling Inventory. *Journal of Counseling Psychology, 41*, 137-148.

Sue, D.W., Arrendondo, P., & McDavis, R. J. (1992). Multicultural counseling competencies and standards: A call to the profession. *Journal of Counseling & Development, 70*, 477-486.

Sue, D. W., Ivey, A. E., & Pedersen, P. B. (Eds.). (1996). *A theory of multicultural counseling and therapy*. Pacific Grove, CA: Brooks/Cole.

Sue, D.W. & Sue, D. (1999). *Counseling the culturally different: Theory and practice* (3rd ed.). New York: John Wiley & Sons.

Thio, A.(1986). *Sociology*. New York: Harper & Row.

Wehrly, B. (1995). *Pathways to multicultural counseling competence: A developmental journey*. Pacific Grove, CA: Brooks/Cole.

# BIOGRAPHICAL SKETCHES FOR AUTHORS

## CHAPTER 1: HISTORICAL CONTEXT OF MULTICULTURALISM IN THE UNITED STATES

**Dr. Jerry Trusty** is an associate professor in the Department of Counselor Education, Counseling Psychology and Rehabilitation Services at Pennsylvania State University. He is Coordinator of the Secondary School Counseling Program in that department. Dr. Trusty received his Ph. D. in counselor education from Mississippi State University. He has experience as a middle-school and high-school counselor. His research interests include educational and career development of adolescents, post-secondary educational choices, counselor-trainees' development, and multicultural counseling.

**Dr. Partick Davis** is an assistant professor of counselor education at University of North Carolina-Greensboro. He received his Ph. D. in counselor education from Texas A&M University-Commerce. He has counseling experience with children, adolescents, adults, and families. Dr. Davis has worked in student affairs settings, hospitals, in substance abuse counseling settings, and in Christian counseling settings. His research interests include cultural influences on youth, post-secondary achievement of African Americans, and treatment issues for adolescent sexual offenders.

**Dr. E. Joan Looby** is Assistant Dean of Education, and Associate Professor of Counselor Education, Mississippi State University. She received her Ph.D. in counselor education from University of Georgia, her M. A. in counseling and educational psychology from University of Illinois at Urbana-Champaign, and her BA from University of the Virgin Islands, St. Thomas, U.S. Virgin Islands. Dr. Looby has over 15 years of clinical experience working with individuals across the developmental spectrum (children, adolescents, adults), and providing individual, group, and family counseling for a wide range of personal, social, and developmental issues. Her research interests include diversity and mental health, spirituality, eating disorders among African American females, sexual harassment, international perceptions of counseling, blindness rehabilitation and African Americans, sexual abuse, and gender issues in counseling.

# CHAPTER 2: CONTEMPORARY ISSUES IN MULTICULTURAL COUNSELING: TRAINING COMPETENT COUNSELORS

**Dr. Tina Q. Richardson** is Associate Professor of Counseling Psychology at Lehigh University, and she is a certified school counselor and a diversity consultant. She received her Masters Degree in 1988 and Ph.D. in 1991 from the University of Maryland, College Park. Her research focuses on violence prevention, identity development, and multicultural counselor training. She is the on the editorial board of the Journal of Counseling & Development and serves as an ad hoc reviewer for the Journal of Multicultural Counseling and Development. She is a board member for several community-based agencies that focus on academic achievement as well as family violence prevention.

**Dr. Elizabeth J. Jacob** is an assistant professor within the Department of Counseling and Human Services at the University of Scranton. She teaches within the undergraduate Human Services program and graduate programs in counseling. Courses taught include Multicultural Counseling, Counseling and Interviewing Skills, Career and Lifestyle Development, Career Seminar, and Internship. Scholarly and professional research and counseling interests are within the area of multiculturalism and diversity issues in counseling. Dr. Jacob's current research agenda explores the role of racial and ethnic identity development in visible racial and ethnic groups (VREG) and its implications for counseling and career development. Other areas of research include an interest in global collaboration and social action and advocacy. Ongoing international collaboration includes providing collaborative summer immersion programs for graduate and undergraduate students in conjunction with Universidad Iberoamericana in Mexico City.

# CHAPTER 3: RACIAL, ETHNIC, AND CULTURAL IDENTITY DEVELOPMENT MODELS

**Dr. Richard C. Henriksen Jr.** is Assistant Professor, School Service Programs, Southwestern Oklahoma State University. He received his Bachelors in Psychology, Master's in Counseling, and Doctorate in Counseling from Texas A&M University-Commerce. He has counseling experience in alcohol and drug abuse treatment settings and in psychiatric settings. He has also worked as a substance abuse prevention specialist. His primary area of research involves developing a theory of Biracial identity development and developing therapeutic interventions for Biracial people.

**Dr. Jerry Trusty** is an associate professor in the Department of Counselor Education, Counseling Psychology and Rehabilitation Services at Pennsylvania State University. He is Coordinator of the Secondary School Counseling Program in that department. He received his Ph. D. in counselor education from Mississippi State University. Dr. Trusty has experience in middle-school and high-school counseling. His research interests include educational and career development of adolescents, career choices, counseling students' development, and multicultural counseling.

## CHAPTER 4: MULTICULTURAL COUNSELING IN SPIRITUAL AND RELIGIOUS CONTEXTS

**Dr. Timothy B. Smith** is Associate Professor of Counseling Psychology at Brigham Young University in Provo, Utah. He received a doctoral degree from Utah State University after completing a research fellowship at Rhodes University in South Africa and an internship at the University of Pennsylvania. He is a licensed psychologist with a small private practice. His research interests include spirituality and mental health, racism and racial tolerance, and factors that enhance interpersonal relationships. He is currently the editor of the *Journal of College Counseling* and of the forthcoming book, *Practicing Multiculturalism* (Allyn & Bacon).

**Dr. P. Scott Richards** has been a faculty member at Brigham Young University (BYU) since 1990 and is currently a professor in the Department of Counseling Psychology and Special Education. He received his Ph.D. in counseling psychology in 1988 from the University of Minnesota. He co-authored *A Spiritual Strategy for Counseling and Psychotherapy* (American Psychological Association (APA), 1997) and co-edited the *Handbook of Psychotherapy and Religious Diversity* (APA, 2000). In 1999, he received the William C. Bier Award from Division 36 of APA for his writings on religious issues in psychology. Dr. Richards is a licensed psychologist and maintains a small private psychotherapy practice at the Center for Change, in Orem, Utah.

## CHAPTER 5: MULTICULTURAL COUNSELING THEORIES

**Ms. Sheilah M. Wilson** is a graduate student in Community Counseling in the department of Educational Psychology at the Northern Arizona University Center for Excellence in Education. She teaches at NAU and offers Divorce and Family Law Mediation services with sensitivities to intervening issues of alcohol, addictions, and abuse. She is listed in Who's Who of American Women.

**Dr. Daya Singh Sandhu** is Professor and Chair of the Educational & Counseling Psychology Department at University of Louisville, KY. He received his doctorate in counselor education from Mississippi State University. He has special interest in multicultural counseling, school counseling, and the role of spirituality in counseling and psychotherapy. Recently, he was honored as one of the twelve pioneers in the field of multicultural counseling.

## CHAPTER 6: COUNSELING ETHNICALLY DIVERSE FAMILIES

**Dr. E. Joan Looby** is Assistant Dean of Education, and Associate Professor of Counselor Education, Mississippi State University. She received her Ph.D. in counselor education from University of Georgia, her master's in counseling and educational psychology from University of Illinois at Urbana-Champaign, and her bachelor's from University of the Virgin Islands, St. Thomas, U.S. Virgin Islands. Dr. Looby has over 15 years of clinical experience working with individuals across the developmental spectrum (children, adolescents, adults), and providing individual, group, and family counseling for a wide range of personal, social, and developmental issues. Her research interests include diversity and mental health, spirituality, eating disorders among African American females, sexual harassment, international perceptions of counseling, blindness rehabilitation and African Americans, sexual abuse, and gender issues in counseling.

**Ms. Tammy T. Webb** is a doctoral candidate at Mississippi State University. She received her master's in clinical social work from Ohio State University, and a B.S. in social science from Coppin State College. She has ten years of clinical experience working with individuals, families, and groups in in-patient and out-patient settings. Her research interests include perceptions of attractiveness among African American men, body image perceptions among women, spirituality, and counselor supervision.

## CHAPTER 7: DISABILITY: AN EMERGING TOPIC IN MULTICULTURAL COUNSELING

**Dr. Liza Conyers** is an assistant professor of Rehabilitation at Penn State University. She received her Ph.D. in Rehabilitation Psychology from the University of Wisconsin-Madison. Dr. Conyers has worked in a number of clinical settings including non-profit community rehabilitation programs (where she helped facilitate the transition of individuals with disabilities from sheltered to competitive employment), an office of students with disabilities, physical medicine and rehabilitation units, college counseling centers, and in community psychiatric rehabilitation agencies. Her research areas are in the area of psychosocial aspects of disability, HIV/AIDS, and employment issues of people with disabilities.

## CHAPTER 8: COUNSELING WITH INDIVIDUALS FROM THE LESBIAN AND GAY CULTURE

**Dr. Mark Pope** is an associate professor in the Division of Counseling & Family Therapy at the University of Missouri - St Louis. He received his M.Ed. from the University of Missouri - Columbia and his Ed.D. from the University of San Francisco in 1989. Dr. Pope is both a Licensed Professional Counselor and a Licensed Clinical Psychologist and his practice specialties include career counseling, addictions counseling, psychological testing, and multicultural counseling. He is a past-president of the National Career Development Association as well as the Association for Gay, Lesbian, and Bisexual Issues in Counseling. His research and scholarly interests include multicultural career counseling, specifically the career development of ethnic, racial, and sexual minorities in the U.S. and internationally. He is a recipient of the 2001 American Counseling Association's Kitty Cole Human Rights Award.

## CHAPTER 9: MULTICULTURAL COUNSELING FOR CAREER DEVELOPMENT

**Dr. Roger Herring** is a professor of counselor education at University of Arkansas-Little Rock. He received his BA from University of North Carolina-Pembroke, his MA and ED.S in psychology and school counseling from Appalachian State University, and his Ed. D. from North Carolina State University. He worked for several years in North Carolina public schools as a teacher, administrator, and school counselor; and he has been a counselor educator for several years. Dr. Herring's research interests include multicultural counseling and education, and ethnic minority adolescents, particularly Native American Indians.

## CHAPTER 10: MULTICULTURAL GROUP COUNSELING

**Dr. Michael Mann** is an assistant professor of counseling at Truman State University in Kirksville, Missouri. He received his Ph.D. in Counseling Psychology from the University of Missouri at Columbia. Dr. Mann has earned Master's degrees from the University of Durham in England, the University of Mississippi, and Emory University. Some of the settings in which he has counseled individuals, groups, and families include university counseling centers, psychiatric facilities, community mental health centers, and international student centers. Some of his research areas and interests include cross-cultural counseling, student adjustment, career development, and rural mental health issues.

**Dr. Changming Duan** is Associate Professor of Counseling Psychology at University of Missouri - Kansas City. She received her Ph.D. degree from University of Maryland at College Park. Her work experience includes working as a staff psychologist at university counseling centers and teaching both masters and doctorate level courses in counseling psychology training programs. Her scholarly work is primarily in the areas of multicultural psychology, counseling process and outcome, and empathy.

## CHAPTER 11: INTERPERSONAL COMMUNICATION SKILLS AS A BASIS FOR MULTICULTURAL COUNSELING

**Dr. M. Sylvia Fernandez** is in private practice and is an adjunct professor for the Department of Counselor Education of Florida Atlantic University, with eight years experience as a counselor educator. Her publications/presentations are in the areas of multiculturalism and supervision of counselors across practice settings. She holds and has held leadership positions in the national and Arkansas divisions of Association for Counselor Education and Supervision and Association for Specialists in Group Work, the Arkansas Counseling association, and the National Board for Certified Counselors. Her masters training is in community mental health and doctorate is in counselor education from Southern Illinois University-Carbondale.

**Dr. Jerry Trusty** is an associate professor in the Department of Counselor Education, Counseling Psychology and Rehabilitation Services at Pennsylvania State University. He is Coordinator of the Secondary School Counseling Program in that department. He received his

Ph. D. in counselor education from Mississippi State University. Dr. Trusty has experience in middle-school and high-school counseling. His research interests include educational and career development of adolescents, career choices, counseling students' development, and multicultural counseling.

**Ms. Reba J. Criswell** is a graduate assistant in the Department of Counseling at Texas A&M University-Commerce where she is pursuing her doctorate in counseling with a specialty in play therapy. She received her M.B.S. and B.A. degrees from Southeastern Oklahoma State University. She has extensive experience working with emotionally disturbed children and adolescents in both school and community settings. Ms. Criswell also maintains a part-time private practice in Durant, Oklahoma. In addition, she has taught as an adjunct instructor at Southeastern Oklahoma State University for a number of years. Her publication areas and research interests include school counseling, play therapy, multicultural counseling, and counselor supervision.

## CHAPTER 12: NON-WESTERN HELPING MODALITIES

**Dr. Roger Herring** is a professor of counselor education at University of Arkansas-Little Rock. He received his BA from University of North Carolina-Pembroke, his MA and ED.S in psychology and school counseling from Appalachian State University, and his Ed. D. from North Carolina State University. He worked for several years in North Carolina public schools as a teacher, administrator, and school counselor; and he has been a counselor educator for several years. Dr. Herring's research interests include multicultural counseling and education, and ethnic minority adolescents, particularly Native American Indians.

**Dr. Carmen Salazar** is an assistant professor and Coordinator of Clinical Training in the Department of Counseling, Texas A&M University-Commerce. She earned a Ph.D. in Counseling from the University of New Mexico in 1999, an M.A. in counseling from University of New Mexico in 1991, and a B.A. in psychology from College of Santa Fe in 1988. Her main areas of interest are research in gender and ethnicity, and professional development in counselor education, with particular focus on faculty of color. She has worked as a counselor with various populations in private practice and agencies in the Albuquerque, New Mexico area.

## CHAPTER 13: SUPERVISION FROM A MULTICULTURAL PERSPECTIVE

**Dr. Karin Jordan** is an Associate Professor and Director/Chair of the Graduate Department of Counseling at George Fox University. She is a Licensed Marriage and Family Therapist and is an Approved Supervisor of the American Association for Marriage and Family Therapy. She has supervised masters and doctoral students and provided post-graduate supervision for several years.

**Dr. Jesse A. Brinson** is an associate professor of counselor education at the University of Nevada, Las Vegas. He received his doctorate in counselor education from Western Michigan University. He has a strong clinical background in multicultural counseling approaches. His research interests include the study of ethnic identity in adolescent drug use.

**Dr. Colleen Peterson** is Director & Clinical Assistant Professor of the Center for Individual, Couple & Family Counseling, University of Nevada--Las Vegas. She received her B.S. in Child Development & Family Relations from Brigham Young University, her M.S. in Marriage & Family Therapy from BYU, and her Ph.D. in Human Ecology, with a specialization in Marriage & Family Therapy, from Kansas State University. Dr. Peterson has experience as a licensed marriage and family therapist in a variety of settings and with a variety of clients (children, adolescents, and adults). Her research and scholarly interests are counseling ethics, clinical supervision, medical family therapy, and outcome research.

# INDEX

# Q